The Materiality of Diplomacy in the Hellenistic-Roman Mediterranean

Edinburgh Studies in Hellenistic History and Culture
Series editors: Benedikt Eckhardt & Andrew Erskine

Embraces the diversity of the Hellenistic world,
from Sicily to Babylonia and beyond

Today, the Hellenistic world is one of the largest and most vibrant fields in the study of antiquity. After centuries at the periphery, sandwiched between Classical Greece and Classical Rome, the period between Alexander's death and the battle of Actium is now thoroughly embedded into the historical study of the ancient world. The many innovations in political and literary culture that mark this period are now much better understood than in earlier, declinist models, and the increasing interconnectedness of the ancient world provides ample material for attempts to broaden the horizon of ancient history beyond the limits of traditional definitions.

The series aims to be a hub for excellent research in this field, consolidating existing strengths and setting research agendas for the future. Ranging from the late fourth to the late first century BCE, it will cover all aspects of Hellenistic history and culture, taking an inclusive approach that does not privilege core regions such as Greece or Macedonia but gives equal weight to developments on the Western and Eastern fringes of the Hellenistic world. By publishing studies on Greece, Sicily and Mesopotamia alongside each other, the series will embrace a holistic approach to the period, demonstrating how specialist knowledge held in various subdisciplines within and beyond Classics needs to be pooled to come to terms with the rapidly accelerating connectivity that characterises the Hellenistic world.

Published in the series:
The Materiality of Diplomacy in the Hellenistic-Roman Mediterranean
Gifts, Bribes, Offerings
Edited by Eduardo Sánchez Moreno and Enrique García Riaza

https://edinburghuniversitypress.com/series-edinburgh-studies-in-hellenistic-history-and-culture

The Materiality of Diplomacy in the Hellenistic-Roman Mediterranean

Gifts, Bribes, Offerings

Edited by Eduardo Sánchez Moreno and
Enrique García Riaza

EDINBURGH
University Press

Edinburgh University Press is one of the leading university presses in the UK. We publish academic books and journals in our selected subject areas across the humanities and social sciences, combining cutting-edge scholarship with high editorial and production values to produce academic works of lasting importance. For more information visit our website: edinburghuniversitypress.com

© editorial matter and organisation Eduardo Sánchez Moreno and Enrique García Riaza, 2024, 2026

© the chapters their several authors 2024, 2026

Grateful acknowledgement is made to the sources listed in the List of Illustrations for permission to reproduce material previously published elsewhere. Every effort has been made to trace the copyright holders, but if any have been inadvertently overlooked, the publisher will be pleased to make the necessary arrangements at the first opportunity.

Edinburgh University Press Ltd
13 Infirmary Street
Edinburgh EH1 1LT

First published in hardback by Edinburgh University Press 2024

Typeset in 10.5/13pt Warnock Pro
by Cheshire Typesetting Ltd, Cuddington, Cheshire, and
printed and bound by CPI Group (UK) Ltd,
Croydon, CR0 4YY

A CIP record for this book is available from the British Library

ISBN 978 1 3995 3038 5 (hardback)
ISBN 978 1 3995 3039 2 (paperback)
ISBN 978 1 3995 3040 8 (webready PDF)
ISBN 978 1 3995 3041 5 (epub)

The right of Eduardo Sánchez Moreno and Enrique García Riaza to be identified as the editor of this work has been asserted in accordance with the Copyright, Designs and Patents Act 1988, and the Copyright and Related Rights Regulations 2003 (SI No. 2498).

Contents

List of Figures vii
Notes on Contributors x

Introduction
Unboxing the Gift: Diplomatic Presents in Their Cultural Contexts 1
Eduardo Sánchez Moreno and Enrique García Riaza

Part I A Background for Gifts in Action: Gracing Gods, Kings and Cities

1 Diplomatic Gifts in the Biblical Context of the Sixth to Fourth Centuries BC: A Systematic Study of Deuteronomistic History (Joshua–2 Kings) 17
   Francesc Ramis Darder

2 Greek Cities and Diplomatic Gifts in the Classical Period 34
   Dominique Lenfant

3 Gifts for the Gods and *Keimēlia*: Some Reflections on Arms as Diplomatic Gifts in the Greek World 57
   María del Mar Gabaldón Martínez

Part II From Asia Minor to Lusitania: The Multiple Use of Gifts in an Interconnected World

4 Crowns to Rome: Honours, Gifts and Hellenistic Diplomacy 77
   Andrew Erskine

5 The Romans and Gifts from the Greeks: The Story of an Ostentatious Rejection 108
   Nathalie Barrandon, Anthony-Marc Sanz and Enrique García Riaza

6 Gift, Debt, Anxiety in Late Hellenistic Times: On the
   Cautiousness and Attitudes of Achaeans, Macedonians and
   Bastarnae towards Diplomatic Presents   130
   Miguel Esteban Payno and Gerard Ventós Rodríguez

7 Buying Goodwill, Granting Rewards: The Roman
   Headquarters as a Space of Diplomatic Interaction   147
   Borja Vertedor Ballesteros

8 From Presents to Bribes: Symbolic and Political Evolution of
   the Diplomatic Gift in Relations between Romans and
   Numidians   168
   Esther Sánchez Medina and Gabriel Roselló Calafell

9 Torques, Horses and Gold: Approaching Diplomatic Gifts
   in Gaul   188
   Alberto Pérez Rubio

10 *Do ut des*: Liberating Hostages and Offering Gifts on the
   Hispanian Front in the Second Punic War   212
   Eduardo Sánchez Moreno and Jorge García Cardiel

11 Gold for the Romans: Booty, Gifts and Bribes during the
   Roman Conquest of the Western Iberian Peninsula   242
   Manuel Salinas de Frías

12 Bonding Gifts: Material Exchange and Political Alliance
   during the Sertorian War   265
   David García Domínguez and Diego Suárez Martínez

   Epilogue   283
   Gifts at the Edges of the World: Diplomatic Exchanges in the
   Roman West and Early Colonial Chile
   Tomás Aguilera Durán

Index   307

Figures

2.1 Procession of gift-bearers: delegation VI (Lydians) carrying bracelets, metal drinking-bowls and amphorae, east side of the Apadana at Persepolis (Wikimedia Commons). 41

2.2 Gold griffin-headed armlet from the Oxus treasure, British Museum (Wikimedia Commons). 42

2.3 Alabaster vase with the inscription 'Xerxes, the Great King' in Persian, Elamite, Akkadian and Egyptian hieroglyphs, Penn Museum B10 (Wikimedia Commons). 42

2.4 Schist statue of Ptah-Hotep, an Egyptian official with a Persian torque, probably from Memphis, Brooklyn Museum (Creative Commons). 43

2.5 Siglos, silver Persian coin (5.43 g), c. 420–375 BC, Sardes mint. Persian king or hero (Classical Numismatic Group 99, Lot: 383; Creative Commons). 45

2.6 Silver Achaemenid phiale, Susa Acropolis (after Curtis & Tallis, 2005: fig. 277). 46

3.1 Bronze Etruscan helmet of the Negau type from the Alpheus River, Olympia. The inscription indicates that it was dedicated to Zeus by Hieron, son of Deinomenes, and the Syracusans after the Battle of Cumae (© The Trustees of the British Museum). 69

4.1 Four men carry a substantial and clearly heavy crown on a *ferculum* as part of the triumphal procession depicted on the small frieze of the Arch of Trajan at Benevento (© Olof Vessberg. National Museums of World Culture – Mediterranean Museum, Stockholm). 97

6.1	Relationship between gift exchange and anxiety (by the authors).	133
7.1	Diagram of the Roman Republican camp, based not only on archaeological evidence but also on literary sources, particularly Polybius, Livy and Appian (by the author).	163
8.1	Coin attributed to Syphax, minted between 213 and 202 BC. Mazard's *CNNM*, n. 12.	172
8.2	Coin attributed to Masinissa, minted between 203 and 148 BC. Mazard's *CNNM*, n. 60.	175
9.1	Statue known as the 'Warrior of Vachères', representation of a Gallic auxiliary from the Province c. 50–30 BC, in which the thick torque that decorates his neck stands out (Barruol, 1996; Pernet & Rouzeau, 2013) (Musée Calvet, Avignon; © Radu Oltean).	198
9.2	Statue known as the 'Warrior of Mondragon', representation of a Gallic aristocrat from the Province at the end of the second century BC or first half of the first century BC, who supports himself on his shield and shows a torque with his right hand (Cavalier & Baudrand, 2018) (Musée Calvet, Avignon; © Radu Oltean).	199
9.3	Torque from Mailly-le-Camp (Musée d'Archéologie Nationale; Wikimedia Commons/Gérald Garitan).	200
9.4	Graffiti on the Mailly-le-Camp torque: 1 – κιντουλλος; 2 – ταουτανοι; 3 – vιτιοβρογεις; 4 – vιτιοβρο; 5 – αυραππιιος; 6 – vιτιοβρογεις (Lejeune, 1969).	201
9.5	Stater minted in the territory of the Suessiones with the legend CRICIRV, and a horse, torque, small wheel and *fibula* on the reverse (Bibliothèque nationale de France).	204
9.6	Bronze of the Carnutes with the legend PIXTILOS. Obverse, a male bust with *fibula* and torque (Bibliothèque nationale de France).	204
9.7	*Potin* minted by the Remi *au personnage dansant*. Obverse, a figure holding a torque; reverse, *fibula* on a quadruped (Bibliothèque nationale de France).	205
10.1	*The Continence of Scipio*, by Federico de Madrazo y Kuntz, 1831 (© Real Academia de Bellas Artes de San Fernando, Madrid).	223
10.2	Silver *paterae*, vases and jewellery from El Castellet de Banyoles, Tivissa, Tarragona (© Museu d'Arqueologia de Catalunya, Barcelona).	227

11.1 Torques from Berzocana, Cáceres (© Ministerio de Cultura
     y Deporte, Gobierno de España). 256
11.2 Torques from the Fuentes de Valdepero (Palencia) hoard
     (© Ministerio de Cultura y Deporte, Gobierno de España). 256
11.3 Pieces (funicular torques, filiform torques, belt plate)
     from the Mogón hoard, Villacarrillo, Jaén (© Ministerio de
     Cultura y Deporte, Gobierno de España). 257
11.4 Treasure and silverware from Abengibre, Albacete
     (© Ministerio de Cultura y Deporte, Gobierno de España). 257

Notes on Contributors

Tomás Aguilera Durán is an Assistant Lecturer in Ancient History at the Autonomous University of Madrid. He specialises in the historiography of ancient Iberia and its ideological reception in modern times, as well as in the perpetuation of classical ethnographic clichés in Western culture, studies which he approaches from a transcultural and postcolonial perspective.

Nathalie Barrandon is Professor of Ancient History at the University of Reims. She is co-director of the project Parabaino: Massacres and Extreme Violence through the Greek and Roman Experiences. She has published important works on Roman Republican expansion in Hispania and on the use of violence in the Graeco-Roman world.

Andrew Erskine is Professor of Ancient History at the University of Edinburgh and a specialist in Roman relations with the Greek and Hellenistic world and in Roman Republican imperialism. He is the author of outstanding contributions on Polybius and Rome, as well as on Hellenistic intellectual culture and Roman oratory.

Miguel Esteban Payno is a 'Juan de la Cierva' Postdoctoral Fellow at the Autonomous University of Madrid. On the basis of a PhD thesis on diplomacy and political communication in Celtiberia, he has recently delved deeper into the analysis of International Relations and the anthropology of diplomacy applied to the societies of the Hellenistic-Roman West.

María del Mar Gabaldón Martínez is a Senior Lecturer in Ancient History at CEU San Pablo University in Madrid, member of the board of the Spanish Association of Military History and former director of *Gladius*, the main Spanish journal devoted to the study of armament and military history. Her main fields of research are the symbolic and ritual aspects of weaponry during Classical Antiquity.

Jorge García Cardiel is a 'Ramón y Cajal' Research Fellow at the Complutense University of Madrid. His main field of study is power and ideology in the Iberian culture and the hybridity process under Roman rule. As member of the Occidens Group, he is currently co-directing a research project on the time of the Punic Wars and its narratives, funded by the State Investigation Agency of Spain.

David García Domínguez is a Predoctoral Researcher in Ancient History at the Autonomous University of Madrid. His research deals with the Roman Civil Wars understood as 'connected histories', within which he is developing a PhD thesis on the Sertorian War and the role of the Hispanic communities in the conflict.

Enrique García Riaza is Professor of Ancient History at the University of the Balearic Islands, Senior Researcher of the Civitas Group and founding member of Libera Res Publica, a network for the study of the Roman Republic, and a member of the Editorial Board of LRP Collection. The political and diplomatic history of the expansion of the Republic is his main subject of study.

Dominique Lenfant is Professor of Ancient History at the University of Strasbourg and Director of the Institut d'histoire grecque. As a Hellenist, historian and translator, she works on the Classical period, and in particular on Graeco-Persian relations, with a focus on the history of diplomacy. She is also director of the journal *Ktèma: Civilisations de l'Orient, de la Grèce et de Rome Antiques.*

Alberto Pérez Rubio holds a PhD in Ancient History from the Autonomous University of Madrid, where he collaborates as an Honorary Member, and he is founder and co-editor of Desperta Ferro Publishing. Interested in ancient warfare, particularly in the Celtic world, his main research deals with the study of military coalitions, diplomacy and connectivity in ancient Gaul.

Francesc Ramis Darder holds a PhD in Theology from the Faculty of Theology of Catalonia. He is a lecturer in Sacred Scripture and History of Israel at the Centre d'Estudis Teològics and at the Institut Superior de Ciències Religioses of Mallorca and former Vice President and Director of Publications of the Spanish Biblical Association. His main research focus is Mesopotamian history and culture in its relationship with the Old Testament.

Gabriel Roselló Calafell is an Assistant Lecturer in Ancient History at the University of the Balearic Islands. He is a specialist in the field of North African diplomatic relations with the Roman Republic, a subject on which he has published important works.

Manuel Salinas de Frías is Professor of Ancient History at the University of Salamanca. Over the decades he has conducted research projects and published extensively on the local communities of the Iberian Peninsula, Roman Republican expansionism and its impact on the political elite, provincial administration, as well as on social and religious issues in Roman Spain.

Esther Sánchez Medina is a Lecturer in Ancient History at the Autonomous University of Madrid, where she teaches on Roman History and Late Antiquity. She has focused her research on North Africa, dealing with political conflict and ethnic, cultural and religious alterities on the margins of the Roman Empire and its historiographical echo.

Eduardo Sánchez Moreno is a Senior Lecturer in Ancient History at the Autonomous University of Madrid, where he leads the consolidated research group Occidens: Power, Conflict and Diplomacy in the Ancient West. His research interests lie in the peoples and cultures of ancient Iberia and the review of imperialism, diplomacy and ethnicity in the framework of Roman Republican overseas expansion.

Anthony-Marc Sanz holds a PhD from the University of Paris I Panthéon-Sorbonne. He is a researcher attached to the Laboratoire ANHIMA Paris–Marseille, UMR 8210, and has an important background in the study of Roman Republican diplomacy, with particular focus on the processes of surrender (*deditio*) and their political and symbolic implications.

Diego Suárez Martínez is a Predoctoral Fellow in Ancient History at the Autonomous University of Madrid. He devotes his attention to the aristocratic discourses of late Iron Age societies, and significantly to the study of single combat as a narrative of power and otherness during the Roman hegemony process over the Mediterranean (third to first century BC).

Gerard Ventós Rodríguez is a Postdoctoral Research Associate at the University of Girona. He has recently defended his PhD on Roman imperialism during the Middle Republic, studying the dynamics of multi-scale conflict and connectivity in the Western Mediterranean regions, to which he has contributed with relevant publications.

Borja Vertedor Ballesteros is a Predoctoral Fellow in Ancient History at the University of the Balearic Islands. He works on the political and diplomatic function of Roman camps during the Republican expansion, dealing specifically with the role of Roman governors and their *consilium*.

Introduction
Unboxing the Gift
Diplomatic Presents in Their Cultural Contexts*

Eduardo Sánchez Moreno and Enrique García Riaza

Unilateral or reciprocal gift-giving is perhaps as old as society itself. The giving of presents involves, in the first instance, the valuation of certain goods for their tangible utility or their intrinsic value. Their donation, however, necessarily implies a transfer to the other, an initial loss which benefits the receiver. Gift-giving is intrinsically a connotative act, a symbolic initiative. The object becomes a present and, as such, constitutes a token. The codes of this sign, its ciphers and implications, are recognisable by both parties – the giver and the receiver – although they do not always have analogous meanings and inferences. The richness of the diplomatic gift derives, in the first place, from this polysemy. At the same time, however, the gift was also selected (or even created) without a primarily practical purpose or functionality, being oriented to a symbolic role as a material manifestation of a state of mind and a political climate. Both dimensions of the diplomatic gift, understood as an offering endowed with political significance, were often combined. Certain goods, characterised by their exceptional value, high opinion of their beauty or their practical utility were selected (and thus imbued with symbolic capital) for this higher mission, losing in this transaction their everyday use and instead being exhibited as

---

* This work has been developed within the coordinated research project PGC2018-096415-B-C21-C22 'El regalo diplomático: simbología, ritualidad y política en el contexto de la expansión romano-republicana (siglos III–I a.C.)', funded by the State Research Agency, Ministry of Science and Innovation, Government of Spain (MCIN/AEI/10.13039/501100011033) and ERDF 'A way of making Europe'. The editors would like to thank Emma Chesterman for the English translations of the chapters, as well as Diego Suárez Martínez and Borja Vertedor Ballesteros for their collaboration in the final editing of the book.

pure status items. The study of the gift through a political prism also offers us a field rich in implications and nuances. Gift-giving can be interpreted as a voluntary mechanism that introduces or facilitates dialogue between interlocutors and, at a second stage, the attraction or alignment of wills, something especially pertinent in the context of ancient Mediterranean imperialism. It therefore plays an important strategic and symbolic role, constituting an instrument of historical (and anthropological) analysis of primary importance.

This book examines the giving or exchange of symbolic elements, considering it to be a practice of exceptional importance for understanding ancient societies. We will focus on a historical period that was crucial because of the intensity of contacts between human groups, cities and states, and is therefore of particular historiographical interest. This is the Hellenistic era, which partially overlaps with the period of the expansion of the Roman Republic in the Mediterranean (third to first centuries BC).

Let us start from a premise. Ever since it was unravelled by M. Mauss in his famous and almost centenarian 'Essai sur le don: forme et raison de l'échange dans les sociétés archaïques', the circulation of gifts – understood as prestige goods that generate a compensatory obligation on the part of the recipient – gives rise to and externalises socially constructed networks of friendship, assistance, domination or bribery.[1] The gift is a nexus through which, symbolically and materially, interpersonal and intercommunity relations are articulated, recognisable in multiple scenarios in the ancient world.[2] This dimension becomes qualitatively important in the context of Roman expansionism in the Mediterranean, in which, in parallel to purely offensive actions, if not complementing them, 'constructivist' behaviour is recorded, seeking cooperation, alliance or aid between political communities.[3] Diplomacy is the alter ego of conflict just as the present is the kind face of persuasion.

---

[1] Mauss, 1925. From the extensive bibliography that the review and critique of the Maussian gift theory (formulated, substantially, on the principle of reciprocity: one rarely gives a gift without expecting something in return) has produced in various disciplines (Anthropology, Sociology, Psychology, History...), we highlight the following: Godelier, 1996; James & Allen, 1998; Osteed, 2002; Algazi et alii, 2003; Sykes, 2005; Magnani, 2007; Liebersohn, 2011; Kustermans, 2021; Brummell, 2022: 3–10; Urakova et alii, 2023.

[2] Among the latest collective contributions: Satlow, 2013; Carlà & Gori, 2014; Cuniberti, 2017.

[3] Burton, 2003; 2010; 2011; Coşkun, 2008; 2017; García Riaza, 2011; Sánchez, 2016; Kemp, 2018; Sánchez Moreno & García Riaza, 2019; cf. Eckstein, 2006; Hoyos, 2013; Burton, 2019.

The practice of gift-giving and euergetism, its diplomatic instrumentality, is a particularly prolific field of study when researching the Greek world. Indeed, with different variables from Homeric times to the Hellenistic period, the *xenía* or ritualised friendship practised by aristocrats, cities and kingdoms had two of its most conspicuous expressions in the giving of gifts and the bestowal of honours.[4] With regard to the Roman Republic, historiographical production is intermittent and scattered. Among the most representative contributions are the works that deal with the reception of diplomatic gifts offered by foreign delegations in the Roman senate,[5] those that examine the role of gifts in the relationships of *amicitia* and patronage of the Roman elite,[6] and the studies on specific items, such as golden crowns and spoils of war.[7] There are also useful systematisations of embassies from kingdoms and cities to Rome throughout the Republican era, based on information from literary sources.[8] The study of gifts has traditionally been limited to the analysis of diplomatic missions to or from Rome, with little or no consideration of their political operability in the various Mediterranean scenarios in which Roman power intervened from the mid-third century BC onwards.[9] We hope that this book will help to address such reductionism.

In a commitment to theoretical and methodological transversality, this volume assumes – from the title itself – a concept that has been used in recent years in the study of more modern stages of the History of Diplomacy and International Relations: 'diplomatic materiality',[10] an analytical category also applicable to the ancient world despite the epistemological and documentary limitations inherent to research on diplomatic praxis in Antiquity. Following H. Rudolph,

> the concept of material culture of diplomacy includes all practices in foreign policy communication in which single artefacts, samples of

---

[4] See among other reference works on the gift and reciprocity in the Greek world: Herman, 1987; Konstan, 1997; Mitchell, 1997; Gill *et alii*, 1998; Mack, 2015; Basile, 2016; Van Berkel, 2020; Domingo Gygax, 2020; Domingo Gygax & Zuiderhoek, 2021; Lenfant, 2022.
[5] Auliard, 2006: 255–72; 2009; Grass, 2015.
[6] Verboven, 2002; 2014; Dixon, 1993; Coffee, 2017: 33–134.
[7] Coudry & Humm, 2009; Östenberg, 2009: 19–127; Coudry, 2012; Helm & Roselaar, 2023.
[8] Canali de Rossi, 1997; 2004–18; Claudon, 2015.
[9] Exceptions to this trend: Burton, 2011: 28–75; Ito, 2015: 22–46; García Riaza, 2021.
[10] Haberlein & Jeggle, 2013; Rudolph & Metzig, 2016; Biedermann *et alii*, 2018; Bauden, 2021; Kjaer, 2022.

artefacts, or else the whole material setting of diplomatic interaction is supposed to be constitutive for creating an intended effect in terms of diplomatic objectives – regardless of whether this effect was accomplished in the end or not. Investigating the material culture of diplomacy means studying a complex web of relations between material objects, human beings, and indoor as well as outdoor spaces to uncover the political, social, and legal significance of ways in which political actors brought artefacts into play during negotiations.[11]

Specifically, the joint assessment of agents, instruments and scenarios, the contextual analysis not only of the subjects but also of the objects that shape the encounter, the communication and resulting interaction, all allow us to obtain a more refined reading of the diplomatic processes that concern us in the following pages. Gifts – active elements endowed with agency, and behind them the dynamics through which they are transferred from hand to hand, or verbally, treasured or rejected by their recipients – invite us to explore the multiple modes of political exchange in the Hellenistic-Roman Mediterranean.

The purpose of this monograph is, therefore, to offer the reader a picture of the complexity of the phenomenon of diplomatic gifts in Antiquity, and especially in the chronological context of the Roman Republican expansion. To this end, the approach to the subject can only be kaleidoscopic. Mediterranean cultural diversity, the continuous processes of change, evolution and mutual influence have generated an enormous wealth of nuances that this scientific study will seek to identify. Far from simplifying approaches, therefore, this book is fully sensitive to this plural reality. From a geographical point of view, a multi-regional analysis has been carried out to highlight the diverse realities that coexisted during the period of expansion of the Roman Republic. In order to understand the practices of political and diplomatic interaction, their genesis has been taken into account, paying particular attention to the background of the Greek and Hellenistic world, which nourished and shaped nascent Roman diplomacy. At a tangential level of analysis, the book assumes and presents in all its richness another dimension of the object of study: the multifactorial character of the giving or exchange of gifts. It is necessary to study not only the physical nature of the goods given as gifts, but also the actors involved in this gesture, the motives that drive it, the conditioning factors that determine or limit it, and the scenarios in which the whole process takes place. The gift should and can be studied from a political perspective, but also from a cultural one, and analysed not only individually, but in a contextualisation

---

[11] Rudolph, 2016: 13. See also Nilsson Hammar *et alii*, 2022.

that takes into account the semantic value of the groups of objects, given as a 'signifying set'. In turn, such a semantic load cannot be univocal for the giver and the receiver if both belong to different cultural spheres, nor can it entail the same implications between the members of both elites and their respective subordinates. It is therefore crucial – and we believe that the book addresses this question – to carry out a historical reconstruction that takes into account all these elements, objective and subjective, in order to gauge the importance of gift exchange in the construction, maintenance and actualisation of networks of cooperation and also rivalry between individuals and collectives.

The book brings together international specialists who approach the question from different chronological, geographical and thematic points of view. An effort has been made to incorporate studies that cover most of the geographic areas and criss-crossing themes significant to the historical period examined.

Part I, 'A Background for Gifts in Action: Gracing Gods, Kings and Cities', consists of three chapters on the Ancient Near East, diplomacy in Classical Greek cities and the role of weapons as diplomatic gifts in the Greek world. This section begins with a chapter by Francesc Ramis Darder entitled 'Diplomatic Gifts in the Biblical Context of the Sixth to Fourth Centuries BC: A Systematic Study of Deuteronomistic History (Joshua–2 Kings)'. The author examines a broad narrative arc, from the conquest of the Palestinian land by the Hebrew hosts from Egypt, commanded by Joshua, to the liberation of the Hebrew monarch, Jeconiah, imprisoned in Babylon. In the Deuteronomistic approach the diplomatic gift is considered from two complementary perspectives: firstly, from the political aspect of the diplomatic relations of Israel and Judah with the eastern countries; and secondly, from the theological point of view that determines Israel's superiority over all nations.

If the Near Eastern sphere is a major element in understanding Mediterranean diplomatic practices, a key factor is the development of Greek diplomacy. To this interesting issue Dominique Lenfant devotes her study 'Greek Cities and Diplomatic Gifts in the Classical Period'. The author examines this practice firstly in the Homeric period, when exchange of gifts was a prominent element in ritualised friendship. In the world of Greek cities of the Classical period, guest-friendship (*xenía*) remained a personal relationship, and ambassadors did not officially receive gifts. They instead received symbolic honours, and not material ones. When Greek cities had diplomatic encounters with the Great King, they were offered sumptuous gifts which were part of a cultural and political code. Greek embassies did not themselves bring gifts to the king, since in the Persian imperial code this was a practice of subject peoples. Greek practice changed outside Athens from the fourth century BC and mainly in the Hellenistic period, since some cities began to offer gifts to visiting ambassadors: hospitality gifts (*xénia*) which were offered officially and fell within both the Greek tradition of guest-friendship (*xenía*) and the politics of civic honours.

A complementary perspective on the same cultural area, focusing on archaeological elements, is contributed by María del Mar Gabaldón Martínez: 'Gifts for the Gods and *Keimēlia*: Some Reflections on Arms as Diplomatic Gifts in the Greek World'. In her view, weapons were much more than tools for combat, and may have been clear symbols of prestige, precious offerings to deities, ceremonial instruments and even objects of worship and relics. This symbolic value of weapons and their use as a language of communication between men and gods explains the fact that many of them come from archaeological contexts defined by their ritual character, such as sanctuaries, particularly in the ancient Greek world. Among the numerous pieces of weaponry found in Greek sanctuaries from the eighth century BC until the Hellenistic period, some pieces of an exotic and special character may well have been diplomatic gifts, in addition to other functions and meanings. The author finally hypothesises that their presence in these spaces would have perpetuated the memory of a pact, thus becoming relics (*keimēlia*), a guise that can be traced back from Homeric times.

Moving into the sphere of Roman Republican expansion, Part II offers a series of case studies, from Asia Minor to Lusitania, underlining the common element of connectivity in turbulent times. This section brings together nine contributions, articulated according to both geo-chronological and thematic criteria.

This section begins with a contribution by Andrew Erskine that goes right into the Hellenistic world, already in contact with the Roman Republic: 'Crowns to Rome: Honours, Gifts and Hellenistic Diplomacy'. The author discusses the case of the representatives of the Attalid king Eumenes who arrived in Rome in the early 180s BC and presented the senate with a gold crown worth 15,000 gold staters. Although in his view this may have been exceptional in its extravagance, it was nevertheless one of numerous crowns to be offered to the Romans by the cities and kings around the Mediterranean. These diplomatic gifts are recorded by the historians Polybius and Livy, but they are still something of a mystery. The chapter thus explores their nature and significance, addressing some key questions. Considering that it is hard to conceive of a literal crown on the scale of the Attalid gift, we must wonder what was meant by a 'crown' in this context. The question also arises of what the gift of a crown says about the relationship between the giver and the recipient. It is also necessary to consider in what circumstances such a crown would be given.

Nathalie Barrandon, Anthony-Marc Sanz and Enrique García Riaza are the authors of the next chapter, which focuses specifically on Republican Rome: 'The Romans and Gifts from the Greeks: The Story of an Ostentatious Rejection'. The aim of this contribution is to offer a reflection on Roman ideological construction at the time of its intervention in the Hellenistic world, with a special focus on the third century BC. From the Roman perspective, the rejection of corruption – a moral quality that justified their claim to hegemony – led to the official refusal of diplomatic gifts. The Roman claim to justify its intervention in the East on the basis of alleged integrity may in turn explain the way in which the tradition concerning a number of episodes from the Pyrrhic War onwards is presented in the sources. The chapter focuses on some cases of total or partial refusal of gifts by Roman individuals, magistrates, senators and *legati*, in order to understand the mechanisms of this historiographical construction.

Miguel Esteban Payno and Gerard Ventós Rodríguez offer an introspective analysis entitled 'Gift, Debt, Anxiety in Late Hellenistic Times: On the Cautiousness and Attitudes of Achaeans, Macedonians and Bastarnae towards Diplomatic Presents'. Their main objective is to identify the reasons for the acceptance or refusal of gifts, a question openly addressed in the political debate of Hellenistic states. The underlying concern was fear of becoming indebted. The duty to compensate for received favours (whether material or symbolic ones) was pointed out by both those who sought benefits from gifts and those who rejected the gifts. The examples provided of the Achaeans, Macedonians and Bastarnae give us an opportunity to reflect on the varying attitudes that states took when reacting to gifts. The background of status anxiety within which actors were involved was a consequence of a quandary: whether to incur a debt and keep a friend or to renounce to that friendship and so save themselves the heavy burden of having to reciprocate. Both options show the assumed acknowledgement that the debt would have to be settled. In their view, gratitude was not a petty, merely rhetorical concept, but promoted and conditioned (preventatively or *a posteriori*) the attitudes of political communities.

This interconnected world, with a strong Hellenistic influence, was articulated through a series of poles of interaction during the Republic's overseas expansion. Undoubtedly one of the most noteworthy of these was the Roman camp, a privileged setting for political and diplomatic contacts as the headquarters and seat of the proto-provincial administration. Borja Vertedor Ballesteros focuses on this important aspect of Roman expansion in 'Buying Goodwill, Granting Rewards: The Roman Headquarters as a Space of Diplomatic Interaction'. The *intra vallum* area hosted diplomatic missions, receiving messengers and ambassadors. The camp and its surroundings were also the venue for high-level political meetings of the *conloquia* type, with the participation of local and regional leaders. The general in chief, assisted by his *consilium*, played a crucial role in a complex ritual of audiences as the unifying force behind these political-diplomatic dynamics. At the same time, the headquarters were the starting point for the dispatch of *legati* in order to create or re-establish bonds of friendship and to interact politically with its surroundings. In these contexts, gift-giving was often used as an instrument of diplomatic status materialisation, or as a tangible expression of goodwill to engage in negotiations and reach cooperation agreements.

Without abandoning the chronological scope of the Middle Republic, the book continues to explore the phenomenon of diplomatic gifts in geographical, political and cultural contexts that were originally far from the Italian reality, but which were affected by the expansion of the Republic. Esther Sánchez Medina and Gabriel Roselló Calafell turn our attention to North Africa with their chapter entitled 'From Presents to Bribes: Symbolic and Political Evolution of the Diplomatic Gift in Relations between Romans and Numidians. Through very different formulae, including bribery, the Republic won the adherence of the Numidian leaders from the final years of the Hannibalic War until the end of the second century BC. Considered an essential element for the understanding of Roman foreign policy, the diplomatic present acquired a specific dimension in this context, where it is possible to analyse its long-term evolution through the review of literary testimony and its contrast with material sources, especially from numismatics. This study thus discusses the differences between the first contacts of the Scipiones and Syphax (214 BC) and the reciprocity that can be observed in the case of Jugurtha and the late Republican elites, almost one hundred years later. The authors conclude that during this period, a paradigm shift is reflected both in the symbolism and in the implications of the objects given, manifesting a parallel evolution within the political relations between the elites of both powers.

The complexity of Gallic diplomatic practices prior to Roman influence and, especially, during the diplomatic and military interventions of the Republic in the first century BC is explored by Alberto Pérez Rubio in 'Torques, Horses and Gold: Approaching Diplomatic Gifts in Gaul'. Based mainly on the accounts of Posidonius, Caesar, Strabo and Livy, and considering also the archaeological and numismatic records, the author discusses some examples of diplomatic gifts in Gaul, the most conspicuous being torques (an ornament imbued with a powerful symbolic significance), weapons and horses. This is the case of the gifts granted by the Roman senate to allied Gallic kings (Cincibilus and Balanus). A similar role may have been played by other elements, such as luxury *fibulae* or even pecuniary gifts. The exchange of presents among Celtic elites and the giving of gifts by Rome should be understood as tokens of prestige and an acknowledgement of status, and were an important mechanism for settling and maintaining diplomatic relationships.

This volume continues with a thematic group of articles focusing on the Iberian Peninsula, an inexhaustible source of information for the study of Roman expansion and interaction with local societies. This section, presented chronologically, begins with the contribution by Eduardo Sánchez Moreno and Jorge García Cardiel: '*Do ut des*: Liberating Hostages and Offering Gifts on the Hispanic Front in the Second Punic War'. The authors begin their study with the following assertion: Romans needed the assistance of the local communities that operated on Hispanian soil during the Second Punic War, so they tried to build bridges that promoted political interaction with their elites – or with certain factions of those elites better disposed towards Roman interests. Among the measures implemented, this chapter focuses on hostage releases and diplomatic gift exchanges: two simultaneous and intertwined actions that operated as signs of the same language, well known to Romans, Carthaginians, Iberians, Celtiberians and Numidians. The three episodes analysed – the release of hostages at Saguntum, the one that took place at Carthago Nova, and the liberation of the young Numidian prince Massiva after the Battle of Baecula – are highly illustrative of the prevailing patterns, but also of the diversity of responses resulting from the changing context and the different political counterparts.

Moving slightly forward in time and expanding the geographical span, Manuel Salinas de Frías comprehensively analyses the phenomenon of wealth acquisition against the backdrop of war on Hispanian territory in 'Gold for the Romans: Booty, Gifts and Bribes during the Roman Conquest of the Western Iberian Peninsula'. His article takes as its starting point a case study: the passage by Diodorus Siculus on the wedding of Viriathus, the Lusitanian leader, in the mid-second century BC. During the wedding, his father-in-law Astolpas exhibited a large quantity of gold and silver, and was rebuked by Viriathus since he entrusted the security of these riches to the Romans and not to him, who was the bearer of the spear. The chapter analyses the existence of these treasures in the area of the western Iberian Peninsula during the wars of Roman conquest and their polysemic function as a diplomatic gift, as a bribe or as loot in the conflict-ridden context of the time, as well as the origin and function of these gold reserves and their role in the diplomacy of local peoples with each other and with the Roman power.

The survey of diplomatic gifts in Hispanian territory concludes with the chapter by David García Domínguez and Diego Suárez Martínez on one of the major conflicts of the first century BC: 'Bonding Gifts: Material Exchange and Political Alliance during the Sertorian War'. The article analyses the logic of gift exchange during that confrontation (82–72 BC). The materiality of the exchanged goods was affected by long-range dynamics of colonial interaction, but the process and meanings of gift-giving were also shaped by the ongoing Roman civil war. The authors hypothesise that the reception of gifts by local dignitaries exteriorised the mutual acknowledgement between their respective *civitates* and Cinnan Rome. At the same time, gifts were meant to build and sustain a hierarchy of power that would benefit both Sertorius and the actual recipients of the presents, members of the elites who would act in the name of their communities. The authors conclude that this double dimension of the gift reveals the complex overlapping of the private and the public spheres in the political practice of the time.

The work as a whole is rounded off with a study in the form of an epilogue, contributed by Tomás Aguilera Durán, that relates, by analogy or contrast, the ancient practice of gift-giving with that corresponding to contemporary colonial models, underlining, in short, the topicality and relevance of the subject: 'Gifts at the Edges of the World: Diplomatic Exchanges in the Roman West and Early Colonial Chile'. This chapter proposes a comparative study of the role of diplomatic gifts in Western Roman expansion and the first stage of the Arauco War (1536–98). The failed Spanish conquest of Central-Southern Chile provides the chance to reflect on key complex colonial phenomena (endemic violence, cultural hybridism and institutionalisation of 'middle ground' territories) in two directions: discursive and ethnohistorical. Firstly, the gift is analysed in the construction per se of the colonial narrative, otherisation of the enemy, and debates about the legitimacy of the war, using classical rhetorical tropes (the sly conqueror, the deceived noble savage or the bloodthirsty barbarian). Secondly, some anthropological and historical interpretations are considered in connection with analogous social and cultural processes derived from the entrenchment of the war: the control of ritual language and progressive mutual adaption, with the standardisation of manners and objects (chaquira necklaces provide the example), the character of the gift in the forging of coalitions and ethnogenesis processes, as well as typological transformations according to social and military changes (from luxury items to horses and weapons).

This volume is the fourth in the Civitas-Occidens Collection and is aimed at offering a new perspective on the importance of cultural contexts for historical reconstruction. We would furthermore also like this work to contribute to shedding light on current issues such as the role of diplomacy and dialogue between cultures as a means of conflict resolution. The reader has in their hands a collective and plural work. The editors express their gratitude to each and every one of the authors. They have worked as a team during the four years of the research project implementation, facing the health challenges of our time without losing heart, and stimulating an intellectual debate that has enriched us all. We are also grateful for the recognition and support of the State Research Agency (Government of Spain)/ERDF (European Union), which financed the activities. The encouragement of Prof. Andrew Erskine has been essential in making this book come to fruition. To conclude, the generous hosting by Edinburgh University Press of the publication of this work is, for us, the most precious of gifts.

Bibliography

Algazi, G., Groebner, V. & Jussen, B. (eds) [2003]. *Negotiating the Gift: Pre-Modern Figurations of Exchange*, Göttingen.

Auliard, C. [2006]. *La diplomatie romaine: l'autre instrument de la conquête. De la fondation à la fin des guerres samnites (753–290 av.-J.C.)*, Rennes.

Auliard, C. [2009]. 'Cadeaux et marchandages diplomatiques à Rome jusqu'au debut de la conquête méditerranéenne', *Veleia*, 26, 63–73.

Basile, G. J. [2016]. '*Xenía*: la amistad-ritualizada de Homero a Heródoto', *Emerita*, 84 (2), 229–50.

Bauden, F. (ed.) [2021]. *Culture matérielle et contacts diplomatiques entre l'Occident latin, Byzance et l'Orient islamique (XIe–XVIe siècle)*, Leiden–Boston.

Berkel, T. A. van [2020]. *The Economics of Friendship: Conceptions of Reciprocity in Classical Greece*, Leiden–Boston.

Biedermann, Z., Gerritsen, A. & Riello, J. (eds) [2018]. *Global Gifts: The Material Culture of Diplomacy in Early Modern Eurasia*, Cambridge.

Brummell, P. [2022]. *Diplomatic Gifts: A History in Fifty Presents*, London.

Burton, P. J. [2003]. '*Clientela* or *Amicitia*? Modeling Roman International Behavior in the Middle Republic (264–146 B.C.)', *Klio*, 85 (2), 333–69.

Burton, P. J. [2010]. 'Culture and Constructivism in International Relations', *International History Review*, 32 (1), 89–97.

Burton, P. J. [2011]. *Friendship and Empire: Roman Diplomacy and Imperialism in the Middle Republic (353–146 BC)*, Cambridge.

Burton, P. J. [2019]. *Roman Imperialism*, Leiden & Boston.

Canali de Rossi, F. [1997]. *Le ambascerie dal mondo greco a Roma in età repubblicana*, Rome.
Canali de Rossi, F. [2004–18]. *Le relazioni diplomatiche di Roma*, Vol. 1: *Dall'età regia alla conquista del primato in Italia (753–265 a.C.)* [2004]. Vol. 2: *Dall'intervento in Sicilia fino alla invasione annibalica (264–216 a.C.)* [2007]. Vol. 3: *Dalla resistenza di Fabio fino alla vittoria di Scipione (215–201 a.C.)* [2013]. Vol. 4: *Dalla liberazione della Grecia alla pace infida con Antioco III (201–194 a.C.)* [2014]. Vol. 5: *Dalla pace infida alla espulsione di Antioco dalla Graecia (194–190 a.C.)* [2017]. Vol. 6: *Dalla spedizione degli Scipioni in Asia alla pace di Apamea (190–188 a.C.)*. Vol. 7: *Problemi e contraccolpi della grande espansione egemonica (188–183 a.C.)*. Vol. 8: *La crisi dinastica macedone e le contese interne della Grecia (182–179 a.C.)*, Rome.
Carlà, F. & Gori, M. (eds) [2014]. *Gift Giving and the 'Embedded' Economy in the Ancient World*, Heidelberg.
Claudon, H. F. [2015]. *Les ambassades des cités grecques d'Asie Mineure auprès des autorités romaines: de la libération des Grecs à la fin du Haut-Empire (196 av. J.-C.–235 apr. J.-C.)*, Paris.
Coffee, N. [2017]. *Gift and Gain: How Money Transformed Ancient Rome*, Oxford.
Coşkun, A. (ed.) [2008]. *Freundschaft und Gefolgschaft in den auswärtigen Beziehungen der Römer (2. Jh. v.Chr.–1. Jh. n. Chr.)*, Frankfurt.
Coşkun, A. [2017]. '*Amicitia, Fides* und *Imperium* der Römer aus konstruktivistischer Perspektive: Überlegungen zu Paul Burton's *Friendship and Empire* (2011)', *Latomus*, 76, 910–24.
Coudry, M. [2012]. 'L'or des vaincus: travestissement et occultation des transactions financières dans la diplomatie de la Rome républicaine', in F. Marco Simón, F. Pina Polo & J. Remesal Rodríguez (eds), *Vae victis! Perdedores en el mundo antiguo*, Barcelona, 113–31.
Coudry, M. & Humm, M. (eds) [2009]. *Praeda: Butin de guerre et société dans la Rome républicaine / Kriegsbeute und Gesellschaft im republikanischen Rom*, Stuttgart.
Cuniberti, G. (ed.) [2017]. *Dono, controdono e corruzione: ricerche storiche e dialogo interdisciplinare*, Alessandria.
Dixon, S. [1993]. 'The Meaning of Gift and Debt in the Roman Elite', *Echos du Monde Classique*, 37 (3), 451–64.
Domingo Gygax, M. [2020]. *Benefaction and Rewards in the Ancient Greek City: The Origins of Euergetism*, Cambridge.
Domingo Gygax, M. & Zuiderhoek, A. (eds) [2021]. *Benefactors and the Polis: The Public Gift in the Greek Cities from the Homeric World to Late Antiquity*, Cambridge.

Eckstein, A. M. [2006]. *Mediterranean Anarchy, Interstate War, and the Rise of Rome*, Berkeley–Los Angeles–London.

García Riaza, E. (ed.) [2011]. *De fronteras a provincias: interacción e integración en Occidente (ss. III–I a.C.)*, Palma de Mallorca.

García Riaza, E. [2021]. 'Secreta spes. Roma y la generación de expectativas en las élites foráneas: algunos casos de estudio en torno al regalo diplomático', in M. D. Dopico Caínzos & M. Villanueva Acuña (eds), *Aut oppressi servient … La intervención de Roma en las comunidades indígenas*, Lugo, 95–115.

Gill, C., Postlethwaite, N. & Seaford, R. (eds) [1998]. *Reciprocity in Ancient Greece*, Oxford.

Godelier, M. [1996]. *L'Énigme du don*, Paris.

Grass, B. [2015]. 'Les présents diplomatiques à Rome (IIIe–Ier siècle av. J.-C.)', in B. Grass & G. Stouder (eds), *La diplomatie romaine sous la République: réflexions sur une pratique*, Besançon, 147–73.

Haberlein, M. & Jeggle, C. (eds) [2013]. *Materielle Grundlagen der Diplomatie: Schenken, Sammeln und Verhandeln in Spätmittelalter und Früher Neuzeit*, Konstanz.

Helm, M. & Roselaar, S.T. (eds.) [2023]. *Spoils in the Roman Republic. Boon and Bane*, Stuttgart.

Herman, G. [1987]. *Ritualised Friendship and the Greek City*, Cambridge.

Hoyos, B. D. (ed.) [2013]. *A Companion to Roman Imperialism*, Leiden–Boston.

Ito, M. [2015]. *Informal Diplomacy and Rome from the First Macedonian War to the Assassination of Ti. Gracchus*, PhD dissertation, University of Edinburgh.

James, W. & Allen, N. J. (eds) [1998]. *Marcel Mauss: A Centenary Tribute*, Oxford.

Kemp, J. [2018]. 'Amicitia, Gift-Exchange and Subsidies in Imperial Roman Diplomacy', in V. D. Mihajlovi & M. A. Jankovic (eds), *Reflections of Roman Imperialism*, Newcastle upon Tyne, 85–105.

Kjaer, L. (ed.) [2022]. *Gift-Giving and Materiality in Europe, 1300–1600: Gifts as Objects*, London.

Konstan, D. [1997]. *Friendship in the Classical World*, Cambridge.

Kustermans, J. [2021]. 'Diplomatic Gifts: An Introduction to the Forum', *Hague Journal of Diplomacy*, 16 (1), 105–9.

Lenfant, D. [2022]. 'The Role of *Xenia* in Diplomatic Relations between Greek Cities and the Persian Empire', in F. Mari & C. Wendt (eds), *Shaping Good Faith: Modes of Communication in Ancient Diplomacy*, Stuttgart, 81–93.

Liebersohn, H. [2011]. *The Return of the Gift: European History of a Global Idea*, Cambridge.

Mack, W. [2015]. *Proxeny and Polis: Institutional Networks in the Ancient Greek World*, Oxford.
Magnani, E. (ed.) [2007]. *Don et sciences sociales: théories et pratiques croisées*, Dijon.
Mauss, M. [1925]. 'Essai sur le don: forme et raison de l'échange dans les sociétés archaïques', *L'Année sociologique*, 1, 30–186. [*The Gift: The Form and Reason for Exchange in Archaic Societies* (translated by W. D. Halls; foreword by Mary Douglas), 1990, London & New York.]
Mitchell, L. G. [1997]. *Greeks Bearing Gifts: The Public Use of Private Relationships in the Greek World (435–323 B.C.)*, Cambridge.
Nilsson Hammar, A., Nyström, D. & Almjär, M. [2022]. *Gender, Materiality, and Politics: Essays on the Making of Power*, Lund.
Osteed, M. (ed.) [2002]. *The Question of the Gift: Essays across Disciplines*, London.
Östenberg, I. [2009]. *Staging the World: Spoils, Captives and Representations in the Roman Triumphal Procession*, Oxford.
Rudolph, H. [2016]. 'Entangled Objects and Hybrid Practices? Material Culture as a New Approach to the History of Diplomacy', in H. Rudolph & G. M. Metzig (eds), *Material Culture in Modern Diplomacy from the 15th to the 20th Century*, Berlin–Boston, 1–28.
Rudolph, H. & Metzig, G. M. (eds) [2016]. *Material Culture in Modern Diplomacy from the 15th to the 20th Century*, Berlin–Boston.
Sánchez, P. [2016]. 'Quand Rome se cherchait de nouveaux alliés: les accords de coopération militaire négociés à l'initiative des Romains sur le théâtre des opérations (IVe–IIIe siècles av. n.è.)', *Ktèma*, 41, 165–90.
Sánchez Moreno, E. & García Riaza, E. (eds) [2019]. *Unidos en armas: coaliciones militares en el Occidente antiguo*, Palma de Mallorca–Madrid.
Satlow, M. (ed.) [2013]. *The Gift in Antiquity*, Oxford.
Sykes, K. [2005]. *Arguing with Anthropology: An Introduction to Critical Theories of the Gift*, London–New York.
Urakova, A., Sowerby, T. A. & Tudor, S. (eds) [2023]. *The Dangers of Gifts from Antiquity to the Digital Age*, New York–London.
Verboven, K. [2002]. *The Economy of Friends: Economic Aspects of 'Amicitia' and Patronage in the Late Republic*, Brussels.
Verboven, K. [2014]. 'Like Bait on a Hook: Ethics, Etics and Emics of Gift-Exchange in the Roman World', in F. Carlà & M. Gori (eds), *Gift Giving and the 'Embedded' Economy in the Ancient World*, Heidelberg, 135–55.

Part I

A Background for Gifts in Action Gracing Gods, Kings and Cities

1
Diplomatic Gifts in the Biblical Context of the Sixth to Fourth Centuries BC
A Systematic Study of Deuteronomistic History (Joshua–2 Kings)*

Francesc Ramis Darder

The objective of this study revolves around the description and analysis of the theme of diplomatic gifts as they figure in Deuteronomistic History. The six biblical books that compose that history (Joshua, Judges, 1 Samuel, 2 Samuel, 1 Kings, 2 Kings) encompass, from a theological perspective, a broad sweep of history. They open with the story of the arrival of the Hebrew host, having fled Egypt and led by Joshua, to take possession of the land of Israel[1] and close with the story of the release of Jeconiah, the King of Judah exiled to Babylon, thanks to the Babylonian king Amel-Marduk.[2] Deuteronomistic History is rooted in different literary sources; it underwent a long, complex process of composition before it reached its definitive form among the scribes of Jerusalem between the mid-fifth and the early fourth centuries BC during the final stages of the Persian period (458–333 BC).[3]

---

* This work has been developed within the research project PGC2018-096415-B-C22 'La expresión diplomática en el Mediterráneo central y oriental bajo la expansión romana: el regalo en su contexto político e institucional', funded by the State Research Agency, Ministry of Science and Innovation, Government of Spain (MCIN/AEI/10.13039/501100011033) and ERDF 'A way of making Europe'.
[1] Jos. 1.1–3.
[2] 2 Kg. 25.27–30.
[3] The process of writing the Deuteronomistic History (Dtr) was complex, and explaining and analysing it goes beyond the remit of this study; for a description of the process, Sicre, 2002: 32–52. Commentators have established four stages in the initial creation of Dtr – Dtr 595/575/560/525 – to which should be added later re-readings and additions until the final stages of the Persian period: Vermeylen, 1978: 122–72; Ramis Darder, 2012: 33–62. For deeper study of the sources, the writing process and the final shape of Deuteronomistic History, see Römer, 2000.

While bearing in mind the lengthy process of composition, we will focus our study on the final version of the biblical source, which appears in the critical edition of the *Biblia Hebraica Stuttgartensia* (BHS).[4] From the methodological perspective, we will assess how continuous reading of Deuteronomistic History reveals the three levels upon which gifts and diplomatic exchange arguably occur. The first level gives a glimpse of the diplomatic exchange between various tribes and social groups that dwelt on Palestinian land; the second reveals the diplomatic gift both between kings of Judah and Israel and between those monarchs and foreign sovereigns; the final level leapfrogs the political aspect of the two previous ones to enter into the theological aspect of gifts that cleanse, from a diplomatic/metaphorical optic, the alliance between God and Israel, His people. It should be appreciated that the biblical bibliography tends to confer limited focus upon the political value of the diplomatic gift, represented by the first two levels, while it tends to perceive with breadth and from the theological perspective the diplomatic/symbolic aspect that can be perceived beneath the relationship between God and Israel, an echo of an alliance; this perspective confirms the innovative aspect of this study, which embraces the three levels mentioned.[5] Having settled the source (the Hebrew biblical text BHS) and the methodology (a continuous reading of Deuteronomistic History), we will establish the structure of the study, so the three levels on which the diplomatic gift and its parallels appear will be described, with particular emphasis on the first two, ending with a brief conclusion.

Diplomatic Exchange between Tribes and Social Actors in Judaean/Israelite Territory

The Book of Joshua begins by narrating, from a theological perspective, the conquest of Jericho by the Hebrews out of Egypt, captained by Joshua.[6] As the story recounts, the leader sent two spies to inspect Jericho; the king of the city was informed and undertook a search, but could not find them

---

[4] Elliger & Rudolf, 1984; regarding the Septuagint, in cases of textual precision: Rahlfs, 1979.

[5] Discussions on the history of Israel barely suggest the importance of the diplomatic gift: see Finkelstein & Mazar, 2007; the theological perspective emphasises the aspect of God's alliance with Israel: see Schmid, 2019.

[6] Jos. 2–7. With regard to the theological perspective and the possible historical allusions present in the texts, see Sicre, 2002: 154–213; Liverani, 2003, 234–41, situates the composition at the end of the fourth century BC and stresses the metaphorical perspective.

because a prostitute, Rahab, had hidden them in her house, which was built into the city walls. The spies and the prostitute made a pact. As Rahab had saved the spies' lives so that the Hebrews could conquer the city, so the Hebrews would protect the lives of the woman and her family when they took Jericho, and would allow them to live among the conquerors. And so it was: once Jericho was occupied, 'Rahab the prostitute, her father's family and all who belonged to her, these Joshua spared. She is still living in Israel even today.'[7] Discernible here, therefore, is an exchange of gifts: in exchange for protecting the informers, Rahab's family remained in Judaean lands alive.

A similar case occurred in the pact between Joshua and the Gibeonites.[8] The Gibeonites were Hivites and lived in the cities of Gibeon, Kephirah, Beeroth and Kiriath Jearim,[9] located in Israelite lands. Knowing about the conquest of Jericho, they went to meet Joshua to plead for a peace agreement to save their lives. They loaded their donkeys with tattered provisions, hidden in old wineskins and saddlebags, wearing worn sandals and patched clothing to get Joshua to believe that they were poor and from a distant country, and wanted to enter into a pact with the Israelites. Joshua fell into the trap; moved by their apparent poverty, and convinced of their foreign origin, he partook of the provisions of the recent arrivals to show, by doing so, that he agreed a pact with the Gibeonites. Joshua later discovered the trick; but, subject to the terms of the pact, he had to keep them within Israel as woodcutters and water-bearers, 'and so they are today'.[10] In exchange for some provisions, brought deceitfully, Joshua thus established a pact with the Gibeonites.

Among the avatars of the conquest of Canaan, Caleb, son of Jephunneh the Kenizzite, recalled to Joshua the promise that he had long ago received from Moses according to which he would be given the land upon which he walked when he explored Caananite territory; to fulfil Moses' promise, Joshua therefore gave him Hebron as his inheritance.[11] Later on, Joshua offered his daughter Aksah in marriage to the man who took Kiriath Sepher; it was captured by Othniel, son of Kenaz, brother of Caleb, who espoused her and also profited from her dowry, the Negev desert; even so, he encouraged his wife to obtain the gift of the springs of water from her father, Caleb.[12] In exchange for his participation in the conquest of

[7] Jos. 6.25.
[8] Jos. 9–11.
[9] Jos. 9.17.
[10] Jos. 9.27.
[11] Jos. 14.6–15; cf. Jdg. 1.12–36.
[12] Jos. 15.16–19.

the Palestinian land, Othniel received Aksah as his wife and governed the Negev, and with great cunning obtained springs of water.

When Joshua completed the conquest of Canaan, he released the Reubenites and Gadites and the half-tribe of Manasseh, who had taken part in the campaign,[13] offering them abundant gifts: 'You are going back to your tents with great wealth, with a great deal of livestock, with silver and gold, bonze and iron and great quantities of clothing';[14] having received the rewards, the tribes returned to the land of Gilead, where they had settled. As payment for their military help, the tribes received donations of land and substantial gifts.

Following on, the Book of Judges describes how Gideon demanded a gift from the Israelites in order to become their protector; each of the Israelites, conquerors of the Midianites, brought the judge a gold ring taken from Midianite booty; as the account relates, 'the weight of the gold rings which he has asked for amounted to seventeen hundred shekels of gold, besides garments worn by the kings of Midian, and besides the collars round their camels' necks';[15] with the offerings, Gideon erected an ephod in Ophrah.[16] Later, when his mother's brothers and the men of Shechem wanted Abimelek to become king of Israel, they brought him seventy shekels of silver from the Temple of Baal-Berit with which to recruit mercenaries to seize the crown and later benefit the citizens of Shechem.[17] Later, the rulers of the Philistines offered Delilah, wife of Samson, 1,100 shekels of silver each to let them trap Samson and thereby seize his land.[18] Another specific aspect of gifts lies in the Israelites' giving of women to the Benjamites so that the tribe would not die out; the Israelites therefore gave the tribe of Benjamin the women who had survived after the Israelite incursion into Jabesh Gilead.[19]

As the Books of Samuel relate, the Philistines, to extricate themselves from a plague inflicted by the God of Israel, decided to return the Ark of the Covenant, which they had taken from the Israelites, accompanied by a peculiar gift: 'corresponding to the number of Philistine chiefs: five

---

[13] Jos. 22.3–5.
[14] Jos. 22.7–8.
[15] Jdg. 8.26–7.
[16] In general terms, a shekel is the equivalent of 11.4 g; a talent of gold corresponds to 34.272 kg. The exact nature of the ephod is still being debated; however, in this case, it alludes to a solid cult object; see Vaux, 1984: 216–19.
[17] Jdg. 9.3–4.
[18] Jdg. 16.5.
[19] Jdg. 21.13–14.

golden tumours and five golden rats.'[20] When Samuel called together all the Hebrew tribes in Mizpah to make Saul king, some scoundrels – according to the text – refused to offer any gift as a symbol of their tribe's submission.[21] When an evil spirit started to torment Saul, the monarch sent messengers to Jesse of Bethlehem for his son David to live in the court. At that time, David was still a shepherd among his father's flocks. When Jesse sent his son to Saul's court, he also sent him a gift of obeisance: 'Jesse took five loaves, a skin of wine and a kid, and sent them to Saul by his son David.'[22] Further on, Abigail, wife of Nabal, the owner of a large estate in Carmel, sent a generous present to David, now an accomplished warrior and leader of a mercenary band, to save his life and later marry him: 'Abigail hastily took two hundred loaves, two skins of wine, five sheep ready prepared, five measures of roasted grain, a hundred bunches of raisins and two hundred cakes of figs and loaded them on donkeys.'[23]

Classical historiography situates the final composition of the episodes mentioned around the late period of the Judaean monarchy (c. 622–587 BC); it considers them aetiological tales composed to explain the presence of foreigners in Palestinian lands (Rahab, Gibeonites), the residence of special Hebrew groups in Judaean lands (Caleb, Othniel) and the presence of Hebrews beyond the borders of the Kingdom of Judah (Gadites, the half tribe of Manasseh). In this way, the sanctuary Rahab gave the Hebrew spies and the provisions brought by the Gibeonites represent foreigners' gifts to the Hebrews so that they could live in Palestinian land; the gift of the sources of water relates the ancestral rule of the Negev clans over the water wells, while the offerings to the tribes of Gilead highlight the participation of all the Israelites in the conquest of Canaan; the gifts also express the peculiarity of some Hebrew clans (Othniel) and the communion of all the tribes in the occupation of Canaan (Reuben, Gad, Manasseh); offering women to various tribes evoked ancestral customs; the gifts offered to Saul, that to David from Jesse, and the gold to Abimelek symbolise the commitment to show loyalty to the king or future monarch, while the bribery of Delilah evokes the habitual purchase of loyalties among the tribes.[24]

Recent historiography, however, offers another interpretative horizon of the above stories. The Judaeans who lived in exile in Babylon (597–538 BC), called from the theological perspective the remnants of

---

[20] 1 Sam. 6.4; 6.7–18.
[21] 1 Sam. 9.27.
[22] 1 Sam. 16.20.
[23] 1 Sam. 25.18.
[24] The aetiological perspective, from Classical exegesis: Vaux, 1996: 560–76; Hermann, 1979: 134–47.

Israel, established a new perspective on the Hebrew religion. When their descendants returned to Jerusalem, from 538 BC,[25] they had to agree terms with the descendants of those who had stayed in Judaean lands during the exile, known as the People of the Land, in order to be able to share the land in harmony. In this way, the story of Rahab evokes the pact by those who returned from exile, represented by the hosts of Joshua, to settle in Jericho; analogously, the Gibeonites' offering highlights the submission of some clans before the authority of the those who returned from exile, again represented by Joshua; the gift of lands received by Othniel and Caleb emphasise the exiles' concessions to the People of the Land to live in the land; the Philistines' offering of golden tumours and rats to the Hebrews reveals the ridicule in which the Judaean religion held pagan idolatry;[26] while the offering of women to the tribe of Benjamin could allude to the need to give wives to the Hebrews who, obeying the legislation promulgated by Ezra and Nehemiah,[27] had divorced their pagan wives (450–398 BC).[28]

Diplomatic Gifts between the Kings of Judah and Israel, and between Them and Foreign Sovereigns

The Deuteronomistic History continues with the Books of Samuel attesting that David held the crown of two states at once, that of Judah in the south of the Palestinian region, and Israel in the north; Davidic territory therefore reached a notable size.[29] Hiram, King of Tyre, then sent an embassy to David with cedar logs, carpenters and stonemasons, to build him a palace;[30] the gifts undoubtedly emphasise, according to the Deuteronomistic approach, Hiram's submission to David's sovereignty. Later on, the Moabites became servants of David, paying him tribute in the form of gifts.[31] Almost immediately, David defeated Hadadezer, King of Zobah; he then took the gold

---

[25] Ezr. 1.14.
[26] Ba. 6.
[27] Ezr. 9.
[28] As it affects the new horizon of Jewish religion during the exile and post-exile period: Becking & Korpel, 1999; Albertz, 2003. On the theological and sociological aspect of the remnants of Israel and the People of the Land: Ramis Darder, 2012: 45–96. To specify references to historical events and theological perspectives of the period immediately after the exile: Sacchi, 2004: 125–230. As it affects the theology and historical evolution of Judaism during the Neo-Babylonian Empire: Lipschits & Blenkinsopp, 2003; García Fernández, 2020: 47–64.
[29] 2 Sam. 2.1–21; 5.1–9.
[30] 2 Sam. 5.20.
[31] 2 Sam. 8.2.

quivers that Hadadezer's servants carried and brought them to Jerusalem.[32] When Tou, sovereign of Jamath, learnt of David's victory over Hadadezer, he quickly sent him, via his son Horam, valuable gifts of gold, silver and bronze, which David consecrated to the God of Israel.[33] Through the mention of gifts, the Deuteronomistic voice attests, from the theological perspective, to the submission to David's authority of the kingdoms neighbouring Judah and Israel.

Over time, David's strength turned to woe and he had to flee Jerusalem. A loyal steward, Ziba, then showered the monarch with gifts to ensure he survived. He gave him donkeys, bread, figs and wine; in exchange, David assured Ziba that he would give him the inheritance of Mephibosheth, an enemy of the king, as a reward for his loyalty.[34] When David arrived at Mahanaim, Shobi, son of Nahash of the Ammonites, Makir, son of Ammiel from Lo Debar, and Barzillai, the Gileadite from Rogelim, brought gifts and victuals to David and his companions in flight: beds, flour, roasted grain, beans, lentils, honey, curds and sheep and goat cheese.[35] The mention of the gifts hides the givers' interest in achieving important posts in David's restored court, as the Scriptures later indicate.[36]

The Books of Kings recount the sovereign exercise of the monarchs of Judah and Israel. The first lines describing Solomon's reign attest to the pact between the King of Jerusalem and the Egyptian Pharoah; to authenticate the alliance, the biblical account underlines how Solomon married Pharoah's daughter and brought her to Jerusalem.[37] Pharoah gave the city of Giza to the king as his daughter's dowry,[38] and, once married, Solomon built her a palace in Jerusalem.[39] To extol Solomon's magnificence, the Deuteronomistic History emphasises the gifts that the subject kingdoms brought him: 'they also provided the barley and straw for the horses and draught animals. Thirty measures of fine flour and sixty measures of meal, ten fattened oxen, twenty free-grazing oxen, one hundred sheep, besides

---

[32] 2 Sam. 8.6.
[33] 2 Sam. 8.9–10.
[34] 2 Sam. 16.1–4.
[35] 2 Sam. 17.27–9.
[36] 2 Sam. 19.32–40. As current historiography indicates, David's strength should be largely relativised. According to some studies, the epic of David constitutes a very late story to emphasise, right from the beginning of the monarchy, the ascendance of the ideal monarch endowed with a messianic aspect; see Finkelstein & Silberman, 2003; Ska, 2020.
[37] 1 Kg. 3.1.
[38] 1 Kg. 9.16.
[39] 1 Kg. 9.24.

deer and gazelles, roebucks and fattened poultry'.[40] Desiring to stress Solomon's royal aura, the narration adds: 'men from all nations came to hear Solomon's wisdom, and received gifts from all the kings in the world, who had heard of his wisdom'.[41] As we can see, the splendour of the gifts constitutes, from a theological perspective, the magnification of Solomon, prototype of the ideal monarch.[42]

The Scriptures lend particular attention to the treaty between Hiram of Tyre and Solomon of Jerusalem. Hiram brought Solomon all the cedar and cypress logs he wanted, while Solomon sent Hiram 20,000 cors of wheat and 20,000 baths of olive oil as provisions for his household.[43] The Scriptures specify that, over time, the relationship between Solomon and Hiram acquired overtones of the Phoenician submitting to the authority of the Hebrew. This is expressed by the value of the successive exchanges of diplomatic gifts between the two sovereigns. Solomon gave Hiram twenty cities in Galilee, while Hiram, King of Tyre, provided Solomon cedar and cypress wood and all the gold that he asked for; in addition to that, Hiram also gave Solomon twenty talents of gold. When Hiram visited the Galilean cities which Solomon had awarded him, however, he called them 'Kabul-Land', that is, wasteland or barren, that which is good for nothing.[44] The gifts brought by the fleet of Tarsis, manned by Phoenician officials, which reached Solomon's court acquired particular significance; the ships sailed into Ophir, whence they brought the king twenty talents of gold,[45] sandalwood of great quality and precious stones;[46] every three years the Tarsis fleet arrived, full of gold, silver, marble, monkeys and peacocks.[47] Hiram's gifts to Solomon emphasise, from the theological perspective, the Phoenician submission to the Hebrews, while the infertile lands of Kabul, given by Solomon to Hiram, also emphasise from a theological perspective

---

[40] 1 Kg. 5.2–3. It is useful to specify that the Hebrew text (BHS) and the Greek (Rahlfs) present two distinct editions or textual traditions; the translation provided here for the gifts mentioned in 2 Kg. 5.2–3 is to a certain extent conjecture, since the Masoretic Text is particularly garbled. The textual difficulty and diversity of traditions may be the result of additions to the text after the final version to emphasise – even more if possible – Solomon's magnificence.

[41] 1 Kg. 5.14.

[42] On the literary and theological process that led to the magnification of Solomon, see Levison, 2001. On the metaphorical character of Solomon's reign and the symbolism of the encounter with the Queen of Sheba, see Wightman, 1990.

[43] 1 Kg. 5.24–6.

[44] 1 Kg. 9.10–14.

[45] 1 Kg. 9.28.

[46] 1 Kg. 10.11.

[47] 1 Kg. 9.28.

the superiority and scorn of the Hebrews of the early fourth century BC towards pagans.

The story of the Queen of Sheba, enthralled by Solomon's wisdom, describes how she arrived in Jerusalem with a caravan of camels and spread splendid gifts before the king: perfumes, quantities of gold and precious stones.[48] Going on, the story repeats and specifies the quality of the offerings – 'a hundred and twenty talents of gold and great quantities of spices and precious stones'[49] – and concludes emphatically: 'no such wealth of spices ever came again as those which the Queen of Sheba gave to King Solomon'.[50] In contrast, the gifts that Solomon offered the sovereign seem simpler, since the story limits itself to indicating that 'King Solomon, in his turn, presented the Queen of Sheba with everything that she expressed a wish for, besides those presents which he gave her with munificence worthy of King Solomon',[51] without specifying the type of offering, nor their quantity nor quality. The final paragraph that praises Solomon's reign could not be more majestic concerning the gifts he received: 'the whole world consulted Solomon [...] and everyone would bring a present with him: things made of silver, things made of gold, robes, armour, spices, horses and mules; and this went on year after year'.[52]

From the description above, we can see that the Phoenician, Hiram, metaphor for the peoples of the sea, the Queen of Sheba, allegory of the eastern sovereign, Pharoah's daughter, echo of the country of the Nile, and to a certain extent the merchants of Kue, Cilicia, evoke the four cardinal points.[53] In this way, the gifts from the noble foreigners declare, from the theological perspective, the undisputed authority of Solomon over the Four Regions of the World, as the Assyrian kings also exhibited in their historical annals.[54] From the theological perspective, the stories mentioned, woven into the narrative in the early fourth century BC, eulogise the figure of Solomon, whom the pagans honoured with gifts, as a symbol of the Ideal

---

[48] 1 Kg. 10.2.
[49] 1 Kg. 10.10a.
[50] 1 Kg. 10.10b.
[51] 1 Kg. 10.13.
[52] 1 Kg. 10.24–5. From the historical perspective of the tenth to ninth centuries BC, we cannot speak of a Phoenician submission before Israel; see Briquet-Chatonnet, 1992; Bunnens, 1976. On the theological and metaphorical perspective on Solomon's reign, see Cook, 2017.
[53] 1 Kg. 10.26–9.
[54] As an example, Solomon's dominion can be compared with the authority of the Assyrian Esarhaddon (680–669 BC) over the Four Regions of the World; see Borger, 1956.

Israel which will rise at the end of time, and to which all the nations will turn at the twilight of history to adore God on top of the Holy Mountain.[55] The gifts therefore emphasise the absolute sovereignty of the God of Israel, represented by the incomparable magnificence of Solomon, the submission of the pagans before Israel, and the contempt of the Hebrews for the idolatry practised by the gentiles.

From the narrative about Solomon's decadence,[56] the Deuteronomistic approach – with the exception of the case of Hadad – puts an end to the theological magnification of the Judaean monarchs to embrace a more historical tone. In Solomon's final years, a leader from the Edomite royal house arose, called Hadad, who was an enemy of the king; the Pharoah of Egypt – at the time also an enemy of Judah – made a pact with the rebel, giving him lands in Egypt and offering him in marriage the sister of his wife, Queen Tahpenes, the Great Lady.[57] We see again how a Pharoah offers a princess in marriage to a foreign king to seal a pact. While she was not a daughter of the Pharoah, as she was in the case of Solomon, there is no confirmation of this event in the Egyptian sources; as occurred with Solomon, the mention therefore achieves the end of certifying the kingly aura of Hadad, enemy of the Hebrew king.[58]

Later, in the fifth year of Rehoboam (931–914 BC), King of Judah, Sheshak (945–925 BC), Pharoah of Egypt, marched against Jerusalem. The city avoided devastation thanks to surrendering a large tribute and offering magnificent gifts to Pharoah: 'he carried off all the treasures of the Temple of Yahweh and the treasures of the royal palace; he took everything away, including all the golden shields which Solomon had made'.[59]

As the Deuteronomistic History indicates, war erupted between Asa, King of Judah (911–870 BC), and Baasha, King of Israel (909–886 BC). In the face of the threat from Baasha, Asa took the silver and gold from the temple treasure in Jerusalem and sent it as a gift to Ben-hadad, the King of

---

[55] Cf. Is. 66.18–23.
[56] 1 Kg. 11.
[57] 1 Kg. 11.19.
[58] The question of the difficulty of offering the sister of the wife of Pharoah in marriage to Hadad, and the daughter of Pharoah in marriage to Solomon, is resolved in a reference article; see Millard, 1991. It should be specified that Tahpenes is not a proper name, but a title equivalent to Great Lady, the title of the queen mother (1 Kg. 15.13).
[59] 1 Kg. 14.25–6. The inscriptions from the Temple of Karnak tell us about Sheshak's campaign against more than a hundred and fifty cities in Israel and Judah. The fact that Jerusalem does not figure in that list seems to indicate that the city had freed itself from the incursion thanks to the payment of tribute and splendid gifts. On Sheshak's attack on Palestine, see Pritchard, 1969: 242–3.

Aram, so that he would break his alliance with Baasha: in response, Ben-hadad withdrew from the alliance and Asa remained free of the Israelite threat.[60] Later, according to the text, Ben-hadad, the King of Syria, accompanied by thirty-two kings, laid siege to Samaria; and afterwards, he sent messengers to King Ahab of Israel (874–853 BC) to say 'I have already sent you an order to hand over your silver and your gold, your wives and your children' to save the city, but the monarch refused.[61] Over time, however, the fortunes of war turned against Ben-hadad, who was obliged to establish a treaty with Ahab. The Syrian sovereign said: 'I shall restore the towns which my father took from your father and you must set up a trading quarter for yourself in Damascus.'[62]

The King of Moab, Mesha, brought Jehoram, King of Israel (848–841 BC), 100,000 lambs and the wool of 100,000 rams;[63] the text thus reveals Mesha's submission to Jehoram.[64] The stories that surround the figure of Elisha recount how the prophet's servants required gifts – sometimes in defiance of that very prophet – from the people whom Elisha had helped. Gehazi, Elisha's servant, thus demanded of Naaman, the commander of the Syrian army, whom Elisha had cured: 'be kind enough to give them a talent of silver and two festal robes'.[65] In a similar way, when Ben-hadad, King of Syria, lay ill, he sent Elisha a gift via Hazael, a servant of his, to beg for health: Hazael went to meet the prophet bearing forty camels with all the best of Damascus as a present.[66] When bands of Arameans invaded and decimated the Israelite territory, the prophet Elisha advised the King of Israel, rather that fighting against the bands, to offer presents to subdue their violence: 'offer them food and water, so that they can eat and drink, and then let them go back to their master'.[67]

The narrative continues with Hazael, enthroned as King of Syria (841–806 BC), marching against Jerusalem. Jehoash, King of Judah

---

[60] 1 Kg. 15.16–19.
[61] 1 Kg. 20.5. The Septuagint inverts the order in the Masoretic Text of 1 Kg. 20–1, which it interweaves between 1 Kg. 20 and 1 Kg. 22. The textual confusion is evidence of the late editing of the texts, while the mention of thirty-three kings (thirty-two plus Ben-hadad) suggests the late and apocalyptic nature that characterises the re-reading of the story. To assess the apocalyptic perspective, see Lipschits *et alii* 2007.
[62] 1 Kg. 20.34.
[63] 2 Kg. 3.4.
[64] The text in fact points to a metaphorical story to magnify Jehoram, since, later, Mesha defeated Omri, sovereign of Israel (885–874 BC), a much more powerful monarch than Jehoram; this is laid out on the Mesha Stele. See Pritchard, 1969: 320–1.
[65] 2 Kg. 5.22.
[66] 2 Kg. 8.7–10.
[67] 2 Kg. 6.21–3.

(835–796 BC), then took all the sacred objects that his predecessors Jehoshaphat, Jehoram and Ahaziah, sovereigns of Judah, had consecrated in the sanctuary, as well as the offerings he himself had consecrated in the temple, together with all the gold from the sanctuary and royal palace; he sent them to Hazael as a gift to stop him attacking Jerusalem.[68]

The rise of Assyria meant that its king, Tiglath-Pileser III (745–721 BC), known as Pul in the Scriptures, invaded Israel; then Menahem, the Israelite sovereign (743–738 BC), offered the Assyrian 1,000 talents of silver as a gift if he allowed him to remain on the Samarian throne.[69] Menahem obtained the money from a tax of fifty shekels of silver on each of the country's wealthy.[70] Later, when Rezin, King of Syria (740–732 BC), threatened Ahaz, King of Judah (736–716 BC), the Judaean monarch took the silver and gold that were in the temple and royal palace in Jerusalem and sent them as a gift to Tiglath-Pileser III to beg his assistance.[71] To prove his subjugation to the Assyrian king, Ahaz also had to remove the podium of the throne that had been erected in the Temple of Jerusalem;[72] he thereby revealed that supreme authority over Jerusalem and the Kingdom of Judah fell to Tiglath-Pileser III.[73] The Assyrian onslaught did not end. Shalmaneser V (726–722 BC) marched against Hoshea, King of Israel (732–724 BC), who, rather than offering tribute, became a vassal; although Hoshea sought help from So, Pharoah of Egypt, the Assyrians conquered Israel and deported its population.[74]

Sennacherib's imperialism also fell upon Judah: the King of Judah, Hezekiah (716–687 BC), was required to offer a tribute of 300 talents of silver and 30 of gold. He had to bestow, moreover, further riches upon Sennacherib, the King of Assyria (704–681 BC), to save Jerusalem from fire; he 'gave him all the silver in the Temple of Yahweh and in the palace treasure; at which time, Hezekiah stripped the facing from the leaves and

---

[68] 2 Kg. 12.18–19. Jehoram's gifts to Hazael to prevent the fall of Jerusalem also figure, to an extent, in the apology of Hazael from Tel Dan; see Pritchard, 1969: 281–2.

[69] 2 Kg. 15.19.

[70] 2 Kg. 15.20.

[71] 2 Kg. 16.7–9.

[72] 2 Kg. 16.18.

[73] The Assyrian attack on the territory of Judah also figures in the Annals of Tiglath-Pileser III; see Pritchard, 1969: 272–4.

[74] 2 Kg. 17.3–4. It should be noted that a Pharoah So is unknown as a sovereign of Egypt; perhaps it should be read as the name of a city, Sais, in the Nile Delta, the home of the Pharoah Tefnakht or his successor Bakenranef, both of debated chronology (726–701 BC). It may refer to an Egyptian general called Sibe by the Assyrians; see Liverani, 2003: 344.

jambs of the Temple of Yahweh".[75] The country of the Nile did not lack animosity towards Judah, either: when Pharoah Neco (609–594 BC) deposed Jehoahaz, King of Judah (609 BC), the new Judaean monarch, Jehoiakim (609–597 BC), taxed by Pharoah, had to provide the Egyptian sovereign with a large quantity of silver and gold to maintain the dynasty.[76] When Nebuchadnezzar II, the King of Babylon (604–562 BC), conquered Jerusalem, he took away all the treasure from the temple and the royal palace, and all the religious objects, as well as a section of the population, whom he deported to Babylon.[77] The temple objects nevertheless acquired the aspect of a material and liturgical hostage, since, when Cyrus II (549–529 BC) conquered Babylon, he allowed the exiled Jews to return to Jerusalem with their cult objects so they could celebrate liturgy again.[78]

In essence, the final section of the Deuteronomistic History[79] emphasises, above all, the political aspect of gifts between monarchs, in contrast to the first section,[80] where the mention of gifts tends to burnish the theological magnificence of the kings. In this way, offering lands and wives seals the pact between Hadad and Pharoah; Rehoboam's gold prevented Jerusalem's downfall at the hands of Sheshak; Asah's gifts to Ben-hadad broke the alliance between Syria and Israel; Asah handed over his wives and children as hostages; the political intervention of the ancient prophets, represented by Elisha, could entail significant gains for their servants; very often, the gift of gold was the political gift that prevented the fall of Jerusalem (Jehoash, Ahaz, Hezekiah, Neco) and of the Kingdom of Israel (Menahem, Hoshea); the temple treasures, plundered by Nebuchadnezzar as security, impeded cultic celebration in Jerusalem and perfected Hebrew captivity in Babylon. The Deuteronomistic perspective nevertheless still preserves the tenor of gifts as an expression of magnificence for figures of royal lineage (Hadad, Jehoram).

---

[75] 2 Kg. 18.13–16. The Assyrian onslaught against Judah also figures in Sennacherib's Annals: see Pritchard, 1969: 287–9.
[76] 2 Kg. 23.35.
[77] 2 Kg. 24.13–25.15. The avatars of the conquest of Jerusalem (597–587 BC) are also attested in the Nebuchadnezzar Chronicle; see Pritchard, 1969: 307–11.
[78] Ezr. 1.7–8.
[79] 2 Kg. 11–25.
[80] Jos. 1–2 Kg. 10.

The Theological Aspect of the Diplomatic Gift, Metaphor of Hebrew Submission to Divine Will

The Deuteronomistic narrative opens with the theological prototype of the diplomatic/religious gift. The Book of Joshua begins with the proclamation of God's promise to the Hebrews who, having fled Egypt, are ready to enter Palestinian land: 'Every place you tread with the soles of your feet I shall give you, as I declared to Moses that I would.'[81] Joshua repeats this promise to the dignitaries from Reuben, Gad and the half-tribe of Manasseh: 'Yahweh your God, in bringing you to rest, has given you the land where we are';[82] and finally, he specifies before all the tribes the theological objective that beats at the heart of God's gift to Israel: 'so that all the peoples of the earth may know how mighty the hand of Yahweh is, and always stand in awe of Yahweh your God.'[83] Having settled on the divine gift of land and established the theological objective, Joshua's hosts began the conquest of Palestine. Once in possession of Jericho and its booty, the troops made a resolution: 'All the silver and all the gold, everything made of bronze or iron, will be consecrated to Yahweh and put in his treasury.'[84] The decision is so rigorous that it determines the sentence of Achan, a dignitary from the tribe of Judah, who had stolen some of the gifts consecrated to God: 'a fine robe from Shinar and two hundred shekels of silver and an ingot of golden weighing fifty shekels.'[85]

The phrase that mentions the objects 'consecrated to Yahweh' alludes to the Hebrew term *herem*; the Hebrew voice relates, in this case, that the booty from the conquest should be offered in its entirety to the Lord as thanks for the gift of Jericho; the offering is realised with the imperative to deposit it in the temple treasury.[86] From the liturgical perspective, the gifts offered to their God by the Hebrews – grateful for the conquest of the land that the divine facilitated – may be understood to suggest the aspect of a

---

[81] Jos. 1.3.
[82] Jos. 1.13.
[83] Jos. 4.24.
[84] Jos. 6.19.
[85] Jos. 7.21.
[86] The word *herem* brings with it, from a theological perspective, notable complexity, since its meaning reveals semantic evolution in the biblical texts. It alludes to a vow made before God (Lv. 27.28), the death penalty for idolatry (Dt. 7.26), the renunciation of booty by the troops so they could deposit it in the temple (Dt. 2.25) and the expulsion of a member of the Judaean assembly (Ezr. 10.8); see Vaux, 1984: 349. The mention of the temple treasury in Jerusalem attests that the text emerged at the end of the fifth or early fourth century BC when Jerusalem's temple treasury was well established. See Sicre, 2002: 79–101.

diplomatic gift with which a lesser sovereign, represented by the Hebrew people, thanked a greater sovereign, symbolised by God himself, for all the help received to conquer a region, while at the same time demonstrating the unarguable submission of the lesser sovereign, Israel, before the superior monarch, the God of Israel. From this perspective, the cult offerings, represented through consecration to the Lord (*herem*), evoked, from a diplomatic standpoint, the gifts through which Israel offered obeisance and submission to the supreme deity who had brought them, as a present, the Palestinian lands.

The story of the conquest of Palestinian land concludes with a robust claim: 'Of all the promises that Yahweh had made to the House of Israel, not one failed; all were fulfilled.'[87] As we can see, however, among the promises announced by Joshua, the ultimate theological objective of God's pact with his people is not fulfilled, for the crowning glory of Hebrew victory consists of all the nations of the world recognising how powerful the hand of the Lord is.[88] As observed in the paragraphs above, the promise came about – from the late Deuteronomistic standpoint – through the journey to Jerusalem by the Queen of Sheba (a metaphor for the East) to shower gifts upon Solomon, beneath whose image she perceived the divine blessing that speaks through the lips of the monarch – 'Blessed be Yahweh your God who has shown you his favour by setting you on the throne of Israel!'[89] – and in the admiration of all nations who come to Jerusalem, who admire the wisdom of Solomon, echo of the ideal monarch, since 'the whole world consulted Solomon [...] and everyone would bring a present [...] year after year.'[90]

Conclusion

This study undertakes a continuous reading of the Deuteronomistic History[91] to assess the features conferred upon the diplomatic gift and its correlating features, which are: bribery, offerings, hostages and security, rewards, purchase of alliances, affirmation of pacts, courtly obeisance, requests for help, provision of booty, compensation, and veneration of an eminent person, among other reasons. The Deuteronomistic History embraces, from a literary and theological perspective, a very long history of

---

[87] Jos. 21.45.
[88] Jos. 4.25.
[89] 1 Kg. 10.9–10.
[90] 1 Kg. 10.24–5.
[91] Jos.–2 Kg.

composition that makes it possible to assess three aspects of the diplomatic gift. The first aspect, based mainly on Jos. 1–2 Kg. 10, assesses the value of the diplomatic gift among the ancient tribes of Judah and Israel, between clans and families, and between individuals. Recent historiography nevertheless tends to perceive these gifts, in general, from the perspective of the pacts and gifts that had to be made by the Judaeans who returned from Jerusalem having suffered the Babylonian exile, referred to theologically as the remnants of Israel, with the Judaeans who stayed in the defunct Kingdom of Judah during the period of the exile known as the People of the Land. The second level on which the Deuteronomistic approach assesses the value of gifts figures principally between the lines of 2 Kg. 11–25. It discusses the nature of gifts between the sovereigns of Judah and Israel that involved vassalage treaties or purchase of alliances, alongside the treaties and bribes that the monarchs cited had to offer foreign monarchs to save their respective reigns. It should be noted that the exchange of diplomatic gifts with foreign kings also figures, with certain variations, in Assyrian and Babylonian documents, as discussed in this study. The third aspect of gifts embraces the theological aspect more strongly, since the Deuteronomistic perspective contemplates the history of Israel as the course of an alliance between God and his people; God, the true King of Israel, therefore receives gifts from his people, represented by their leaders,[92] an echo of the diplomatic gift that a lesser monarch offers, in the name of his nation, to a King of greater magnificence: God, the King of Israel.[93]

Bibliography

Albertz, R. [2003]. *Israel in Exile: The History and Literature of the Sixth Century B.C.E.*, Atlanta, GA.

Becking, B. & Korpel, M. [1999]. *The Crisis of Israelite Religion: Transformations of Religious Tradition in Exilic and Post-Exilic Times*, Leiden.

Borger, R. [1956]. 'Die Inschriften Asarhaddons Königs von Assyrien', *Granz*, 57, 87–9.

Briquet-Chatonnet, F. [1992]. *Les relations entre les cités de la côte phénicienne et les royaumes d'Israel et de Juda*, Leuven.

Bunnens, G. [1976]. 'Commerce et diplomatie phéniciens au temps de Hiram Ier de Tyr', *JESHO*, 19, 1–31.

Cook, S. [2017]. *The Solomon Narratives in the Context of the Hebrew Bible*, London.

---

[92] Jos. 1.
[93] Is. 43.15.

Elliger, K. & Rudolph, W. (eds) [1984]. *Biblia Hebraica Stuttgartensia*, Stuttgart.
Finkelstein, I. & Mazar, A. [2007]. *The Quest for the Historical Israel: Debating Archaeology and the History of Early Israel*, Atlanta, GA.
Finkelstein, I. & Silberman, N. [2003]. *The Bible Unearthed: Archeology's New Vision of Ancient Israel and the Origins of Its Sacred Texts*, New York.
García Fernández, M. [2020]. 'Extranjeros y forasteros en el corpus profético', in G. Seijas (ed.), *Sal de tu tierra: estudios sobre el extranjero en el Antiguo Testamento*, Madrid, 47–64.
Hermann, S. [1979]. *Historia de Israel*, Salamanca.
Levison, B. [2001]. 'The Reconceptualization of Kingship in Deuteronomy and Deuteronomistic History's Transformation of Torah', *VT*, 51, 510–34.
Lipschits, O. & Blenkinsopp, J. (eds) [2003]. *Judah and the Judeans in the Neo-Babylonian Period*, Winona Lake, IN.
Lipschits, O., Knoppers, G. & Albertz, R. (eds) [2007]. *Judah and the Judeans in the Fourth Century B.C.E.*, Winona Lake, IN.
Liverani, M. [2003]. *Oltre la Bibbia: storia antica di Israele*, Rome.
Millard, R. [1991]. 'Text and Archeology: Weighing the Evidence. The Case of King Solomon', *PEQ*, 123, 19–27.
Pritchard, J. (ed.) [1969]. *Ancient Near Eastern Texts Relating to the Old Testament*, Princeton, NJ.
Rahlfs, A. (ed.) [1979]. *Septuaginta*, Stuttgart.
Ramis Darder, F. [2012]. *La Comunidad del Amén: identidad y misión del Resto de Israel*, Salamanca.
Römer, T. [2000]. *The Future of the Deuteronomistic History*, Leuven.
Sacchi, P. [2004]. *Historia del judaísmo en la época del Segundo Templo*, Madrid.
Schmid, K. [2019]. *Historia literaria del Antiguo Testamento*, Madrid.
Sicre, J. [2002]. *Josué*, Estella.
Ska, J. L. [2020]. *Introducción a la lectura del Pentateuco*, Estella.
Vaux, R. [1984]. *Instituciones del Antiguo Testamento*, Barcelona.
Vaux, R. [1996]. *Histoire ancienne d'Israel*, Paris.
Vermeylen, J. [1978]. *Du Prophète Isaïe à l'Apocalyptique*, Paris.
Wightman, G. [1990]. 'The Myth of Solomon', *BASOR*, 277–8, 5–22.

2

Greek Cities and Diplomatic Gifts in the Classical Period*

Dominique Lenfant

Regardless of time or place, offering gifts is a highly codified practice. In Ancient Greece, as in any chronocultural context, one did not offer anything to anyone without a defined function.[1] As a general rule, a diplomatic gift means a gift given by a state to the delegate of another state during an official visit. It has a political dimension, and a highly symbolic value. It expresses satisfaction with the attitude of the counterpart, but it is also looking to the future, aiming to consolidate a link and promote goodwill. It is offered to an individual, but one functioning as a delegate of his state, and is supposed to foster a good relationship between individuals, and above all between their states. Diplomatic gifts are not a universal practice; because of their individual nature, they are undoubtedly more common between monarchs. In the Greek world, offering gifts to a foreigner who had been granted hospitality was a practice which is evidenced very early in literature, and notably in the *Odyssey*. From that time on, indeed, there was even a specific Greek term, *xénia*, to mean such 'hospitality gifts'.[2] Could such gifts have a properly diplomatic role, however? Did such a practice

---

* This work has been developed within the research project PGC2018-096415-B-C22 'La expresión diplomática en el Mediterráneo central y oriental bajo la expansión romana: el regalo en su contexto político e institucional', funded by the State Research Agency, Ministry of Science and Innovation, Government of Spain (MCIN/AEI/10.13039/501100011033) and ERDF 'A way of making Europe'.

[1] Satlow, 2013: 1–2.

[2] *Xénia* (ξένια) in the neuter plural form (*xeínia* in the Homeric language) may mean the gifts given to a guest by his host, whereas *xenía* (ξενία) in the feminine singular may mean the hospitality shown towards a guest.

inaugurate a model that was followed later in the Classical city, moreover, when the political framework had profoundly changed?

After reviewing the uses of hospitality gifts as attested in Homeric epic, this chapter will show that they did not survive as such in diplomatic relations between Greek cities in Classical times, but that Greeks still had to deal with diplomatic gifts in their relations with kingdoms outside the world of the cities: the Thracian Odrysian Kingdom, the Kingdom of Macedonia, and above all the Persian Empire. It will be the major concern here to explain the reactions of Greek ambassadors and their cities to such cultural differences.

Private Hospitality and Gifts for Foreign Guests

Offering gifts to a foreign guest appears as a common practice in the Homeric world.[3] There the *xeínia* included, firstly, the food provided on-site (hospitality meals), and also material presents – such as valuable pieces of tableware, clothing or weapons – which were lasting and were taken away by the guest when leaving (hospitality gifts).[4] It must be noted, however, that the host expected to receive the same benefits if he became the guest of his current guest one day.[5]

In fact, what we commonly call hospitality, for lack of a better word, was in Ancient Greece part of a larger system with particular codes: it was far from being understood as an act of unselfish generosity, a purely unilateral and occasional behaviour (as is meant with the modern word 'hospitality'), but rather as a way to establish a specific, durable and hereditary relationship, with a precise – quasi-ritual – set of rules. This is why Gabriel Herman equates *xenía* with 'ritualised friendship' rather than with 'hospitality'. The first rule was that the establishment of the relationship included a solemn, performative declaration and the exchange of gifts.[6] Gifts were indeed supposed to be reciprocal, even if gift and 'counter-gift' were often staggered in time, with a counter-gift being delayed.[7] The second was that there were duties arising from the sort of agreement concluded with this social ritual – duties like hospitality and solidarity (as far as it did not conflict with patriotic loyalty). Gifts therefore not only had a material

---

[3] See on *xenía* in general Herman, 1987. On 'hospitality exchanges' in Homer: Scheid-Tissinier, 1994: 115–76 (on the granting of hospitality gifts: 164–70).
[4] See e.g. Menelaus' gifts to his guest Telemachus: Scheid-Tissinier, 1994: 167–8.
[5] See e.g. Hom. *Od.* 24.265–86: when the one to whom you gave is dead, you gave him gifts 'in vain'.
[6] See Herman, 1987: 58–69 on the 'initiation ritual'.
[7] Scheid-Tissinier, 1994: 158.

dimension, but also a strong symbolic one: they were a way of establishing a long-lasting link. The resulting relationship was between men, but also between their families. The Homeric epic attests this elite social behaviour quite precisely through various examples, but while it depicts a very specific world, the same type of relationships continued to exist for centuries after the emergence of the city.

Before addressing the diplomacy of cities and its relation to gifts, it is worth noting that in epic, gifts unquestionably had a major role in creating connections between heroes who were often kings or sons of kings, but did not play any role in diplomatic encounters per se. In the scenes of negotiation between heroes, gifts are strikingly absent.[8]

Diplomatic Envoys between Greek Cities: The Granting of Honours

Material gifts are absent in the diplomacy of Classical cities as well. In most cases, decisions were taken there by collective bodies, assemblies and councils, whereas diplomatic envoys were not professionals, nor even annual magistrates, but just citizens elected by those bodies for a single and specific mission. They were elected without being sure of selection for any future exchange; they had no special decision-making powers in their cities before or after the mission, but were simply, at the most, rather influential persons in the decision-making process.[9]

Envoys, however, were not chosen at random, since cities knew perfectly well that some citizens had a better chance of success than others. They consequently elected men with a prestigious status, whether that was political, social, cultural or athletic, in a way that honoured or impressed the other city;[10] men with good skills of persuasion and eloquence;[11] men who were supposed to inspire trust in the other city (some citizens of Sparta or Athens were chosen several times for the same destination – Thebes, Argos, Athens or Sparta).[12] A good indication of this affinity is the title of *proxenos*, which could be granted to a citizen by another city and made him an ideal interlocutor with that state:[13] as an 'official host',

---

[8] On these scenes, see Wéry, 1967; Karavites, 1987; 1992; 2008.
[9] For the selection of diplomatic envoys and their limited powers, see Mosley, 1973: 43–9.
[10] Kienast, 1973: 532–3.
[11] Mosley, 1973: 58; Piccirilli, 2022.
[12] Mosley, 1973: 51–2, 58.
[13] On proxeny, see Gschnitzer 1973; Kienast, 1973: 581–7; Mack 2015. On proxeny as an exclusively Greek institution, which could not have had any role in Graeco-Persian

he was supposed to protect in his own city the citizens of the foreign city who gave him this title, and also to further the interests of that state. This explains why a *proxenos* was frequently sent as an ambassador to the city which had made him *proxenos*.[14] Sometimes, moreover, the personal relationship of an envoy with a citizen of another state might appear as a possible asset, especially the fact that they were tied by a *xenía*-relationship:[15] for example, the Lacedaemonian Endios, who was sent as an ambassador to Athens several times, had a *xenía*-relationship with Alcibiades' family. In 420 BC, he was clearly received at home by Alcibiades, who then had the opportunity to speak in private with Sparta's envoys.[16] It is possible that on this occasion, Alcibiades and Endios exchanged gifts, as was usual between *xenoi* not only when they sealed the relationship, but also when they met and wanted to renew the bond.[17] This, however, was in no way a public action: the city did not offer gifts to the visiting diplomatic envoys.[18]

What the city granted at most in material terms to the visiting ambassadors was a hospitality meal called *xénia*. The word indicates some filiation with the meal which was offered by heroes in the Homeric epic to foreign private guests.[19] The civic *xénia* was, however, offered at the hearth of the city – in its town hall (called the *prytaneion* or *hestia* depending on the city)[20] – the day after the reception of the diplomatic envoys at the assembly: the invitation formula is regularly included in decrees about diplomatic agreements.[21] Such a material delivery certainly had a high symbolic

diplomatic relations, see Lenfant, 2016. A citizen could also become *proxenos* as a descendant of an earlier *proxenos*. See the example of Callias (Xen. *Hell.* 5.4.22–3).

[14] See Kienast, 1973: 583. On the Athenian Callias as *proxenos* of the Lacedaemonians (Xen. *Hell.* 6.3.4) sent as diplomatic envoy to Sparta: Xen. *Hell.* 5.4.22–3. On Demosthenes, *proxenos* of the Thebans, sent to Thebes as ambassador in 339: Aeschin. 2.141.

[15] Kienast, 1973: 582.

[16] Thuc. 8.6.3 (*xenía*-relationship); 5.44–5 (embassy in 420 BC); Diod. Sic. 13.52.2 (in 410 BC).

[17] Herman, 1987: 60–6, 70.

[18] Cinalli, 2015 thinks that the *xénia* to which cities invited visiting envoys included not only a meal, but also a larger ceremony with a sacrifice and other elements, such as gifts. She does not, however, give any compelling examples or conclusive proof.

[19] Herman, 1987: 136 (where the meal offered by the city is defined as 'an institutionalised version of the feasting which sealed guest-friendship').

[20] For example, Rhodes & Osborne, 2003: 44. Other examples: Kienast, 1973: 566.

[21] One of the oldest extant epigraphical examples is in the Athenian treaty with Selymbria in 407 BC (Osborne & Rhodes, 2017: 520–1). See, as early as 425 BC, the parody in Aristophanes' *Acharnians* 124. General statement: Pollux 9.40. Kienast, 1973: 566.

dimension, since it communicated the city's benevolence and satisfaction with the diplomatic exchange.

What the city granted above all to diplomatic envoys when it was satisfied with the outcome of the negotiations, and what remained even after the completion of the mission, was, however, honours and titles. Such honours could be public praise,[22] the reservation of front seats in the theatre,[23] and above all the title of *proxenos*. The last was granted to a foreign diplomatic envoy in order to thank him for his action and to favour his designation for future negotiations. As stated above, the *proxenos* also had to protect in his own city the citizens of the city who honoured him.[24] This was purely an honour, entailing no material gain, which in addition imposed duties such as receiving citizens on an official visit in their own home.[25]

Material gifts were infrequent, even more so those which were perennial and had a market value: foliage crowns were sometimes awarded, but gold crowns were rarely granted to foreign envoys.[26] In a word, as a general rule, in Greek cities, ambassadors did not receive any diplomatic gifts.[27]

Greek Cities and Diplomatic Gifts in Powerful Kingdoms: Facing other Cultures

Against this background, Greeks discovered quite different habits in their diplomatic relations with powerful kings, especially with the Great King of the Persian Empire and, to a lesser extent, with the King of Macedonia. The difference with these states was, firstly, that diplomatic envoys met a monarch, and not a collective body, council or assembly, as they did with the cities – a monarch who received them at his court, like a Homeric king, and alone decided if he wanted to offer gifts to his visitors. Secondly, he was far richer than any Greek city. Lastly, he belonged to another cultural system.

---

[22] Kienast, 1973: 566.
[23] Kienast, 1973: 568. See Aeschin. 2.55 and 110 (for Macedonian envoys).
[24] For references, see above, n. 13.
[25] E.g. Callias receiving Spartan envoys in 378 BC (Xen. *Hell.* 5.4.22). Kienast, 1973: 568 also mentions citizenship as an honour (rarely) granted to ambassadors.
[26] Kienast, 1973: 567.
[27] Kienast, 1973: 568–9 indicates that Greek practice changed outside Athens from the fourth century BC, and mainly in the Hellenistic period, since some cities began to offer hospitality gifts (*xénia*) to visiting ambassadors, gifts which obviously consisted of money.

At the Macedonian Court: Xénia or Bribes

The case of Macedonia is hard to assess, since it is mainly attested in polemical contexts, through the biased accusations of Demosthenes after he took part in the Athenian embassy to the Macedonian court in 346 BC. Before the Athenian judges, he attempted to denounce the results of the embassy and make other envoys responsible for them, accusing his colleagues, especially Aeschines, of taking bribes.[28] It is clear from his account that Philip, King of Macedonia, offered material gifts to all the members of the Athenian embassy[29], in particular money (χρήματα, *chrēmata*), and that he presented these gifts as *xénia*, 'hospitality gifts'. Demosthenes himself did not deny that he accepted the gift: he just pretended that he had asked Philip to take that money as ransom for freeing the Athenian prisoners. The Athenian obviously wanted to display a noble cause before his citizens and to avoid being suspected of taking bribes or even profiting personally. By contrast, he interpreted the gifts given to his colleagues as bribes, especially those offered to Philocrates and Aeschines, who obviously accepted them.[30] According to him, another attitude was possible, and would have helped the envoys gain respect from the king: the attitude of the Theban ambassadors, who refused to accept Philip's gifts – money, captives, silver and gold drinking-cups – but instead made the very polite comment that they did not need these gifts to be the friends and *xenoi* (private guest-friends) of Philip.[31] This confirms that *xenía* was the common framework to which the King of Macedonia and Greek envoys referred.

In a word, the Macedonian case is known through a biased discourse, which suggests that the king there drew upon traditional Greek practices (*xenía*) to conceal the fact that he tried to tempt, or even to bribe the diplomatic envoys. At any rate, the latter interpretation is that of Demosthenes when it suits him (since, when he himself accepted gifts, they were no longer bribes).

Greek Ambassadors at the Persian Court: Encountering a Foreign Institution

Greek envoys at the Persian court provide a wider field of investigation, since there is more evidence – on diplomatic gifts as well as on the wider

---

[28] Dem. 19.110 and 167.
[29] Dem. 19.166–8.
[30] Dem. 19.114, 119, 245 (Philocrates); 110, 167 (Aeschines).
[31] Dem. 19.139.

practice of gift-giving within the Persian Empire. Evidence is also more diverse and even reliable, since, unlike that on envoys to the Macedonian king, it is not confined to polemical or apologetical purposes. There is another particular feature, as – even more than with Macedonia – a major cultural difference was at work: gift-giving reflected a different code in the political and social ritual of Greeks and Persians, and the gap was likely to have an impact on the possible interpretations on the exchange of gifts between them.[32]

Gift-Giving in the Persian Empire

Gift-giving was a customary practice in the Persian Empire.[33] It is, at least, attested around the king, who was *par excellence* the one who offered and received gifts, in both cases openly, even ostentatiously.[34] Gifts served as a symbolic manifestation of the relationship between the king and his subjects, individuals or delegates of a subject people of the empire. On the one hand, subject peoples had to provide gifts (*dōra*) to the king in addition to tribute (*phoros*).[35] This was undoubtedly an obligation, which had an economic dimension, but also a symbolic and political meaning. The Palace of Persepolis has a famous stone relief depicting delegations from the entire empire as gift-bearers converging in procession to the king (Figure 2.1). The gifts they carry include weapons, silver and gold vessels, jewellery, woven fabrics, and animals. It clearly shows that gifts were there to symbolise the devotion and submission of subject peoples, and consequently the acknowledged superiority of the king. On the other hand, the king himself sometimes offered gifts to some of his subjects, at least in particular circumstances. He did it at some royal ceremonies, for example on the occasion of his accession to the throne, or during his birthday banquet, and he also – and above all – used gifts to reward or honour men who served him. These gifts were of a specific nature, and included beautiful robes, gold torques and gold bracelets (Figure 2.2), which were even considered a sort of royal monopoly. In the *Cyropaedia*, Xenophon writes that Cyrus began the practice of lavish giving that continued among kings even to his day, adding:

> Who is there that is known to adorn his friends with more beautiful robes than does the king? Whose gifts are so readily recognised as some

[32] For the following discussion, see Lenfant, 2017 for further references and details.
[33] Lenfant, 2017: 42–4.
[34] See Sancisi-Weerdenburg, 1989; Briant, 1996: 78–81, 314–35, 406–10 and *passim*.
[35] Sancisi-Weerdenburg, 1989: 129–30; Briant, 1996: 79–80.

of those which the king gives, such as bracelets, necklaces, and horses with gold-studded bridles? For, as everybody knows, no one over there is allowed to have such things except those to whom the king has given them.[36]

Some archaeological pieces are likely to testify to this practice. There are, for example, luxury Achaemenid vessels with the name of King Xerxes or Artaxerxes inscribed, and it has been argued that these were gifts given by the King and clearly identified as such, gifts designed to demonstrate the favour of the King (Figure 2.3).[37] More strikingly, a statue of the Egyptian Ptah-Hotep represents him with a Persian torque (Figure 2.4), which, according to Amélie Kuhrt, was 'undoubtedly granted him by the Persian king', so that it is 'very likely that he personally served Darius at the Achaemenid court'.[38] Such gifts then had a dual value, that of their material price (they were luxury goods, made of rare and valuable materials and finely crafted by the best craftsmen), and that of their symbolic meaning (they meant that the beneficiary enjoyed royal favour).

Figure 2.1 Procession of gift bearers: delegation VI (Lydians) carrying bracelets, metal drinking-bowls and amphorae, east side of the Apadana at Persepolis (Wikimedia Commons).

---

[36] Xen. *Cyr.* 8.2.7–8.
[37] Sancisi-Weerdenburg, 1989: 142 n. 14; Herman, 1987: 66–7; Miller, 1997: 129.
[38] Kuhrt, 2007: 660.

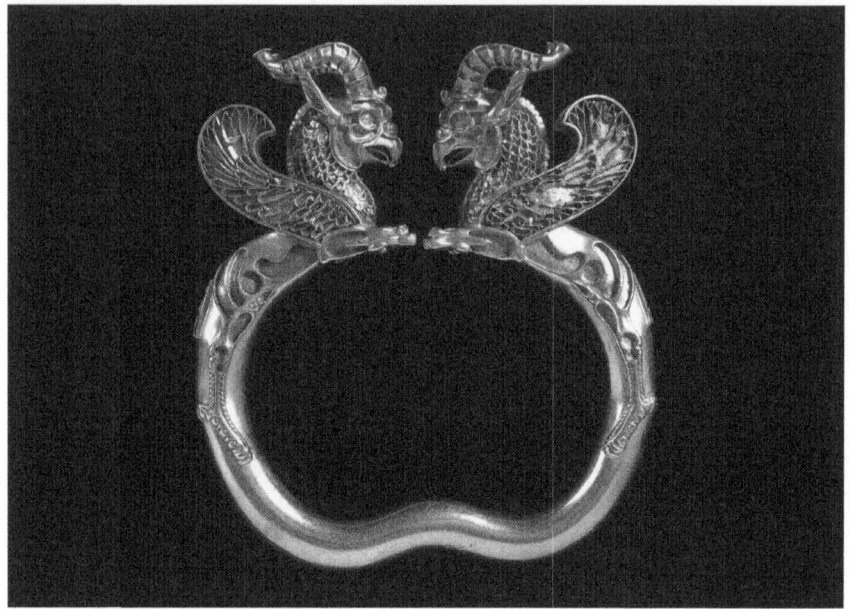

Figure 2.2 Gold griffin-headed armlet from the Oxus treasure, British Museum (Wikimedia Commons).

Figure 2.3 Alabaster vase with the inscription 'Xerxes, the Great King' in Persian, Elamite, Akkadian and Egyptian hieroglyphs, Penn Museum B10 (Wikimedia Commons).

Figure 2.4 Schist statue of Ptah-hotep, an Egyptian official with a Persian torque, probably from Memphis, Brooklyn Museum (Creative Commons).

It is clear, then, that within the Persian Empire gifts to the king and gifts from the king were not of the same nature, and that they were not an object of an exchange in line with the logic of gift and counter-gift. For the subject peoples, gift-giving was an obligation, while for the King it was an expression of goodwill. In both cases, however, it served to show royal power and hierarchy within the empire.

Gifts in Persian Diplomatic Relations with Greek Cities

Against this background, what was the role of gifts in the external relations of the empire, and more specifically, in diplomatic relations with peoples who were not its subjects? We lack evidence on Persian diplomacy with states other than Greek cities, and consequently on the role of gifts in such cases. Some Achaemenid objects found outside the empire have been proposed as possible evidence of the Great King's gift-giving to diplomatic interlocutors: Brosius mentions in this respect 'the superb silver vessel from Thrace crafted in Achaemenid style or the grave finds from Pazyryk in southern Siberia' as possible results of diplomatic exchange with the Odrysian Kingdom of Thrace and the nomadic Scythians of the Russian steppes.[39] It is certainly an attractive proposition, but must remain nothing but a hypothesis. Firstly, the very notion of an Achaemenid style has been seriously questioned, *inter alia* concerning silverware found in

---

[39] Brosius, 2012: 151.

Thrace.⁴⁰ Secondly, even if such objects had a definite Achaemenid origin, the possibility could not be excluded that they were private gifts, not necessarily from the King – or were even the result of a commercial or financial transaction. An example of such a possible transaction is actually given by the Athenian Demos, the son of Pyrilampes, who owned a gold phiale offered by the Great King, and tried to use it as a pledge to borrow money from his fellow citizen Aristophanes.⁴¹ Our evidence is therefore Greek, and concerns Persian contacts with Greeks. This makes it possible to draw a substantial and coherent picture.

As a starting point, it seems clear that Greek embassies from independent cities did not themselves bring gifts to the King. Two reasons may explain this. Firstly, it was not common practice amongst themselves – although that was probably not the main reason, because Greeks also knew how to adapt when necessary. According to Thucydides, in winter 429/8, Athenians sent to Sitalkes, the King of the Odrysian Thracians, 'ambassadors and gifts (*dōra*)', because they knew that such was the custom, and the local king had this expectation.⁴² The second possible reason has to do with Persian institutions, since in the Achaemenid imperial code, gifts were not required from visiting envoys except for those of subject peoples, as the Greeks were very well aware.

By contrast, there is no doubt that for the King it was customary to offer presents to diplomatic envoys visiting him, whether they were Greeks or non-Greeks.⁴³ Firstly, Aelian gives a list of 'gifts given from the King to the ambassadors coming to him, whether they came from the Greeks or from elsewhere' which includes silver coins, silver cups (phiales), valuable bracelets, torques, glaives and clothes.⁴⁴ Secondly, other Greek authors, when telling the story of the reception of an embassy, allude to gifts in a

---

⁴⁰ Dupont, 2015.
⁴¹ Lys. 19.25–6. On Demos' *phiale*, see Lenfant, 2022: 88–90, with earlier bibliography.
⁴² Thuc. 2.101.1 (δῶρα δὲ καὶ πρέσβεις ἔπεμψαν αὐτῷ). On the custom of gift-receiving: Thuc. 2.97.4. Gift-giving in the Odrysian kingdom has been discussed above all as a form of tribute paid in the sphere of Odrysian domination. See Rufin Solas, 2016.
⁴³ As discussed above, we do not have precise evidence about non-Greek ambassadors to the court, but, when recording his list of gifts (see next note), Aelian, *VH* 1.22 states that they were granted to ambassadors coming from Greece as well as elsewhere.
⁴⁴ Δῶρα τὰ ἐκ βασιλέως διδόμενα τοῖς παρ' αὐτὸν ἥκουσι πρεσβευταῖς, εἴτε παρὰ τῶν Ἑλλήνων ἀφίκοιντο εἴτε ἑτέρωθεν, ταῦτ' ἦν. τάλαντον μὲν ἑκάστῳ Βαβυλώνιον ἐπισήμου ἀργυρίου, ταλαντιαῖαι δὲ φιάλαι δύο ἀργυραῖ. δύναται δὲ τὸ τάλαντον τὸ Βαβυλώνιον δύο καὶ ἑβδομήκοντα μνᾶς Ἀττικάς. ψέλια δὲ καὶ ἀκινάκην ἐδίδου καὶ στρεπτόν, χιλίων δαρεικῶν ἄξια ταῦτα, καὶ στολὴν ἐπ' αὐτοῖς Μηδικήν· ὄνομα δὲ τῇ στολῇ δωροφορική (Aelian, *VH* 1.22).

way that makes them appear as an institution in such circumstances.⁴⁵ This list of apparently standard gifts suggests quite a precise cultural code. Like the gifts which were granted by the King to some of his subjects (and listed by Xenophon in the *Cyropaedia*, as discussed above), these were typically Persian luxury goods – objects which are well known to us through archaeology (Figures 2.5 and 2.6).⁴⁶ Some Greek stories about embassies also refer to other sorts of gifts, which were probably more extraordinary for the Persian court itself and especially so for Greeks. They include the peacocks received by the Athenian Pyrilampes, a gift which meant the first introduction of this animal into Europe, in the second half of the fifth century BC.⁴⁷ Such extraordinary gifts probably came in addition to the other, more customary presents, and served to express the King's liking for the beneficiary.

Figure 2.5 Siglos, silver Persian coin (5.43 g), c. 420–375 BC, Sardes mint. Persian king or hero (Classical Numismatic Group 99, Lot: 383; Creative Commons).

---

⁴⁵ Xen. *Hell.* 7.1.38 mentions τὰ δῶρα, 'the gifts', and Plut. *Pelop.* 30.7 δῶρα ... τῶν νομιζομένων, 'gifts ... among those which were customary'.
⁴⁶ See also, for example, in *Pracht und Prunk*, 2006: silver coins (73–5), bracelets (126, 207, 230), silver phiales (191, 194–7), torques (208), glaive (*akinakēs*; 209).
⁴⁷ See Plat. *Charmid.* 158a; Plut. *Per.* 13, 15; Aristoph. *Ach.* 61–3; Athen. 9.397c–d; Aelian, *NA* 5.21. Miller, 1997: 189–92.

Figure 2.6 Silver Achaemenid phiale, Susa Acropolis (after Curtis & Tallis, 2005: fig. 277).

Greek Reactions to a Different Custom

Greek ambassadors were thus facing a world with different rules from their own. As discussed above, Greeks at that time could certainly have been conscious of the Homeric epics, with 'hospitality gifts' offered to foreign visitors when they were about to leave,[48] but these concerned exchanges between individuals rather than official delegations, as they still existed in the context of *xenía*-relationships. Cities which sent or received diplomatic envoys did not offer gifts, and did not have a practice equivalent to that of the Persians. This raises a question about the reaction of Greek ambassadors when they were granted presents by the Great King.

Greeks were well aware of the diversity of customs and conventions regarding gift-giving. Thucydides expressly contrasts the custom of the Thracian Odrysians, who required that presents (*dōra*) be given to the King of the Odrysians,[49] with that prevailing in the Persian kingdom, where the

---

[48] Harvey, 1985: 105–7 thinks that this well-known precedent might have prepared Greek minds for the Persian custom.

[49] Thuc. 2.97.3–4 even states that this was the practice with the Odrysian chiefs and nobles, and also elsewhere in Thrace. It should be recalled that Thucydides had Thracian connections and interests, and probably a direct knowledge of local habits.

King offered them himself.⁵⁰ In the diplomatic field, they often had to be flexible in their dealings with local customs. As already seen, this was what the Athenians themselves did in 429/8 when they wanted to contact the Odrysian king.⁵¹ Such flexibility can also be seen in their diplomatic relations with the Persian king.

Initially, one might think that it would not be difficult to adapt to a practice consisting of receiving gifts, but things were not that simple. Extant Greek narratives on the attitude of Greek ambassadors at the Persian court certainly show that most of them accepted the King's gifts, but they also reveal that some of them refused to accept them. Such was the case of the Arcadian Antiochus, who came to the palace of Susa in 367 BC, along with other delegations from Greek cities in Europe, such as Sparta, Thebes, Athens and Elis, seeking that the Persian king favour their interests in the power struggle between them.⁵² Antiochus, considering that the Arcadians whom he represented had received less than the neighbouring city of Elis, refused to accept the King's gifts.⁵³ Even if Xenophon does not say so explicitly, there is every reason to believe that, in contrast, all the other diplomatic envoys present, coming from Sparta, Thebes, Elis or Athens, accepted the King's gifts, as was certainly the norm.⁵⁴ Both reactions were meaningful in the context of a coded protocol: accepting the King's gifts was simply the norm, while refusing them was a way of expressing discontent.⁵⁵ There is no reason to believe that the Greeks demonstrated any cultural misunderstanding about this system.⁵⁶

In the same way, it is far from certain that the Greeks understood gifts from the King as a way of sealing a personal guest-friendship (*xenía*)

---

⁵⁰ Thuc. 2.97.4 (κατεστήσαντο γὰρ τοὐναντίον τῆς Περσῶν βασιλείας τὸν νόμον, ὄντα μὲν καὶ τοῖς ἄλλοις Θραξί, λαμβάνειν μᾶλλον ἢ διδόναι).
⁵¹ Thuc. 2.101.1 (δῶρα δὲ καὶ πρέσβεις ἔπεμψαν αὐτῷ).
⁵² Xen. *Hell.* 7.1.33–8.
⁵³ Xen. *Hell.* 7.1.38 (ὁ δὲ Ἀντίοχος, ὅτι ἠλαττοῦτο τὸ Ἀρκαδικόν, οὔτε τὰ δῶρα ἐδέξατο ...).
⁵⁴ Xenophon mentions Antiochus' attitude as if it were an exception. Plutarch, in turn, expressly states that the Athenian Timagoras (*Art.* 22.9–12; *Pelop.* 30.9) and the Theban Pelopidas received gifts (*Pelop.* 30.7–8).
⁵⁵ Lenfant, 2017: 50–1, 64–5.
⁵⁶ The hypothesis of cultural misunderstanding has been proposed unconvincingly by Mitchell, 1997. According to her, Greeks misunderstood Persian hospitality by interpreting it as corruption (p. 132), or they wrongly believed in an equal hospitality relationship with the King while the Persian ruler could only consider an unequal relationship (p. 127). My reservations on this thesis have been expressed in more detail in Lenfant, 2017: 52–4.

between an ambassador and the King.⁵⁷ It is true that according to Greek authors, some individuals, whether Greek or not, were *xenoi* of the King. These 'private guests' are, however, not said to have been diplomatic envoys or to have received gifts.⁵⁸ It also appears that the King's gifts to diplomatic envoys did not meet the usual requirements for sealing a *xenía*-relationship; that is, a personal relationship of a contractual nature implying an equal exchange and a permanent obligation.⁵⁹ In fact, firstly, the ambassador did not give any gift to the King, even on a deferred basis; secondly, he did not enter into a personal or familial obligation to host the Great King at home; and thirdly, he did not enjoy a similar status to the King, especially as he only represented his state for a very limited time. We have seen that, according to Demosthenes, the King of Macedonia, Philip, referred to the institution of *xenía* when he offered gifts to Greek ambassadors, and that this reference was a way to disguise an attempt at corruption, and to have the ambassadors accept bribes without being suspected of dishonesty by their citizens. In other words, this was not a real *xenía*-relationship, and in any case such a reference to *xenía* is not attested for the gifts offered by the Great King. It should be noted that these presents are never called *xénia*, 'hospitality gifts', but instead *dōra*, 'gifts'. Admittedly, this is not enough to prove that the relationship was not seen as *xenía*, since even gifts linked to a *xenía*-relationship could be called *dōra*, but the absence of the specific word *xénia* deprives us of a positive clue.⁶⁰ If the gifts received by diplomatic envoys were indeed perceived by the Greeks as *xénia*, it would be at most in the sense of hospitality gifts offered to a foreign guest punctually received, without creating a personal link, in a way sometimes attested in the Homeric world as well as in Classical cities.⁶¹ All in all, Greeks did not connect the gifts granted by the King to their envoys with *xenía*, because they knew perfectly well that they were facing a different system: the Persian practice of granting special gifts to ambassadors visiting the court.

---

⁵⁷ For a full discussion, see Lenfant, 2017: 54–9; 2022: 86–90. In contrast, Vickers, 1984: 50, Herman, 1987: 65 and Bivar, 1999: 382–3 interpret the relationship between the Great King and Pyrilampes (followed by his son Demos) as *xenía*.
⁵⁸ On the possible exception of Ismenias of Thebes, who was tried for being the King's *xenos* by enemies who wanted his condemnation, see Lenfant, 2017: 59 n. 87; 2022: 87–8.
⁵⁹ See Herman, 1987.
⁶⁰ Lenfant, 2017: 56–7.
⁶¹ See Lenfant, 2017: 54–9.

Royal Gifts and Suspicions of Bribery

Despite this knowledge, envoys who received gifts were exposed in their own cities to the charge of bribery. The gifts received during their diplomatic mission were offered to them personally (they were not intended to be deposited in their city's treasury),[62] and this was not alien to the Greeks, since they themselves often granted honours to visiting envoys. Gifts could, nevertheless, seem ambiguous, as the vocabulary itself suggests, since *dōra* means either 'gifts' or 'bribes' according to the context. The question implied is that of the intention behind the gift and its acceptance, of the possible expectation of a return that entailed acting against one's civic duty. While *dōra* is ambiguous, the verb *dōrodokein* is unequivocal: although its etymological meaning is 'to accept a gift', in Classical times it always meant 'to take bribes'.[63] Accusations of bribery were especially common in a city like Athens, where they were directed against citizens in the various public offices and roles they could hold.[64] Among diplomatic envoys, the most exposed to suspicion and accusation were those who were sent as embassies to the Macedonian or the Persian courts.[65] This is probably due to the specific conditions of such embassies: firstly, in both cases, the king owned considerable wealth, and could dispose of it as he pleased without being accountable to anyone; secondly, unlike in a democratic city like Athens, negotiations were not conducted in public; finally, ambassadors received food and shelter from the king – unlike in the cities, where they had to find private hospitality[66] – and their sojourn often lasted some time, which opened many opportunities for secret contact.

It is difficult for us to know whether diplomatic envoys sometimes took bribes, since, on the one hand, bribery by nature requires secrecy, and when it is really successful, does not come to be known, and, on the other hand, our evidence is not only patchy but also – and above all – biased. What we do know are the accusations, and these accusations need to be

---

[62] Cartledge, 1990: 57 assumes that the lawsuit for which Antiphon wrote his speech *Against Erasistratus on Peacocks* in 411 BC was brought against Demos for seizing public property – that is to say, his father's diplomatic gift, the peacocks that he had received as a diplomatic envoy. This hypothesis is, however, highly speculative (we don't know who brought this lawsuit, against whom and for what reason), and it could be an anachronism, since there is nothing to suggest that the diplomatic gift was not considered a private gift.
[63] Harvey, 1985: 83, *contra* Herman, 1987: 76 and Taylor, 2001b: 161.
[64] Harvey, 1985: 89–90; Taylor, 2001a: 58–61; Bettalli, 2017; Cuniberti, 2017.
[65] Perlman, 1976: 231–2; Taylor, 2001b: 162.
[66] Kienast, 1973: 566–72.

considered with caution, since they come to us through various literary texts with their own background, foundations and agenda.

Caution is first needed when reading late evidence, strongly impacted by dubious sources and biased by a specific, moralist agenda. An important example is that of the gifts that, according to Plutarch, the Athenian Timagoras received during his diplomatic mission to Susa in 367 BC – on the same occasion as the one when the Arcadian Antiochus refused the customary royal presents. Plutarch, along with all our ancient sources, does not fail to recall that Timagoras was condemned to death after returning to his home country. The author distinguishes himself, however, by listing an impressive series of extraordinary gifts he had received: not only a very large sum of money (10,000 darics), but also a variety of luxury services: splendid suppers at the court,[67] and, for his return journey to the coast, bearers to carry him, a couch with bedding and servants to make it, and a herd of eighty cows in order to supply him with the cow's milk necessary for his health.[68] To this list given in *Artaxerxes*, in *Pelopidas* Plutarch adds silver coins and herdsmen for the cows, as well as wages for the bearers.[69] All this largesse is called *dōreai* by Plutarch, since it includes not only gifts in cash or kind, but also privileged services.[70]

The story is certainly colourful, and it has struck readers of all periods, including modern scholars, some of whom see it as an illustration of Persian extravagance and luxury, as well as of bribes taken by Greek envoys. The enormity of these gifts, however, may also seem rather suspect: 10,000 darics equates to no less than 84 kg of gold, and eighty cows to provide milk for one man is especially puzzling. Assuming that the king aimed at ostentation, in practical terms the displacement of cows over hundreds and hundreds of miles is unrealistic, and if it were possible it would have slowed down the ambassadors' progress considerably, since cows cannot move at the pace of a horse-drawn carriage. Another clue

---

[67] Plut. *Art.* 22.11: δεῖπνον ἐπέμπετο λαμπρότατον, 'he used to send him a most splendid supper'.

[68] Plut. *Art.* 22.9–10, 'he gave him ten thousand darics, and eighty milk cows to follow in his train because he was sick and required cow's milk; and besides, he sent him a couch, with bedding for it, and servants to make the bed (on the grounds that the Greeks had not learned the art of making beds), and bearers to carry him down to the sea-coast, enfeebled as he was' (μυρίους τε δαρεικοὺς ἔδωκε, καὶ γάλακτος βοείου δεομένῳ δι' ἀσθένειαν ὀγδοήκοντα βοῦς ἀμέλγεσθαι παρηκολούθουν· ἔτι δὲ κλίνην καὶ στρώματα καὶ τοὺς στρωννύντας ἔπεμψεν, ὡς οὐ μεμαθηκότων Ἑλλήνων ὑποστρωννύναι, καὶ φορεῖς τοὺς κομίζοντας αὐτὸν μέχρι θαλάσσης μαλακῶς ἔχοντα; trans. B. Perrin).

[69] Plut. *Pelop.* 30.10–11.

[70] Plut. *Pelop.* 30.9: τῷ πλήθει τῶν δωρεῶν.

that encourages scepticism is the striking contrast between Plutarch's late versions and that of Demosthenes more than four centuries earlier. The Athenian orator is the first extant source to describe Timagoras as taking bribes, and he merely mentions a gift of 40 talents.[71] This is certainly a considerable sum, and the equivalent of the 10,000 darics later mentioned by Plutarch,[72] but he mentions not a word about the conspicuous complements listed in *Artaxerxes* and *Pelopidas*, admittedly supposed to have mainly concerned the return trip through Asia. Thirdly, several centuries after Demosthenes, some authors certainly refer to the condemnation of Timagoras, but without explaining it with bribery or gifts: according to Valerius Maximus (first century AD) and Athenaeus (second century AD), the Athenians convicted him for having performed *proskunēsis* (for having prostrated himself) before the King.[73] At first glance, the whole picture may seem rather confused, and it would obviously be misguided to add together all the faults mentioned and give credence to each of them[74] with the idea that each author would just have retained what suited him. In fact, Timagoras' case is used as an *exemplum*, an edifying example, a useful precedent, that can be adapted to the needs of each author. All record that he suffered the death penalty after his return from his mission to the Persian court, but one can play with the charges. In his judicial oration, *On the False Embassy*, where he charges Aeschines with taking bribes during their shared embassy to Philip, Demosthenes urges the judges to be strict, and needs a precedent wherein a diplomatic envoy was convicted of bribery – an ancient, respectable example to follow.[75] Far later, with his *Memorable Deeds and Sayings*, Valerius Maximus practises another type of writing, composing a collection of inspiring examples from which speech writers can draw, and he classifies them according to their theme. Timagoras is meant to illustrate a case of severity.[76] Athenaeus, for his part, mentions Timagoras in a section on flattery,[77] for which *proskunēsis* before the Great King may appear quite fitting. Plutarch, in both *Artaxerxes* and *Pelopidas*, contrasts Timagoras the immoral envoy, a traitor to his homeland, or even

---

[71] Dem. 19.137.
[72] Equating to 240,000 Attic drachmas.
[73] Val. Max. 6.3.ext.2; Athen. 6.251b.
[74] This is just what the authors of the tenth-century Byzantine encyclopedia, the *Suda*, did (*s.v.* Τιμαγόρας T 591).
[75] Perlman, 1976: 229.
[76] Val. Max. 6.3. ext.2. Note that Timagoras is said to have encountered Darius (instead of Artaxerxes II), a mistake that betrays the poor quality of the information.
[77] Athen. 6.251a–b, drawing on Hegesander of Delphi, whose literary agenda is poorly known, but the *OCD* defines his work as 'a collection of unreliable anecdotes'.

to Greece, with righteous, patriotic envoys like Pelopidas or Ismenias. He makes him an illustration of bad, despicable behaviour.

Given Plutarch's extensive modern readership, and because of the many striking details he gives on Timagoras, his version is the most widespread, but it is worth turning to earlier, contemporary evidence. If we go back to the oldest extant source, Xenophon's *Hellenica*, it happens to be a historical account which was written very soon after Timagoras' embassy.[78] This does not mean that it is neutral,[79] but it is likely to be the least biased of our extant sources (the author does not need to produce an edifying example, or strive to make people laugh). In fact, it is probably reproducing the true terms of the lawsuit brought against Timagoras by Leon, his fellow ambassador who was with him in Susa.[80] Xenophon's sober narrative shows the disagreement between the two Athenians: Timagoras supported Pelopidas, the ambassador of the rival city of Thebes, and was held just after him in honour by the King, while Leon expressed his discontent with the stipulations decided by the King. And 'when the ambassadors returned to their home countries, the Athenians put Timagoras to death, because Leon had brought formal charges that Timagoras had failed to share quarters with him and had taken advice with Pelopidas in all matters'.[81] In other words, the death sentence is explained by Timagoras' betrayal of Athens for the benefit of Thebes – and there is no mention at all of bribery or special gifts with respect to the Athenian,[82] since this was not the major concern. Timagoras probably received gifts like other ambassadors, but this was not the reason for his condemnation.

This is not to say that Plutarch entirely invented his story. It is tempting to think that he borrowed some data on Timagoras' gifts from a now lost comedy. The clues supporting this view are, firstly, that the eighty cows might result from the eccentric character of comic assertions; secondly, that allegations of bribery were very common in Old Attic comedy, just as in judicial oratory, and with the same dubious foundations;[83] thirdly, that we specifically know of a comedy which satirised real Athenian ambassadors

---

[78] The embassy was sent in 367 BC, the *Hellenica* covers until 362 BC, and Xenophon died around 355 BC.
[79] Bearzot, 2008–9 = 2011 convincingly highlights the anti-Theban bias of this version.
[80] Bearzot, 2008–9 = 2011 shows the historical superiority of Xenophon's narrative here, as well as the fact that Leon obviously was his source ('Xenophon's partiality for Leon, the convergence of their political ideas, and the reconstruction of Timagoras' case in political and not moralistic terms', 2011: 35).
[81] Xen. *Hell.* 7.1.35–8.
[82] See Hofstetter, 1972: 104; 1978: 183, and above all Bearzot, 2008–9 = 2011: 35.
[83] Taylor, 2001a: 54–5.

as taking bribes at the Persian court;[84] and fourthly, that Plutarch has sometimes taken comic caricatures as historical facts.[85]

In any case, although Plutarch's narrative on Timagoras and Demosthenes' speech *On the False Embassy* are well known, they should not become the tree that hides the forest. Not only are they suspect in many respects, but they are also unrepresentative exceptions, since trials against ambassadors seem to be quite rare, and their convictions even rarer.[86] According to Mosley,[87] out of the 110 Athenian embassies known to us, only 5 led to a trial for *parapresbeia* (misconduct on an embassy) and, of those, three trials resulted in a guilty verdict – for 12 ambassadors out of 500, that is to say for 2 per cent of them. These convictions sanctioned them for treason, and not the fact of their having received gifts in itself.[88]

Naturally, betrayal could be fostered by gifts, and it is not my intention to say that Greeks and especially Athenians did not condemn bribery: they did, of course. Philocrates, one of Demosthenes' and Aeschines' embassy colleagues in 346 BC, was tried and found guilty of *dōrodokia*.[89] Greeks did, however, admit that ambassadors could receive gifts as long as it did not jeopardise their mission and the defence of their country's interests.[90] In brief, accepting a gift was not blameworthy in itself.

Conclusion

It was not the practice of Classical Greek cities to offer material gifts to visiting ambassadors; neither was it the custom for the ambassadors to bring them. Beyond the sphere of the cities, nevertheless, Greeks happened to meet other institutions: that of the Odrysian king, who expected to receive gifts from his official visitors; that of the Macedonian king, who pretended to refer to the old practice of *xenía*, and offered presents to ambassadors,

---

[84] The *Presbeis* (*The Ambassadors*) of the comic poet Plato mocked Epicrates and Phormisius as getting 'a great many bribes from the king – golden saucers and silver platters' (fr. 127 Kassel-Austin = Athen. 6.229f). Note that in reality, as far as we know, they were not accused in court. See Lenfant, 2017: 47, 62, 64.
[85] Lenfant, 2003.
[86] Scholars have often stated, on the contrary, that the conviction of ambassadors for bribery was not rare (for example, Hofstetter, 1972: 102–3; Briant, 1996: 688; Mitchell, 1997: 132).
[87] Mosley, 1973: 41.
[88] Mosley, 1973: 41; Perlman, 1976: 225, 231; Lenfant, 2017: 64–5.
[89] Dem 19.114–16; Hyper. 4.29; Aeschin. 2.6; 3.78–9; Din. 1.28.
[90] Kienast, 1973: 570 quotes Dem. 21.113 and Lys. 21.22, and denounces as false Demosthenes' biased claim that it was forbidden to accept a gift (Dem. 19.7, anxious to charge Aeschines). See also Harvey, 1985: 108–13.

Athenians and Thebans, presumably to blandish them, or even to corrupt them in his favour; and that of the Persian king, whose custom it was to offer gifts to every ambassador visiting his court, whatever the result of the negotiations, following a long-standing court practice that was for him an opportunity to display its economic and political power.

The Greeks from European cities understood these foreign customs and behaviours, and, although they did not imitate them in their own countries, they knew how to adapt to them abroad. In the best-known case, that of the Persian Empire, Greek ambassadors knew how accepting or refusing gifts was a means of expressing their satisfaction or disappointment in the diplomatic results. It is plausible that the Macedonian Philip tried to bribe – or even succeeded in bribing – some of the ambassadors visiting his court by offering them gifts. It is not impossible that the Persian king also tried, especially through exceptional gifts, to conciliate some foreign ambassadors or to reward them for their attitude. In any case, however, what cities then condemned was eventual betrayal by their envoys, not the gifts they had received as such. The citizens the ambassadors represented could certainly feel envious and make fun of the luxury that their envoys had enjoyed in the empire,[91] but neither in court nor socially did they condemn these ambassadors just for having received gifts. Pyrilampes was even so far from concealing his peacocks that thirty years after their arrival in Athens, his son Demos still organised fee-paying visits attended by people from far and wide, sold peacocks and peacock eggs, and some twenty years later still, boasted in Athens that he owned a gold phiale that he had received from the Great King.

Bibliography

Bearzot, C. [2008–9]. 'L'ambasceria ateniese a Susa (367 a.C.)', *Hormos* 1, 100–10.

Bearzot, C. [2011]. 'Xenophon on the Athenian Embassy to Susa (367 BC)', *Historika: Studi di storia greca e romana*, 1, 21–37.

Bettalli, M. [2017]. 'Ricchezza, corruzione, incompetenza: il mestiere di stratego nell' Atene del IV secolo a.C.', in G. Cuniberti (ed.), *Dono, controdono e corruzione: ricerche storiche e dialogo interdisciplinare*, Alessandria, 179–96.

Bivar, A. D. H. [1999]. 'ΣΥΜΒΟΛΟΝ: A Noteworthy Use for a Persian Gold Phiale', in G. R. Tsetskhladze (ed.), *Ancient Greeks West and East* (*Mnemosyne*, Suppl. 196), Leiden–Boston–Cologne, 379–84.

Briant, P. [1996]. *Histoire de l'Empire perse*, Paris.

---

[91] See Aristophanes' *Acharnians* and Plato Comicus' *Ambassadors*.

Brosius, M. [2012]. 'Persian Diplomacy between "Pax Persica" and "Zero-Tolerance"', in J. Wilker (ed.), *Maintaining Peace and Interstate Stability in Archaic and Classical Greece*, Mainz, 150–64.

Cartledge, P. [1990]. 'Fowl Play: A Curious Lawsuit in Classical Athens (Antiphon XVI, frr. 57–9 Thalheim)', in P. Cartledge, P. Millett & S. Todd (eds), *Nomos: Essays in Athenian Law, Politics and Society*, Cambridge, 41–61.

Cinalli, A. [2015]. *Τὰ ξένια: la cerimonia di ospitalita cittadina*, Rome.

Cuniberti, G. [2017]. 'Il dono, la persuasione, la democrazia: percezione e negazione della *dorodokia*', in G. Cuniberti (ed.), *Dono, controdono e corruzione: ricerche storiche e dialogo interdisciplinare*, Alessandria, 197–218.

Curtis, J. and Tallis, N. [2005]. *Forgotten Empire: The World of Ancient Persia*, London.

Dupont, P. [2015]. 'Le règne des "persianismes"', in J.-L. Martinez *et alii* (eds), *L'épopée des rois thraces: des guerres médiques aux invasions celtes, 479–278 av. J.-C. Découvertes archéologiques en Bulgarie*, Paris, 230–2.

Gschnitzer, F. [1973]. *s.v.* Proxenos, *RE* Suppl. 13, 629–730.

Harvey, F. D. [1985]. '*Dona ferentes*: Some Aspects of Bribery in Greek Politics', in P. Cartledge & F. D. Harvey (eds), *Crux: Essays in Greek History presented to G. E. M. de Ste. Croix*, London, 76–117.

Herman, G. [1987]. *Ritualised Friendship and the Greek City*, Cambridge.

Hofstetter, J. [1972]. 'Zu den griechischen Gesandschaften nach Persien', in G. Walser (ed.), *Beiträge zur Achämenidengeschichte*, Historia Einzelschriften, 18, 94–107.

Hofstetter, J. [1978]. *Die Griechen in Persien: Prosopographie der Griechen im persischen Reich vor Alexander*, Berlin.

Karavites, P. [1987]. 'Diplomatic Envoys in the Homeric World', *RIDA*, 34, 41–100.

Karavites, P. [1992]. *Promise-Giving and Treaty-Making: Homer and the Near East*, Leiden.

Karavites, P. [2008]. *Homer and the Bronze Age: The Reflection of Humanistic Ideals in Diplomatic Practices*, Piscataway, NJ.

Kienast, D. [1973]. *s.v.* Presbeia, *RE* Suppl. 13, 499–628.

Kuhrt, A. [2007]. *The Persian Empire: A Corpus of Sources from the Achaemenid Period*, New York–London.

Lenfant, D. [2003]. 'De l'usage des comiques comme source historique: les *Vies* de Plutarque et la Comédie Ancienne', in G. Lachenaud & D. Longrée (eds), *Grecs et Romains aux prises avec l'histoire: représentations, récits et idéologie*, Rennes, 391–414.

Lenfant, D. [2016]. 'Le rôle de la proxénie dans les relations diplomatiques entre Grecs et Perses', *Ktèma*, 41, 275–87.

Lenfant, D. [2017]. 'Liens personnels, pots-de-vin ou protocole? Les dons du roi de Perse aux ambassadeurs grecs', in G. Cuniberti (ed.), *Dono, controdono e corruzione: ricerche storiche e dialogo interdisciplinare*, Alessandria, 41–69.

Lenfant, D. [2022]. 'The Role of *Xenia* in Diplomatic Relations between Greek Cities and the Persian Empire', in F. Mari & C. Wendt (eds), *Shaping Good Faith: Modes of Communication in Ancient Diplomacy*, Stuttgart, 81–93.

Mack, W. [2015]. *Proxeny and Polis: Institutional Networks in the Ancient Greek World*, Oxford.

Miller, M. [1997]. *Athens and Persia in the Fifth Century BC: A Study in Cultural Receptivity*, Cambridge.

Mitchell, M. [1997]. *Greeks Bearing Gifts: The Public Use of Private Relationships in the Greek World, 435–323 BC*, Cambridge.

Mosley, D. J. [1973]. *Envoys and Diplomacy in Ancient Greece*, Historia Einzelschriften, 22, Wiesbaden.

Osborne, R. & Rhodes, P. J. [2017]. *Greek Historical Inscriptions, 478–404 BC*, Oxford.

Perlman, S. [1976]. 'On Bribing Athenian Ambassadors', *Greek, Roman and Byzantine Studies*, 17 (3), 223–33.

Piccirilli, L. [2022]. *L'invenzione della diplomazia nella Grecia antica*, Rome.

Pracht und Prunk [2006]. *Pracht und Prunk der Grosskönige: das persische Weltreich*, Historisches Museum der Pfalz Speyer, Stuttgart.

Rhodes, P. J. & Osborne, R. [2003]. *Greek Historical Inscriptions 404–323 BC*, Oxford.

Rufin Solas, A. [2016], '*Phoroi* et *dôra* chez les Thraces', *Revue numismatique*, 75–94.

Sancisi-Weerdenburg, H. [1989]. 'Gifts in the Persian Empire', in P. Briant & C. Herrenschmidt (eds), *Le tribut dans l'empire perse*, Paris, 129–46.

Satlow, M. L. (ed.) [2013]. *The Gift in Antiquity*, Malden–Oxford.

Scheid-Tissinier, E. [1994]. *Les usages du don chez Homère: vocabulaire et pratiques*, Nancy.

Taylor, C. [2001a]. 'Bribery in Athenian Politics Part I: Accusations, Allegations, and Slander', *Greece & Rome*, 48 (1), 53–66.

Taylor, C. [2001b]. 'Bribery in Athenian Politics Part II: Ancient Reaction and Perceptions', *Greece & Rome*, 48 (2), 154–72.

Vickers, M. [1984]. 'Demus' Gold Phiale (Lysias 19.25)', *AJAH*, 9 (1), 48–53.

Wéry, L.-M. [1967]. 'Le fonctionnement de la diplomatie à l'époque homérique', *RIDA*, 14, 169–205.

3

Gifts for the Gods and *Keimēlia*
Some Reflections on Arms as Diplomatic Gifts in the Greek World*

María del Mar Gabaldón Martínez

In 1584, King Philip II of Spain received the first Japanese embassy to visit Europe at the Royal Monastery of San Lorenzo del Escorial. As a gift, the representatives of this embassy presented two suits of armour and various weapons, which were sent to the Royal Alcázar of Madrid to be kept, given their value and exoticism, in the palace's *Guardajoyas* (treasury). Ten years later these gifts were transferred to the Royal Armoury, which at the end of the sixteenth century was one of the finest examples of the splendour of the Habsburg dynasty and which housed, preserved and exhibited, as treasures, the weaponry of the monarchs and their ancestors, diplomatic gifts and military trophies.[1]

Throughout history, arms have played a prominent role as diplomatic gifts, not only for their extrinsic value (their beauty, sumptuousness, exoticism) but also for the intrinsic dimension, as emblematic and prestigious objects, as well as symbols of authority.[2] This exchange of weapons (and other items of military equipment) was a custom rooted in Antiquity. The practical giving and exchange of these gifts would take place in the context

---

* This work has been developed within the research project PGC2018-096415-B-C22 'La expresión diplomática en el Mediterráneo central y oriental bajo la expansión romana: el regalo en su contexto político e institucional', funded by the State Research Agency, Ministry of Science and Innovation, Government of Spain (MCIN/AEI/10.13039/501100011033) and ERDF 'A way of making Europe'.
[1] Soler del Campo, 2003.
[2] Arms communicate authority, strength and prestige, and are therefore suitable objects for exchange (since they define both the person who gives them and the recipient of the gift). Arms can therefore be defined or categorised as 'diplomatic objects', as can golden wreaths, clothing, belts and horses.

of a ritual staging, governed by rules and gestures, which could take place in a special space, such as sanctuary, since divine sanction for the exchange was a maxim in the ancient Mediterranean.[3]

Undoubtedly, as E. Sánchez Moreno states, for the Iron Age, the exchange of weapons (as well as sumptuary objects, horses ...) was a highly effective diplomatic instrument for sealing agreements, attracting allies outside the group, extending client networks, ensuring loyalty and, in short, consolidating the power of the chiefdoms.[4]

This universal practice was already well established in Homeric times, where the concept of the gift was not associated with property but with social relations. It acted as a symbol of personal, social and political identification.[5] As M. I. Finley indicates,

> gift-giving too was part of the network of competitive, honorific activity. And in both directions: it was as honourable to give as to receive. One measure of a man's true worth was how much he could give away in treasure. Heroes boasted of the gifts they had received and of those they have given as signs of their prowess. That is why gift-objects had genealogies.[6]

In the Homeric world, moreover, the exchange of gifts was framed by a formality, by rules, gestures and discourse. In this respect, hospitality, one of the most characteristic institutions of Homeric society, was the key to aristocratic exchange;[7] a hospitality that was articulated and renewed through the exchange of gifts,[8] such as weapons. In Book 6 of the *Iliad*, the Argive

---

[3] Perea Caveda, 2003: 150.
[4] Sánchez Moreno, 2011: 174. On this question, see also Quesada Sanz, 2007: 88.
[5] Perea Caveda, 2003: 150. On Homer and the subject of gifts, the bibliography is very wide. See the classic work by Finley, 1979 (originally 1954); Morris, 1986; Herman, 1987: 60–1; Hooker, 1989; Perea Caveda, 2003; Duce Pastor, 2013; Seiradaki, 2014. In ancient Greece, gifts continued to play an important part in diplomacy in the Classical and Hellenistic periods (Mitchell, 1997; Grainer, 2019: 69).
[6] Finley, 1979: 120–1.
[7] Perea Caveda, 2003: 154–6; Duce Pastor, 2013: 55–7.
[8] This type of exchange could occur in the context of banquets and celebrations. In fact, festivals and banquets were the most propitious moments to give gifts. Returning to the sixteenth century, during his baptismal celebrations, Emperor Charles V in Ghent was given gifts that were emblematic and 'figurative of future dignities', such as the golden helmet, sword and arms offered to him by various European nobles (Checa Cremades, 1986: 34–5).

Glaucus and Lydian Diomedes thus exchange arms as a sign of their pledge and bond.[9]

In the Homeric poems we have several other examples of the exchange of arms. The *Odyssey*, for example, relates how Alcinous, King of the Phaeacians, ordered the other leaders to entertain his guest Odysseus, and Euryalus to be especially kind with his words.[10] The latter also gave Odysseus a rich bronze sword with a silver hilt.[11] For his part, the hero Meriones, son of Molus of Crete, gave Odysseus a bow, a quiver, a sword and a boar-tusk helmet.[12] Homer specifies that this helmet had passed through several hands and generations before covering Odysseus' head.[13] This special 'biography' and 'long life' of the object, charged with memory, conferred even greater value upon it.[14] It would therefore have been a unique gift, a prestige item with the highest intrinsic value, given its long history. A gift evoking the past 'obviously shed greater glory on both donor and recipient'.[15] 'The biographic narrative attached to the object', moreover, 'makes it a very suitable object for a gift that will help to preserve the name and fame of the owners for posterity'.[16] Many prestige goods which evoked past histories were in fact endowed with special characteristics. This was the case with Meriones' helmet, described in detail in the *Iliad*,[17] and the

---

[9] *Il.* 6.224–36.
[10] The function of words – suitable and friendly language – should be emphasised here as a sort of non-material diplomatic gift. For example, *Od.* 15.51–5.
[11] *Od.* 8.400–6: a sword which, as Euryalus observes, would be very valuable to Odysseus. According to F. Quesada Sanz (2003: 136), the description of the weapon fits perfectly with the rich bronze swords of the Bronze Age, weapons that no longer existed at the time the Homeric poems were written.
[12] *Il.* 10.261–5. Quesada Sanz, 2003: 136.
[13] *Il.* 10.265–70. As indicated by J. Grethlein (2008: 37, 40), the boar-tusk helmet went through three different modes of exchange as it was handed down over three generations: theft, hospitality gift and inheritance. This author emphasises here that in Homeric epic, arms and other items of military equipment figure as the objects that accumulate the most history. See also Seiradaki, 2014: 160.
[14] Meriones' helmet is a very elaborate piece of military equipment that has a long history. Its unique workmanship, combined with its extensive history of different owners, turns it into a symbol of prestige that dignifies Odysseus and his nocturnal spy mission to the Trojan camp. For the question of the 'biography of objects' in the Homeric poems, and their connection with memory, see Crielaard, 2002; 2003; Grethlein, 2008; Seiradaki, 2014. For the Greek world in general, see Boardman, 2004; Reiterman, 2014; Crielaard, 2015; Reiterman, 2016.
[15] Finley, 1979: 121.
[16] Crielaard, 2015: 354.
[17] *Il.* 10.261–5.

gold cups of Diomedes and Nestor.[18] The same can be said of the silver krater with which Menelaus presented Telemachus, which had been made by Hephaestus, and given by the hero Phaedimus, King of the Sidonians, when Menelaus was his guest. In fact, the King of Sparta said that this krater was the most beautiful and valuable object in his possession,[19] for both its extrinsic and intrinsic value: as an object that evoked a past, which was received as a gift, and made by the god Hephaestus.[20]

This genealogy of gifted objects cumulatively conferred the qualities of their previous owners (sanctity, prestige, authority), which emphasised that the relationship between the object and its owner was reciprocal.[21] This was the case with the well-known sceptre of Agamemnon, a gift from Zeus himself, made by Hephaestus, given by Zeus to Pelops, from whom it passed to Atreus, from Atreus to Thyestes and then to Agamemnon, grandson of Pelops,[22] until it presumably became a sacred relic in Chaeronea.[23] In short, the transmission of gifts over generations conferred upon them striking additional value.[24] They were 'objects with history' that built their curriculum in these processes of circulation as aristocratic gifts in a context of reciprocity of gift and counter-gift.[25] As A. S. Reiterman indicates, the temporal sequence of these objects is important in the reading of their memory. She thus distinguishes between three types of temporal distances: those that came from a very distant mythical past (as we see in many examples in the Homeric narratives), those that had a closer past, perhaps of one generation or two, and those whose origin corresponded to the lived memory of a generation.[26]

At a certain point this transmission stopped and the goods, given their prestige, were amortised: they were therefore kept, treasured and preserved,[27] or deposited in a ritualised context such as a grave or shrine.[28]

---

[18] *Il.* 6.220; 11.632–5.
[19] *Od.* 4.613–19.
[20] As J. Grethlein (2008: 36) highlights, 'the significance of several objects is even heightened by their divine origin ... Therefore, biographies seem to be attached only to precious items; inversely, biographies render objects significant.'
[21] Crielaard, 2002: 250; 2003: 54; Grethlein, 2008: 36, 40–1.
[22] *Il.* 2.100–9.
[23] Paus. 9.40.11. Finley, 1979: 112; Crielaard, 2003: 53.
[24] Crielaard, 2002: 250.
[25] Ruiz Rodríguez, 2020: 146.
[26] Reiterman, 2016: 7.
[27] Although they could return to circulation.
[28] This does not mean that their history was erased. Crielaard, 2015: 364.

These objects that circulated and amortised were the *keimēlia*, objects that, produced in any given present, recalled ancient times.[29] As M. I. Finley wrote,

> the Greek word customarily rendered by 'treasure' is *keimelion*, literally something that can be laid away. In the poems treasure was of bronze, iron, gold, less often of silver ... Such objects had some direct use value and they could provide aesthetic satisfaction, too – characteristically expressed by reference to the costliness of the raw materials and to the craftsmanship applied to them – but neither function was of real moment compared to their value as symbolic wealth or prestige wealth. The twin uses of treasure were in possessing it and in giving it away, paradoxical as that may appear. Until the appropriate occasion for a gift presented itself, most treasure was kept hidden under lock and key. It was not 'used' in the narrow sense of that word.[30]

In Homeric epic, the term appears more frequently in the plural, and is described as undifferentiated collections of treasures, whether valuable objects stored in the homes of wealthy men, booty or gifts acquired through friendships. In fact, owning *keimēlia* seems to have been one of the criteria for belonging to the Homeric aristocracy.[31]

The word *keimēlion*, furthermore, has a connotation of remembrance ('relic'). Preserving an object was thus a way of retaining the memory of an event. Penelope therefore protected Odysseus' treasure, which included the bow and arrows kept as relics and given to him by his host Iphitos of Messene (gifts with a story behind them, moreover).[32] In turn, Odysseus offered him a sword and his spear as *dōra*, as the start of a friendship.[33] Homer expressly states that the King of Ithaca did not take the gift of the bow to Troy and left it as a relic in remembrance (*mnēma*) of the pact, the alliance, he had made with his foreign host. That is, the gift (the bow and the quiver of arrows) became an 'object of memory' of a past and present event, the evocation of a friendship.[34] For that reason, it was preserved as

---

[29] Ruiz Rodríguez, 2020: 145.
[30] Finley, 1979: 61. For the definition of *keimēlion* as 'treasure' and 'relic', see also Reiterman, 2016: 19–20.
[31] Reiterman, 2016: 21.
[32] Crielaard, 2002: 250; 2003: 56.
[33] *Od.* 21.9–41.
[34] The gifts received by a guest recalled the man who had welcomed him if the latter had offered him his friendship. *Od.* 15.51–5.

a *keimēlion*.³⁵ In this episode these gifts, which sanctioned a commitment, are kept under guard, hidden under lock and key. They are not displayed, perhaps because of their special importance or fineness.³⁶ This contrasts with what we know about the display of arms in the Homeric megaron,³⁷ where weapons were hung on the walls, like the old shield of Laertes, Odysseus' father.³⁸

The safekeeping and exhibition of arms given as a sanction for a commitment recalls the armour described at the start of this chapter, which the Japanese embassy presented to King Philip II in 1584. This armour was kept in the treasury of the Alcázar and later exhibited in the Royal Armoury as a symbol of prestige and a memento of a friendship.³⁹ In the same way, in the times of the Homeric heroes, gifts were treasured as a memory of a pact, and friendship, and then, after a time, they could be exhibited or given as gifts again, as they were perceived as objects with an important symbolic significance.

Arms in Sanctuaries, Gifts for the Gods and Relics

In the Greek world, sanctuaries were 'places of memory' (*lieux de mémoire*) that accommodated offerings and relics which evoked past characters and events (real or mythical). In the words of Reiterman,

> The Hellenes were a memorious people who contemplated the peoples and events of their past, as well as the relationship of the past to the present. Material and visual culture were keys to their commemorative *ethos*. At Greek cities and sanctuaries across the Mediterranean, inhabitants expressed deep interest in the physical remains of the past, whether real or invented. Often physical remains, both monuments and purported relics, served as proofs of the roles of different communities within pan-Mediterranean myth and history.⁴⁰

---

³⁵ Grethlein, 2008: 38; Reiterman, 2016: 22.
³⁶ *Od*. 21. 6–11.
³⁷ Arms were displayed hanging on the walls of noble halls from the Bronze Age to the Classical period (Van Wees, 1998: 363–6; Quesada Sanz, 2003: 138; Gabaldón Martínez, 2005: 144–5).
³⁸ *Od*. 22.182–6.
³⁹ In the Middle Ages, church treasuries also preserved and displayed arms and other pieces that were emblematic of the monarchs and used as ceremonial objects (Ruiz Souza, 2001).
⁴⁰ Reiterman, 2016: 5–6.

Indeed, Greek sanctuaries became settings in which objects commemorating a rich past could be displayed and kept in their temples and treasuries, which in turn conferred prestige and exclusivity upon the sanctuaries. Temple inventories thus recorded offerings (real or fictitious), many of them from famous visitors, which were 'preserved' in their treasuries, as if they were museums.[41] In this sense, weapons represented a prominent group of offerings in the sanctuaries. This was so much the case that it has even been said that Greek temples were veritable 'war museums'.[42] The dedication of arms and other items of military equipment in sanctuaries was a common practice from the Archaic period, and we have an abundance of historical, archaeological and epigraphic evidence.[43]

The presence of weaponry as offerings in cult spaces is a clear testimony to the ritual value of weapons and armour in the Greek world. Weapons were dedicated, above all, as an offering of the panoply of the vanquished collected on the battlefield, as offerings of the victor's personal weapons, donated to the deities as a token of gratitude after victory, or as an amortisation of one's own weapons after their use following a long military career.[44] In the latter sense, the weapons deposited in the shrines become *keimēlia*, i.e. objects that had been used for a long time and were finally kept and preserved in a place of worship. The shrine, moreover, guaranteed the preservation of the memory of the offerer through the consecrated arms.[45]

Of particular interest are the weapons of the mythical heroes of the Trojan War mentioned in the written sources and in temple inventories (particularly those of Delos and Lindos) as a reference to the long tradition of the dedication of weapons in some sanctuaries, or as an expression of the desire to enrich their prestige. This occurred to the point of becoming almost a fashion, since the fame of the donors would have been shared with

---

[41] Harris, 1995; Boardman, 2004: 115–17; Gabaldón Martínez, 2005: 92; Shaya, 2005; Reiterman, 2016; 6, 8; Graells Fabregat, 2017a: 156–8.

[42] Snodgrass, 1980: 63.

[43] In recent years, much research has been written on this subject from different perspectives: Jackson, 1991; Gabaldón Martínez, 2004; 2005; Larson, 2009; Gabaldón Martínez, 2010; Baitinger, 2011; La Torre, 2011; Baitinger, 2016a; 2016b; Graells Fabregat, 2016; 2017a; 2017b; Baitinger, 2018.

[44] As was the case, for example, with Aristomenes' shield, dedicated in the Sanctuary of Trophonius in Lebadaea (Paus. 4.16.7), and Alexander the Great's spear and cuirass, which, according to Pausanias (8.28.1), could still be found in the Sanctuary of Asclepius at Gortys (as relics). On the offering of personal arms, see the epigrams in the Palatine Anthology: *Anth. Pal.* 6.9, 52, 75, 81, 84–6, 91, 97, 122–4, 125, 127–9, 141, 163, 264.

[45] For example, *Anth. Pal.* 6.125, 6.128.

that of the sanctuaries that guarded them, as if they were relics, 'objects with history'.[46] Cult spaces could thus construct a prestigious image by weaving legends and traditions that linked them to emblematic figures and their arms. In this way, shrines and temples were builders of memory.

In fact, the well-known Chronicle of Lindos, a long Rhodian inscription from 99 BC,[47] lists forty-two offerings, beginning with those dedicated by mythical and famous figures, thus demonstrating the importance and prestige of the Temple of Athena Lindia and of the city of Lindos itself, in Rhodes.[48] According to this inscription, Lindos, the eponymous hero, gave the tutelary goddess a bowl; Heracles two shields; Menelaus donated the helmet of Paris; and the archer Teucer left the quiver of Pandarus at Lindos. Meriones' silver quiver was also found in the list.

Several sources also mention these relic-arms of legendary personages kept in sanctuaries.[49] According to Pausanias, the sword of Memnon was found in the Temple of Asclepius at Nicomedia[50] and Pelops' gold-hilted sword could be seen in the Treasury of the Sicyonians at Olympia.[51] Achilles' spear was kept in the Sanctuary of Athena at Phaselis[52] and that of Meleager in the Sanctuary of Apollo at Sicyon.[53] Other relic-arms were Diomedes' shield, found, according to Callimachus, in the Sanctuary of

---

[46] Pritchett, 1979: 243–5; Gabaldón Martínez, 2004: 28–9; Graells Fabregat, 2017a: 148.
[47] This is a large stele from the acropolis at Lindos. When this chronicle was composed in 99 BC, the sanctuary had become a museum which preserved 'objects with history' as *keimēlia*. See Pritchett, 1979: 245; Shaya, 2005.
[48] The epigraphic text begins with a decree in which the Lindian authorities decided to entrust two citizens of the city with the task of drafting an account of the offerings at the temple. This was not simply a catalogue of offerings, however, but a detailed description of those objects along with the data of who made the offering. For the Chronicle of Lindos see, for example, Boardman, 2004: 115–17; Shaya, 2005; Massar, 2006.
[49] Heroes' arms possessed a high symbolic value. Their origin was on occasions divine: Achilles' arms were forged by Hephaestus, at the request of Thetis, like Aeneas', who received a panoply thanks to his mother, Aphrodite. On the other hand, the transfer of arms equated to the distinction of heroic relationship: Heracles, at the moment of death on the pyre, therefore gave his bow to Philoctetes – a weapon which was deposited, according to tradition, in the Sanctuary of Apollo Alaios at Crimissa. Apollod. *Epit.* 6.15b; Gabaldón Martínez, 2005: 48, 128, n. 427.
[50] Paus. 3.3.8.
[51] Paus. 6.19.6.
[52] Paus. 3.3.8.
[53] Pausanias records many testimonies of relics in Greek sanctuaries; his sources were often local guides (Pretzler, 2007: 55, 118–48).

Athena at Argos,[54] and the cuirass (*hoplon*) of Timomachus, the legendary Theban leader, which was kept in the Sanctuary of Apollo and Hyacinthus at Amyclae, where it was displayed in the procession that took place during the annual festival of the Hyacinthia.[55]

These relics kept in cult spaces could be reused for propaganda purposes. Arrian narrates a legend according to which Alexander the Great made sacrifices in the Temple of Athena at Ilion, where he consecrated his armour, taking in exchange some of the weapons kept there from the time of the Trojan War, which would accompany him in battle.[56] This was undoubtedly a symbolic gesture of a propagandistic nature that connected the Macedonian monarch with the heroes of Troy, particularly Achilles, through the supposed relics preserved as *keimēlia* in the Temple of Athena, while conferring upon him authority and also special protection in combat.[57]

In short, through relics, sanctuaries increased their prestige as custodians of objects that belonged to famous people, while at the same time reinforcing their historical and mythical antiquity.[58] It should be noted that most relics were objects of prestige – such as weapons, vessels and jewellery – used in the remote past which become sacred pieces for the fact of having been owned or dedicated by a famous personage (real or mythical), which even received cult (as was the case of the so-called sceptre, or spear, of Agamemnon),[59] or formed part of the cult and were used in

---

[54] Callim. *Hymn* 5. Pritchett, 1979: 246–7. Among the mythical arms dedicated in sanctuaries, the shield stands out, principal weapon and emblem of the panoply. In the Sanctuary of Apollo in Sicyon, therefore, were found the sword and shield of Agamemnon (Ampelius, *L.m.* 8.5). In an Iapigian sanctuary, Menelaus 'hung' a shield as a present (Lycoph. *Alex.* 850–3). In the Sanctuary of Athena in Odysseia (Iberia), Odysseus dedicated shields and ship prows (Strab. 3.4.3). The Trojan, Euphorbus, dedicated a shield in the Sanctuary of Apollo at Miletus (Diog. Laert. 8.5).

[55] Arist. fr. 532 Rose; Pritchett, 1979: 247; Gabaldón Martínez, 2005: 40; Baitinger, 2011: 10; Graells Fabregat, 2016: 55; Kõiv, 2020.

[56] Arr. *Anab.* 1.11.7–8. In this case, it is interesting to emphasise how weaponry 'provides a good illustration of how personality and qualities of previous and present owners adhere to a particular object' (Crielaard, 2003: 54).

[57] The Greeks believed that many objects kept in the sanctuaries had been dedicated by legendary characters. As described by Pritchett (1979: 245): 'Just as devout medieval pilgrims contemplated with uncritical faith relics of early Christians, so the Greeks believed that many objects in their temples had been dedicated by heroes.'

[58] Boardman, 2004: 117.

[59] Paus. 9.40.11–12. The veneration of relic-arms occurred in some cultures in Antiquity. For example, in ancient Mesopotamia temples contained sacred arms which were considered genuine cult objects (perhaps relics?), as some texts from Mari and Ugarit indicate. For more examples, see Gabaldón Martínez, 2004: 28. In the Middle Ages,

sanctuary ceremonies (such as the armour of Timomachus at Amyclae).[60] At the same time, it is significant that the prestige goods preserved by the shrines as relics were largely pieces of military equipment and sumptuary objects (above all, vessels such as kraters and phiales)[61] and therefore belonged to the same category of objects that the Homeric heroes mostly exchanged as *dōra* (and which formed part of the *keimēlia*). For this reason, we can say that they were gifts fit for the gods.

Arms as Diplomatic Gifts in Greek Sanctuaries

The list in the Chronicle of Lindos mentions gifts made by historical figures to the Rhodian sanctuary for religious and propagandistic (and perhaps diplomatic) reasons.[62] For example, Pyrrhus dedicated his armour, possibly after defeating Antigonus II Gonatas in 274 BC.[63] Hieron II similarly consecrated his weapons at the Rhodian sanctuary, and shortly afterwards, around 211 BC, Philip V offered there ten shields, ten swords and ten helmets from the spoils of his enemies.

Without doubt, however, among the numerous diplomatic gifts sent by foreign kings, the best known are those made by the Egyptian king Amasis sometime in the mid-sixth century BC to the Temple of Athena Lindia and also to Sparta.[64] As Herodotus tells us, among other objects, he offered as a gift to the Temple of Athena Lindia a striking linen corselet.[65] This beautiful *linothōrax* eventually became a relic since, as Pliny reports, it was still admired centuries later, although it was in a very poor state of preservation due to constant handling by visitors, who wanted to touch it and see it up close to verify the legend about its fine weave and the high thread count that formed its structure.[66] Given his philhellenism, Amasis' dedication is a

---

relic-arms were also symbols of royal authority, as was the case for the 'Holy Lance' of St Maurice, used in coronations of the emperors of the Holy Roman Empire from Otto the Great (Blough, 2016).

[60] Pritchett, 1979: 247.
[61] As we know from the Chronicle of Lindos, the eponymous hero gave Athena Lindia a bowl, Cadmus dedicated a bronze lebes, and King Minos a silver cup (Pritchett, 1979: 243).
[62] See Pritchett, 1979: 245.
[63] After defeating Antigonus' army, Pyrrhus dedicated the Galatian mercenaries' shields to Athena Itonia, and those of the Macedonians to Zeus at Dodona (Paus. 1.13.3).
[64] Hdt. 2.182; 3.47.
[65] On this offering, see Pritchett, 1979: 224; on the sanctuary see Gabaldón Martínez, 2005: 63; Baitinger, 2011: 63–6; for Amasis' diplomatic dedication in the Sanctuary of Lindos see F. and M. Vickers, 1984; for the *linothōrax* see Graells Fabregat, 2016: 55.
[66] Plin. *NH* 19.2.12.

clear example of a gift given to the Rhodian sanctuary as a diplomatic gift,[67] and because Rhodes was on the trade route between the Aegean and Egypt. The Egyptian Pharaoh also sent diplomatic gifts to other Greek cities. As F. and M. Vickers have pointed out,

> at least four other communities were singled out as beneficiaries of such instruments of Amasis' foreign policy: Cyrene, Delphi, Samos and Sparta. His largesse, at least in retrospect, seems to have been carefully calculated to establish *xenía* with politically influential centres in widely different areas of the Greek world.[68]

At the end of the seventh century BC, the Egyptian King Necho II of the twenty-sixth-century dynasty, following his military victories in Syria, sent the armour he had worn in those battles to the oracular Temple of Apollo at Didyma.[69] According to M. Verčik and U. Güder, Necho II offered this gift to Apollo Didymeus in thanks for the help of Greek and Carian mercenaries in his military campaigns, as well as for a propagandistic and perhaps also diplomatic purpose.[70] The supraregional dimension of the oracle of the Branchides, moreover, made it possible to link the local with the international. In fact, the presence of weapons in this sanctuary reflects two prominent features of Ionia in the Archaic period: conflict and internationality.[71]

In order to win the favour of the divinity[72] at the oracular sanctuary of Didyma, the powerful King Croesus of Lydia also dedicated numerous valuable gifts,[73] as he did at Delphi, where among his offerings was a great golden shield, consecrated in the Temple of Athena Pronaia.[74] Herodotus

---

[67] This was a political (not military) gift. The offering of cuirasses in sanctuaries represented, moreover, a practice undertaken by prominent owners, bearing in mind their high value as a protective item and as a species of symbolic substitution, or alter ego, of the offerer. See Graells Fabregat, 2016: 61; 2017a: 153. The linen cuirass, moreover, 'becomes in this context a token of peace and, at the same time, a magnificent example of Egypt's most characteristic industry' (F. and M. Vickers, 1984: 125).
[68] F. and M. Vickers, 1984: 122. On this subject, see also Kaplan, 2006: 134, 145–6; 2016.
[69] Hdt. 2.159. See Pritchett, 1979: 271; Kaplan, 2006: 134. For the presence of arms in the sanctuary, see Baitinger, 2011: 33; Verčik, 2018; Verčik and Güder, 2021.
[70] Verčik and Güder, 2021: 191, 206.
[71] Verčik, 2018: 21–2.
[72] With both a religious and a political motivation.
[73] Hdt 1.92; 5.36.
[74] Hdt. 1.92. It has been suggested that 'Croesus is depicted as putting himself in a *xenía*-relationship with the god, wherein he exchanges his gifts, the dedications, for a response, indeed, for a statement support' (Kaplan, 2006: 143).

also relates that even in his day the shield and spear of solid gold, which Croesus had dedicated to the mythical seer Amphiaraus, were still to be found as relics in the Temple of Apollo Ismenios at Thebes.[75] The offering of arms made of precious metals, such as Croesus' golden shields, was associated with prominent leaders.[76] These were non-functional weapons (*ex-voto par destination*[77]), which combined their intrinsic value and symbolism – especially the shield, as the emblematic weapon of the panoply[78] – with their economic and decorative value,[79] which could turn them into worthy political and diplomatic gifts, such as were the golden wreaths[80] and the metal vessels.[81] These diplomatic gifts show that shrines could be spaces of mediation, 'localities where relationships with the outside world were materialised. It is also clear that by having access to local polis sanctuaries, foreigners in fact had access to the heart of the poleis.'[82] The gifts dedicated by some foreign rulers at the great Greek sanctuaries such as Delphi were, moreover, kept in treasuries, guarded and administered by allied states, 'showing that dedications could create interconnections on more than one level.'[83]

Finally, of particular interest are the offerings that the rulers of Sicily made at Greek temples, especially at Olympia, such as the three linen cuirasses that Gelon dedicated probably after defeating the Carthaginians at the Battle of Himera in 480 BC and which, according to Pausanias, were still

---

[75] Hdt. 1.52. On these gifts, see Kaplan, 2006: 132–3; Bassi, 2014.
[76] Pritchett, 1979: 271–2, 278.
[77] Morel, 1992.
[78] On the symbolic dimension of the gold shield in the Temple of Apollo Ismenius in Thebes and its connection with a heroic past, see Mozhajsky & Pichugina, 2020.
[79] Pausanias (5.10.4) speaks of a gold shield with an engraved Gorgon hanging on the pediment of the Temple of Zeus in Olympia, undoubtedly a tithe following the victory of Tanagra in 457 BC. After expulsing the Galatians from Delphi in 280 BC, the Aetolians dedicated golden shields in the sanctuary (Paus. 10.19.4). In Greek sanctuaries, miniature shields made of gold and silver were also offered (Gabaldón Martínez, 2010: 203). During the Roman Republic, Flamininus dedicated silver shields at Delphi following his victory over Philip V of Macedon in 197 BC (Plut. *Flam.* 12.5–6).
[80] Gold crowns frequently appear as a category of diplomatic gift, above all in the Hellenistic period. See the chapter by A. Erskine in this volume.
[81] Like, for example, the beautiful bronze krater that the Spartans sent to King Croesus of Lydia after making a hospitality pact and alliance with him (Hdt. 1.69–70). See Mitchell, 1997: 22.
[82] Crielaard, 2009: 67.
[83] Crielaard, 2015: 353.

Figure 3.1 Bronze Etruscan helmet of the Negau type from the Alpheus River, Olympia. The inscription indicates that it was dedicated to Zeus by Hieron, son of Deinomenes, and the Syracusans after the Battle of Cumae (© The Trustees of the British Museum).

preserved in the second century AD in the Treasury of the Syracusans,[84] as well as the helmets which Hieron I, tyrant of Syracuse, dedicated at Olympia after his victory over the Etruscans in the naval Battle of Cumae (475 BC; Figure 3.1).[85] These were dedications of enemy weapons (*spolia hostium*) to commemorate military victories, but at the same time were political and diplomatic gifts, given the strong ties (cultural, religious and political) that connected the Siceliot rulers to the sanctuary, as Pindar's

---

[84] Paus. 6.19.7. As indicated by Graells Fabregat (2016: 63), the relationship between these cuirasses and important individuals, the long duration of their display, their care and preservation, and the place chosen for their political use (the Treasury of the Syracusans) makes it necessary to relate these *spolia opima* with important enemies, whose defeat was celebrated and recorded, becoming the collective memory of the community and as such worthy of being preserved, although this implied extensive restoration or replacement over the centuries.

[85] On this dedication, see Gabaldón Martínez, 2005: 68; Baitinger, 2011; 2016a: 111; 2016b: 69–70. In detail, see Graells Fabregat, 2019. 'Votive gifts from Sicily and southern Italy are most prominent among the objects discovered in Greek sanctuaries, especially Olympia, the most significant location for such material in Greece' (Baitinger, 2016a: 111).

Triumphal Odes and the buildings and monuments built at Olympia by the Sicilian cities remind us.[86]

Conclusion

In the Homeric universe, friendship pacts (*xenía*), sanctioned by the deities, were sealed with reciprocal gifts (such as pieces of military equipment). These *dōra* could become *keimēlia*, wealth that circulated and could be hoarded, given their value extrinsically (as prestige goods) and intrinsically (as objects with memory, that evoked a history).[87]

From the Archaic period, the dedication of arms at sanctuaries, whether as an evocation of mythical times and legendary characters or as royal offerings, became a way of remembering past events (battles, victories, treaties). In this way, many of these arms became relics, *keimēlia*: objects that stored memory, that were horded, displayed, cared for and preserved over a long period in the sanctuaries, either for belonging to a famous person (mythical[88] or historical); for their exoticism, such as the striking *linothōrax* that Pharaoh Amasis sent as a diplomatic gift to the Sanctuary of Athena Lindia; as a memento of an important military exploit, such as the linen cuirass that Gelon dedicated at Olympia after his victory at Himera; or as a demonstration and evocation of the power and wealth of the donor, such as the golden shields offered by King Croesus of Lydia at Delphi and Thebes.

Bibliography

Baitinger, H. [2011]. *Waffenweihungen in griechischen Heiligtümern*, Mainz.

Baitinger, H. [2016a]. 'Votive Gifts from Sicily and Southern Italy in Olympia and Other Greek Sanctuaries', *Archaeological Reports*, 62, 111–24.

Baitinger, H. [2016b]. 'Fremde Waffen in griechischen Heiligtümern', in M. Egg, A. Naso & R. Rollinger (eds), *Waffen für die Gotter: Waffenweihungen in Archäologie und Geschichte*, Mainz, 67–85.

---

[86] Paus. 6.19.9; 6.19. 11; 6.19.15. For Sicilian cities' votive gifts in Olympia, see Baitinger, 2016a; Graells Fabregat, 2019: 40–2.

[87] 'The pan-Hellenic resonance of the Homeric epics, which served as status markers of elite culture for many centuries, suggests that these and other capacities of long-lived objects might have been adopted into mainstream practice in the historical period' (Reiterman, 2016: 22).

[88] Emphasising here the function of sanctuaries as creators of traditions and legends to strengthen their prestige.

Baitinger, H. [2018]. 'La dedica di armi e armature nei santuari greci: una sintesi', in R. Graells & F. Longo (eds), *Armi votive in Magna Grecia*, Mainz, 1–20.
Bassi, K. [2014]. 'Croesus' Offerings and the Value of the Past in Herodotus' Histories', in C. Pieper & J. Ker (ed.), *Valuing the Past in the Greco-Roman World* (*Mnemosyne*, Suppl. 369), Leiden, 173–96.
Boardman, J. [2004]. *Archaeologia della Nostalgia: come i greci reinventaron il loro pasato*, Genoa.
Blough, K. [2016]. 'The Lance of St Maurice as a Component of the Early Ottonian Campaign against Paganism', *Early Medieval Europe*, 24 (3), 338–61.
Checa Cremades, F. [1986]. 'Regalos y obras de arte en las sociedades del Renacimiento y del Barroco', *Revista de Occidente*, 67, 31–40.
Crielaard, J. P. [2002]. 'Past or Present? Epic Poetry, Aristocratic Self-Representation and the Concept of Time in the Eighth and Seventh Centuries BC', in F. Montanari (ed.), *Omero tremila anni dopo*, Rome, 239–95.
Crielaard, J. P. [2003]. 'The Cultural Biography of Material Goods in Homer's Epics', *Gaia*, 7, 49–62.
Crielaard, J. P. [2009]. 'The Ionian in the Archaic Period: Shifting Identities in a Changing World. Ethnic Constructs in Antiquity: The Role of Power and Tradition', in T. Derks & N. Roymans (eds), *Ethnic Constructs in Antiquity: The Role of Power and Tradition*, Amsterdam, 37–84.
Crielaard, J. P. [2015]. 'Powerful Things in Motion: A Biographical Approach to Eastern Elite Goods in Greek Sanctuaries', in E. Kistler, B. Öhlinger, M. Mohr & M. Hoernes (eds), *Sanctuaries and the Power of Consumption: Networking and the Formation of Elites in the Archaic Western Mediterranean World*, Wiesbaden–Göttingen, 351–72.
Duce Pastor, E. [2013]. 'El comercio noble homérico en la Odisea y su vertiente femenina', *Antesteria*, 2, 51–65.
Finley, M. [1979, orig. 1954]. *The World of Odysseus*, London.
Gabaldón Martínez, M. [2003]. 'El trofeo y los rituales de victoria como símbolos de poder en el mundo helenístico', *CuPAUAM*, 28–9, 127–43.
Gabaldón Martínez, M. [2004]. *Ritos de armas en la Edad del Hierro: armamento y lugares de culto en el antiguo mediterráneo y el mundo celta*, Madrid.
Gabaldón Martínez, M. [2005]. *Rituales de armas y de Victoria: lugares de culto y armamento en el mundo griego*, BAR, S1354, Oxford.
Gabaldón Martínez, M. [2010]. '*Sacra loca* y armamento: algunas reflexiones en torno a la presencia de armas no funcionales en contextos rituales', *Gladius*, 30, 191–212.

Graells Fabregat, R. [2016]. 'Las corazas incorruptas y la permanencia en exposición de algunas armas en santuarios (s. VI a.C.–II d.C.)', *Ostraka*, 25, 53–66.

Graells Fabregat, R. [2017a]. 'Armi mitiche, storiche e realli nei santuari', in R. Graells, F. Longo & G. Zuchtriegel (eds), *Le armi di Athena: il santuario settentrionale di Paestum*, Naples, 147–62.

Graells Fabregat, R. [2017b]. 'Armi nei santuari: esibire, conservare, defunzionalizzare, ricordare', in R. Graells, F. Longo & G. Zuchtriegel (eds), *Le armi di Athena: il santuario settentrionale di Paestum*, Naples, 163–79.

Graells Fabregat, R. [2019]. 'Da *Onatas* a *Laphyra*: tre elmi di Cuma offerti a Olimpia', *ArchClass*, 70, 29–53.

Grainer, J. D. [2019]. *Great Power Diplomacy in the Hellenistic World*, New York.

Grethlein, J. [2008]. 'Memory and Material Objects in the *Iliad* and the *Odyssey*', *JHS*, 128, 27–51.

Harris, D. [1995]. *The Treasures of the Parthenon and Erectheion*, Oxford.

Herman, G. [1987]. *Ritualised Friendship and the Greek City*, Cambridge.

Hooker, J. T. [1989]. 'Gifts in Homer', *BICS*, 36, 79–90.

Jackson, A. H. [1991]. 'Hoplites and the Gods: The Dedication of Captured Arms and Armour', in V. D. Hanson (ed.), *Hoplites: The Classical Greek Battle Experience*. London–New York.

Kaplan, P. [2006]. 'Dedications to Greek Sanctuaries by Foreign Kings in the Eighth through Sixth Centuries BCE', *Historia: Zeitschrift für alte Geschichte*, 55 (2), 129–52.

Kaplan, P. [2016]. 'The Ring of Polycrates: Friendship and Alliance in the East Mediterranean', *Journal of Ancient History*, 4 (2), 132–57.

Kõiv, M. [2020]. 'Amyklai: Rituals, Traditions and the Origins of Spartan State', in R. Kulesza & N. Sekunda (eds), *Studies on Ancient Sparta*, Gdańsk, 129–63.

La Torre, G. [2011]. 'Le lance di Temesa e le offerte di armi nei santuari di Magna Grecia e Sicilia in epoca arcaica', *Quaderni di Archaeologia*, 1, 67–104.

Larson, J. [2009]. 'Arms and Armor in the Sanctuaries of Goddesses: A Quantitative Approach', in C. Prêtre (ed.), *Le donateur, l'offrande et la déesse: systèmes votifs dans les sanctuaires de déesses du monde grec* (*Kernos*, Suppl. 23), Liège, 123–33.

Massar, N. [2006]. 'La "Chronique de Lindos": un catalogue à la gloire du sanctuaire d'Athéna Lindia', *Kernos*, 19, 229–43.

Mitchell, L. G. [1997]. *Greeks Bearing Gifts: The Public Use of Private Relationships in the Greek World 435–323 BC*, Oxford.

Morel, J. P. [1992]. 'Ex-voto par transformation, ex-voto par destination (à propos du dépôt votif de Fondo Ruozzo à Teano)', in M. M. Mactoux & E. Geny (eds), *Mélanges Pierre Lévêque*, Vol. 6: *Religion*, Paris, 221–32.

Morris, I. [1986]. 'Gift and Commodity in Archaic Greece', *Man*, NS 21 (1), 1–17.
Mozhajsky, A. Y. & Pichugina, V. K. [2020]. 'The Greek Shield as a Metal Artifact and its Reflection in the Story of the Croesus' Gifts in Thebes', *Nonferrous Metals*, 2, 79–83.
Perea Caveda, A. [2003]. 'Artesanos y mercaderes: la sanción divina del intercambio', in P. Cabrera & R. Olmos (eds), *Sobre la Odisea: visiones desde el mito y la arqueología*, Madrid, 147–60.
Pretzler, M. [2007]. *Pausanias: Travel Writing in Ancient Greece. Classical Literature and Society*, London.
Pritchett, W. K. [1979]. *The Greek State at War*, Vol. 3, Berkeley–London.
Quesada Sanz, F. [2003]. 'Lavar con sangre la humillación: armas y valores del guerrero en la Odisea', in P. Cabrera & R. Olmos (eds), *Sobre la Odisea: visiones desde el mito y la arqueología*, Madrid, 125–45.
Quesada Sanz, F. [2007]. '¿Héroes? de dos culturas: importaciones metálicas ibéricas en territorio vettón', in M. Barril & E. Galán (eds), *Ecos del Mediterráneo: el mundo ibérico y la cultura vettona*, Ávila, 87–93.
Reiterman, A. S. [2014]. '*Keimēlia* in Context: Toward an Understanding of the Value of Antiquities in the Past', in C. Pieper & J. Ker (ed.), *Valuing the Past in the Greco-Roman World* (*Mnemosyne*, Suppl. 369), Leiden, 146–72.
Reiterman, A. S. [2016]. *Keimēlia: Objects Curated in the Ancient Mediterranean (8th–5th Century BC)*, Publicly Accessible Penn Dissertations, 2545, University of Pennsylvania.
Ringheim, H. L. [2020]. 'Hera and the Sea: Decoding Dedications at the Samian Heraion', *Studia Hercynia*, 23 (1), 11–25.
Ruiz Rodríguez, A. [2020]. '*Keimelia, anastasis* y otras formas de memoria en la cultura de los iberos del sur', in J. M. Noguera, I. López & L. Baena (eds), *Satyrica signa: estudios de Arqueología Clásica en homenaje al profesor Pedro Rodríguez Oliva*, Granada, 143–54.
Ruiz Souza, J. C. [2001]. 'Botín de guerra y tesoro sagrado', in I. Bango (ed.), *Maravillas de la España medieval: tesoro sagrado y monarquía*, León, 31–9.
Sánchez Moreno, E. [2011]. 'Rebaños, armas, regalos: expresión e identidad de las elites vetonas', in G. Ruiz Zapatero & J. Álvarez-Sanchis (eds), *Castros y verracos: las gentes de la Edad del Hierro en el occidente de Iberia*, Ávila, 159–89.
Seiradaki, E. [2014]. *The Arms of Achilles: Re-exchange in the Iliad*. PhD dissertation, University of Toronto.
Shaya, J. [2005]. 'The Greek Temple as Museum: The Case of the Legendary Treasure of Athena from Lindos', *AJA*, 103 (3), 423–42.
Snodgrass, A. [1980]. *Archaic Greece: The Age of Experiment*, London.

Soler del Campo, A. [2003]. 'Embajadas japonesas en la Real Armería', in M. Alfonso & C. Martínez (eds), *Oriente en Palacio: tesoros asiáticos en las colecciones reales españolas*, Madrid, 58–67.

Van Wees, H. [1998]. 'Greeks Bearing Arms: The State, the Leisure Class and the Display of Weapons in Archaic Greece', in N. Fisher & H. Van Wees (eds), *Archaic Greece: New Approaches and New Evidence*, London, 333–78.

Verčik, M. [2018]. 'The Ionians at War? Die Waffenweihungen in den ionischen Heiligtümern und das Apollon-Heiligtum von Didyma', *Studia Hercynia* 21 (2), 7–26.

Verčik, M. & Güder, U. [2021]. 'Searching for Necho's Armour in Didyma: An Archaeological and Archeometallurgical Study on the Archaic Armour Scales', in G. Bardelli & R. Graells (eds), *Ancient Weapons: New Research Perspectives on Weapons and Warfare*, Mainz, 191–212.

Vickers, F. & Vickers, M. [1984]: 'Amasis and Lindos', *BICS*, 31, 119–30.

Part II

From Asia Minor to Lusitania

The Multiple Use of Gifts in an Interconnected World

4

Crowns to Rome
Honours, Gifts and Hellenistic Diplomacy*

Andrew Erskine

Rome's victories, first in the Punic Wars and then against the kingdoms of the Hellenistic East, made it the focal point of the Mediterranean. Year after year embassies undertook the often arduous and dangerous journey to Rome to demonstrate their loyalty or make requests. Success was not guaranteed. Ambassadors had to navigate an unfamiliar political system, canvassing individual senators in advance of their appearance before the senate, drawing attention to past support for Rome or perhaps highlighting kinship between their two states. They could also bring gifts, an affirmation of friendship and allegiance. The most striking and most visible of the gifts brought by embassies from the Greek world was the gold crown. Such crowns in one form or another had been a feature of international relations since the late fifth century BC and stood on the borderline between diplomatic and honorific culture.[1]

The first half of the second century BC offers a particular good opportunity to study the part played by crowns (*stephanoi*) in diplomacy. Not only was this a crucial time in the history of the eastern Mediterranean, during which cities and states had to come to terms with a new dominant power,

---

* This work has been developed within the research project PGC2018-096415-B-C22 'La expresión diplomática en el Mediterráneo central y oriental bajo la expansión romana: el regalo en su contexto político e institucional', funded by the State Research Agency, Ministry of Science and Innovation, Government of Spain (MCIN/AEI/10.13039/501100011033) and ERDF 'A way of making Europe'.
[1] This chapter has benefited greatly from some careful reading by my colleagues Mirko Canevaro, Benedikt Eckhardt and Keith Rutter. I am grateful also to the Leverhulme Trust for the fellowship that gave me the time to write it.

but diplomatic activity is well represented in the evidence.[2] Central is the history of Rome's rise to power written by the contemporary Achaean politician Polybius of Megalopolis. Although a substantial part of this history is now lost, we are fortunate that many of Polybius' accounts of diplomatic exchanges are preserved in the Byzantine collection *On Embassies*, one of several thematic collections of excerpts of historical texts overseen by Constantine Porphyrogenitus.[3] Alongside Polybius and often drawing on him, there is Livy's history, which provides a continuous narrative from the beginning of the Hannibalic War to the end of the Macedonian kingdom, concluding with the visit of Prusias of Bithynia to the senate in 167 BC. These historical accounts can be supplemented by contemporary epigraphic testimony.

Crowns to Rome

Both kings and cities are to be found sending gold crowns to Rome. There the crowns would be dedicated on the Capitol, home to the great Temple of Jupiter Optimus Maximus, also known as Jupiter Capitolinus. One of the earliest instances comes from the middle of the Second Macedonian War (200–196 BC) against Philip V.[4] In 198 BC an embassy arrived in Rome from its leading ally in the war, Attalus I of Pergamum. This embassy came to offer the king's thanks for Roman assistance in forcing Antiochus III to leave Attalid territory alone. In a vivid visual expression of Attalid gratitude the ambassadors brought an impressive gold crown to be placed on the Capitol, said by Livy to weigh 246 Roman pounds (*coronam auream ducentum quadraginta sex pondo*). While this gesture might be interpreted as symbolising Attalid subservience to Rome, it also needs to be noted that the Roman intervention was prompted by Attalus' threat to withdraw his forces from the war.[5] Such a gesture of thanks thus restored the balance, but it foreshadowed the increasingly unequal relationship that would develop between Rome and the Attalids. The embassy was one of many they would

---

[2] The evidence for embassies to Rome is collected in Canali de Rossi, 1997.
[3] Zecchini, 2005 for Polybius' treatment of embassies. The complete edited text of the *Excerpta de legationibus* is to be found in De Boor, 1903, the embassies to Rome appearing in part 2.
[4] Livy reports several earlier dedications of gold crowns in Rome, all from the west; on their authenticity, see the end of this section.
[5] Livy 32.8.8–15, 32.27.1. Some (Ma, 1999: 279–81, reviewing the arguments) suggest that Antiochus' invasion was an annalistic invention, but even if this backdrop to the embassy is questioned, there is no need to discard the embassy itself. Cf., in favour of Livy's account, Gruen, 1984: 539.

send to Rome. Twenty-six are recorded between the First Macedonian War and the end of the dynasty in 133 BC.⁶ How many of these were accompanied by such extravagant offerings we do not know, but the Attalids sent at least one more gold crown to Rome. This occurred in 184/3 BC during the reign of Attalus' son and successor Eumenes II, who ruled a far more extensive kingdom than his father but only because of a Roman decision to assign him a large portion of the territory in Asia Minor that had formerly been subject to the Seleucids. The embassy was led by Eumenes' youngest brother Athenaeus and had a very clear objective; it was to bring complaints against Philip V of Macedon. The latter's son Demetrius was in Rome as part of a Macedonian embassy sent to counter these charges. The valuable crown brought by Athenaeus and presented to the senate was surely intended to give the Attalids an advantage over Philip's representatives. This crown, reports Polybius, was worth 15,000 gold staters (ἀπὸ μυρίων καὶ πεντακισχιλίων χρυσῶν).⁷ The embassy makes a brief appearance in Livy but with no reference to any crown, an omission which helps to show the serendipitous character of the surviving evidence for the use of crowns in Greek diplomacy.

In examining these crowns it is important to distinguish between a state's justification for the award and its diplomatic objective. Sometimes our sources are helpful here, sometimes they are not. The public justification tends to involve gratitude for or celebration of past Roman actions, whereas the diplomatic objective will look to the future, in ways that may be specific, for instance Roman assistance in solving a particular problem, or general, such as ensuring friendly relations with Rome. Attalus' embassy, as presented by Livy, focused on gratitude, whereas Polybius' account of Eumenes' embassy tells only about the diplomatic objective. Gratitude too is the reason given by Appian for Greek cities sending ambassadors with gold crowns in the aftermath of the Second Macedonian War, but he also observes that these cities sought to be counted as Roman allies, so even as they are giving thanks they are looking to the future. Appian is the only source to mention crowns in this context, but the general sense of gratitude expressed to Rome for freeing the cities of the Greek mainland from Macedonian domination is well attested.⁸ In 191 BC Philip V, now aligned with the Romans, sent an embassy to Rome to congratulate them on their

⁶ Erskine, forthcoming, section 5.
⁷ Polyb. 23.1.4–7; for χρυσοῦς as a gold stater, Le Rider & de Callataÿ, 2006: 30; LSJ, s.v. χρύσεος.
⁸ App. *Mac.* 9.4; these crowns are perhaps to be linked with the 114 gold crowns that decorated Flamininus' triumph in 194, described as *dona civitatium* (Livy 34.52.8–9). Gratitude: Polyb. 18.46, Plut. *Flam.* 10–12, SIG³ 592.

victory over Antiochus III at Thermopylae. He asked, according to Livy, 'for permission to sacrifice on the Capitol and place a gift made from gold in the temple of Jupiter Optimus Maximus'. The gift was a gold crown, which weighed 100 Roman pounds. Zonaras, whose account was based on Dio Cassius, refers to it as a 'victory crown'. Yet Philip had other objectives, one of which was the return of his son Demetrius, who was held in Rome as a hostage. This the embassy successfully accomplished.[9]

Offering a gold crown might be perceived to give a state a competitive edge over its rivals, but it was a costly way of conducting diplomacy, so not something that could be done too often. But times of crisis would justify such measures. It is no coincidence that five examples cluster round the Third Macedonian War (171–168 BC), undertaken by Rome against Philip's successor, Perseus.[10] Boeotian Thisbe provides rare epigraphic evidence, although in the form of a *senatus consultum* rather than a decree from Thisbe itself, so we are not given direct access to the reasons why the Thisbaeans voted a crown to Rome. The city had been loyal to Macedon, but after surrendering to the advancing army of C. Lucretius Gallus pro-Roman citizens were put in charge.[11] These citizens proposed to dedicate a crown on the Capitol, but the circumstances of the proposal are obscure. The senatorial decree reads:

> So regarding the matters about which the same men [Thisbaean ambassadors] made speeches, that the gold, which they had collected for a crown in order that they might dedicate the crown on the Capitol, might be given back to them, as they explained, in order for them to dedicate this crown on the Capitol. It was resolved thus to give it back.[12]

It is not clear when the gold was collected and who had taken it. The anti-Roman citizens have been suggested, but for the Romans to be able to return the gold they must have been in possession of it themselves at the time of the decree, which offers an interesting perspective on the symbolic

---

[9] Livy 36.35.12–13 (*centum pondo coronam auream*), Zon. 9.19 (Cass. Dio, book 19); it is possible that Livy's source here is not Polybius, who in the brief excerpt (21.3.1–3) on the embassy does not mention the crown, Walbank, 1979: 91.

[10] For the Third Macedonian War as a time of crisis, Erskine, 2020: 75–8.

[11] Polyb. 27.5, Livy 42.46.7 and 63.12. Polybius' text incorrectly reads Θήβας for Θίσβας, as Mommsen observed, Walbank, 1979: 298; this in turn influenced the text of Livy: Briscoe, 2012: 312. On the events, Sherk, 1969: 28–31.

[12] *RDGE* 2, lines 31–5.

value placed on crowns.¹³ The Romans were here returning gold to the Thisbaeans, so it could then be given back to them in the form of a crown. It can also be observed that this embassy came to Rome not with a crown but only the idea of one.

Although the Third Macedonian War was fought in mainland Greece, it had repercussions further afield. Three embassies from communities in Asia Minor are reported by Livy to have brought crowns to Rome to be lodged on the Capitol in the Temple of Jupiter. In 170 BC an embassy from Alabanda brought a gold crown of 50 Roman pounds, and one from Lampsacus brought another weighing 80 Roman pounds; the following year a delegation from Pamphylia is said to have carried into the senate house a gold crown made out of 20,000 *philippeioi*, requesting that they be allowed to place it as an offering in the Temple of Jupiter.¹⁴ The *philippeios* was a common term for a gold stater, which took its name from the Macedonian king Philip II.¹⁵ The accuracy of Livy's information has been questioned. Lampsacus is wrongly said to have been subject to Macedon, and the figure of 20,000 *philippeioi* in the case of Pamphylia seems exceptionally high for a relatively poor region, but whether or not the details are correct in any particular case is less important than the overall impression of the role played by crowns in the Greek diplomacy with Rome.¹⁶ The example from the Carian city of Alabanda adds an extra element, linking the bestowal of a crown with ruler cult. When presenting their crown, the ambassadors are said to have spoken about how the Alabandans had built a temple to 'the city of Rome' (*urbs Roma*) and established annual games in honour of the divinity.¹⁷ This recalls a late fourth-century BC decree from Scepsis in the Troad, which honoured Antigonus Monophthalmus with a sacred precinct, an altar, a festival and crowns for himself and his sons.¹⁸ In all three cases, Alabanda, Lampsacus and Pamphylia, the Romans

---

¹³ Masri, 2016: 336 for Roman control of the gold; Sherk, 1969: 30 thinks it was originally seized by anti-Romans.
¹⁴ Alabanda and Lampsacus: Livy 43.6.5–10; Pamphylia: Livy 44.14.3–4.
¹⁵ De Callataÿ, 2012: 177.
¹⁶ Lampsacus: Briscoe, 2012: 407–8; Pamphylia: Briscoe, 2012: 507, who rejects the figure of 20,000 as either corrupt or 'an annalistic falsehood', suggesting the latter is more likely.
¹⁷ Mellor, 1975: 41–2, who notes that this is the only reference to the cult of Roma in Livy, would date its inception to the early 180s after Apamea; Briscoe, 2012: 407 would prefer a later date. It could, however, have developed in stages, first the games, then later the temple, as was also the case with the cult of Antigonus at Scepsis; see next note.
¹⁸ *OGIS* 6, lines 20–31; cf. also *I.Priene* 14 (for Lysimachus), Polyb. 5.86.10 (crowns and cult honours to Ptolemy IV).

responded by giving gifts to the ambassadors and promising continuing friendship.

Rhodes was one of Rome's oldest friends in the east and it had been rewarded after the war against Antiochus III with control over Caria and Lycia, but its relationship with Rome had since been deteriorating. This was said to have begun in the early 170s BC when the Rhodians escorted Perseus' Seleucid bride to Macedon, but Rhodian actions during the Third Macedonian War only made relations worse. They were now anxious that Rome would make war on them. It was partly out of relief that this did not happen that they voted Rome a gold crown worth 10,000 gold staters (στέφανον ἀπὸ μυρίων χρυσῶν), but the embassy sent to deliver the crown also had another objective, to ensure the continuing security of Rhodes by obtaining an alliance, something that it had hitherto avoided. When they heard that the Romans had announced that Lycia and Caria were to be set free, they feared, writes Polybius, 'that the gift of the crown had been futile and so too were their hopes of an alliance'.[19] When, a few years earlier in 170, Carian Alabanda had sent its embassy to Rome, it may already have been anticipating this situation, hence its extravagant gift.[20] But whatever ulterior purpose the Alabandans had as they sought to foster Roman goodwill in the future, their crown could be presented as essentially honorific, to be understood alongside cult honours for the goddess Roma. The Rhodians, on the other hand, were motivated by a combination of relief (that they were not at war) and fear (about what might happen next); the crown, implies Polybius, was aimed at fending off Roman anger and ill will.[21]

Crowns were also sent to Rome by kings seeking support for their rule, a reflection of the changing power dynamics wrought by Rome's increasing influence in the eastern Mediterranean. Several kings in the late 160s and early 150s BC resorted to this strategy. The Seleucid Demetrius, who had been held for many years as a hostage in Rome, escaped from the city

---

[19] Polyb. 30.5; cf. Livy 45.25.4–10; at 20,000 gold pieces (*coronam viginti milium aureorum*) Livy's crown is twice the value of Polybius'. Walbank, 1979: 421 suggests that the Polybian excerptor is responsible for the error, because the Rhodians would not have given a crown that was half the value of one given previously by the Pamphylians. Briscoe, 2012: 684 accepts Walbank's argument, but in doing so is inconsistent with his own argument, because he has already rejected the Pamphylian figure as very likely incorrect (2012: 507). If we accept that Briscoe is right to reject Livy's figure for the Pamphylian crown, then Polybius' figure for the Rhodian one becomes less problematic.

[20] Mellor, 1975: 43. Note how the Alabandans launch a campaign into Rhodes' Carian territory at this time, Polyb. 30.5.16, Livy 45.25.13.

[21] For Roman anger, Erskine 2015, esp. 109, 114–15, 126; it would take several more embassies for the Rhodians to get their alliance, Polyb. 30.23.2–3, 30.31.20.

and claimed his father's throne. This did, however, involve overthrowing and executing the child who with the backing of Rome was the current occupant. Anxious about the Roman reaction, he sent an embassy with a crown of 10,000 gold staters to Rome (πρέσβεις στέφανόν ... κομίζοντες ἀπὸ μυρίων χρυσῶν). Acceptance of the crown by the senate gave some degree of reassurance, although the Roman answer was distinctly cautious.[22] Not long beforehand the new Cappadocian king, Ariarathes V, had also sent an equally expensive gold crown to Rome. The senate responded with gifts, a sceptre and an ivory chair, gifts which had been bestowed on other kings.[23] Their significance is unclear, but the ivory chair, as the seat of a Roman curule magistrate, may have been intended as a way of recognising a king's authority while symbolically and subtly expressing his kingship as an extension of Roman power.[24] Ariarathes may have been motivated by the need to demonstrate Roman support in the face of any possible challenges to the succession. Such concern was not misplaced. Shortly afterwards he was toppled by his brother Orophernes, who duly sent another crown to the senate. On this occasion our sources do not say whether or not the crown was gold, but it is a safe assumption that it was.[25] Again the protagonists are seen using the gift of a crown as a means of getting a competitive advantage over their rivals.[26]

This section has concentrated on gold crowns brought to Rome by Greek kings and cities in the second century BC, once Rome was seen as a significant player in the politics of the east. Livy does, however, record several earlier dedications of gold crowns in Rome, all of which come from the west, but their historicity can be questioned. In the fifth century BC the Latins both alone and later with the neighbouring Hernici are said to have dedicated gold crowns to Jupiter Capitolinus. Such an early date is implausible; either Livy or his source has surely projected later practices on to earlier times.[27] In 343 BC a Carthaginian embassy was said to have come with a gold crown to congratulate the Romans on their achievements against the Samnites. It is possible that this reflects Carthaginian experience of the practice elsewhere in the Mediterranean; Athens had offered crowns to Dionysius of Syracuse and his sons in the 360s BC, an act which, given their Sicilian interests, may not have gone unnoticed among the Carthaginians.

[22] Polyb. 31.33, 32.2; App. *Syr.* 8.47; Diod. Sic. 31.29.1.
[23] Braund, 1984: 27–9, Walbank, 1979: 518–19.
[24] Polyb. 31.32.3, 32.1.1–3; Diod. Sic. 31.28.
[25] Polyb. 32.10.
[26] For the complicated manoeuvres undertaken by these three figures, see Habicht, 1989: 356–9.
[27] Livy 2.22.7, 3.57.7, on which Masri, 2016: 331–2, Oakley, 1998: 359–60.

At the same time the only function of the embassy in Livy's narrative is to demonstrate the impact of Roman military success, not only in Italy but also overseas.[28] Closer to our second-century examples, both in time and style, is the case of Saguntum, a coastal city in the Iberian Peninsula which had been captured by Hannibal in the lead-up to the Second Punic War and was subsequently recaptured by Rome. In 205 ambassadors came to Rome to express their gratitude for everything the Romans had done for their city and request permission to dedicate a gold crown to Jupiter Capitolinus. Their speech, as presented by Livy, closes with a request that the senate ratify and confirm the advantages given to them by the Roman commanders in Hispania. As with the Greek embassies discussed above, the Saguntines were both giving thanks and looking to the future. It is plausible that Saguntum did indeed offer a crown. Although Saguntum was an Iberian city, it had longstanding links with the Greek world.[29] Pliny also records a gold crown given to Gaius Aelius, tribune of the plebs in 285, by the south Italian city of Thurii for helping it against the Lucanians, but this is an award to an individual rather than Rome itself.[30]

Our largely narrative sources focus on the arrival of the embassy and crown in Rome, so they reveal little about the process that led to the decision to send the crown. Instead they highlight the embassy itself and what it hoped to achieve in Rome. In monarchies the decision to send a crown would have been a matter for discussion between the king and his advisers, but in a polis there would have been an established procedure for the granting of crowns. The matter would have been debated and voted upon in the assembly. Only in the case of the Rhodians do we learn about this aspect of the process. Polybius is here concerned not only with the reception of the embassy in Rome, but with the fearful uncertainty of the Rhodian people themselves. They have debated the matter and voted, and they reflect on whether or not their decree offering the crown will be effective. No second-century decree authorising the gift of a crown to the Romans survives, but there is a relevant decree from Mytilene which dates from Augustus' reign. It necessarily reflects the transformation of Roman

[28] Livy 7.38.1–2; Oakley, 1998: 360 accepts it, while acknowledging the possibility that it is invented. Dionysius: Rhodes & Osborne, 2003: no. 33. An earlier Carthaginian crown to Gelon's wife Demarate (Diod. Sic. 11.26.3) is persuasively rejected as a Hellenistic construct by Rutter, 1993: 179–81.
[29] Livy 28.39; the ambassadors may even have addressed the senate in Greek, Pina Polo, 2013: 256–7; see also Torregaray Pagola, 2005 for Hispanian embassies to Rome, including the Saguntine one.
[30] Plin. *NH* 34.15.1, who reports that Aelius was the recipient of the first statue in Rome awarded by foreigners.

politics in the latter part of the first century, honouring Augustus while also thanking the senate for its kindness. The beginning is in poor condition, but it is clear that the first part of the surviving text concerns cult honours for Augustus; there is a fragmentary mention of 'benefactions' and details of the duties of the ambassadors, including delivery of a crown made out of 2,000 gold pieces. What benefactions the Mytilenians are grateful for is not apparent from the decree as it survives, but it has been plausibly suggested that it is a response to Roman assistance after the earthquake of 26 BC.[31] Like the Alabandan decision discussed above, this crown is closely linked to cult honours, this time for Augustus rather than Roma.

Despite the limitations of the epigraphic evidence for crowns to Rome, it is possible to fill the gaps to some extent by examining comparable decrees, that is to say Greek decrees where the recipient of the crown was not Rome but a king or another city. This will help us to understand the decision-making process. What we will see when we examine these in the next section is that such decrees are not simply about diplomatic expediency, they are also honorific in character.

Crowns and Greek Honorific Culture

The cities and kings that brought these gold crowns to Rome were working in a well-established Greek tradition. The use of crowns as honorific rewards for achievement of various kinds had a long history. They had been given to the victors in the so-called 'crowned' contests (*stephanitai agones*), the Nemean, Isthmian, Pythian and Olympic, since the very early years of those festivals. There the athletes received crowns, sometimes referred to as wreaths, that were made of foliage, such as laurel or olive, rather than ones made of gold.[32] Elsewhere, however, gold crowns gradually came to be awarded, although still imitating the form of the vegetative crown. Such crowns are found given by states to foreign individuals or to other states, a practice that first appears in our evidence in the latter part of the fifth century BC. In 423 BC, during the Peloponnesian War, the people of Scione in northern Greece crowned the Spartan general Brasidas with a gold crown on the grounds that he was liberating Greece;[33] in 410 BC, the Athenians rewarded Thrasybulus of Calydon in the same way for his role in

---

[31] *OGIS* 456, on which Rowe 2002: 133–5 and Jones, 2015: 102–5 (who connects it with the earthquake).
[32] Blech, 1982: 109–53; on crowned contests: Mari & Stirpe, 2021.
[33] Thuc. 4.121.1, on which Hornblower, 1996: 380; Scionian faith in Brasidas did not, however, save them from complete destruction at the hands of the Athenians shortly afterwards, punishment for their revolt, Thuc. 4.122.6, 5.32.1.

the assassination of the oligarchic general Phrynichus.[34] Later gold crowns were awarded by cities to their own citizens, but the focus in this chapter is only on their role in international relations.[35]

A mid-fourth-century Athenian speech offers a valuable insight into the meaning and use of gold crowns. It was written by Demosthenes and delivered by a certain Diodorus as part of the trial of the Athenian politician Androtion. Among the many accusations brought against him was one that concerned gold crowns that had been dedicated in the Temple of Athena. Earlier in his career Androtion had overseen the melting down of these crowns and their conversion into sacred vessels of various forms.[36] Androtion was probably not exceptional in recycling dedications in this way, only unlucky to find his actions the subject of Demosthenic polemic.[37] The crowns in question had been awarded by other Greek states to Athens or to an individual such as Conon and then dedicated to the goddess. The speech focuses on the honour that the crowns represent and on the way that they encourage emulation and love of honour (*philotimia*).[38] To melt them down takes away the memory of that honour and replaces them with wealth alone. Androtion, the speaker claims, 'is so dim that he does not know that crowns are evidence of excellence (*aretē*), while bowls and such like are evidence of wealth'. It is this very *aretē* that is singled out in surviving honorific decrees.[39] He continues 'every crown, however small it may be, is as much an incentive to honour as a large one'.[40] In this way, therefore, the giving of a crown was a means of honouring a person or a state, and the subsequent dedication of the crown to a divinity was appropriate recognition of that honour.

Although decrees that award crowns to Rome may not survive, there are many decrees that award crowns to other states or individuals that do survive, and these help to throw light on the way these honours were justified. The person or city being given the crown has to be shown to merit it. Before the honours are outlined, the decree will first draw attention to

---

[34] Osborne & Rhodes, 2017: 182. On early Athenian awards of gold crowns, Scafuro, 2009: 66–8.

[35] For Athens, see Engen, 2010: 158, Henry, 1983: 23. For a useful overview of crowns in the late Classical and Hellenistic periods, Rutter, 1993: 179–81.

[36] Dem. 22.69–76, on which Giannadaki, 2020: 355–81.

[37] Harris, 1995: 32–5 brings together the evidence for melting down Parthenon treasures.

[38] For the importance of *philotimia*, Canevaro, 2016: 78–86.

[39] Whitehead, 1993, where *aretē* is one of the cardinal virtues; cf. Rhodes & Osborne, 2003: no. 64, lines 32–3, ἀρετῆς καὶ εὐνοίας ἕνεκα τῆς εἰς τὸν δῆμον τὸν Ἀθηναίων.

[40] Dem. 22.75.

the achievements or qualities of the honorand. Such decrees, however, are not only about the past; they also look forward, explicitly or implicitly, to the future, anticipating that the honorand's positive attitude will continue. They are, as Stephen Lambert nicely puts it, 'monumentalised diplomacy'.[41] A gold crown is an investment in the future, but it needs to be understood in the context of a continuing relationship.[42] Some examples should illustrate the way they operate.

In 311 BC Antigonus Monophthalmus wrote to the city of Scepsis in the Troad to tell its citizens how during negotiations with his rival warlords he had insisted that Greek freedom should be upheld and that this should be formally incorporated into any agreement. In response Scepsis gave cult honours to him and gold crowns to him and his sons. The resolution of the *dēmos* begins: 'since Antigonus has been responsible for great goods for the city and for the rest of the Greeks, to praise Antigonus and rejoice with him at what has been accomplished', and it continues 'In order that Antigonus may be honoured in a way that is worthy of what has been accomplished and that the *dēmos* may be seen to return thanks for the good things it has hitherto received, be it ...' So Antigonus is honoured for what he has done and the Scepsians show that they are the type of people who know how to honour benefactors. But the decree also says that the city should 'rejoice with the Greeks at the fact that, being free and autonomous, they will continue for the future to exist in peace', so the past is taken as an indicator of the future. Thus, although Antigonus is honoured for what he has already achieved, he is also presented as a guarantor of future Greek freedom.[43]

In 287 BC the Athenians freed their city from Antigonid control, although they were unable to expel the garrison from the Piraeus; free but constrained, therefore, they were in dire need of grain, as several honorific decrees of the period attest.[44] One of these decrees honours the Paeonian ruler Audoleon with a gold crown and Athenian citizenship. It lists several reasons for making this award: Audoleon's support for Athenian freedom, his assistance to Athenians living in and visiting his kingdom, and his substantial gift of 7,500 *medimnoi* of grain, roughly two shiploads' worth. Furthermore Audoleon is praised for 'his excellence *(aretē)* and his goodwill *(eunoia)* towards the *dēmos* of the Athenians'. In this case too there is

---

[41] Lambert, 2006: 117.
[42] Canevaro, 2016: 77–97, cf. also Ma, 1999: 201–6 on honours for Hellenistic kings; Gygax, 2016: 19–57 brings out the anticipatory character of honours but tends to interpret them in an overly instrumental manner.
[43] *OGIS* 5 (letter), 6 (decree). For other gold crowns voted to Antigonus, Billows, 1997: 258.
[44] Oliver, 2007: 236–7 with n. 41 on the epigraphic evidence.

explicit reference to what will happen next: Audoleon 'has announced that in the future he will be of service by working together with them for the recovery of the Piraeus and the freedom of the city'.[45] So again the decree looks to past achievements to justify the award while locating these within a pattern of continuing favourable behaviour.

Crowns were not only bestowed on individuals; they were also given to cities and even leagues. A conceptual shift is taking place here. Crowning a man is easy to understand, but once the recipient is a city the act is moving into the area of metaphor and the city is becoming personified. Rome is the most notable example of this happening, but precedents can be found as far back as the fourth century BC in Athens, at that time the hegemon of the Second Athenian Confederacy, which was both the recipient of crowns from states such as Andros and Miletos and the giver of crowns to others such as Tenedos. Some survive only in the Athenian temple inventories, others are known from inscribed decrees, some of which are better preserved than others.[46] Cities might also bestow a crown on the *dēmos* of another city to thank it for providing judges to resolve an internal dispute, the so-called foreign judges. Decrees of second-century Smyrna attest to this practice.[47] In the mid-third century Chios voted 'the largest gold crown according to the law' to the Aetolian League.[48] The decree explains that it is being passed in response to the Aetolian decision to offer Chios a seat on the Amphictyonic Council, but it also makes clear this is the latest in a series of measures that have improved relations between the two, notably an *isopoliteia* agreement and an exemption for Chians from Aetolian plundering. There is no explicit reference to the future, but the whole tenor of the decree is looking forward; the *isopoliteia*, the exemption and the place on the council only make sense with reference to the future. The idea of one city crowning another could also be depicted in sculpture. After the Rhodian earthquake in the early 220s BC the Syracusan rulers' gifts included not only a massive aid package but also a set of statues representing the *dēmos* of Syracuse crowning the *dēmos* of Rhodes.

---

[45] *IG* II² 654; Oliver, 2007: 124–5. For fourth-century decrees offering crowns to foreigners, Lambert, 2006.

[46] Rutishauser, 2014, drawing particularly on the Athenian temple inventories examined by Harris, 1995.

[47] *I.Kaunos* 17.14–20, with Caunian acknowledgement of the crown in *I.Kaunos* 19; Hamon, 1999, supplementing XII 8 269 from Thasos.

[48] Moretti, *ISE* ii.78, lines 25–6, with 35–40. Its value depends on how the text is restored; Wilhelm put δραχμῶν, but Moretti prefers χρυσῶν, the latter more appropriate to μεγίστωι. Cf. also *IG* XI.2 199B, line 23, *dēmos* of Naxians crowns *dēmos* of Delians.

Whether this sculptural group memorialised the giving of an actual crown is not recorded.[49]

The decrees normally made arrangements for the proclamation of the crowns at one of the city festivals.[50] At Scepsis they were to be proclaimed at the festival in honour of Antigonus, while the Athenian honours for Audoleon would be announced at the Great Dionysia. The Chians were particularly keen to publicise the crown they had awarded to the Aetolian League, no doubt eager to advertise not only the crown but also their accession to the Amphictyonic Council. After it had been proclaimed at the Dionysia in Chios the same thing was also to be done at two Aetolian festivals and at the Pythia at Delphi.[51] Where there is a reference to the making of the crowns, it tends to be cursory, indicating only who is responsible.[52]

Gold crowns were relatively high-value items, so it must have been tempting for recipients to take advantage of this and use them to improve their financial situation. In most cases, however, there is no evidence at all for what happened to the crown once it had been given to the state or individual honoured. What limited evidence that there is suggests that the appropriate action was to dedicate the crown to a deity, thus taking the gold out of circulation. The inventories of the treasurers of Athena list many crowns that had been given to Athens by Greek states during the fourth century, especially its allies in the Second Athenian Confederacy. In some cases the crowns were offered directly to the goddess Athena, but in others they were given to the *dēmos* or *boulē*. Yet all are dedicated in the Parthenon.[53] It may be that it was simply expected that the recipient would dedicate it in the main sanctuary of the state. Melting the crowns down was certainly not out of the question, as Androtion's actions show, but in his case the crown remained the property of the goddess. In a rare instance where the final destination of the crown is indicated, it is the honorand who makes the decision; crowns had been awarded to the members of the

---

[49] Polyb. 5.89.8; interestingly, despite the monarchic character of the regime, the Syracusan rulers Hieron and Gelon chose to emphasise the *dēmos*. The act of crowning sometimes appears in relief sculpture on Attic honorific decrees, Lawton, 1995: 30–3.

[50] McLean, 2002: 239.

[51] Scepsis: *OGIS* 6, lines 30–1; Athens: *IG* II² 654, lines 41–3 (cf. honours for Pharnaces, *IG* II³.1 1258, lines 24–7); Chios: Moretti, *ISE* ii.78, lines 23–45, 39–43.

[52] For Athens, see Henry, 1983: 34–5, citing *IG* II² 212, lines 26–9 (Rhodes & Osborne, 2003: no. 64); *IG* II² 223.B, lines 13–14; *IG* II² 555, lines 26–9; cf. also *IG* II² 654, lines 43–5; for Chios, Moretti, *ISE* ii.78, lines 35–7.

[53] Harris, 1995: 238, Rutishauser, 2014: 69; Aeschin. *In Ctes.* 46–7 says that crowns given to Athens and Athenian citizens by foreign states were expected to be dedicated to Athena.

Spartocid ruling family in the Black Sea, who asked that they be dedicated to Athena Polias in Athens, but it is not known how often this occurred.[54] So the dedication of Greek crowns on the Capitol in Rome may be following an established pattern, but there is one noticeable difference. Greek ambassadors are several times represented as requesting that their crowns be placed in the Temple of Jupiter Optimus Maximus, which may suggest that, although this was something that was desirable, it could not be taken for granted.[55] It is a request that reflects a recognition that Romans did things differently.

Demosthenes' speech against Androtion mentions the practice of adding inscriptions to the crowns that are dedicated to the goddess:

> Consider, men of Athens, how noble and admirable were the inscriptions that he has destroyed for all time and how impious and terrible were those he wrote in their place. For you have all seen, I think, the writing below the rings of the crowns: 'From the allies for the people on account of their bravery and justice', or 'From the allies a prize of valour for Athena', and from individual cities, 'From such-and-such city for the *dēmos*, having been saved by the *dēmos*', for example 'The Euboeans, having been freed, crowned the *dēmos*'.[56]

There are very few decrees that have anything to say about the process of inscription, so it is uncertain when and by whom they were inscribed. It may have been a stand rather than the body of the crown itself that was inscribed.[57] Nor should we assume that the practice was consistent from place to place. An early third-century decree from Cos honouring the cities of Thessaly does include, in a rather fragmented form, the text to be inscribed on the crown.[58] On the other hand, when the crown given to the Spartocids was dedicated, the decision about the text of the inscription

---

[54] Rhodes & Osborne, 2003: no. 64 with discussion. The text does not explicitly say that the crowns are to be gold, but at 1,000 drachmas it is the standard amount for an Athenian gold crown for a foreigner (cf. Henry, 1983: 24, Engen, 2010, 159–61); furthermore it is supplementary to an earlier lost decree in which the decision about the crown was originally made. This was a continuing relationship over generations; see Dem. 20.29–40 for honours for their father Leucon (on which Canevaro, 2016: 240–51) and later the early third-century crown for Spartocus III, *SIG*³ 370.

[55] See 'Arrival in Rome', below.

[56] Dem. 22.72; cf. Dem. 24.180–1, where the text is largely the same.

[57] Giannadaki 2020: 368 argues in favour of a stand on the basis of the language used. On the other hand, the two inscriptions cited in nn. 58 and 59 imply the crown itself, as does the suggestion in Demosthenes that the inscription itself was melted down.

[58] *SEG* 55.922.

appears to have been made by the Athenians. 'Since they [Spartocus and Paerisades] are dedicating the crowns to Athena Polias, the *athlothetai* shall dedicate the crowns in the temple with the inscription: "Spartocus and Paerisades, sons of Leucon, dedicated to Athena, after having been crowned by the people of Athens".'[59]

The crowns that came to Rome were brought there by both cities and kings. The civic decrees examined in this section give an insight into the political and cultural world that produced these gifts, at least insofar as the cities are concerned. Kings and rulers, on the other hand, were under no such obligation to leave a public record of the decision-making process. To understand what was going on at the court we can only extrapolate from the civic evidence that we have and the reports of royal embassies in Rome. Cities were relatively secure in contrast to kings, who were always at risk of being overthrown, especially in the volatile second century, as Ariarathes V knew to his cost. So for kings and other sole rulers there was an even stronger need to invest in the future.

The Crown

Before turning to the crown's arrival in Rome, it is useful to consider what the crown was. Those that were sent to Athens were without doubt gold versions of the traditional foliage crown. One of Androtion's justifications for melting down the crowns in the treasury was said to be that the leaves were falling off, an excuse roundly mocked by Demosthenes, who said that he was talking as if they were made of roses or violets rather than gold.[60] The elegant crowns with intricate gold leaves that have been found in Macedonian and Tarantine tombs give some sense of what an honorific crown may have looked like.[61] None of these, however, compare in weight with those brought to Rome. The heaviest surviving crown, dating from the fourth century BC, comes from the Macedonian royal tombs at Vergina and weighs just over 700 g.[62]

The standard amount allocated for a gold crown to honour a foreigner in Athens was 1,000 silver drachmas, which probably included the cost not

---

[59] Rhodes & Osborne, 2003: no. 64, lines 33–8.
[60] Dem. 22.70; for the fragility of crowns, Giannadaki, 2020: 360–1; the problem of detached leaves is also mentioned in the treasury inventory, Harris, 1995: 33.
[61] Kyriakou, 2014; Masiello, 1984; gold wreaths are also found in fourth- and third-century Thracian tombs, reflecting Greek influence, although adapted to the local context, Tonkova, 2013.
[62] De Callataÿ, 2017: 203; Kyriakou, 2014: 264–5.

only of the gold but also its production.⁶³ To put this in context, the hull of a trireme cost around 5,000–6,000 drachmas, so the cost of the crown would have represented a substantial but not outlandish sum.⁶⁴ The Hellenistic period, however, saw an escalation in the value of the crowns that were awarded to rulers. There is a lack of consistency in the way that these costs were expressed, which makes comparison difficult, but the overall impression is clear. In 311 Scepsis gave Antigonus 'a gold crown of a hundred gold staters' (χρυσῶι στεφάνωι [ἀπὸ στατήρ]ων χρυσῶν ἑκατόν]), but that was dwarfed by the 'gold crown of a thousand gold staters' (στεφά[ν]ωι [χρυσῶι] ἀπὸ χρυσῶν χιλίων) given by Priene to Lysimachus just over twenty years later. Around 280 BC the League of Islanders voted and delivered a 'gold crown of a thousand staters as a prize of excellence' (χρυ[σῶι] στεφάνωι ἀριστεί[ωι ἀπὸ] στα[τήρ]ωγ χ[ι]λίων) to Ptolemy II, which, assuming these are gold staters, would be an equal of the Prienean crown.⁶⁵ Taking a stater to weigh 8.6 g, according to the common Attic standard, the crown for Antigonus would have weighed 860 g. while the other two would have been over 8 kg each, although the cost of manufacture may have reduced these weights.⁶⁶ They would, therefore, have been significantly heavier than the fragile crowns that were stored on the Acropolis, although Antigonus' crown would have been not dissimilar to the large crown found at Vergina.⁶⁷ At the same time, however, lesser individuals still received more moderate honours, as is attested by a Delian decree bestowing a 1,000-drachma crown on the Sidonian king Diocles.⁶⁸ The increase in the value of honorific crowns in the Hellenistic period reflects the vast amount of gold that had come into circulation as a result of Alexander's seizure of the Persian treasuries, but the immense power and wealth of the new kingdoms must also have put pressure on Greek states to offer something

---

⁶³ Engen, 2010: 159 with n. 53; Lewis, 1968: 106–7; Athenian citizens tended to get crowns costing 500 drachmas, Henry, 1983: 24.
⁶⁴ For the comparison, Engen, 2010: 160.
⁶⁵ Scepsis: *OGIS* 6, lines 25–30; Priene: *OGIS* 11, lines 12–15; League of Islanders: *Syll.*³ 390, lines 42–6. For χρυσοῦς as a gold stater, see n. 7 above.
⁶⁶ For the Attic standard, Le Rider & de Callataÿ, 2006: 28–9, 287; for the lighter Ptolemaic stater, see n. 92 below.
⁶⁷ The Athenian temple inventories give the weights of numerous gold crowns in drachmas; see the catalogue in Harris, 1995. Crowns weighing c. 40 drachmas in gold are likely to have cost 500 silver drachmas, and those weighing c. 80 drachmas in gold would have cost 1,000 silver drachmas (Lewis, 1968), roughly 170 g and 340 g respectively.
⁶⁸ *SIG*³ 391.

more impressive.⁶⁹ The spectacular procession in Ptolemaic Alexandria described by Callixenus of Rhodes was awash with gold, including thousands of gold crowns, at least some of which would have been brought by embassies such as the one from the League of Islanders.⁷⁰ Callixenus no doubt exaggerated, but even so his description reflects a perception of the Hellenistic kings as extraordinarily rich.

When recording the value of the crowns that were sent to Rome, Polybius and Greek sources tend to use gold staters, while Livy prefers Roman pounds. It is possible that Livy is converting Polybius' figures into pounds, but it is more likely that where he uses pounds he is drawing on a Roman source. It would be good to be able to compare Polybian and Livian accounts directly, but of the four embassies where Livy uses pounds to describe the crown only one of these appears in Polybius. This is Philip's embassy of 191 BC, but Polybius does not mention a crown at all. Given the brevity of the Polybian excerpt we should be cautious about drawing conclusions, but a Roman source for the crown is a plausible explanation for why the two differ.⁷¹ Both Polybius and Livy do describe the Rhodian decision to send a crown to Rome after the Third Macedonian War. In this case Livy does not give its weight in pounds, but comparison brings different problems. While Polybius writes that the Rhodians voted a crown of 10,000 gold staters (στέφανον ἀπὸ μυρίων χρυσῶν), Livy says they voted one of 20,000 gold *aurei* (*coronam viginti milium aureorum*). Regardless of whether the numerical error lies with the Polybian excerptor or with the text of Livy, the similarity in the form of the description does suggest that Livy did not try to convert Polybius' figures into pounds.⁷² We can suggest, therefore, albeit tentatively, that where Livy is giving the weight in pounds he is following a Roman, non-Polybian tradition. Given that the Capitol was one of the places for the standardisation of Roman weights, it

---

⁶⁹ Scholars (e.g. de Callataÿ, 2017; Holt, 2016: 164–77) may disagree on the amount that was monetised, but the amount of gold in any form was clearly huge.

⁷⁰ Crowns appear throughout the procession, but note esp. Athen. 5.201c–e, 202b, 202d (3,200 crowns) with commentary in Rice, 1983. For crowns to Alexandria, Shear 1978: 33–5; see also the mid-third-century decree in honour of Boulagoras of Samos, *SEG* I.366, lines 28–36, and Ptolemy III's letter to Xanthos, *SEG* 36: 1218 (Bousquet, 1986).

⁷¹ Livy 36.35.12–13, Polyb. 21.3.1–2, on which Walbank, 1979: 91 and Briscoe, 1981: 273, the latter noting that this is a transition passage between Polybius and Roman annalistic sources.

⁷² Polyb. 30.5.4, Livy 45.25.7; on the textual issue, see n. 19 above. Similarly at 44.14.3–4 *philippeiorum* Latinises φιλιππείων, which again suggests Polybius as the source.

is possible that any crowns dedicated at the Temple of Jupiter were weighed on arrival there.⁷³

The gold crowns brought to Rome appear to be significantly more costly than any known to have been given to other Hellenistic rulers. Polybius records three crowns valued at 10,000 gold staters and one at 15,000, which at 8.6 g a stater convert into 86 kg and 129 kg respectively (or c. 190 lbs and 285 lbs). Any estimates of weight, however, must recognise that other elements may also have contributed to the value of the crowns, such as the cost of production and possible decoration with precious stones.⁷⁴ Attalus I's gift of a crown, said by Livy to weigh 246 pounds, at a conversion rate of 327 g to the Roman pound would be just over 80 kg (or 177 lbs), roughly equivalent to a 10,000-stater crown.⁷⁵ The crowns given by Alabanda, Lampsacus and Philip V are more moderate at 50, 80 and 100 pounds, but still substantial.⁷⁶ Even Alabanda's at around 16 kg is almost twice the weight of the crowns given by Priene to Lysimachus or the League of Islanders to Ptolemy. If we accept Livy's two crowns at 20,000 gold staters from Pamphylia and Rhodes, then the figures are even higher, but it is hard to see how a relatively poor region like Pamphylia could raise such a sum.⁷⁷ So if we convert them all (in an admittedly rough and ready way) into kilograms, then we can see a range from 16 kg to an impressive 129 kg. This is a lot of gold, and we may wonder about the accuracy of the figures. In this respect the evidence of civic decrees and historical texts is not comparable. Civic decrees record exactly what the city plans to spend on the gold crown that it is awarding, which means that we can be confident that the figures for Priene and the League of Islanders are reliable. But those that are found in historical works do not have the same authority. A historian is concerned with the embassy and its purpose, but the value of any crown is of only secondary interest, easily susceptible to exaggeration in the telling.

Archaeologically, large gold objects have had a hard time surviving. There would have been a strong temptation to melt them down when the

---

⁷³ For standardisation of weights, Riggsby, 2019: 100–1.

⁷⁴ Le Rider & de Callataÿ, 2006: 176 n. 2; precious stones are found decorating a gold candelabrum brought to Rome by Seleucid representatives in the early first century BC, Cic. *Verr.* 2.4.64, 71.

⁷⁵ For the conversion rate, Riggsby, 2019: 102 and 129.

⁷⁶ Livy gives the figures in the form *coronam auream quinqaginta pondo* etc., which Walbank, 1979: 422 mistakenly takes to refer to staters rather than pounds.

⁷⁷ Contrasting the Pamphylians with Ariarathes, Demetrius and the Rhodians, who all invested 10,000 staters in their crowns, Briscoe, 2012: 507 writes: 'It is incredible that the much poorer Pamphylians could have raised 20,000 and the figure must be rejected.'

need arose. Those that do survive tend to be from tombs, but even here they were at risk. Since Antiquity grave robbers have targeted the tombs of the rich and powerful in search of precious objects. Plutarch tells how Pyrrhus' Galatian mercenaries ransacked the tombs of the Macedonian kings at Aegae, modern Vergina.[78] Despite their efforts, however, the heaviest gold object to be found in the Greek world comes from Vergina, the gold larnax from the supposed tomb of Philip II, which weighs around 11 kg.[79]

Some scholars have questioned whether these were crowns at all. John Briscoe, commenting on the Pamphylian gold crown at Livy 44.14.3, says simply that it was 'a gift of money, not a real crown'.[80] It is certainly the case that the terms στεφανόω and στέφανος do develop by extension a broader range of meanings.[81] In Ptolemaic Egypt, for instance, cleruchs would pay a tax known as the 'gold crown' (χρυσικὸς στέφανος).[82] It is possible that the origins of this tax lay in collecting money for real gold crowns to honour the king, perhaps for display in the Ptolemaia. Polybius too occasionally employs the terms in ways that cannot signify literal crowns. The verb στεφανόω is used by him to refer not only to the act of wreathing or crowning but also to that of honouring. Thus he writes that 'the Gerraeans honoured (ἐστεφάνωσαν) king Antiochus with five hundred talents of silver, a thousand of frankincense and two hundred of what is known as *staktē*'.[83] The noun στέφανος can stand for some form of payment. He reports Greeks giving what are described as 'crowns' to Roman commanders in the field, thus the Ambraciots give a 'crown of 150 talents' (στέφανος ἀπὸ ταλάντων ἑκατὸν καὶ πεντήκοντα) to Fulvius after he occupied their city in 189 BC and stripped it of its artworks. This crown, however, is not said by Polybius to be gold.[84] Talents usually represent weight in silver; 150 silver talents

---

[78] Plut. *Pyrrh.* 26.6–7; cf. Strabo 8.6.23.
[79] De Callataÿ, 2017: 203–4 on surviving gold objects, including the 12 kg mask of Tutankhamun.
[80] Briscoe, 2012: 507; it is clear from his note on the Alabandan embassy at Livy 43.6.6 (p. 407) that he believes all the crowns brought to Rome by embassies were in fact 'gifts of money'. Walbank's notes on the Pergamene crown (23.1.7) and Ariarathes' crown (31.23.3) both refer back to his note on 20.12.5, where he writes that στέφανος 'often has the meaning of a gift of precious metal, coined or uncoined, presented as a mark of homage' (Walbank, 1979: 86).
[81] Welles, 1934: 363.
[82] Fischer-Bovet, 2014: 224, cf. Bowman, 1967.
[83] Polyb. 13.9.5; cf. Diod. Sic. 20.84.3; for this shift in meaning, cf. also Gengler, 2017: 42.
[84] Polyb. 21.30.10; Livy (38.9.13), unsure how to interpret this, turns it into a 'gold crown of 150 pounds' (*coronam auream ... centum et quinquaginta pondo*). Another example in Polybius (21.36) is a crown of 50 talents given by Sagalassus to Manlius,

would have weighed almost 3,900 kg. Even if Polybius had meant that this was 150 silver talents worth of gold, on the basis of a gold to silver ratio of 1:10, this would be still be close to 390 kg.[85] So, even allowing that the figure might be inflated, this looks as if it was bullion rather than an actual crown, and silver rather than gold.[86] Nonetheless, Roman commanders did receive genuine gold crowns from Greek cities, crowns which would later decorate their triumphs.[87] Indeed, when gold crowns did appear in Roman triumphs, Livy makes a clear distinction between them and other forms of gold.[88] Curiously, he reports gold crowns in several triumphs from Hispania and Liguria in the second half of the 180s BC. Whether this is to be explained by westerners borrowing a Greek practice, Greek cities in the east celebrating Roman victories by contributing crowns to the triumph or some other factor is unclear.[89]

The Greek embassies arriving in Rome were operating within a tradition that stretched back at least to the fourth century, one in which crowns were brought and then dedicated in a sanctuary. In Rome their final destination was the Temple of Jupiter Capitolinus. The crowns may have got bigger and heavier, but they were still crowns. Once the move had been made to include cities among the recipients of crowns, then it is fair to assume that the size of the crown awarded no longer had to be limited by the size of a human head. Depictions of substantial crowns carried in later triumphal processions are found on two relief sculptures from the Roman Imperial period. On a frieze of the Arch of Trajan at Benevento

together with 20,000 *medimnoi* of barley, and 20,000 of wheat; again there is no reference to gold (cf. also Antiochus IV's 50-talent crown at 28.22.3). Given that Manlius was already plundering their territory, the Sagalassans, like the Ambraciots, had little choice. Moagetes of Cibyra may have offered Manlius the traditional gold crown (15 talents) but ended up paying silver bullion (Polyb. 21.34.3–13). It was also possible to offer both a crown and gold, as Erythrae did to an early Antiochus, *OGIS* 223, lines 3–5, although the text does not specify from what material the crown was made.

[85] Calculations based on equivalents given by de Lisle, 2021: 109, while explaining Diod. Sic. 20.79.5.

[86] Östenberg, 2009: 123–4 with n. 629 treats it as a genuine gold crown, but she follows Livy's figure of 150 pounds rather than Polybius' 150 talents. Sherk's restoration of 200 talents for a gold crown in Sulla's letter to Stratonicea (*RDGE* 18, lines 30–3) goes back to Dittenberger (*OGIS* 441) and nineteenth-century scholars (cf. Böckh, 1851: 38–42), who believed there was a 'small talent' that was applied specifically to gold; this was based on the statement of Pollux (*Onom.* 4.173) that ὁ δὲ χρυσοῦς στατὴρ δύο ἦγε δραχμὰς Ἀττικάς, τὸ δὲ τάλαντον τρεῖς χρυσοῦς (cf. also *Etym. Magn.* 744, 38–40, citing the comic poet Philemon).

[87] Östenberg, 2009: 119–27 collects the evidence for the use of crowns in triumphs.

[88] Livy 37.59, 39.5, 39.7, 39.29.

[89] Livy 39.42.3–4, 40.16.11, 40.34.8, 40.43.6, on which Östenberg, 2009: 123–4.

Figure 4.1 Four men carry a substantial and clearly heavy crown on a *ferculum* as part of the triumphal procession depicted on the small frieze of the Arch of Trajan at Benevento (© Olof Vessberg. National Museums of World Culture – Mediterranean Museum, Stockholm).

four men carry a *ferculum* upon which sits a very large and weighty crown (Figure 4.1), while a similar group appears on a relief from Naples.[90] Among the many crowns in Callixenus' description of the procession in Alexandria one stands out in particular: 'on the throne of Ptolemy Soter there lay a crown made from ten thousand gold staters (στέφανος ἐπέκειτο ἐκ μυρίων κατεσκευασμένος χρυσῶν)'. It is possible that 'ten thousand' here is simply intended to emphasise its inordinate value, but it may be a precise figure taken from royal records, which can be compared with those which we have observed on honorific decrees.[91] If so, this crown could have weighed 60 kg or more and thus would have been considerably larger than those from Priene and the League of Islanders, making it closer to some of the crowns said by Polybius to have been brought to Rome.[92]

---

[90] Östenberg, 2009: 120–1, illustrated in figures 11 and 12.
[91] Athen. 5.202b, on which Rice, 1983: 118.
[92] The Ptolemaic stater was lighter than the standard Attic weight of 8.6 g, the Ptolemaic three-stater gold coin, the *trichryson*, weighing 17.85 g, Lorber, 2018: 34, Le Rider &

These were not the only large gold gifts that came to Rome. Kings in particular, unconstrained by civic honorific tradition, may have been more versatile in their choice of diplomatic gifts.[93] In 216 BC, soon after C. Flaminius' disastrous defeat at Trasimene, the Syracusan ruler Hieron, who not that long previously had been lavishing his gifts on the Rhodians, sent an embassy with a gold statue of Victory to Rome. This Nike statue, according to Livy, weighed 220 Roman pounds, a little less than the 10,000-stater gold crowns which were later said to have been brought to Rome.[94] As a statue it appears to have been acceptable to the senate in a way that gold bullion was not. On several occasions Livy says that the senate turned down gifts of gold, including a large quantity of gold and silver from Ptolemy V in 191 BC for the war against Antiochus, as well as other gifts, such as supplies of grain.[95] The acceptance of Hieron's statue was justified by placing it in the Temple of Jupiter Capitolinus. Thus it was accepted not as gold but as a symbol.[96] The same would be true of the gold crowns. The reality of these gold crowns as crowns is further reinforced by Jewish evidence. Both 1 Maccabees and Josephus reproduce letters said to be from Roman magistrates, each of which acknowledges the receipt of a valuable gold shield, brought to Rome by a Jewish embassy. These shields sound like an imitation of the crowns brought by Greek embassies, the choice of the shield as the gift being explained by its meaning in Jewish tradition, but imitation would not make sense if the Greeks were only bringing bullion.[97] The authenticity of these letters has been questioned, but it is the Jewish perception of Greek practice that is important.

de Callataÿ, 2006: 176–7 with n. 2. If Callixenus was using a Ptolemaic rather than Attic standard, then this crown would have weighed approximately 60 kg rather than 86 kg.

[93] Cf. Seleucid gold gifts to the Temple of Apollo at Didyma, *RC* 5 (*OGIS* 214); for other royal gold gifts to Rome, see n. 96 below.

[94] Livy 22.37.5–6, on which Meadows, 1998: 127–8, Burton, 2011: 166–8. Rhodes: Polyb. 5.88.5–8.

[95] Livy 22.37.11, 36.4.1; Burton, 2011: 168, 187–90. Livy 22.32.4–9 reports gifts of gold bowls from Naples, all but one of which were rejected, but in this case the Neapolitans made clear that this was intended as financial assistance for the cash-strapped Romans; cf. also the delegation from Paestum shortly afterwards, Livy 22.36.9.

[96] Other crafted gold objects were accepted when dedicated in temples: cf. gold vases from Antiochus IV, Livy 42.6.8–11; a Nike from the Seleucid usurper Tryphon (although only accepted and inscribed in the name of his murdered predecessor Antiochus VI), Diod. Sic. 33.28a; cf. also the gold candelabrum brought to Rome by Seleucid princes for dedication in the restored Temple of Jupiter: Cic. *Verr.* 2.4.67.

[97] 1 Macc. 14.24, 15.18–20; Joseph. *AJ* 14.146–8, on which Zollschan, 2017: 81–2, 234–8.

Arrival in Rome

An embassy to Rome was a challenging endeavour.[98] If all went well, it might look something like those described by a Rhodian ambassador in a speech to the senate as reported by Livy:

> Formerly, after the Carthaginians had been defeated, after Philip and Antiochus had been overcome, when we visited Rome, we went from our state accommodation to the senate house to offer our congratulations, and from senate house up to the Capitol carrying gifts for your gods.[99]

Here we have the key components of the ideal visit to Rome: sponsored accommodation, a speech in the senate and a dedication on the Capitol, all of which are found in various forms in the evidence for those bringing gold crowns to Rome. But embassies did not always go as smoothly as this, as the Rhodian speaker knew well. Out of favour with the Romans, his embassy had to put up with 'a shabby lodging-house, difficulty finding accommodation even with money and being ordered to remain outside the city in a manner that was more appropriate to enemies'.[100] Furthermore, before their big speech in the senate, ambassadors would need to lobby senators to win them over in advance, something all the more necessary if there was a rival embassy, as, for instance, with the competing embassies of the Attalid Athenaeus and the Macedonian Demetrius in 184/3 BC.[101]

Embassies tended to gather in Rome at the beginning of the consular year.[102] The gift of a gold crown would not only make an embassy stand out, it would also make an impression on the other Greeks present. The ambassadors would ostentatiously bring their crown into the senate house itself before beginning their address.[103] This would be likely to follow Hellenistic practice elsewhere. When cities bestowed crowns on kings, they would present the decree to the king and give a speech

---

[98] For the diplomatic visit to Rome: Westall, 2015; Ferrary, 2007; Torregaray Pagola, 2005; Erskine, 1994.
[99] Livy 45.22.1.
[100] Livy 45.22.2. For problems faced by embassies, see Brennan, 2009.
[101] See the first section above ('Crowns to Rome'). For lobbying see *SIG*³ 656, lines 20–7.
[102] Ferrary, 2007: 118.
[103] Cf. Livy 44.14.3: *Pamphylii legati coronam auream ... in curiam intulerunt*. For the theatricality of diplomatic visits to Rome, Torregaray Pagola, 2005: 29–30, 43–53; Westall, 2015.

that repeated the main points of the decree, as is clear from royal letters acknowledging honours bestowed.[104] The speech which Livy attributes to the Saguntines when they brought their crown to Rome may be very like the kind of speech delivered in the senate, even if it does not accurately reflect what was said by the Saguntines themselves. It follows the pattern of a decree, first the motivation for the award, then thanks and congratulations, after which comes the request to carry the gold crown to the Capitol for Jupiter Capitolinus. Finally they ask for confirmation of all the benefits they have received from the Roman commanders in Hispania.[105] Echoes of this pattern are still present some centuries later, when Menander Rhetor offered a guide on how to present a crown to the emperor. After some rather over-the-top flattery, the speaker should move on to the emperor's achievement in war and peace before concluding along the lines: 'For these reasons the city crowns you, returning thanks for the benefits that we receive every day, while at the same time begging and beseeching you, encouraged by your all-embracing humanity, that it will not fail in its object.'[106]

Repeatedly Livy describes the visiting embassies as requesting to be allowed to present their crown as an offering to Jupiter; sometimes this is combined with a request to sacrifice on the Capitol, although it is likely that these two requests regularly went hand in hand.[107] Polybius, on the other hand, makes no mention of Jupiter Capitolinus or of any request in this context. He does, however, say several times that the crown was 'for Rome' (τῇ Ῥώμῃ), the significance of which is not clear. The goddess Roma has been suggested, but this was a Greek, not a Roman cult, so not present in Rome. More plausible is the suggestion that Polybius is making a reference to the Roman people and that he has in mind Jupiter Capitolinus.[108] Although Polybius does not say anything about a request to the senate, he makes clear that the embassy could not take for granted that their gift would be accepted. Ariarathes' crown is only accepted after Tiberius

---

[104] For instance, Lysimachus to Priene, *OGIS* 12 (*RC* 6), Eumenes to League of the Ionians, *OGIS* 763 (*RC* 52); cf. Ma, 1999: 201.
[105] Livy 28.39.2–11.
[106] Men. Rhet. 2.12 (422.5–423.5).
[107] Livy 28.39.15–18 (Saguntum), 36.35.12–13 (Philip V), 43.6.5–7 (Alabanda and Lampsacus), 44.14.3 (Pamphylians). Even where a request is not explicitly attested, Livy reports that the crown was placed on the Capitol: Livy 32.27.1 (Attalus I); cf. App. *Mac.* 9.4.
[108] Polyb. 30.5.4, 31.32.3, 32.2.1, 32.10.4; Walbank, 1979: 421–2, Grass, 2015: 158–9 n. 63. A Locrian coin from c. 275 shows a seated figure identified as ΡΩΜΑ being crowned by the personified Pistis; Head 1911: 103–4, Rutter 2001: 181 (no. 2347).

Gracchus vouches for the claims of the king's ambassadors. Demetrius offers a crown together with a captured assassin, but after much thought the senate decides to take only the crown.[109] The fragmentary nature of Polybius' text means that the fate of the Rhodian crown is not known. They did not get their alliance on this occasion and would have to wait another few years, but it is important not to confuse the state's objective with the publicly announced honorific motive. The fact that they feared that gift was in vain may suggest that the crown stayed in Rome.[110]

As part of its response the senate would often decree *munera* to visiting ambassadors. For instance, each of the ambassadors from Lampasacus and Alabanda received 2,000 *asses*, as did those from Pamphylia. The purpose of this money has been debated. Was it a straightforward gift, or was it intended to cover travel or accommodation expenses in some way? Attractive is the suggestion that it was a Roman contribution to any sacrifice for which the senate had granted permission; in these cases it would be the sacrifice to Jupiter Capitolinus during the dedication of the crown. The Romans thus not only permit the sacrifice, they also participate, making it a shared endeavour and a mark of acceptance, something the frustrated Rhodian ambassadors failed to achieve.[111] Such *munera*, however, were specifically given to the ambassadors and were only indirectly gifts to the state represented by the ambassadors.[112]

Once permission to deposit the crown on the Capitoline Hill was granted, a formal procession would have made its way there. We can imagine the crown carried on a *ferculum* in the manner of the triumphal relief from Beneventum. In contrast to the privacy of the senate house this was a public, visual statement of the honour in which the visitors held Rome and also of their own place within the expanding structure of Roman power. This was diplomacy with spectacle, as the visiting embassy, accompanied by Roman magistrates, escorted the dazzling gold crown to the temple of Rome's highest god.[113] It shows Greeks, both cities and kings, adjusting to a new world order in which Rome is dominant, but the direction of influence was not only one way. At the same time, Rome and Jupiter Capitolinus are being incorporated into the Hellenistic world. The awarding of gold crowns was a Greek honorific institution, as was the practice of dedicating

---

[109] Ariarathes: Polyb. 32.1.2–3; Dem. 32.2.1–3.
[110] Polyb. 30.5.16; Masri, 2016: 338 ponders various scenarios; she seems to think that because they did not get an alliance they could not have dedicated the crown on the Capitol, but not all dedications involved alliances.
[111] Grass, 2015.
[112] Ito, 2015: 22–46.
[113] Masri, 2016: 337; Livy 45.22.1, Joseph. *AJ* 14.386.

them in a temple. For Greeks the god and his temple epitomised Rome.[114] It is striking that for the two centuries before Augustus evidence for foreign dealings with Jupiter Capitolinus, whether in the form of dedications, treaties or sacrifices, comes almost exclusively from the Greek world.[115] The god attracted the attention of Greeks in the eastern Mediterranean as early as the first half of the third century, if a Rhodian inscription mentioning Jupiter Capitolinus in the context of an embassy to Rome is correctly dated.[116]

When gold crowns were brought to Rome by Greek ambassadors, they were working in a tradition that would have been familiar to the citizens of any Greek city. Crowns continued to be used throughout the Hellenistic period to honour prominent figures, whether citizens or non-citizens. Most of the time these crowns were of moderate size, being closer to the crowns given by Athens to its foreign benefactors, but the elevated status and wealth of the new Hellenistic kings called forth more valuable (and weightier) crowns. Such gifts continued to be framed in terms of honour, highlighting the achievements and benefactions of the honorand, but they were also part of an exchange that looked forwards as well as backwards. As such they fitted well in the context of diplomacy and easily found a place within the emerging new world order of the second century BC. The crowns taken to Rome were on a different scale from their predecessors and reflected Greek perceptions of Roman power as it imposed its will not only on the Greek cities of the east but also on the once dominant kings. The decision to make such a costly award would not have been taken lightly, but it was a choice freely made in response to circumstances. Later this would change, especially with the emergence of the emperor. Not only did the practice spread to other parts of the empire but increasingly there was an expectation that Rome's subjects should offer crowns to the emperor. So what was ostensibly a gift was also an obligation which the emperor could remit if he wished.[117]

---

[114] See also the way it appears in Greek inscriptions, *OGIS* 762, line 14 (Cibyra); *SEG* 9.7, line 24–5 (Ptolemy VIII's will); *SIG*³ 694 (Pergamum), hence also the dedicatory inscriptions located on the Capitol, *ILLRP* 174–81 with Lintott, 1978.

[115] See the list in Masri, 2016: 344–5; exceptions are Saguntum (205), Masinissa of Numidia (168) and Bocchus of Mauretania (91).

[116] The inscription was originally dated to c. 200 BC by Kontorini, 1983 (*SEG* 33 (1983) no. 637), but that date has now been persuasively challenged in favour of c. 280–70, Badoud, 2015–16: 244, Harris, 2017: 21.

[117] For this later development of the crown, see Millar, 1977: 140–3.

Bibliography

Badoud, N. [2015–16]. 'Note sur trois inscriptions mentionnant des Rhodiens morts à la guerre', *Bulletin de correspondance hellénique*, 139–40, 237–46.
Billows, R. [1997]. *Antigonos the One-Eyed and the Creation of the Hellenistic State*, Berkeley.
Blech, M. [1982]. *Studien zum Kranz bei den Griechen*, Berlin.
Böckh, A. [1851]. *Die Staatshaushaltung der Athener*, 2nd edn, Berlin.
Boor, C. de [1903]. *Excerpta historica iussu imp. Constantini Porphyrogeniti confecta*, Vol. 1: *Excerpta de legationibus*, Berlin.
Bousquet, J. [1986]. 'Lettre de Ptolémée Évergète à Xanthos de Lycie', *Revue des études grecques*, 99, 22–32.
Bowman, A. [1967]. 'The Crown Tax in Roman Egypt', *Bulletin of the American Society of Papyrologists*, 4, 59–74.
Braund, D. [1984]. *Rome and the Friendly King: The Character of the Client Kingship*, London.
Brennan, T. C. [2009]. 'Embassies Gone Wrong: Roman Diplomacy in the Constantinian *Excerpta de legationibus*', in C. Eilers (ed.), *Diplomats and Diplomacy in the Roman World*, Leiden, 171–92.
Briscoe, J. [1973]. *A Commentary on Livy, Books xxxi–xxxiii*, Oxford.
Briscoe, J. [1981]. *A Commentary on Livy, Books xxxiv–xxxvii*, Oxford.
Briscoe, J. [2008]. *A Commentary on Livy, Books 38–40*, Oxford.
Briscoe, J. [2012]. *A Commentary on Livy, Books 41–45*, Oxford.
Burton, P. [2011]. *Friendship and Empire: Roman Diplomacy and Imperialism in the Middle Republic (353–146 BC)*, Cambridge.
Canali de Rossi, F. [1997]. *Le ambascerie dal mondo greco a Roma*, Rome.
Canevaro, M. [2016]. *Demostene, 'Contro Leptine': introduzione, traduzione e commento storico*, Berlin.
de Callataÿ, F. [2012]. 'Royal Hellenistic Coinages: From Alexander to Mithradates', in W. E. Metcalf (ed.), *The Oxford Handbook of Greek and Roman Coinage*, Oxford, 175–90.
de Callataÿ, F. [2017]. 'Gold Jewellery and Gold Coinage in Ancient Greece: Towards a Quantified Pattern', in K. Liampi, C. Papaevangelou-Genakos & D. Plantzos (eds), *Coinage/Jewellery: Uses – Interactions – Symbolisms from Antiquity to the Present*, Athens, 197–223.
de Lisle, C. [2021]. *Agathokles of Syracuse: Sicilian Tyrant and Hellenistic King*, Oxford.
Engen, D. T. [2010]. *Honor and Profit: Athenian Trade Policy and the Economy and Society of Greece, 415–307 B.C.E.*, Ann Arbor.
Erskine, A. [1994]. 'Greek Embassies and the City of Rome', *Classics Ireland*, 1, 47–53.

Erskine, A. [2015]. 'Polybius and the Anger of the Romans', in D. Cairns & L. Fulkerson (eds), *Emotions between Greece and Rome*, London, 105–27.

Erskine, A. [2020]. 'Changes of Fortune: Polybius and the Transformation of Greece', in I. Kuin & J. Klooster (eds), *After the Crisis: Remembrance, Re-anchoring, and Recovery in the Ancient World*, London, 65–82.

Erskine, A. [Forthcoming]. 'Showing Rome the Way: The Attalids and Their Friends in the West', in G. Pezzini, S. Rebeggiani & T. Nelson (eds), *Pergamon and Rome: Culture, Identity, Influence*, Oxford.

Ferrary, J.-L. [2007]. 'Les ambassadeurs grecs au Sénat romain', in M. Sot (ed.), *L'audience: rituels et cadres spatiaux dans l'Antiquité et le haut Moyen Âge*, Paris, 113–22 (reprinted in J.-L. Ferrary, *Rome et le monde grec: choix d'écrits*, Paris, 2017, ch. 14).

Fischer-Bovet, C. [2014]. *Army and Society in Ptolemaic Egypt*, Cambridge.

Gengler, O. [2017]. 'Praise and Honour', in A. Heller & O. M. van Nijf (eds), *The Politics of Honour in the Greek Cities of the Roman Empire*, Leiden, 31–58.

Giannadaki, I. [2020]. *A Commentary on Demosthenes' Against Androtion*, Oxford.

Grass, B. [2015]. 'Les présents diplomatiques à Rome (IIIe–Ier siècle av. J.-C.)', in B. Grass & G. Stouder (eds), *La diplomatie romaine sous la République: réflexions sur une pratique. Actes des rencontres de Paris (21–22 juin 2013) et Genève (31 octobre–1er novembre 2013)*, Besançon, 147–73.

Gruen, E. [1984]. *The Hellenistic World and the Coming of Rome*, Berkeley.

Gygax, M. D. [2016]. *Benefaction and Rewards in the Ancient Greek City: The Origins of Euergetism*, Cambridge.

Habicht, C. [1989]. 'The Seleucids and Their Rivals', in A. E. Astin, F. W. Walbank, M. W. Frederiksen and R. M. Ogilvie (eds), *The Cambridge Ancient History*, Vol. 8: *Rome and the Mediterranean to 133 B.C.*, Cambridge, 324–87.

Hamon, P. [1999]. 'Juges thasiens à Smyrne: I. Smyrna 582 complété', *Bulletin de correspondance hellénique*, 123, 175–94.

Harris, D. [1995]. *The Treasures of the Parthenon and Erechtheion*, Oxford.

Harris, W. V. [2017]. 'Rome at Sea: The Beginnings of Roman Naval Power', *Greece & Rome*, 64, 14–26.

Head, B. V. [1911]. *Historia numorum: A Handbook of Greek Numismatics*, 2nd edn, Oxford.

Henry, A. S. [1983]. *Honours and Privileges in Athenian Decrees*, Hildesheim.

Holt, F. L. [2016]. *The Treasures of Alexander the Great: How One Man's Wealth Shaped the World*, New York.

Hornblower, S. [1996]. *A Commentary on Thucydides*, Vol. 1: *Books IV–V*, Oxford.

Ito, M. [2015]. *Informal Diplomacy and Rome from the First Macedonian War to the Assassination of Ti. Gracchus*, PhD dissertation, University of Edinburgh.

Jones, C. P. [2015]. 'The Earthquake of 26 BCE in Decrees of Mytilene and Chios', *Chiron*, 45, 101–22.

Kontorini, V. [1983]. 'Rome et Rhodes au tournant du IIIe s. av. J.-C. d'après une inscription inédite de Rhodes', *JRS*, 73, 24–32.

Kyriakou, A. [2014]. 'Exceptional Burials at the Sanctuary of Eukleia at Aegae (Vergina): The Gold Oak Wreath', *Annual of the British School at Athens*, 109, 251–85.

Lambert, S. D. [2006]. 'Athenian State Laws and Decrees, 352/1–322/1: III Decrees Honouring Foreigners. A. Citizenship, Proxeny and Euergesy', *Zeitschrift für Papyrologie und Epigraphik*, 158, 115–58.

Lawton, C. L. [1995]. *Attic Document Reliefs: Art and Politics in Ancient Athens*, Oxford.

Le Rider, G. & de Callataÿ, F. [2006]. *Les Séleucides et les Ptolémées: l'héritage monétaire et financier d'Alexandre le Grand*, Monaco.

Lewis, D. M. [1968]. 'New Evidence for the Gold–Silver Ratio', in C. Kraay & G. Jenkins (eds), *Essays in Greek Coinage Presented to Stanley Robinson*, Oxford, 105–10.

Lintott, A. W. [1978]. 'The Capitoline Dedications to Jupiter and the Roman People', *ZPE*, 30, 137–44.

Lorber, C. [2018]. *Coins of the Ptolemaic Empire*, part I: *Ptolemy I through Ptolemy IV*, New York.

Ma, J. [1999]. *Antiochos III and the Cities of Western Asia Minor*, Oxford.

McLean, B. H. [2002]. *An Introduction to Greek Epigraphy of the Hellenistic and Roman Periods: From Alexander the Great to the Reign of Constantine (323 BC–AD 337)*, Ann Arbor.

Mari, M. & Stirpe, P. [2021]. 'The Greek Crown Games', in T. Scanlon & A. Futrell (eds), *The Oxford Handbook of Sport and Spectacle in the Ancient World*, Oxford, 87–97.

Masiello, L. [1984]. 'Corone', in E. M. de Juliis (ed.), *Gli ori di Taranto in età ellenistica*, Milan, 69–108.

Masri, L. [2016]. 'Rome, Diplomacy, and the Rituals of Empire: Foreign Sacrifice to Jupiter Capitolinus', *Historia*, 65, 325–47.

Meadows, A. [1998]. 'The Mars/Eagle and Thunderbolt Gold and Ptolemaic Involvement in the Second Punic War', in A. Burnett, U. Wartenberg & R. Witschonke (eds), *Coins of Macedonia and Rome: Essays in Honour of Charles Hersh*, London, 125–34.

Mellor, R. [1975]. ΘΕΑ ΡΩΜΗ: *The Worship of the Goddess Roma in the Greek World*, Gottingen.

Millar, F. [1977]. *The Emperor in the Roman World (31 BC–AD 337)*, London.

Oakley, S. P. [1998]. *A Commentary on Livy, Books VI–X*, Oxford.

Oliver, G. [2007]. *War, Food, and Politics in Early Hellenistic Athens*, Oxford.

Osborne, R. & Rhodes, P. J. [2017]. *Greek Historical Inscriptions, 478–404 BC*, Oxford.
Östenberg, I. [2009]. *Staging the World: Spoils, Captives, and Representations in the Roman Triumphal Procession*, Oxford.
Pina Polo, F. [2013]. 'Foreign Eloquence in the Roman Senate', in C. Steel & H. van der Blom (eds), *Community and Communication: Oratory and Politics in Republican Rome*, Oxford, 247–66.
Rhodes, P. J. & Osborne, R. [2003]. *Greek Historical Inscriptions 404–323 BC*, Oxford.
Rice, E. E. [1983]. *The Grand Procession of Ptolemy Philadelphus*, Oxford.
Riggsby, A. [2019]. *Mosaics of Knowledge: Representing Information in the Roman World*, Oxford.
Rowe, G. [2002]. *Princes and Political Cultures: The New Tiberian Senatorial Decrees*, Ann Arbor.
Rutishauser, B. [2014]. 'Crowning the Polis: Island Gifts and Aegean Politics', in G. Bonnin & E. Le Quéré (eds), *Pouvoirs, îles et mer: formes et modalités de l'hégémonie dans les Cyclades antiques (VIIe s. a.C.–IIIe s. p.C.)*, Paris, 69–80.
Rutter, N. K. [1993]. 'The Myth of the "Demarateion"', *Chiron*, 23, 171–88.
Rutter, N. K. [2001]. *Historia numorum: Italy*, London.
Scafuro, A. [2009]. 'The Crowning of Amphiaraos', in L. Mitchell & L. Rubinstein (eds), *Greek History and Epigraphy: Essays in Honour of P. J. Rhodes*, Swansea, 59–86.
Shear, T. L. [1978]. *Kallias of Sphettos and the Revolt of Athens in 286 B.C.* (*Hesperia* Suppl., 17), Princeton, NJ.
Sherk, R. K. [1969]. *Roman Documents from the Greek East*, Baltimore.
Tonkova, M. D. [2013]. 'Gold Wreaths from Thrace', in V. Sirbu & R. Stefanescu (eds), *The Thracians and Their Neighbors in the Bronze and Iron Ages*, Brașov, 413–45.
Torregaray Pagola, E. [2005]. 'Embajadas y embajadores entre Hispania y Roma en la obra de Tito Livio', in E. Torregaray Pagola & J. Santos Yanguas (eds) *Diplomacia y autorrepresentación en la Roma antigua*, Vitoria, 25–62.
Walbank, F. W. [1979]. *A Historical Commentary on Polybius*, Vol. 3: *Commentary on Books XIX–XL*, Oxford.
Welles, C. B. [1934]. *Royal Correspondence in the Hellenistic Period*, New Haven.
Westall, R. [2015]. '"Moving through Town": Foreign Dignitaries in Rome in the Middle and Late Republic', in I. Östenberg, S. Malmberg & J. Bjørnebye (eds), *The Moving City: Processions, Passages and Promenades in Ancient Rome*, London, 23–36.
Whitehead, D. [1993]. 'Cardinal Virtues: The Language of Public Approbation in Democratic Athens', *Classica et Mediaevalia*, 44, 37–75.

Zecchini, G. [2005]. 'Ambasciate e ambasciatori in Polibio', in E. Torregaray Pagola & J. Santos Yanguas (eds), *Diplomacia y autorrepresentación en la Roma antiqua*, Vitoria, 11–23.

Zollschan, L. [2017]. *Rome and Judaea: International Law Relations, 162–100 BCE*, London.

5

The Romans and Gifts from the Greeks
The Story of an Ostentatious Rejection*

Nathalie Barrandon, Anthony-Marc Sanz and Enrique García Riaza

In 197 BC, victorious over Philip V at Cynoscephalae and outraged by Aetolian pretensions, the proconsul T. Quinctius Flamininus decided to concede the Macedonian ambassadors a fortnight's truce and proposed holding a meeting with the king. According to Polybius, his Greek interlocutors saw in this indulgence towards the vanquished the fruit of corruption: Philip must have bought Flamininus through the ambassadors, which was demonstrated by the cordiality with which he treated them.[1] Polybius explains the origin of these rumours in the following way:

> For since by this time bribery and the notion that no one should do anything gratis were very prevalent in Greece, and so to speak quite current coin among the Aetolians, they could not believe that Flamininus'

---

* This work has been developed within the research project PGC2018-096415-B-C22 'La expresión diplomática en el Mediterráneo central y oriental bajo la expansión romana: el regalo en su contexto político e institucional', funded by the State Research Agency, Ministry of Science and Innovation, Government of Spain (MCIN/AEI/10.13039/501100011033) and ERDF 'A way of making Europe'.

[1] Polyb. 18.34.8: '... and calculated that it was probable that Philip would offer a very large sum owing to his actual situation and Flamininus would not be able to resist the temptation' (trans. W. R. Paton). Livy 33.11.7 only mentions unrealistic suspicions about Flamininus: *donis regis imminere credebant invicti ab ea cupiditate animi virum*. Plutarch's narrative in *Flam.* 9.6–7 also recounts the rumours and reveals their diplomatic interest: this was to pressure Philip, continuing the mobilisation of the Greek allies, which was perhaps not in vain, since Flamininus ended up convening the allies to explain to them the planned peace (Livy 33.12). For an initial exploration of this passage and its significance in the Polybian opus, see Baronowski, 2011: 157.

complete change of attitude toward Philip could have been brought about without a bribe, since they were ignorant of the Roman principles and practice in this matter ...[2]

Behind Philip's supposed gesture, it is easy to envisage the offering of gifts – a practice well attested in the Greek diplomatic context – with a counter-example evaluated by Polybius: Philopoemen refusing the Spartans' gifts in 191 BC.[3] For that historian – and on this point – the Romans were an exception, and his observations echoed a passage in his famous Book 6, dedicated to the Roman constitution. In that work, he specified 'the laws and customs' of the Romans in respect of money: 'among the Romans nothing is considered more disgraceful than to accept bribes and seek gain from improper channels.'[4]

For this reason, for the Romans, receiving, like giving, always implied a *quid pro quo*, a trade-off:[5] in a diplomatic context, receiving a gift could mean nothing other than letting oneself be corrupted. Polybius himself understood this so well that he refused the gifts offered by the ten senatorial legates when they resolved Greek affairs in 145 BC.[6] In his eyes, and undoubtedly in the eyes of many of his contemporaries, it was therefore understood that the ideal Roman refused to be bought with gifts.

In fact, in highlighting the moral contrast with particular Greeks, Polybius was merely echoing a discourse constructed from the earliest contacts between Rome and the great Hellenistic powers. From at least the

---

[2] Polyb. 18.34.7: ἤδη γὰρ κατὰ τὴν Ἑλλάδα τῆς δωροδοκίας ἐπιπολαζούσης καὶ τοῦ μηδένα μηδὲν δωρεὰν πράττειν, καὶ τοῦ χαρακτῆρος τούτου νομιστευομένου παρὰ τοῖς Αἰτωλοῖς, οὐκ ἐδύναντο πιστεύειν διότι χωρὶς δώρων ἡ τηλικαύτη μεταβολὴ γέγονε τοῦ Τίτου πρὸς τὸν Φίλιππον, οὐκ εἰδότες τὰ Ῥωμαίων ἔθη καὶ νόμιμα περὶ τοῦτο τὸ μέρος.

[3] Or 192 BC; cf. Walbank, 1979: 85–7. Philopoemen rejected the gifts, not to oppose Greek practice, but because he had to reserve it – in his eyes – for his enemies and not his friends: Polyb. 20.12.3–6; see also Plut. *Phil.* 15, who underscores his great dignity and simplicity of life; and Paus. 8.51.2, who enables us to understand Philopoemen's maxim; it implies that he had to bribe the last possible traitors first.

[4] Polyb. 6.56.1: Καὶ μὴν τὰ περὶ τοὺς χρηματισμοὺς ἔθη καὶ νόμιμα βελτίω παρὰ Ῥωμαίοις ἐστὶν ἢ παρὰ Καρχηδονίοις παρ' οἷς μὲν γὰρ οὐδὲν αἰσχρὸν τῶν ἀνηκόντων πρὸς κέρδος, παρ' οἷς δ' οὐδὲν αἴσχιον τοῦ δωροδοκεῖσθαι καὶ τοῦ πλεονεκτεῖν ἀπὸ τῶν μὴ καθηκόντων καθ' ὅσον γὰρ ἐν καλῷ τίθενται τὸν ἀπὸ τοῦ κρατίστου χρηματισμόν, κατὰ τοσοῦτο πάλιν ἐν ὀνείδει ποιοῦνται τὴν ἐκ τῶν ἀπειρημένων πλεονεξίαν. Cf. Walbank, 1967: 594.

[5] In his portrait of Scipio Aemilianus, Polybius alludes to a custom which is not unlike the rejection of a gift, relating to Aemilia: 'Such conduct would naturally be admired anywhere, but in Rome it was a marvel; for absolutely no one there ever gives away anything to anyone if he can help it' (Polyb. 31.26.9, trans. W. R. Paton).

[6] Polyb. 39.4.

third century BC, the governing aristocracy of the Roman Republic affirmed its values and identity in a complex dialogue with the Greek world, a dialogue in which the question of money and wealth took centre stage. This affirmation was undertaken within the framework of the *regimen morum*, by which the censors set themselves up as judges of the conduct of its most eminent members. While it clearly Hellenised, the aristocracy made frugality a central element of its *ēthos*, in contrast to the *luxuria* which was seen as a feature of Greek otherness.[7] This ideal behaviour, however, constructed by the Romans and received as such by many of their interlocutors, is attributed to the representatives of Rome from the first moments of their encounter with the Greeks. Indeed, episodes are known in which Roman senators and magistrates ostensibly refused gifts intended for them as individuals during the conquest of the Greek cities and the Pyrrhic War in the first third of the third century BC, and then during Roman intervention in the East in the first third of the second century BC.[8] The sources relating these events need to be treated carefully, in the sense that it is not easy to discern what is authentic behaviour – particularly for the oldest episodes – and what is a reinterpretation of events a posteriori. We therefore propose to return to the study of these episodes in order to try to clarify in each case the origin of the reason for the Romans' rejection of diplomatic gifts, the representations associated with this rejection, and the meaning attributed to it by our sources.

The Roman Senate, Pyrrhus and Ptolemy II: Between Corrupting Temptation and Collective Discipline

The earliest attested episodes of the refusal of diplomatic gifts date back to the period of Roman expansion in southern Italy, which ended with Tarentum's surrender in 272 BC. These episodes involved the Roman senate

---

[7] On the censors' moral control, associated with the adoption of the *lex Ovinia* in the second half of the fourth century BC, see Humm, 2005 and Passet, 2011. On the central question of the relationship with *luxuria* and the complex process of the construction of identity in relation to the Greek benchmark, perfectly integrated at the same time as it was set up as Other, see more specifically Passet, 2011: 142ff., in the wake of the works by the scholars of the Centre Louis Gernet with F. Dupont and, later, P. Veyne. On the Hellenisation of the Roman aristocracy, see Humm, 2007.

[8] That is, at a point prior to the supposed degeneration indicated in Polyb. 18.35 around the middle of the second century BC. It should be taken into account that this study focuses only on the gifts given to the Romans as individuals, and not to Rome as a city – that is, to its gods – a practice which is attested much earlier and does not imply the theme of corruption in the same terms. For an initial approach to diplomatic gifts, see Auliard, 2009.

and its members in their early contacts with Hellenistic monarchs. Pyrrhus' intervention in Italy, requested by Tarentum (280–275 BC), represents a decisive stage in this phase of the conquest. With the Epirote monarch, it was not a peaceful contact, but above all a confrontation, interspersed with sequences of diplomatic negotiations which never led to the conclusion of a peace.[9]

It is in this context that the first episode of the senate's refusal of diplomatic gifts took place. Before analysing it, however, it should be noted that the information about these successes that has come down to us *in extenso* is late, and has as its principal reference the biography of the Epirote monarch written by Plutarch, data that complement those of various other sources.[10] The image they convey is that of a Roman Republic whose elites placed moral rectitude (*ēthos*) and the defence of *fides* at the height of their value system.[11] The existence of early documentation, however – the speech made by Ap. Claudius Caecus against peace with Pyrrhus – has been convincingly argued. This speech was probably published in its entirety shortly after its author's death.[12] The influence of this text on the Roman view of events and attitudes was decisive in the construction of later historiographical narratives (a point to which we will return later).

The episode that interests us is Cineas' *legatio* to the senate after the Roman defeat at Heraclea (280 BC).[13] According to Plutarch (based

---

[9] The sequence of diplomatic moves throughout the conflict is difficult to reconstruct, and we will not linger over that question here. See for the sources *StV* no. 467 and Torelli, 1978: 137ff. and the full analysis by Lefkowitz, 1959; cf. Passerini 1943. This was not the first diplomatic contact with a Hellenistic king in Italy, since Rome had already concluded a treaty (*foedus*) with Alexander Molossus during his intervention in Italy in 332 (Just. 12.2.12; Livy 8.17.10; Paus. 1.11.7), but the confrontation between two mentalities and two different diplomatic praxes was much more decisive in the case of Pyrrhus' activity: Lévêque, 1957: 543, citing J. Pirenne. Cf. Schettino, 2009: 173–4.

[10] See on this the classic study by Lévêque, 1957: 15–79 and, recently, Kent, 2020. On the models in the historiographical reconstruction of the figure of Pyrrhus, Rodríguez Horrillo, 2016.

[11] This can be elicited from the epistolary exchange between Pyrrhus and P. Valerius Laevinus, who rejected his peace proposals after the Battle of Heraclea (Dion. Hal. *Ant. Rom.* 19.9–10); from C. Fabricius Luscinus' promise to return to Pyrrhus the Roman prisoners who had been permitted to participate in the Saturnalia (Plut. *Pyrrh.* 20.10–11; App. *Sam.* 4–5; Stouder, 2007 and 2009); and from the rejection of Pyrrhus' doctor's proposal to kill him (Plut. *Pyrrh.* 21.1–6; see also App. *Sam.* 11.1 and Livy's tradition: Lévêque, 1957: 364).

[12] Humm, 2005: 61–73; Passet, 2011: 273.

[13] Plut. *Pyrrh.* 18.2; Just. *Epit.* 18.2.7; App. *Sam.* 11. On the sequence of events, we follow Lévêque, 1957: 359–70: after Heraclea would have been Fabricius' (only)

on Dionysius of Halicarnassus and Hieronymus of Cardia),[14] Pyrrhus' ambassador, on his arrival in Rome, 'had conferences with the men in authority, and sent their wives and children gifts in the name of his King' (ἐνετύγχανε τοῖς δυνατοῖς, καὶ δῶρα παισὶν αὐτῶν καὶ γυναιξὶν ἔπεμψε παρὰ τοῦ βασιλέως).[15] The identity of these δυνατοί is unknown to us. The term alludes to 'power and influence', so it tends to be identified with members of the senate, and especially with magistrates in office. It is, however, possible that some of the intended recipients also belonged to other orders. Perhaps a passage in Pliny hints at this when it alludes to Cineas' ability to remember the names of the senators and knights in Rome the day after his arrival in that city.[16] It seems clear that he also held conversations with groups of merchants, conscious, no doubt, of their increasing ability to influence the political agenda, although the naturalist admittedly does not refer to gifts in these cases.[17]

The sources agree that the gifts were rejected, with the bearers refused permission to enter the houses of the recipients. It is possible that this rejection was not a spontaneous initiative, nor an immediate decision. Plutarch, after alluding to this initial refusal, indicates that the Romans made the acceptance of the gifts conditional upon the definitive signing of the peace treaties, information which implies the existence of a certain general political coherence in the attitude towards the Epirote gifts. Arguably, Cineas' visit took place in a climate comparable to a situation of *indutiae* or truce: a space for negotiation in which war was suspended. In Lévêque's opinion,[18] Rome's weak military situation after the defeat at Heraclea, and the visit of Pyrrhus' skilful ambassador offering peace, would have generated an initial atmosphere of receptivity, reinforced by Cineas' proposal

---

mission, followed by Cineas' first embassy, whilst Cineas' second visit to Rome would have taken place after Ausculum; see also Kent, 2020: 62–81.

[14] See A. Erskine's introduction in the English translation by Waterfield, 2016: 210–14.
[15] Plut. *Pyrrh.* 18.2, trans. B. Perrin.
[16] *Cineas Pyrrhi regis legatus senatui et equestri ordini Romae postero die quam advenerat* (Plin. *NH* 7.24 (88); cf. Sen. *Controv.* 1.19); Lévêque, 1957: 346–7 and 347 n. 1.
[17] Plut. *Pyrrh.* 19.6 alludes, in fact, to conversations with the ἄριστοι to understand Roman institutions better. Appian (*Sam.* 11.1) indicates, in turn, that 'Cineas was told that Romans loved money and gifts, and their women had long wielded great influence. So he brought with him many gifts both for men and women' (trans. H. White). Of little assistance is the rather hyperbolic account of Valerius Maximus (4.3.14), who, however, alludes to *legati* – plural – charged with the distribution of the gifts throughout the houses, and to the diversity of gifts, adapted to the tastes of the recipients (*et magni pretii et varii generis a legatis eius tam virorum quam feminarum apta usui munera circa domos ferrentur*).
[18] Lévêque, 1957: 347.

to return the prisoners. It should particularly be taken into account that Epirote diplomatic activity at least succeeded in dividing Roman public opinion, generating debate in the senate. There would have been a majority initially inclined to peace, according to Plutarch: a group that would have been considering accepting the gifts.[19] The possibility should also be considered that the exchange of gifts of prestige among the Roman aristocracy was a custom inherited from the Italic cultural tradition, and modified via a strong Hellenisation. On the other hand, it is possible that a section of the Roman elite had already adopted a pragmatic position, considering it possible that Pyrrhus could win against Rome, and that a peace agreement was the best of the possible solutions to the conflict.

Finally, the victory of the more hard-line members, condensed by the sources in the emblematic figure of Ap. Claudius Caecus, brought the end of the truce and, therefore, the formal resumption of the war. Returning to the reconstruction of events, it should arguably be considered that not all the gifts would initially have been rejected, and that the general return of the gifts could have been ordered at that moment, as a graphic manifestation of the breakdown of the negotiations.

As indicated above, M. Humm has argued for the historicity of Claudius' speech to the senate, as well as the existence of a written version.[20] This publication would have been put into verse in Ennius' *Annales* (written in the first third of the second century BC), mentioned by Cicero. Among the earliest uses of the transcription (or recreation) of this speech would be that of the *Anonimum Vaticanum*, perhaps through Timaeus of Tauromenium. For Humm the problem is rooted in identifying the moment the image of Claudius as a defender of Roman dignity was created: the fabrication, in essence, of an *exemplum* that would later be picked up and amplified by various sources. In any case, Claudius' position and his rejection of the gifts served to illustrate the collective discipline of an aristocracy that seemed disposed to put the service of the state above family interests. In short, the episode of Pyrrhus' gifts constitutes in historiography the genesis of a diplomatic line in which moral integrity was defined as the cornerstone of the defence of the *dignitas* of the Roman people.

A second notable and well-documented episode involves Roman senators collectively confronting the question of diplomatic gifts. It took place

---

[19] Plut. *Pyrrh.* 18.7; Kent, 2020: 68: 'Pyrrhus was attempting to take advantage of the disputes that existed within the political leadership of Rome's elites ... The internal political turmoil was no doubt significant in the face of Cineas' mission, and the king's envoy sought to bend it to his favour.'

[20] Humm, 2005: 61–73.

shortly after Pyrrhus' final departure, in 275 BC, when Rome was about to complete its conquest of southern Italy and thus establish itself definitively as a great power in the Greek world. This time, however, the context was that of peaceful diplomatic exchanges, which took place between Rome and the Lagid kingdom of Egypt from 273 BC.[21] According to Dio Cassius, the initiative came from Ptolemy II Philadelphus: informed of Rome's victory over Pyrrhus, he felt the need to send an embassy to conclude a formal agreement (ὁμολογία) with the state that promised to be the emerging power in the West.[22] The exact motives and aims of this move remain conjectural, although they must certainly have been related to Alexandria's geopolitical and economic interests in the Greek world as a whole.[23] In any case, Dio Cassius indicates that Ptolemy took care to strengthen his arguments with his interlocutors, loading his embassy with gifts (δῶρα), gifts which we may assume were destined for Rome, although we do not know of what they consisted or what the senate decided about them.[24]

Rome's diplomatic response to this initiative is clearer in the sources. According to a tradition probably of annalistic origin and related in particular by Dionysius of Halicarnassus and Valerius Maximus, Rome sent an embassy composed of three high-ranking personalities to Alexandria: the consul Q. Fabius Maximus Gurges, who led the *legatio*, as well as N. Fabius Pictor and Q. Ogulnius.[25] The care with which the senate designated its envoys, chosen from among the Fabii and Ogulnii *gentes*, known for their philhellenic inclinations, also indicates the importance it attached to the success of this mission with a Hellenistic monarch of the first rank, whose

---

[21] On this diplomatic contact, see Torelli, 1978: 216–19 and Lampela, 1998: 33–51.
[22] Cass. Dio 10 fr. 41 = Zonar. 8.61.
[23] See the reconstruction in Lampela, 1998, which takes into account Ptolemy II's interest in Pyrrhus remaining in Macedonia, as well as the need to guarantee his trade relations in Magna Graecia and perhaps even the recruitment of mercenaries in the West – all this without compromising his status as defender of the Greeks; in any case, these arguments all advocate for him seeking an official *foedus* with Rome.
[24] Indeed, it was the custom to offer gifts to the city's gods, especially to Jupiter Capitolinus, to congratulate it upon its victory, which is probably what Ptolemy did here, as he had just heard of its success against Pyrrhus. Those gifts are therefore beyond the remit of our study. See Masri, 2014 and 2016.
[25] Dion. Hal. *Ant. Rom.* 20.14; Val. Max. 4.3.9. The information may be traceable back to Q. Fabius Pictor, the first annalist known in Rome, who could have extracted it both from the senatorial archives and from the tradition of the Fabii, a family to which two members of the embassy belonged; a Greek source such as Timaeus of Tauromenium, however, cannot be discarded, according to Lampela, 1998: 33 n. 29.

favour it was obviously anxious to obtain.[26] The same tradition relates that, during their stay in Alexandria, Ptolemy offered them *privatim* a series of gifts (δῶρα/*munera*).[27] Justin specifies, however, that they refused them upon arrival, and that when Ptolemy offered them gold crowns at a dinner, they set them upon the king's statues the next day.[28] Justin's reference is probably a late tradition, which is not echoed in either Dionysius of Halicarnassus or Valerius Maximus. According to them, the *legati* were responsible instead for bringing the gifts from Alexandria to Rome, but once their report had been presented to the senate, they hurried to deliver them to the *aerarium*.[29] It was then that the senate decreed that some of these gifts be given to each of the ambassadors, and probably had it approved by a *lex de donis regis Ptolemaei*.[30]

This last detail offers a wealth of conclusions for more than one reason. Firstly, it reinforces the authenticity of an episode that analysts could find in the senatorial and legislative archives. Secondly, if the senate and Roman people had to decide to return Ptolemy's *dona*, it was because the legates had first received, accepted and brought them with them to Rome, and then wanted to dispose of them publicly because they felt they could not keep them as individuals. The sequence attested by the ancient authors is thus well supported, especially since it can be explained logically in its context. On the one hand, the diplomatic configuration that connected the king and Rome, unlike the one established between Rome and Pyrrhus a few years earlier, explains the behaviour of the *legati*. The Roman ambassadors, who knew about Greek customs and wanted their mission to succeed, evidently did not commit the error of displeasing their host by refusing his

---

[26] On his *cursus*, see Pittia, 2002: 452ff.: Ogulnius was, for example, one of the ten *legati* sent to Epidaurus in search of Asclepius in 292 BC.

[27] Dion. Hal. *Ant. Rom.* 20.14; Val. Max. 4.3.9: *munera quae ab eo priuatim acceperant ...*

[28] Just. *Epit.* 18.2.9: *nam missi a senatu Aegyptum legati cum ingentia a Ptolemeo rege missa munera spreuissent, interiectis diebus ad cenam invitatis aureae coronae missae sunt, quas illis ominis causa receptas postera die statuit regis imposuerunt.*

[29] Dion. Hal. *Ant. Rom.* 20.14; Val. Max. 4.3.9: *munera ... aerarium ... detulerunt, scilicet de publico ministerio nihil cuiquam praeter laudem bene administrati officii accedere debere iudicantes.*

[30] Dion. Hal. *Ant. Rom.* 20.14 and especially Val. Max. 4.3.9: *iam illud humanitatis senatus et attentae maiorum disciplinae indicium est. data sunt enim legatis quae in aerarium reposuerant, non solum partum conscriptorum decreto, sed etiam populi permissu eaque legata quaestores prompta uni cuique distribuerunt,* the basis upon which Rotondi, 1922 no. 234 postulates the existence of the aforementioned *lex*.

gifts.³¹ It is clear that Rome was interested in concluding a formal alliance with Egypt.³² On the other hand, the gesture of these same *legati* on their return to Rome attests to the progression of a model of behaviour which Roman senators seemed increasingly keen to adopt: the rejection of corrupting wealth in the name of an aristocratic *ēthos* that ordained not only the repudiation of any form of remuneration that was not honour, but also, undoubtedly, an assertive rejection of *luxuria*.

The analysis of these first two episodes allows us to propose some conclusions. Firstly, the ancient sources, probably quite close to the events, of family and senatorial origin, reveal to us the behaviour of the senators when they were offered gifts for the first time by the Hellenistic kings. The correct understanding of their material and diplomatic interests may have obliged them to accept them in order to win the favour of these powerful monarchs. It seems, however, that their moral code led them to see it as an act of diplomatic corruption. The censure of individual enrichment was increasingly seen as a central element of their own value system. This rejection was presented as one of the foundations of their aspiration to command posts. In other words, the repudiation of diplomatic gifts was already becoming a moral imperative in Roman ruling circles.

M'. Curius Dentatus and C. Fabricius Luscinus: The Genesis of a Model of Diplomatic Behaviour

The value system at play in the above cases is much more clearly articulated in other episodes that also involve the refusal of diplomatic gifts. Although tradition also links them to the period of the last wars of conquest in southern Italy, they differ from the ones we have just analysed both in their characteristics and in their genealogy. Indeed, on this occasion it is not the senate or its members, but individual figures who interacted, moreover,

---

[31] This clearly contradicts Justin's evidence, so it can reasonably be supposed that it is the result of an a posteriori distortion of the Alexandrian episode in the light of the behaviour of the *legati* when they returned to Rome, and in order to reinforce their ideal image as frugal and incorruptible ambassadors.

[32] The agreement reached is described as a *societas*, that is, a military alliance, by Livy, *Per.* 14. On the interpretation of the contents of what was probably a *foedus*, see Lampela 1998, against the traditional conception of an informal friendship. The double issue of decadrachmae with the effigy of Arsinoe II and of didrachmae of Rome and Victory, evidently coordinated by the two states, confirms this accord. The idea is strengthened when it is taken into account that it was during the consulship of the same Q. Ogulnius Gallus and of C. Fabius Pictor, brother of the *legatus* N. Fabius Pictor, in 269, when the silver coin was introduced.

with interlocutors who were not necessarily Greek. These individuals are presented as *exempla*, and have profiles that have been reworked by a tradition whose genesis must be analysed separately.

The first episode in this category presents the famous M'. Curius Dentatus refusing to accept the gold offered by the Samnites. He is attested in the sources from early on, as he is already identified by Ennius, who, in the epic of the *Annales*, was clearly inspired by Dentatus' negative response to describe him as someone 'whom no man made yield for iron or gold'.[33] His canonical version is certainly to be found in the work of his contemporary, Cato the Elder, moreover, who did not hesitate to use his example to present himself as the champion of frugality in the context of the political struggle in Rome. Indeed, everything suggests that this is the source from which Cicero draws when he evokes the *exemplum*, widely popularised at the end of the Republican era and tirelessly regurgitated in the Imperial period by authors such as Valerius Maximus, Pliny the Elder and Plutarch.[34]

In fact, the diplomatic nature of the episode itself can only be affirmed with certainty if it is accepted that it occurred immediately after the Roman victory over the Samnites and was therefore part of a manoeuvre by the latter to buy peace. This contextualisation seems reasonable, but is only clearly indicated in one of the versions collected by Plutarch, that of the *Apophthegmata*.[35] Once this diplomatic dimension is admitted, it is necessary to clarify its date in the long series of events that mark the last wars of conquest in southern Italy. In fact, it could go back to Dentatus' first consulship, when he triumphed over the Samnites and Sabines, in 290 BC. A series of elements, however, points instead to the date of his second consulship and his triumph over the Samnites and Pyrrhus, that is, 275 BC; or even to his third consulship, in 274 BC. According to the Catonian version

---

[33] Enn. *Ann.* 373 V³ = 209 W: *quem nemo ferro potuit superare nec auro*.

[34] Cic. *Rep.* 3.6 and 40; *Sen.* 55; Val. Max. 4.3.5; Plin. *NH* 19.87; Plut. *Apophth. M'. Curii* 2; *Cat. Mai.* 2.2; see also the secondary sources listed by Torelli, 1978: 61–4 and Martin 2019. For the Catonian origin of the canonical version of the episode, which possibly dates back to the *Origenes*, see Berrendonner, 2001; see also Pasco-Pranger, 2015; for the political use the censor made of it in the context of the second century, see Passet, 2011: 270ff.; 2020.

[35] Plut. *Apophth. M'. Curii* 2. Aside from this mention, there is no reason to discard the hypothesis that the Samnites' action took place *before*, rather than *after*, the conclusion of the peace, and that therefore it had a completely different meaning, for example in relation to the client relationships established in the context of the 'patronat par conquête': Cic. *Rep.* 2.40 establishes a clear connection between this episode and the client relationships between the conquered and their conqueror; cf. Eilers, 2002: 56–8, who demonstrates that the name Dentatus was mistakenly substituted by Fabricius in the tradition pertaining to this relationship.

of the event, it was after his three triumphs that Dentatus received the Samnite delegation, and therefore not before 275 BC, and this in his villa in Sabina, which he had logically only been able to acquire after the conquest and subdivision of this territory, which he himself had led in 290 BC.[36] The general context of the series of episodes of refusal of diplomatic gifts that we are concerned with in this study, insofar as it clearly belongs in the 'Pyrrhic' phase of Rome's later wars of conquest in the peninsula, also points in this direction.

According to the story's rationale, the Samnites' approach was clearly intended to obtain from the victor a plea in their favour when peace and their fate were discussed in the senate. All the traditions record Dentatus' response, however, saying he preferred to command those who have gold rather than possess it himself, thus appearing to reject what seemed to him to be corruption.[37] This response intimately associates the legitimacy of commanding (*imperare*), the fruit of the Romans' valour, with their virtues of *continentia* and *disciplina*.[38] Tradition reinforces that with the frugal behaviour of the Roman, moreover, who was supposed to be satisfied with a modest meal of turnips on wooden plates.[39] These virtues are in turn illustrated by another famous episode attributed to him, that of the distribution of the Sabine lands, over which he presided, and on the occasion of which he refused to receive more than the statutory seven *iugera*.[40] All the traditions linked to Dentatus, probably as early as Cato's day, thus clearly associated the legitimacy of Roman domination with their virtues, among which were those that dictated frugality. These virtues therefore had to be taken into consideration and imitated in order for the Romans to remain worthy of exercising power.[41]

---

[36] Cic. *Cat. Mai.* 55 and Plut. *Cat. Mai.* 2.1–2.

[37] See for example Cic. *Cat. Mai.* 55: *non enim aurum habere praeclarum sibi videri dixit, sed iis qui haberent aurum imperare*; and also Val. Max. 4.3.5, who specifically has Curius denounce the Samnites' attempt at corruption: *supervacuae, inquit, ne dicam ineptae legationis ministri, narrate Samnitibus M'. Curium malle locupletibus imperare quam ipsum fieri locupletem atque istud ut pretiosum, ita malo hominum excogitatum munus refertote et mementote me nec acie vinci nec pecunia corrumpi posse*.

[38] See in particular Cic. *Cat. Mai.* 55: *cuius quidem ego villam contemplans – abest enim non longe a me – admirari satis non possum vel hominis ipsius continentiam vel templorum disciplinam*; Val. Max. 4.3.5 in a chapter *de abstinentia et continentia*: *M'. autem Curius, exactissima norma Romanae frugalitatis idemque fortitudinis perspectissimum specimen* ...

[39] On wooden vessels, Val. Max. 4.3.5; on the plate of turnips, Plut. *Apophth. M'. Curii* 2; *Cat. Mai.* 2.1–2.

[40] On this episode, Torelli, 1978: 52–5.

[41] See, for example, Cato's behaviour according to Plut. *Cat. Mai.* 2.3.

In the tradition of the *exempla*, however, this first case was in turn closely associated with another, this time featuring Pyrrhus: the episode of Fabricius refusing the gifts of the King of Epirus. This association between the two episodes probably stems from a Catonian literary tradition, as indicated above.[42] After the Roman defeat at Heraclea and the progress of the episode of Cineas' embassy analysed above, Fabricius Luscinus was sent to Pyrrhus at the head of a senatorial *legatio* to negotiate the return of the Roman prisoners.[43] Plutarch attributes to Fabricius a long series of moral traits: austerity, temperance, prudence, loyalty and honesty. Austerity because he refused the valuable gifts offered to him; temperance because he remained calm when surprised by the sound of the elephants; prudence in his conversations during banquets; loyalty because he kept his promises to reinstate the prisoners; and, finally, honesty because of his denunciation of the offer of treason made by Pyrrhus' physician.[44] The *topos* of austerity is presented in Plutarch, using contrast to reinforce it by presenting Fabricius as an excellent soldier but an immensely poor man.

Pyrrhus offered him a sum of gold 'in the name and as a token of friendship and hospitality' (φιλίας δέ τι καὶ ξενίας ἐπονομάζων τοῦτο σύμβολον).[45] The anecdote is brought to its full literary development by Dionysius of Halicarnassus, who, unlike Plutarch, does allude to the political motivation of the gift (in silver and gold): to get Fabricius to convince the senate of the virtues of the peace proposed by the King of Epirus.[46] For Lefkowitz,[47] the offer of gifts constituted in itself a symptom of the weakness of Pyrrhus' political position. It was a peace, in short, that would have meant the Roman renunciation of its southern expansionism – an impossible peace as well, since, by that time, the Italian power had reached an agreement with Carthage to expel Pyrrhus, their common enemy, from the West. Dionysius of Halicarnassus' treatment of the subject consists of a

---

[42] Berrendonner, 2001; Martin, 2019.
[43] Lévêque, 1957: 359–70; Schettino, 2009; Stouder, 2007 and 2009; Kent, 2020: 76–9.
[44] Plut. *Pyrrh.* 20.1–21.6.
[45] Plut. *Pyrrh.* 20.1; cf. App. *Sam.* 10.4. See complete sources in Lefkowitz, 1959: 171 n. 48.
[46] See likewise Just. *Epit.* 18.2.6-7: *dum haec aguntur, legatus a senatu Romano Fabricius Luscinus missus pacem cum Pyrrho conponit. ad quam confirmandam Cineas Romam cum ingentibus a Pyrrho donis missus neminem, cuius domus muneribus pateret, inuenit.*
[47] Lefkowitz, 1959: 158. Cf. Auliard, 2009: 64, who situates it among 'les tentatives de corruption', like the Samnite offerings made to M'. Curius Dentatus ten years later. He adds, about Fabricius, 'Dans la plus pure tradition stoïcienne, les auteurs qui relatent l'événement insistent sur le mépris avec lequel le légat romain refusa les propositions du roi.'

long hymn to austerity as an identifying virtue of Republican Rome, again a collective *ēthos* that is presented in veiled terms as an ideological justification for territorial conquests: 'for the sake of a good reputation scorned even the riches gained in an honest manner, just as did Valerius Publicola and very many others besides, men through whom our commonwealth has become so great'.[48] *Continentia* as a moral value reappears illustrated on the occasion of Luscinus' own later exercise of censorship, sharing to some extent the Catonian cliché.[49]

The analysis of these two episodes, strongly structured around exemplary figures, allows us to broaden the conclusions of the previous section. The Roman ruling elites are known to have recalled the period of the Pyrrhic Wars as the departure point for the assertion of a diplomatic morality that advocated *continentia* in matters of individual gifts. It was, however, at a later stage of the tradition – which we can clearly link to Ennius and especially to Cato at the beginning of the second century BC – that other episodes of this period were reinvented in the name of the same morality, but according to different models. Instead of presenting the imperative to refuse gifts as emanating from a collective and impersonal morality imposed on the ruling elites, the tradition tried to convince of its relevance through the example of famous Romans who assumed it with greater rigour because they had internalised it perfectly within the framework of an ethic structured around frugality. It remains to be discussed how effective this exemplary behaviour was at a time when Rome was intervening decisively in Eastern affairs.

Exemplary Behaviour in a Context of Military Supremacy and Unprecedented Wealth: The Early Second Century BC

Roman *continentia* did not refer only to refusing gifts in the form of precious metals, as the future Africanus did after the capture of Carthago Nova. Scipio, according to Livy, is said to have refused to abuse a young woman offered by his men. He then returned her to her betrothed, the Celtiberian chief Alucius, and finally refused her kinsmen's gold. More specifically, he accepted it in order to return it as a dowry.[50] Although

---

[48] Dion. Hal. *Ant. Rom.* 19.14–18 (trans. E. Cary).
[49] As censor in 275 BC, he expelled P. Cornelius Rufinus from the senate for having accumulated silver vases, a decision widely recorded in the ancient sources (see *MRR* I: 196).
[50] Livy 26.50: gold was offered primarily to pay ransoms, and later as a gift. Polyb. 10.18–19 does not speak of gold received, but rather of the rejection of the young woman, to demonstrate Scipio's *continentia* and *temperantia*. Cf. also Sil. *Pun.*

this episode, unlike those analysed so far, does not fall within the context of diplomacy between Romans and Greeks, Scipio's gesture would have been intended for the latter, according to P. François.[51] In the case of Polybius, certainly, the East as the intended recipient of Scipio's image of integrity is clear. The evidence of the period of the first third of the second century BC, besides being historical, takes on a different hue with the historian's Graeco-Roman perspective. It will, however, be necessary to place this in its Roman context by returning in particular to the actions of Cato.

To describe Scipio's position with regard to diplomatic gifts, Polybius returned not to the scene that took place at Carthago Nova, but to one that occurred in 190 BC on the banks of the Hellespont, during the Syrian War. As official negotiations were failing, Antiochus' ambassador, Heraclides of Byzantium, addressed Scipio individually. As well as reiterating the king's instructions (not detailed here), he offered to return his son to him without a ransom and to offer him immediately a sum of his own choosing, and later a share of the royal revenues. Scipio accepted the first offer, which was compatible with Roman diplomacy, but not the second.[52] His severity replicated that of the *consilium* with regard to the truce offers.[53] The fact that Scipio's attitude is viewed positively is interesting given that the cases brought against him and his brother on their return from the war suggested financial malpractice.[54]

15.268–82 and Val. Max. 4.3.1 (who describes the girl as Indibilis' fiancée). For a list of the sources and their analysis, cf. François, 2006. See in this volume the chapter by E. Sánchez Moreno and J. García Cardiel, on the politico-diplomatic dialogue on the Hispanian front at the time of the Second Punic War and the historiographic construction of Scipionic *continentia* as an *exemplum*.

[51] François, 2006: 324: 'Avec l'Africain, le système référentiel romain de l'exemplum jusque-là interne et limité à l'histoire nationale, s'élargit à la dimension du monde hellénistique ... Si Scipion adresse un message, ce n'est pas à ses concitoyens mais aux populations helléniques ou hellénisées ... Les guerres puniques sont un conflit dans lequel l'hellénisme est un enjeu et en même temps un instrument, voire un pierre de touche: dans le bassin méditerranéen hellénisé du IIIe siècle, c'est en affirmant et en montrant avoir sa place et jouer son rôle dans ce monde et dans cette culture que l'on peut espérer emporter un succès durable.'

[52] Polyb. 21.3.15. The account in Livy 37.36 is similar. In the speech that he attributes to Scipio, the latter emphasised his status as a public figure, implying a firm rejection; cf. also Diod. Sic. 29 fr. 10; App. *Syr.* 29. Walbank, 1979: 107–8.

[53] For an analysis of the embassy, see Berrendonner, 2016: the failure to recognise Greek culpability was used to justify the *consilium*'s intransigence towards the king's proposals.

[54] On the details of these procedures, see Brizzi, 2006. On this occasion, Scipio made another ostentatious gesture by publicly ripping up his brother's accounts.

Like Flamininus before him, it was important for Scipio not to be suspected of diplomatic corruption. This generation followed the pattern of individual behaviour outlined above, while participating in its formation. Polybius attests that the practice of refusing diplomatic gifts continued in the period of Rome's early involvement in eastern Mediterranean affairs. Following his account of Flamininus, the historian digresses with two other *exempla*: Aemilius Paullus and Scipio Aemilianus. Paradoxically, however, it is no longer a question of diplomatic negotiations, but of victory and the principle of not enriching oneself personally.[55] There is no such paradox if the *exemplum* of Dentatus is taken into account, but Polybius does not refer to him. On the other hand, the proof of Aemilius Paullus' integrity is given at another point in the narrative, when he specifies the 'poverty' of the inheritance left by him, despite the considerable booty brought to Rome.[56] This refusal to enjoy the booty had already been proclaimed by Cato in his campaigns in Hispania in 195 BC,[57] but Polybius chooses to compare Aemilius Paullus with the Athenian Aristides and the Theban Epaminondas.[58] The Roman's behaviour would have been more remarkable, since the wealth amassed far exceeded that of the Greeks (and certainly that of Cato). Scipio Aemilianus went even further than his father in also showing generosity. Indeed, this is a higher dimension in the moral relationship with wealth,[59] since he had to face greater temptations.[60] It was thus argued that the Romans had not conquered the world out of greed. Polybius integrates this idea into the theoretical reflection on the cycle of constitutions and the valorisation of Roman institutions in Book 6. Along the lines of Platonic thought on *tryphē* (luxury), he states that the aristocrats' desire for money and their sexual appetite explain the degeneration of the aristocratic regime, and then the democratic one, where corruption reigned.[61] According to Polybius, if Rome remained preserved from such a

[55] Polyb. 18.35.
[56] Polyb. 31.22–3.
[57] Plut. *Cat. Mai.* 10.4 and Cato, *Dierum dictarum de consulatu suo*, fr. 55 M², according to Plut. *Cat. Mai.* 10.5.
[58] Cf. also the moral features Plutarch confers upon the two Greeks, with the idea of a necessary detachment from material goods to be a great statesman in the purest Stoic tradition.
[59] For a detailed analysis, see Eckstein, 1995: 79–82. Cf. also Diod. Sic. 37.3.4.
[60] On the vices of some generals as a counterpoint to this *ēthos*, cf. Polyb. 3.81.4–9. Polyb. 9.10 also develops a long criticism of the Romans who stripped the conquered of their works of art, which unlike gold and silver are not useful for imposing rule. This could only taint future relations between Rome and the provinces.
[61] Polyb. 6.2.8–9. For an analysis of these passages and Polybius' moral vision of enrichment, see Eckstein, 1995: 70–5 and Baronowski, 2011: 154–9.

fate, it was thanks to exemplary generals, but he considered this theoretical evolution to be a possibility for the future.[62]

In this first third of the second century BC, Valerius Maximus gives another example of the refusal of diplomatic gifts: that of Q. Aelius Tubero, son-in-law of Aemilius Paullus, upon receiving an Aetolian embassy. The reference to Dentatus and Fabricius is explicit in recording that they ate from earthenware dishes.[63] Valerius Maximus also recalls that Cato travelled through Hispania with three slaves and a simple cloak of goatskins, and that he was satisfied with frugal meals.[64] Was this kind of behaviour a way of distinguishing a general from an ambassador? These two attitudes are presented in a chapter in which *continentia* (of Scipio, Cato the Younger and Germanicus) in the face of carnal pleasures is linked to money (with numerous examples). This catalogue of attitudes resonates with Polybius' theoretical assertion, when studying the evolution of the constitutions, on the importance of individual behaviour. In contrast, Valerius Maximus did not use Flamininus as an example. It is clear that with this anecdote about the liberator of the Greeks, Polybius wanted to mark a caesura; that this war was followed by a form of decadence, also denounced by Cato at the

---

[62] Polyb. 6.8.5–7: ὅταν γὰρ πολλοὺς καὶ μεγάλους κινδύνους διωσαμένη πολιτεία μετὰ ταῦτα εἰς ὑπεροχὴν καὶ δυναστείαν ἀδήριτον ἀφίκηται, φανερὸν ὡς εἰσοικιζομένης εἰς αὐτὴν ἐπὶ πολὺ τῆς εὐδαιμονίας συμβαίνει τοὺς μὲν βίους γίνεσθαι πολυτελεστέρους, τοὺς δ' ἄνδρας φιλονεικοτέρους τοῦ δέοντος περί τε τὰς ἀρχὰς καὶ τὰς ἄλλας ἐπιβολάς. ὧν προβαινόντων ἐπὶ πλέον ἄρξει μὲν τῆς ἐπὶ τὸ χεῖρον μεταβολῆς ἡ φιλαρχία καὶ τὸ τῆς ἀδοξίας ὄνειδος, πρὸς δὲ τούτοις ἡ περὶ τοὺς βίους ἀλαζονεία καὶ πολυτέλεια, ... οὗ γενομένου ... ('When a state has weathered many great perils and subsequently attains to supremacy and uncontested sovereignty, it is evident that under the influence of long established prosperity, life becomes more extravagant and the citizens more fierce in their rivalry regarding office and other objects than they ought to be. As these defects go on increasing, the beginning of the change for the worse will be due to love of office and the disgrace entailed by obscurity, as well as to extravagance and purse-proud display ... When this happens ...', trans. W. R. Paton).

[63] Val. Max. 4.3. Plin. *NH* 33.50 (142) also recalls that he was contented with the silver cups that Aemilius Paullus offered him as his only wealth. Passet, 2011: 288–9: this anecdote, constructed by Tubero himself or by Aemilius Paullus' entourage, converted him into 'a real Roman, true to the ancient customs of the *Antiqui*, our virtuous ancestors'. It is said that his son reproduced his father's behaviour, but in the context of a public banquet to prepare for election to the praetorship, which led him to fail; frugality should be private, Passet, 2010.

[64] He also asserts that Scipio Aemilianus was accompanied by only a few slaves, even when he was on a diplomatic mission. On this point and on the frugality imposed by Scipio upon his army in Hispania, cf. Plut. *Apophth. Reg.* 201.

end of the narrative.⁶⁵ This reinforces the idea that the behaviour of the Romans was constructed in contrast to that of enemies motivated solely by greed (the Aetolians *par excellence*) who did not understand the relationship between frugality and military power. Polybius thus reflects an *ēthos* shared by many Roman aristocrats of his time, mixing Roman identity with Greek philosophy. Cicero believed that Scipio Aemilianus and his friends combined the virtues of Dentatus with the teachings of Socrates, achieving an incomparable degree of excellence.⁶⁶ According to Plutarch, Cato's conviction about a necessary and virtuous frugality, like that of Dentatus, was reinforced by his stay with the Pythagorean Nearchus, and by the words of Plato.⁶⁷

Cato would have expressed his position publicly for the first time during his quaestorship: he reproached Scipio – the future Africanus – for corrupting the simpleness of the soldiers, inciting them to pleasures and luxury with his profligacy.⁶⁸ Livy also makes the connection between *sumptus* (expense) and *luxuria*, in narrating the speech in favour of the *lex Oppia* that Cato supposedly delivered in 195 BC.⁶⁹ This speech denounced the political role that women attempted to have, but the main argument was based on the decadence linked to the enrichment of all Romans. This is followed by a reference to Cineas, who, if he were to enter Rome that day, would find his proposals favourably received.⁷⁰ Numerous military metaphors are used to integrate women into an overall reflection on Roman morality.⁷¹ This speech is considered a pastiche, freely composed

---

[65] He situated it following the last Macedonian War, after the influx of riches; cf. Polyb. 31.25.

[66] Cic. *Rep.* 3.4–6.

[67] Plut. *Cat. Mai.* 2.

[68] Plut. *Cat. Mai.* 3.5. This mention is historically problematic, since Cato's quaestorship dates to 204 BC, according to Cic. *Sen.* 10; *Brut.* 60 and Livy 29.25.10. The denunciation of the actions of Q. Pleminius in Locri, and therefore Scipio's in terms of his army, dates from 205 BC, which may throw doubt on the date of his quaestorship, however. The point that we want to make here is to highlight the moral dimension of the reproaches made to Scipio. It should also be noted that during his command in Sardinia, in 198 BC, Cato reduced or suppressed the representation expenses that the allies paid the praetor (Livy 32.27.2–4).

[69] Livy 34.4.9: *ne ullus modus sumptibus, ne luxuriae sit.*

[70] App. *Sam.* 11.1 also refers to the women's role in encouraging the acceptance of Cineas' gifts.

[71] Livy 34.2–3; the vocabulary used (*agmen, obsidere, expugnare*) echoes the idea that, as well as gold, women desired to emulate the ride in the triumphal chariot (*velut triumphantes de lege victa*).

by Livy,[72] with prophetic value and/or as an echo of Augustus' legislation.[73] The denunciation of *luxuria* and the unconditional rejection of diplomatic gifts may also be an echo of the story of Tarpeia, told by the Paduan historian: she is said to have handed Rome to the Sabines, 'corrupted by Tatius' gold'.[74] Should women, like the best Roman citizens, behave in an exemplary manner, showing temperance? With Curius Dentatus as a model, it is not surprising that sumptuary laws, regulating in particular 'l'art de la table', were one of Cato's battles. Without going into the details of these laws, which have been well studied,[75] we will note the argument of M. Coudry, according to whom the control of female adornment may have originated in Greek legislation, but not in the Roman sumptuary laws.[76] If luxury had been a political issue since Fabricius Luscinus' censorship, enrichment following Roman victories in the East brought a dimension of reality to its repression: frugality, an ideal of individual behaviour,[77] became a collective issue, in a discourse argued by Cato, just as the first rejection of diplomatic gifts, those brought by Cineas, had been collective.

The first quarter of the second century therefore seems decisive in the development of a discourse on the necessary display of integrity by a number of well-known generals in the exercise of their diplomatic and military activities. All this was at a time when their presence in Greece and their victories were considered by some to be responsible for an alteration of Roman customs.[78] In Roman thought, there was a close relationship between the rejection of diplomatic corruption and frugality; between enrichment in war and the decline of traditions. But from the middle of the second century BC onwards, the rejection of gifts became secondary in

---

[72] Ferrary, 1988: 577–8 and n. 20.
[73] Mineo, 2006: 326–8.
[74] Livy 1.11.6: *huius filiam virginem auro corrumpit Tatius*. Dion. Hal. *Ant. Rom.* 2.38–9 preserves another version, more credible in terms of the honours later rendered by the city to Tarpeia: she wanted to give the gold to the Romans.
[75] Passet, 2011 and Zecchini, 2016. Coudry, 2007: the *lex Porcia de sumptu provinciali* is known only from allusion and, therefore, may not have been the work of Cato the Elder, but he spoke clearly against the repeal of the *lex Orchia*, which limited the number of diners at senators' tables and is dated to 182 (or 181).
[76] Coudry, 2004.
[77] Passet, 2011: 21 and 83.
[78] On the idea that this was effectively a question of period in terms of sumptuary laws of the first quarter of the second century in relation to the Second Punic War, see Zecchini, 2016. On the overall impact of the Roman conquests of the second century, see Lintott, 1972.

diplomatic stakes, which makes sense in the context of the new balance of power between Rome and its interlocutors.[79]

Conclusion

Ultimately, literary references to the rejection of gifts by Roman elites must be analysed in the ideological and political context of a singular period extending from early third century BC to the aftermath of Pydna (168 BC). . This period is characterised by the qualitative leap entailed by Rome's direct contact with Hellenistic diplomatic practice. The rejection of gifts is one more manifestation of a set of moral traits that revolved around frugality as a constitutive element of the Roman *ēthos*, turned into cultural heritage by aristocratic families. This conception is already very extensive in late sources, but it has, in our opinion, ancient origins. It can be dated back at least to the Epirote gifts of 280 BC and the Ptolemaic ones of 273 BC. Beyond the Roman aristocracy's usual channels of transmission, Ennius and Cato seem to have played a key role in formalising this tradition around individual *exempla* – Curius Dentatus, Fabricius Luscinus – by proposing, as it were, a series of ready-made behaviours. From the beginning of the second century BC, the *topos* was thus enriched through a dual process. On the one hand, successive historiographical layers were responsible for the expansion of the pre-existing themes. On the other hand, this image of austerity was projected in a self-interested way on to new characters – Aemilius Paullus, Scipio Aemilianus – with Polybius' invaluable contribution: continence and discipline were presented as typically Roman values that determined behaviour, both in diplomatic matters and in other areas, and thus justified and legitimised the empire.

Bibliography

Auliard, C. [2009]. 'Cadeaux et marchandages diplomatiques à Rome jusqu'au début de la conquête méditerranéenne', *Veleia*, 26, 63–73.
Baronowski, D. W. [2011]. *Polybius and Roman Imperialism*, London.
Berrendonner, C. [2001] 'La formation de la tradition sur M'. Curius Dentatus et C. Fabricius Luscinus: un homme nouveau peut-il être un grand homme?',

---

[79] As early as 172, Decimius, a legate from the senate, was reproached for having received money from the princes of Illyria (Livy 42.45.8). During the Mithridatic War, gifts from Ptolemy and Tigranes were rejected, but Lucullus kept a ring, and Claudius a cup (Plut. *Luc.* 2.6–9; 3.1 and 21.8). In the war against Sertorius, the provincials showered Metellus with crowns and offered him gold trophies to simulate a triumph (Plut. *Sert.* 22.2–4).

in M. Coudry & T. Späth (eds), *L'invention des grands hommes de la Rome antique = Die Konstruktion der grossen Männer Altroms: actes du colloque du Collegium Beatus Rhenanus, Augst, 16–18 septembre 1999*, Paris, 97–116.

Berrendonner, C. [2016]. 'Le nerf de la guerre? Les clauses financières des accords diplomatiques conclus par les responsables publics romains sur les théâtres d'opération militaires à l'époque républicaine', *Ktèma: civilisations de l'Orient, de la Grèce et de Rome antiques*, 41, 223–41.

Brizzi, G. [2006]. 'Per una rilettura del processo degli Scipioni: aspetti politici e istituzionali', *Rivista storica dell' antichità*, 36, 49–76.

Coudry, M. [2004]. 'Loi et société: la singularité des lois somptuaires de Rome', *Cahiers du Centre Gustave Glotz*, 15, 135–71.

Coudry, M. [2007]. 'Loi Orchia somptuaire (pl. sc.)', in J.-L. Ferrary & P. Moreau (eds), *Lepor: Leges Populi Romani*. Paris: http://telma.irht.cnrs.fr/outils/lepor/notice571/. Published 28 November 2014.

Coudry, M. [2016]. 'Lois somptuaires et comportement économique des élites de la Rome républicaine', *Mélanges de l'École française de Rome. Antiquité*, 128 (1): *Le luxe et les lois somptuaires dans la Rome antique*. https://journals.openedition.org/mefra/3180.

Eckstein, A. M. [1995]. *Moral Vision in The Histories of Polybius*, Berkeley–Los Angeles–London.

Eilers, C. [2002]. *Roman Patrons of Greek Cities*, Oxford.

Ferrary, J.-L. [1988]. *Philhellénisme et impérialisme: aspects idéologiques de la conquête romaine du monde hellénistique, de la seconde guerre de Macédoine à la guerre contre Mithridate*, Rome.

François, P. [2006]. '*Externo more*: Scipion l'Africain et l'hellénisation', *Pallas*, 70, 313–28.

Humm, M. [2005]. *Appius Claudius Caecus: La République accomplie*, Rome.

Humm, M. [2007]. '*Forma virtutei parisuma fuit*: les valeurs helléniques de l'aristocratie romaine à l'époque (médio-) républicaine (IVe–IIIe siècles)', in H.-L. Fernoux & C. Stein (eds), *Aristocratie antique: modèles et exemplarité sociale*, Dijon, 101–26.

Kent, P. A. [2020]. *A History of the Pyrrhic War*, London.

Lampela, A. [1998]. *Rome and the Ptolemies of Egypt: The Development of Their Political Relations, 270–80 B.C.*, Helsinki.

Lefkowitz, M. R. [1959]. 'Pyrrhus' negotiations with the Romans 280–279 B.C.', *HSPh*, 64, 147–77.

Lévêque, P. [1957]. *Pyrrhos*, Paris.

Lintott, A. W. [1972]. 'Imperial Expansion and Moral Decline in the Roman Republic', *Historia: Zeitschrift für alte Geschichte* 21 (4), 626–38.

Martin, P. M. [2019]. 'Dentatus et Fabricius: couplage, surimpression, utilisation', *Revue des études anciennes*, 121 (1), 93–113.

Masri, L. [2014]. *The Rituals of Empire: Religion and Diplomacy in Republican Rome*, PhD dissertation, University of Chicago.

Masri, L. [2016]. 'Rome, Diplomacy, and the Rituals of Empire: Foreign Sacrifice to Jupiter Capitolinus', *Historia: Zeitschrift für alte Geschichte*, 65 (3), 325–47.

Minéo, B. [2006]. *Tite-Live et l'histoire de Rome*, Paris.

Pasco-Pranger, M. [2015]. 'Finding Examples at Home: Cato, Curius Dentatus, and the Origins of Roman Literary Exemplarity', *Classical Antiquity*, 34 (2), 296–321.

Passerini, A. [1943]. 'Sulle trattative dei Romani con Pirro', *Athenaeum*, 21, 92–112.

Passet, L. [2010]. 'Frugalité et banquet offert au peuple à l'occasion de funérailles: la vaisselle de terre et les peaux de bouc de Quintus Aelius Tubéron', *Ktèma: civilisations de l'Orient, de la Grèce et de Rome antiques*, 35, 51–67.

Passet, L. [2011]. *Refus du luxe et frugalité à Rome: histoire d'un combat politique (fin du IIIe siècle av. J.-C. – fin du IIe siècle av. J.-C.)*, PhD dissertation, Université Lumière-Lyon 2. HAL Id: tel-01168050, https://theses.hal.science/tel-01168050v1.

Passet, L. [2020]. 'Frugality as a Political Language in the Second Century BCE: The Strategies of Cato the Elder and Scipio Aemilianus', in I. Gildenhard & C. Viglietti (eds), *Roman Frugality: Modes of Moderation from the Archaic Age to the Early Empire and Beyond*, Cambridge–New York, 192–212.

Pittia, S. (ed.) [2002]. *Denys d'Halicarnasse: Rome et la conquête de l'Italie aux IVe et IIIe s. avant J.-C.*, Paris.

Polybius [1970]. *Histoire*, trans., ed. and comm. Denis Roussel, Paris.

Rodríguez Horrillo, M. A. [2016]. 'Tendencias literarias en la historiografía de la guerra de Pirro con Roma', *Fortunatae*, 27, 145–61.

Rotondi, G. [1922]. *Leges publicae populi Romani*, Milan.

Schettino, M. T. [2009]. 'Pyrrhos en Italie: la construction de l'image du premier ennemi venu de l'Orient grec', *Pallas*, 79 (monogr. *Pyrrhus en Occident*), 173–84.

Stouder, G. [2007]. 'Déconvenues diplomatiques et philologiques de Fabricius: les rapports de Rome avec les peuples et cités d'Italie entre 285 et 280 av. J.-C. à la lumière d'un fragment de Dion Cassius', *DHA*, 33 (1), 47–70.

Stouder, G. [2009]. 'Le rôle de Fabricius dans les négociations avec Pyrrhus ou l'émergence de la figure de l'ambassadeur à Rome', *Pallas*, 79 (monogr. *Pyrrhus en Occident*), 185–201.

StV = Schmitt, H. H. [1969]. *Die Verträge der griechisch-römischen Welt, von 338 bis 200 v. Chr.*, Vol. 3, Munich.

Torelli, M. R. [1978]. *Rerum Romanarum fontes ab anno CCXCII AD annum CCLXV a. Ch. n.* (Bibl. degli studi classici e orientali 14), Pisa.

Walbank, F. W. [1967]. *A Historical Commentary on Polybius*, Vol. 2, Oxford.

Walbank, F. W. [1979]. *A Historical Commentary on Polybius*, Vol. 3, Oxford.

Waterfield, R. [2016]. *Plutarch: Hellenistic Lives*, with introduction and notes by A. Erskine, Oxford.

Zecchini, G. [2016]. 'Ideologia suntuaria romana', *Mélanges de l'École française de Rome – Antiquité*, 128 (1). http://journals.openedition.org/mefra/3168; DOI: https://doi.org/10.4000/mefra.3168. Published 18 February 2016.

6
Gift, Debt, Anxiety in Late Hellenistic Times
On the Cautiousness and Attitudes of Achaeans, Macedonians and Bastarnae towards Diplomatic Presents*

Miguel Esteban Payno and
Gerard Ventós Rodríguez

The final decades of the third century BC and the early ones of the next witnessed turbulent political and diplomatic activity in Greece and its vicinity. The already dynamic and tumultuous competitive relationship between the Hellenistic kings was escalated by the entrance of a new participant: Rome. This world was shaping up to be heterogeneous and, above all, multipolar.[1] Poleis, confederations, large (and small) kingdoms, Romans and 'barbarians' (Galatians, Thracians, Illyrians, Bastarnae) constituted the pieces on a complex chequerboard in which competing interests often clashed and in which various languages had to coexist and overlap. While the kings continued to play a fundamental role in 'international politics',[2] they were obliged to depend on other smaller entities, such as leagues and cities,[3] which tried to secure their own agenda in the midst of the struggle between giants. In this context, diplomatic practice and the mechanisms associated with it played an essential role.

As this monograph explores, diplomatic gifts were a common resource in contexts of interaction in the ancient Mediterranean. Through a series of cases drawn from around continental Greece in the early second century BC, this work will examine the reaction aroused in the recipient

---

* This work has been developed within the research project PGC2018-096415-B-C22 'La expresión diplomática en el Mediterráneo central y oriental bajo la expansión romana: el regalo en su contexto político e institucional', funded by the State Research Agency, Ministry of Science and Innovation, Government of Spain (MCIN/AEI/10.13039/501100011033) and ERDF 'A way of making Europe'.

[1] Eckstein, 2006.
[2] Grainger, 2017.
[3] Strootman, 2020.

by the (supposed) intentionality of the giver and how this perception could have conditioned the acceptance or, above all, the rejection of the gift offered.

In 'Essai sur le don', M. Mauss described how, in the anthropological act of gifting, three obligations come into play: that of giving, that of receiving and that of reciprocating.[4] These three compulsions constitute the fundamental pillars of every circuit of gift exchange, known as the *exchange phenomenon*.[5] The cultural particularities of each society undoubtedly shape the nuances with which these obligations are understood,[6] but, even taking these differences into account, the pillars mentioned are a constant that anthropology has believed it can trace practically universally. The ancient tradition does not diverge from this canon. As M. L. Satlow and P. J. Burton have indicated, authors such as Seneca were capable of reflecting actively and recognising these three fundamentals.[7]

This chapter starts from the position that these qualities of gift exchange must have applied also to so-called 'diplomatic gifts'.[8] Analysis of some episodes reveals, however, a notable flexibility around these obligations, above all regarding that of acceptance.

The gift can be situated temporally in two categories: at the beginning or during the course of a cycle of exchange; that is, it can be an inaugural act or a further link in perpetuating a chain that already exists.[9] From this perspective, the obligation to accept the gift seems somewhat flexible – or not too compulsory – in the first case, while the second brings greater dilemmas. In the Greek mentality, gift exchange, as G. Herman has already indicated, constituted a key benchmark in rituals that began a friendly relationship.[10] The offer and eventual rejection of the gift in this initial phase occurred in the *reconnaissance dance*, understood as a process of reciprocal approaching and weighing up,[11] in which either of the *potential friends* could decide to accept, intensify or cease the rapprochement.[12]

---

[4] Mauss, 2002: 50–5.
[5] Lévi-Strauss, 1950: xxxvii–xli.
[6] Pitt-Rivers, 1977: 108.
[7] Sen. *Ben.* 1.4.3: *libenter dare, libenter accipere, libenter reddere et magnum ipsis certamen proponere, eos, quibus obligati sunt, re animoque non tantum aequare sed vincere, quia, qui referre gratiam debet, numquam consequitur, nisi praecessit.* Cf. Burton, 2011: 32; Satlow, 2013: 2.
[8] See Domingo Gygax, 2013: 46; Satlow, 2013: 4.
[9] Sykes, 2005: 59.
[10] Herman, 1987: 58–69.
[11] Rodin, 1984: 38.
[12] Burton, 2011: 34.

Either party could, at any time, symbolically step back and suspend the process of founding their friendship.

In contrast, it was more difficult to fit possible rejection into the course of a prolonged relationship. The dichotomy between accepting or rejecting a gift enters, moreover, into what P. Bourdieu called *le jeu de l'honneur*.[13] This is a phenomenon, again, traceable in the ancient Mediterranean. Herman identified these features in Archaic Greek thought, describing how an individual's capacity to respond adequately to the exigencies imposed by the gift acted as a real 'measure of his moral quality'.[14] In turn, Cicero also understood the exchange (of gifts) as an *honesta certatio* ('honourable competition').[15] This honour game obliged the participants – givers and receivers – to adhere to certain behaviours in which they weighed themselves up in relation to their interlocutor: the game should necessarily only have taken place between equals, since to challenge (or accept the challenge of) an inferior or superior brought dishonour.[16]

The course of the *reconaissance dance* and the inauguration of a new relationship generated a state of anxiety in its participants. In this case, there are two key aspects of that anxiety that interest us. On the one hand – as a *jeu de l'honneur* – it generated *status anxiety* in the face of the imminent competition for ascendancy.[17] On the other hand, as Burton also points out, anxiety was experienced as a consequence of mutual expectations, ultimately of the need to trust the other to reciprocate, opening oneself to the risk that this might not happen.[18] This latter circumstance was, furthermore, extendable not only to the inaugural events of a relationship, but also throughout the duration of its evolution. This is what Bourdieu indicates when he highlights how, in all social acts, even the most routine, uncertainty exists.[19] The person who gives can never be sure either that their gift will be accepted, or that it will be reciprocated. In short, any cycle of gift exchange, whatever its time span, is characterised by the participants' anxiety (Figure 6.1).

---

[13] Bourdieu, 1980: 170.
[14] Herman, 1987: 76, cf. 61.
[15] Cic. *Amic.* 32, *Off.* 2.69; See Burton, 2011: 37, 58, 67–8.
[16] Bourdieu, 1980: 170–1. Taking the categories defined by Sahlins, 1967: 191–6, this *honesta certatio* coincides with 'balance reciprocity', understood as an exchange between individuals of equivalent rank. Cf. the adaptation made to the Graeco-Roman world by Crook, 2013.
[17] Burton, 2011: 69–75.
[18] Burton, 2011: 39–40.
[19] Bourdieu, 1980: 168.

GIFT, DEBT, ANXIETY IN LATE HELLENISTIC TIMES 133

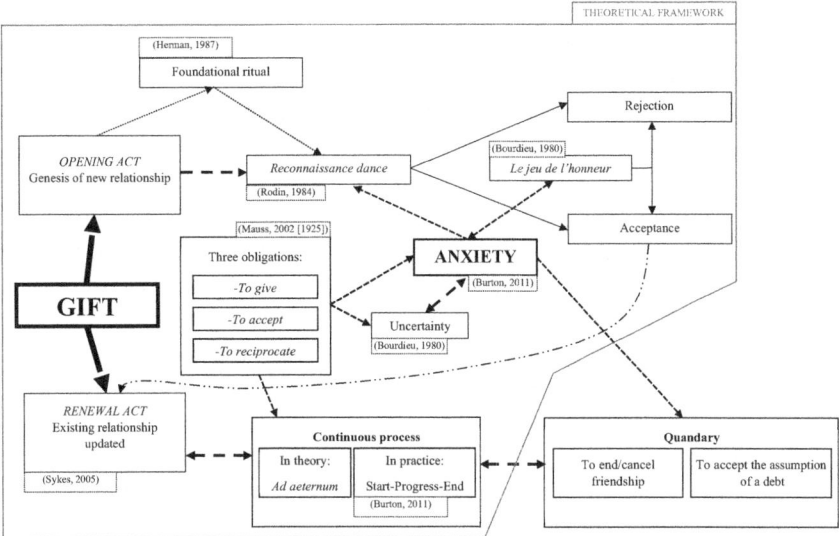

Figure 6.1 Relationship between gift exchange and anxiety (by the authors).

Finally, although the theory that can be inferred from the donation–acceptance–reciprocation cycle is of a social phenomenon *ad aeternum* in which the relationship extends without time limit, the practical reality underscores that ties were born and died when it was no longer possible (or desirable) to maintain them. Burton seems correct in his opinion, applying psychological principles, that relationships of friendship are created, evolve and are destroyed.[20] This factor adds, if possible, a greater complexity – and level of anxiety – to decisions taken over gift exchange. The recipient has to consider, in short, how far it is better to preserve a friendship – which could be long-lived – at the expense of incurring a debt, which may be undesirable, or whether it is better to relinquish a well-established connection specifically to avoid incurring such a debt.

We will begin by assessing the case of the Achaean League through two episodes respectively led by Philopoemen when he took an embassy to Sparta, and by the whole Achaean assembly and in particular by Apollonidas and Cassander when they received an offer from Eumenes of Pergamum. In both cases, the attitude of the recipient suggests a very high level of awareness of the principle of reciprocity. The importance of repaying what

---

[20] Burton, 2011.

was received was well recognised in the Greek world, including in the Hellenistic period, as various inscriptions indicate.[21]

P. Veyne pointed out several decades ago that the Achaeans were reluctant to accept foreign gifts, and carefully explored the reasons for that. In accepting, they would be either at the mercy of the interests of the giver, or ungrateful.[22] As Z. Crook indicates, 'to receive a benefaction is to be obligated to someone', and this is not an ideal situation.[23] The person who sought or received a gift is therefore in an inferior position and 'is forced to compromise his *eleutheria* (freedom) by adapting his behaviour to gratify his potential benefactor, on whose favours he is dependant'.[24]

The issue is, however, that the Achaeans only rejected foreign gifts *sometimes*.[25] This is perhaps the most pertinent detail. If the Achaean League had consistently refused any attempt from another to offer gifts, this would imply a 'state policy' (if such an expression may be used). The fact that only some circumstances led to the rejection makes it necessary to examine the motives and impact of this attitude.

The episode involving Philopoemen[26] is of particular interest because of the speech Polybius puts in the mouth of the *stratēgos*.[27] Wanting to honour the Achaean leader, the Spartans charged Timolaus, because he was close to him, to communicate to him the Lacedaemonians' intentions of decorating him with a crown. In the presence of the Spartan *synedrion*, Philopoemen rejected the gift, stating that, while he felt honoured by the offering, in practice to wear it upset him.[28] Philopoemen's rejection should not appear strange, since, according to another of Polybius' passages, a law

---

[21] Domingo Gygax, 2013: 45. Among other examples, *Syll.*³ 354: ὅπως ἅπα<ν>τες εἰδῶσιν ὅτι ὁ δῆμος ἐπίσταται χάριτας ἀποδιδόναι τοῖς εὐεργετοῦσιν αὐτόν; *Syll.*³ 493: ὅπως οὖν εἰδῶσι πάντες ὅτι ὁ δῆμος ὁ τῶν Ἱστιαιέων ἐπίσταται τιμᾶν τοὺς εὐεργετοῦντας αὐτόν.

[22] Veyne, 1990: 103.

[23] Crook, 2013: 64. Plutarch himself recognises and echoes this theoretical maxim; Plut. *Phil.* 21.6.

[24] Millett, 1989: 33; See Crook, 2013: 69.

[25] Under the same magistrates and at the same assembly, after rejecting Eumenes' offer, the Achaeans simultaneously accepted Ptolemy's gifts – Polyb. 22.9.3 – and perhaps also those of Seleucus. On the latter there are discrepancies between the versions in Polyb. 22.9.13 and Diod. Sic. 29.17. See below.

[26] Polyb. 20.12.

[27] As is common in Polybius, this is not a textual reproduction of the full speech, but a summary of its main points: cf. Polyb. 36.1; see Rosillo-López, 2011.

[28] This is a speech that fractures the 'common miscognition' around gifts; see Bourdieu, 1997; cf. Sykes, 2005: *passim*.

prohibited the acceptance of foreign gifts (from monarchs).[29] In any case, his speech highlights the difficult position in which a gift's recipient would find himself. Philopoemen situated *parrhēsia* (freedom of speech) as one of the first victims of the debt. For Crook, the lack of this freedom implies the absence of a symmetrical relationship.[30] In fact, the Achaean's apology includes the justification that defending Spartan interests before the Achaean assembly would be more feasible without this lack of *parrhēsia* – presumably because the moral authority to argue politically in favour of the Spartans would not be compromised by a publicly known debt to them on his part.

The threat to *eleutheria*, in this case collective, may also be observed in the concerns and caution that suffuse the debates in the Achaean assembly of 185 BC. In that year, the Achaean League faced a diplomatic offensive by the kings – Eumenes, Seleucus and Ptolemy – who sought to win its favour. It is important to remember that gifts did not only generate power relationships, they were also given and received in already established power relationships.[31] The decisions taken at the point of accepting or rejecting a gift should therefore be framed in a wider context in which what is at play could be a relationship that remains operational for (much) longer.

The monarchs' heavy spending in their bids to win Achaean friendship demonstrates their great interest in establishing a strong,[32] stable connection.[33] In relation to the events of 185 BC, it is notable that some of the gifts were by nature both sumptuous and functional. Leaving to one side the money offered by Eumenes, which will be discussed shortly, it is very striking that both Seleucus' and Ptolemy's presents had a pronounced military aspect. Among other things, Ptolemy brought six thousand peltast

---

[29] Polyb. 22.8.3. The law prohibited private citizens and magistrates receiving gifts from kings, but the prohibition was perhaps also extended to other external givers. In any case, although the law did not expressly forbid offerings from other cities, it is probable that the same factors as those that motivated the caution about monarchs weighed morally.

[30] Crook, 2013: 69–70.

[31] Domingo Gygax, 2013: 46.

[32] Herman, 1987: 77: 'the value of the gift was unabashedly recognised as an index of the attachment between giver and recipient'.

[33] The fulfilment of Ptolemy's pledge occurred over several years, from 185 BC when six thousand bronze shields and 200 talents in coins were sent (Polyb. 22.9.3, 24.6.5) until at least 180, when ten fully equipped penteconters were given (Polyb. 24.6.1). All this, it should be noted, comprised only one single episode (another one) in the renewal of alliance in a much longer relationship yet, in which multiple pacts had been signed (Polyb. 22.9.5–12) and which would go on to last still longer (Polyb. 24.6.1).

shields.[34] Seleucus presented ten ships.[35] Aside from the symbolic value that the act of *giving* could have, the choice of offerings with a clear military function in the context of the marked international tension which characterised the Hellenistic Mediterranean[36] surely entailed overlapping meanings. On the one hand, it increased the intrinsic value of the gift by providing useful and opportune military resources for the (most probable) war.[37] In this way, the degree of debt and potential yield in favour of the giver was greater.[38] On the other hand, taking into account that these gifts fell within the context of the renewal of military alliances, a more pragmatic reading in strategic terms may perhaps be proposed. The logistical difficulties of all military campaigns in Antiquity meant that any response to an enemy attack could be overly delayed. Preventative preparations for war (including in favour of allies) could therefore include, over time, an advantage for the interested party in augmenting their military allies' capacity for resistance in the face of a possible surprise strike, as well as in improving their operational and mobilisational capabilities. Gifts may therefore have subtly played an important role to this end.

The current objective, nevertheless, is to analyse not so much the interests of those kings as the reactions of the Achaeans, especially where they show differing attitudes. They did not systematically reject all gifts. While the attempt by the King of Pergamum met Achaean opposition (see below), for example, Ptolemy's attempt successfully managed to achieve his intention of renewing the alliance between the two parties.[39] In the case of Seleucus, discrepancies exist between the versions of Polybius and Diodorus. The variation between the two texts is rooted, moreover, not in the renewal of friendship with the king, which both historians agree was ratified by the assemby, but specifically in the acceptance of the gift. Diodorus says that the Achaeans accepted the gift[40] but leaves the nature of the gift unspecified. Polybius, however, reports the gift consisted of ten ships, which the

---

[34] Polyb. 22.9.3, 24.6.5. To which, five years later, were added the ten pentéconters mentioned in the previous note.
[35] Polyb. 22.7.4.
[36] Eckstein, 2006; 2008.
[37] On the frequency of war in this period, see Chaniotis, 2005: 5–12.
[38] It also makes very clear the *military* nature of the relationship: 'How people give and receive is a matter of what kind of relationships they imagine they make and keep with each other' (Sykes, 2005: 59).
[39] A success which, nevertheless, encountered some obstacles due to the confusion, condemned by Aristaenus, over which alliance specifically had been renewed; see Polyb. 22.9.5–12.
[40] Diod. Sic. 29.17.

Achaeans rejected.⁴¹ The proximity of Polybius to the events – his father was a witness at first hand⁴² – perhaps supports his version.⁴³ If it is correct, the Achaean attitude is revelatory, since it shows a desire for diplomatic balance when it came to receiving and ratifying the renewal of old alliances with the Seleucid king, but sidestepped the debt that the acceptance of the gift would impose upon them. It constituted, ultimately, a manoeuvre to preserve the League's *eleutheria* and a strategy for retaining a symmetrical relationship.

Eumenes' venture, as previously noted, received a greater wholesale rejection, at least as it is related by Polybius. In his case, as in that of Seleucus, the gifts were not accepted, but on this occasion the Megalopolitan presents much more explicit arguments through the speeches of Apollonidas of Sicyon and Cassander of Aegina. The former delivers a harsh criticism. The king's offering, 20 talents, was trying to finance the functioning of the Achaean *boulē*. Apollonidas decried not only that it would be illegal, but also that it constituted a lure – δέλεαρ – which would leave them at the mercy of the king's pleasure, since 'either the interests of the kings will take precedence over our own; or, if this is not so, we shall appear to everyone to be ungrateful in acting against our paymasters.'⁴⁴ As in the case with Philopoemen, this was a defence of the Achaean League's *parrhēsia* and *eleutheria* and, above all, an absolute refusal to put themselves in a situation of indebtedness. Other motives that were less 'autonomist' and perhaps indeed more 'classist' should nevertheless not be ruled out. Á. M. Moreno Leoni has proposed, in fact, that the king's attempt to fund a *misthos* (payment for public service) could be read as a way of radically altering the social bases who had access to this institution.⁴⁵ Apollonidas' reaction could therefore conform to certain oligarchic interests. He pointed out to his compatriots, moreover, that Eumenes' attempt would be followed by other kings, which in turn anticipated and pre-empted Seleucus' gift, which has been discussed above and which would take place immediately afterwards.

Cassander of Aegina's speech involves a twist, since the rejection of the gift comes with a demand. He required of the monarch's emissaries

---

⁴¹ Polyb. 22.7.4, 22.9.13.
⁴² Polyb. 22.9.2, 22.9.11, 24.6.4.
⁴³ Polybius' version is, furthermore, slightly more detailed, specifying the type of gift both in the offering and in the rejection, while Diodorus limits himself to using much more generic concepts: τὴν συμμαχίαν ἀνενεώσαντο καὶ τὴν δωρεὰν προσεδέξαντο.
⁴⁴ Polyb. 22.8.7, trans. W. R. Paton.
⁴⁵ Moreno Leoni, 2009.

as a condition of friendship that Eumenes free the Aeginetans,[46] who following various treaties had been subjugated by King Attalus.[47] The deft diplomatic manoeuvre entailed by this position puts the burden (and anxiety) of meeting those expectations back on to the king's shoulders. In some ways, it recalls the strategy that M. Domingo Gygax identifies in the relationships between kings and other Hellenistic states. He demonstrates that some poleis employed gifts 'in a manipulative fashion' when '[they] portrayed what were actually gifts aiming at reciprocation as countergifts'.[48] This case is clearly not of that type of episode, since the Achaeans were not offering any kind of gift, no (disproportionate) honour to Eumenes, which did occur on other occasions.[49] Cassander's attitude, nevertheless, bears similarities because, ultimately, what he sought was to reinterpret and profit from the figure of patron–benefactor that the monarch was trying to project. In this way, Cassander exploited the king's own intentionality, redirecting it (or at least, trying to do so) towards where he – and the Achaeans – wanted it. While Eumenes wanted to show himself as a benefactor in support of the League, the Achaeans corrected him in how and what he had to do to be one in reality. Cassander's speech thus succeeded not only in neutralising the diplomatic offensive of a gift which would have left the Achaean *boulē* indebted, but also in cutting short the king's attempt by situating him instead as a prey to anxiety. It was the monarch who came to be under pressure to *have to satisfy* the expectations of the image of benefactor which he himself attempted to convey. It does not seem, however, that Cassander's manoeuvre bore fruit, as Aegina continued under Attalid control.[50]

---

[46] It is no surprise that this initiative was taken by an Aeginetan – perhaps exiled? – but who undoubtedly had Achaean *sympoliteia*; Moreno Leoni, 2009.

[47] The original passage, which would have been narrated in Book 9 or 10, has been lost, but Polybius gives some details in this story (22.8.9–11): the Romans had taken the island, which they would have ceded through pacts to the Aetolians, and they in turn would have sold it to the King of Pergamum in exchange for 20 talents.

[48] Domingo Gygax, 2013: 52. It has recently been highlighted that the relationship between poleis and kingdoms was, fundamentally, one of mutual dependence based on *philia* and that, on occasions, cities managed to exploit it in their favour; Strootman, 2020, esp. 163.

[49] As occurred in 170 BC, when they debated the appropriateness (or otherwise) of restoring a series of honours to Eumenes: Polyb. 28.7. This particular episode demonstrates the precarious balance between favours, gifts and honour, and the many efforts made (and positions taken) to achieve an equilibrium in the complicated relationship between the Achaean League and the Attalids.

[50] Over a decade later, in 172 BC, the island remained under the control of the King of Pergamum, as implied by the fact that it was there that a gravely injured Eumenes

In any case, what is revealed by both Apollonidas' and Cassander's attitudes, and also, previously, that of Philopoemen, is the clear recognition that accepting a gift or favour implied a binding obligation to reciprocate.[51] Although, in the cases discussed, the Achaean League and its leaders were the (potential) recipients, there is evidence that when the roles were reversed, the Achaeans tried to exploit the favours that they had bestowed. The behaviour of Philopoemen himself can be interpreted in this way in relation to the thorny issue of the Spartan exiles after the defeat of Nabis. According to Plutarch, Philopoemen opposed the Roman request for the return of the exiles because he wanted the Spartans to be indebted to the Achaeans and not the Romans.[52]

The final case to analyse sits within the context of the Third Macedonian War.[53] The confrontation between Rome and the Macedonian kingdom constitutes without any doubt a paradigmatic case, since the literary sources assemble a large amount of information around the diplomatic praxis deployed by both powers.[54] Prior to the escalation of the conflict and subsequent fighting, numerous embassies from both sides and Greek cities, as well as legates from various political entities around the Hellenistic world, met to strengthen links, reinforce friendships, denounce abuses and/or request help in the face of a growing threat from one side or the other. In this case, rather than focusing on the Roman diplomatic praxis, we will study the policy deployed by the Macedonian king and his interlocutors.

We know from the sources that Perseus agreed various alliances, of which those of the greatest interest for this chapter are his negotiations with the Bastarnian chiefs. In 168 BC, with the war underway, Perseus attempted to recruit a group of 20,000 Bastarnian mercenaries who had spread through Illyria in the time of Philip V, who had signed an alliance with them and intended to settle them in Dardania.[55] According to Livy's

---

was taken to recover; Livy 42.16.6–7. It would continue under the rule of Attalus II. On the Attalid domination of Aegina, see Allen, 1971.

[51] An idea that, according to Plutarch, Philopoemen had already previously manipulated, after the capture of Megalopolis by Cleomenes: Plut. *Phil.* 5.2.

[52] Plut. *Phil.* 17.4; cf. Moreno Leoni, 2009.

[53] On the causes of the war, Polyb. 22.18.10; cf. 3.11.5–8; see Eckstein, 2010, 239. See also App. *Mac.* 11.1; cf. Polyb. 25.3.1–8; see Gruen, 1984: 408–36; Grainger, 2017: 213–24; Eckstein, 2010: 240; Burton, 2017.

[54] See Gruen, 1984: 412; cf. Grainger, 2017: 213.

[55] Delev, 2015: 66–7. A comparative analysis of the literary sources enables us to clarify the tribe to which these soldiers belonged, the Bastarnae, as can be deduced from the presence of Clondicus in the failed negotiations with Perseus (Cloelius in App. *Mac.* 18.2–3). The ancient sources diverge over the ethnic origin of the Bastarnae. Some authors argue a Germanic origin (Strabo 7.3.17; Plin. *NH* 4.25.81; Tac. *Germ.*

account, Perseus agreed with the leaders a sum specified as 10 gold coins per horseman, 5 per infantryman, and 1,000 for the *dux*.[56] Be that as it may, while at first this may appear to be the simple procurement of a mercenary army, a close analysis of the literary account allows us to weave a different history, given that the diplomatic relationship between Macedonia and the Bastarnae was not limited only to this episode, but reveals a long tradition of collaboration.[57]

For his first move, with the intention of consolidating the alliance, Perseus invited the Bastarnian chiefs to a meeting at his camp, then situated on the shores of the Axios River.[58] Perseus had ordered the cities and villages along the route to provide supplies and provisions to victual the Bastarnian troops that had to travel to that spot. The description that Livy gives of the preparation for the encounter is not insignificant, given that the monarch would acquire from the start a greater status thanks to his generosity, boasting the position of benefactor, and accompanying the act with the greatest publicity and display, as the preparation of the supplies and the presence of half his troops demonstrate. The importance of space is striking in this respect, since it adds an important psychological factor, with the pressure and anxiety that befell the beneficiary, who found himself

---

46.1), while others claim Gaulish descent (Livy 44.26.2–14; cf. 40.57–8; Plut. *Aem.* 9.4; Polyb. 29.9.13 ; Diod. Sic. 30.19.1). Appian refers to a group of Getae (App. *Mac.* 18.1). For the debate, see Walbank, 1979: 282, 369.

[56] The reference to the recruitment of these mercenary soldiers is in Livy 44.26.3–4; Plut. *Aem.* 12.4; App. *Mac.* 18.1. In terms of the stipulated payment, Plutarch differs from Appian and Livy, claiming that the payment of 1,000 talents was for each of the leaders and not only for the *dux*: Plut. *Aem.* 12.4. In contrast, Diodorus (30.19.1) lowers the figure to 500 talents. For a longer analysis, see Briscoe, 2012: 550–1.

[57] During the reign of Philip V, embassies were sent to the Bastarnae with the intention of agreeing an alliance, auxiliaries and hostages of noble lineage. Livy noted the desire to consolidate that alliance with a marriage between one of Philip V's sons and a noble Bastarnian (Livy 40.5.10). The extended diplomatic relationship between Antigonus, a member of the Macedonian court, and Cotto, a notable Bastarnian, gives the same impression. It seems that Philip V had already negotiated with the Bastarnae, bringing them offerings to encourage them to sack the territories of the Dardanians and settle in them. The Macedonian king's intention was for the Gauls to sack Italy from Dardania, although this seems unlikely and the story could be a product of Roman propaganda, Livy 40.57.4–9, Hammond & Walbank, 1988: 468, 470–1; Quillin, 2004: 775. Before the death of Philip V and the coronation of the new king, part of the Bastarnian troops returned north, but 30,000 remained in the region, led by Clondicus (Livy 40.58.7–8).

[58] The river system of the Axios River provided the boundaries of the original nucleus of the kingdom of Macedonia and was an important route into the interior: Thomas, 2010: 68.

with the obligation to reciprocate or reject the offering in the face of the unfavourable public.⁵⁹

Perseus likewise intended to offer the chiefs horses, phalerae and military capes.⁶⁰ Given that the sources speak about the importance of the cavalry for the Bastarnae,⁶¹ giving their leaders horses clearly shows Perseus' knowledge of the diplomatic praxis and his capacity to adapt to his interlocutor. It should be emphasised that, in the period we are studying, there is no evidence in the literary or epigraphic record of any Hellenistic monarch and/or Greek city that used horses as a gift for any another Hellenic interlocutor. It does, however, appear that during the Classical period, horses could have been a key element in diplomatic relationships established by Macedonia, since the region was known, alongside Thessaly, for horse-rearing and for the calibre of its cavalry.⁶² This fact was fundamental in a political speech by Demosthenes, wherein the Athenian accused some notable Olynthians of having received gifts from Philip II, among which horses stand out.⁶³ Extrapolating this reading to the whole of the Greek world in the fourth century BC, Xenophon observes the same practice in his *Anabasis*, although it should be emphasised that in the majority of occasions, the interlocutors belonged to the Persian sphere, where the horse was considered a gift of honour and was regularly given.⁶⁴ Be that as it may, although the Greek world could occasionally give horses, this does not disprove the exploitation of the high symbolic value that the horse had among Celtic and/or Germanic peoples. Perseus therefore knew how to interpret the diplomatic language

---

⁵⁹ Various psychological studies demonstrate the importance of space, the physical environment and the audience upon individuals. See Thirer & Rampey, 1979: 1048; Lyman & Scott, 1967: 238–44.

⁶⁰ Livy 44.26.6; cf. App. *Mac.* 18.2.

⁶¹ Livy 44.26.3; Plut. *Aem.* 9.4.

⁶² Errington, 1990: 7–8. On horses as gifts, see in this volume the chapter by A. Pérez Rubio.

⁶³ Dem. 19.265. It should be taken into account, however, that Olynthus was a Thracian city of Greek descent, formed in part by citizens who originated from Chalcis. The fact that this was a Thracian context could explain the gift of horses, a common present in the region, Xen. *An.* 7.2.2, 7.3.26. To explore this theme further, see Herman, 1987: 73–97. In a totally different context, Perseus used horses as an element of prestige, giving them to his troops as war booty, Livy 42.61.1–2. Antenor, prefect of Perseus' navy, likewise sent ten horses to the city of Thessalonica, taken from Eumenes as booty (Livy 44.28.15).

⁶⁴ Xen. *An.* 1.2.27, 4.7.27. One particular example should be highlighted, that of Thimbron, the Lacedaemonian commander of the mercenary troops, who gave a horse to Xenophon, Xen. *An.* 7.8.6.

of the Bastarnae to perfection, in this way drawing himself closer to the characteristics of the other participant.

There is a case, finally, for suggesting that the meeting proposed by Perseus constituted an inaugural act – the phase known as the *reconnaissance dance* – that attempted to assess the position of the interlocutor and begin a relationship, with the intention of winning reciprocity which would, ultimately, result in military assistance. As discussed above, the Bastarnae had certainly forged a relationship with King Philip V, but his death, in Livy's words, completely disrupted things from developing as planned,[65] for which reason Perseus had to make a pact with them again.[66] Be that as it may, nobody could ensure for the king that his offer would receive a response. According to Livy, Antigonus, Perseus' envoy, informed the Bastarnian mercenaries about the gifts that awaited them at the camp, as well as the abundance of provisions that they would encounter along the route. The chiefs nevertheless declined the invitation, since Antigonus did not bring with him the agreed payment. The fact of fighting for a foreign power in exchange for a salary does not, of course, imply adhesion to its political ideas, but the Bastarnians' response had much greater repercussions, given that it terminated the rapprochement between the two parties and brought new pressure to bear on Perseus, the theoretical benefactor and interlocutor of higher status because of his position as creditor.

As Bourdieu identified, a sense of honour is present in the exchange of gifts, and mutual recognition exists only when the exchange is reciprocal. For this very reason, when the chieftain Clondicus declined to meet Perseus and, by extension, receive the gifts, the monarch was dishonoured, because he received a slight from his interlocutor, thus inverting the asymmetry in the relationship. Although the sources work hard to single out the figure

---

[65] Livy 40.57.3.

[66] On this point, Livy's account is ambiguous. Initial reading of the narrative seems to suggest that the violent action against Dardania by the Bastarnae pertained to their uncontrolled behaviour once they heard of the death of King Philip V (Livy 40.57.2–9, 40.58.1–2). The Roman legates sent to Macedonia therefore spoke upon their return of the war that was taking place in Dardania. Spokesmen of King Perseus justified themselves, arguing that the king had made no pact with the Bastarnae, nor was he responsible for their actions. It seems that the senate could not condemn the king, but warned him to stick to the treaties (Livy 41.19.4–6). In a later passage, however, Livy claims that it was King Perseus who introduced the Bastarnae to Dardania (Livy 41.23.12), which would entail the existence of a previous agreement before the encounter of 168 BC. This final point contradicts the other versions, which claim that it was in the final days of Philip V that the Bastarnae entered Dardania (Livy 40.5.10; cf. 40.57.2–9). Livy's final story therefore seems to be a narrative construct, with the objective of demonstrating that Perseus was preparing for war immediately after ascending to the throne.

of Perseus negatively, describing him as an obstinate and arrogant person both in combat and in diplomatic practice, and, therefore, attribute the failure of the negotiation to Perseus' austerity,[67] it seems much more plausible to argue that the king, after three years of war and having made an enormous logistical and economic effort, did not want to cede in the face of what he considered extortion and a dishonourable act.[68]

Taken together, the episodes analysed makes it possible to prove that the rejection of diplomatic gifts was not unusual in contexts of negotiation during the early decades of the second century BC. The attitudes that can be identified reveal the latent anxiety in this *jeu de l'honneur* that is the exchange of gifts. Deliberation on the consequences of offering and accepting gifts is a constant in the attitudes of the Hellenistic kings and their interlocutors. The act of *giving* can be interpreted as 'a gamble' in which nobody wishes to lose, in which the potential benefits come with a high risk of disrepute or debt.

The decision adopted by the Achaeans and Bastarnae is, arguably, eloquent. The willingness to accept the moral and reputational cost of rejecting an offered gift reveals the level of awareness that existed around its symbolic and social implications, including transcending the context of an immediate political pragmatism, among political actors in the ancient Mediterranean. It is striking, moreover, that these actions are attested in a context like the second century BC, in which progressive Roman intervention and the final death throes of forays by Hellenistic kings put cities and federations in difficult situations.

There are, then, five main conclusions that can be drawn from this analysis.

First, all the actors seem to have been very well versed in a common 'code of conduct' about the norms of reciprocity. Knowing these rules – or precisely because of knowing them – they occasionally violated them. The premise of receiving was thus frequently infringed, as can be confirmed by the Achaean opposition to receiving any gifts from kings, and the retreat the Bastarnae made from their rapprochement with Perseus.

Second, rejection of the offer of gifts is attested at all phases of a relationship. Some episodes, such as that of the Bastarnae towards Perseus, took place in the inaugural phase, in the *reconaissance dance* (although a previous relationship would have existed with Philip V) in which the

---

[67] Livy 44.26.1–3. The theme of Perseus' greed and cruelty is repeated in Diod. Sic. 30.19.1, 30.21.2 and Plut. *Aem.* 8.6, 9.1, 12.2–7 and App. *Mac.* 16, which surely draw from the narrative of Polyb. 29.8.2, 29.9.12–13.

[68] Livy 44.26.12–13; Hammond & Walbank, 1988: 535.

interlocutors were still sounding each other out. This amounted, therefore, to an early termination of the relationship. On other occasions, however, gifts were declined in contexts of long-term relationships, as occurred between the Achaeans and some Hellenistic kings. The refusal ultimately was not limited to the early stages, but occurred within a specific geopolitical context and was determined by the agendas of that moment. In certain situations, it was preferable to escape a debt, although this could threaten a long-term friendly relationship.

Third, the givers exploited the gifts, and this exploitation also encompassed the strategic choice of *what* was given and *to whom*. The Hellenistic monarchs chose the type of gift according to the recipient, bearing in mind not only their own codes, but also those of the intended recipient. This can be seen when Perseus chose to give arms and horses to the Bastarnian leaders. The choice could also be made in evident pragmatism, as when Seleucus and Ptolemy offered the Achaean League arms, which de facto strengthened their military allies.

Fourth, in the case of the Achaeans, there was a constant preoccupation about guaranteeing a wide margin of *parrhēsia* and *eleutheria* for the League. Both in the episodes involving Philopoemen and in the great diplomatic offensive of 185 BC, the reticence when it came to accepting certain gifts from certain givers bore an obvious objective of preserving the political autonomy of the confederation. This attitude nevertheless constituted part of a broader strategy which, despite everything, managed to ensure that relationships with allied kings were nurtured. The relationship with the Ptolemaic kingdom, from whom they did accept considerable offerings, therefore remained healthy over a long period of time. In the case of the Seleucid king, the refusal of his gift did not prevent continuing agreements to collaborate.

Fifth, the episodes analysed suggest that attempts to give were often understood as an 'offensive'. For this reason they were countered, even reversing the asymmetry between the interlocutors. This can be seen in the situation in which Perseus and Eumenes found themselves. The Macedonian saw his great investment bear no fruit and suffered the dishonour of a lack of reciprocation despite his vast deployment of resources. The Attalid not only failed to achieve his objective, but his emissaries also left the Achaean assembly without the support of the League and with a new demand for the king.

In summary, it may be said that anxiety and expectation formed a double-edged sword that swung between the offeror (uncertainty about acceptance, risk of rejection, social dishonour) and the offered (contraction of debt, consideration of risks and probable benefits).

Bibliography

Allen, R. E. [1971]. 'Attalos I and Aigina', *Annual of the British School at Athens*, 66, 1–12.
Bourdieu, P. [1980]. *Le sens pratique*, Paris.
Bourdieu, P. [1997]. 'Marginalia – Some Additional Notes on the Gift', in A. D. Schrift (ed.), *The Logic of the Gift: Toward an Ethic of Generosity*, London–New York, 235–41.
Briscoe, J. [2012]. *A Commentary on Livy, Books 41–45*, Oxford–New York.
Burton, P. J. [2011]. *Friendship and Empire: Roman Diplomacy and Imperialism in the Middle Republic (353–146 BC)*, Cambridge.
Burton, P. J. [2017]. *Rome and the Third Macedonian War*, Cambridge.
Chaniotis, A. [2005]. *War in the Hellenistic World: A Social and Cultural History*, Oxford–Malden–Victoria.
Crook, Z. [2013]. 'Fictive Giftship and Fictive Friendship in Greco-Roman Society', in M. L. Satlow (ed.), *The Gift in Antiquity*, Oxford, 61–76.
Delev, P. [2015]. 'From Koroupedion to the Third Mithridatic War', in J. Valeva, E. Nankov and D. Graninger (eds), *A Companion to Ancient Thrace*, Oxford–Malden–Chichester, 59–74.
Domingo Gygax, M. [2013]. 'Gift-Giving and Power Relationships in Greek Social Praxis and Public Discourse', in M. L. Satlow (ed.), *The Gift in Antiquity*, Oxford, 45–60.
Eckstein, A. M. [2006]. *Mediterranean Anarchy, Interstate War, and the Rise of Rome*, Berkeley–Los Angeles–London.
Eckstein, A. M. [2008]. *Rome Enters the Greek East: From Anarchy to Hierarchy in the Hellenistic Mediterranean, 230–170 B.C.*, Malden–Oxford–Chichester.
Eckstein, A. M. [2010]. 'Macedonia and Rome, 221–146 BC', in J. Roisman & I. Worthington (eds), *A Companion to Ancient Macedonia*, Oxford–Malden–Chichester, 225–50.
Errington, R. M. [1990]. *History of Macedonia*, Berkeley.
Grainger, J. D. [2017]. *Great Power Diplomacy in the Hellenistic World*, Oxford.
Gruen, E. S. [1984]. *The Hellenistic World and the Coming of Rome*, Vol. 2, Berkeley.
Hammond, N. G. L. & Walbank, F. W. [1988]. *A History of Macedonia*, Vol. 3, New York.
Herman, G. [1987]. *Ritualised Friendship and the Greek City*, Cambridge.
Lévi-Strauss, C. [1950]. 'Introduction a l'oeuvre de Marcel Mauss', in *Sociologie et anthropologie*, Paris, ix–lii.
Lyman, S. M. & Scott, M. B. [1967]. 'Territoriality: A Neglected Sociological Dimension', *Social Problems*, 15 (2), 236–49.

Mauss, M. [2002]. *The Gift: The Form and Reason for Exchange in Archaic Societies*, London–New York. [1925].
Millett, P. [1989]. 'Patronage and Its Avoidance in Classical Athens', in A. Wallace-Hadrill (ed.), *Patronage in Ancient Society*, London–New York, 15–47.
Moreno Leoni, Á. M. [2009]. 'Algunas observaciones sobre el régimen político de la confederación aquea helenística: actores e instituciones (s. III–II a.C.)', in *XII Jornadas Interescuelas/Departamentos de Historia*, San Carlos de Bariloche.
Pitt-Rivers, J. [1977]. 'The Law of Hospitality', in *The Fate of Shechem or The Politics of Sex: Essays in the Anthropology of the Mediterranean*, Cambridge, 94–112.
Quillin, J. M. [2004]. 'Information and Empire: Domestic Fear Propaganda in Republican Rome, 200–149 B.C.E.', *Journal of Institutional and Theoretical Economics*, 160, 765–85.
Rodin, M. J. [1984]. 'Non-engagement, Failure to Engage, and Disengagement', in S. W. Duck (ed.), *Personal Relationships 4: Dissolving Personal Relationships*, London, 31–50.
Rosillo-López, C. [2011]. 'Los embajadores en las *Historias* de Polibio: entre la crónica y la búsqueda de apoyos', in J. M. Cortés Copete, R. Gordillo Hervás and E. Muñiz Grijalvo (eds), *Grecia ante los imperios: V Reunión de historiadores del mundo griego*, Seville, 329–34.
Sahlins, M. [1967]. *Stone Age Economics*, Chicago–New York.
Satlow, M. L. [2013]. 'Introduction', in M. L. Satlow (ed.), *The Gift in Antiquity*, Oxford, 1–11.
Strootman, R. [2020]. '"To be magnanimous and grateful": The Entanglement of Cities and Empires in the Hellenistic Aegean', in M. Domingo Gygax & A. Zuiderhoek (eds), *Benefactors and the Polis: The Public Gift in the Greek Cities from Homeric World to Late Antiquity*, Cambridge–New York, 137–78.
Sykes, K. [2005]. *Arguing with Anthropology. An Introduction to Critical Theories of the Gift*, London–New York.
Thirer, J. & Rampey, M. S. [1979]. 'Effects of Abusive Spectators' Behavior on Performance of Home and Visiting Intercollegiate Basketball Teams', *Perceptual and Motor Skills*, 48, 1047–53.
Thomas, C. G. [2010]. 'The Physical Kingdom', in J. Roisman & I. Worthington (eds), *A Companion to Ancient Macedonia*, Oxford–Malden–Chichester, 63–80.
Veyne, P. [1990]. *Bread and Circuses: Historical Sociology and Political Pluralism*, London.
Walbank, F. W. [1979]. *A Historical Commentary on Polybius*, Vol. 3: *Commentary on Books 19–40*, Oxford.

7

Buying Goodwill, Granting Rewards
The Roman Headquarters as a Space of Diplomatic Interaction*

Borja Vertedor Ballesteros

Beyond its military duties, the Roman camp or headquarters – understood as the commander in chief's base, whether that was the military compound itself, the winter quarters or a city – functioned in the Roman period as an administrative hub and political centre. For this reason, it also acted as a space for interaction with the local authorities.

This was the stage where diplomatic missions, heralds and *legati* were received. The camp was also the base for bilateral meetings between dignitaries of different political entities and the commander in chief. In turn, it was configured as a centre which dispatched representatives of the Roman provincial authority to cities and kingdoms within its own provinces and even from other regions. In this way, the various actors consistently came together in one Roman headquarters, which was itinerant because of its military facet, so they could interact in a more immediate way. In parallel, the agreements reached in this camp environment were circumscribed by the objective and subjective conditions of the war context.[1] Ultimately, the

---

* This work has been developed within the research project PGC2018-096415-B-C22 'La expresión diplomática en el Mediterráneo central y oriental bajo la expansión romana: el regalo en su contexto político e institucional', funded by the State Research Agency, Ministry of Science and Innovation, Government of Spain (MCIN/AEI/10.13039/501100011033) and ERDF 'A way of making Europe'.

[1] We have little epigraphic evidence for the Middle Republican period; however, there are various pieces that illustrate a politico-diplomatic process in a Roman camp. One of them, the Lascuta Bronze (*CIL* II 5041; *ELRH* no. U1, 191–5), reads at the end of the inscription: *act(um) in castreis*. The Ascoli Bronze (*CIL* I 709) likewise on two occasions records the formula *donavit in castreis apud Asculum*.

representation of Rome in the provinces through the Roman headquarters elevated that space to the forefront of diplomatic activity.²

There is a lot of evidence for the role of camps as the arena for receiving embassies. One example which encompasses various aspects that are characteristic of this function is that transmitted by Livy in the context of the victory over Perseus in 168 BC. After the Battle of Pydna, the Roman troops moved to Pella and set up camp next to the city.³ Here they received various *legationes* which came to express their congratulations to the Roman people.⁴

The camp also hosted *conloquia*, as indicated above: high-level political conversations in which local and regional leaders participated; the conduct of *concilia* should also be noted. These bilateral meetings saw dialogues and negotiations of various natures, among which were appeals for truces, surrenders, the handing over of rewards and requests for friendship and alliance. The convention of these coordinating fora also demonstrated the diplomatic enthusiasm of the general in charge of the expeditionary armies.⁵

An example of these interlocutions, specifically of surrender or submission (*in fidem*), is the visit of 112 horsemen from the Campanian nobility to the Roman camp in Suessula, commanded by the praetor Gnaeus Fulvius. The nobles came from Capua, which in 213 BC was still on the Carthaginian side, under the pretext of plundering enemy territory. Their secret destination, however, was the Roman military compound. Once there, they stopped at the guard post, revealed their identity and requested an interview with the praetor. Informed of the event, the praetor ordered that ten of the horsemen enter his presence unarmed. In the course of the meeting, they presented their requests to the magistrate, which focused on the recovery of their possessions after the capture of Capua:

---

² This chapter follows Díaz Fernández, 2015, esp. 34, that a *provincia* is understood as the jurisdiction mandated to a holder of *imperium*. Likewise, see Cadiou & Moret, 2004 for the specific case of Hispania, especially during the Roman conquest, and the conception of a mobile border.

³ On the Roman camp's capacity as a centre for receiving embassies, both in the west and in the east, for this latter space see Claudon, 2015; Grainger, 2017. Cf. Torregaray Pagola, 2020.

⁴ *per quos dies ad Peliam stativa fuerunt, legationes frequentes quae ad gratulandum convenerant, maxime ex Thessalia, auditae sunt* (Livy 44.46.9). For an example of *legationes* in the Gaulish world, see García Riaza, 2020.

⁵ These meetings would have helped consolidate support networks, both military and logistic, without which the conquest of Carthago Nova, for example, is inexplicable: García Riaza, 2016: 256.

a hundred and twelve noble Campanian horsemen, setting out from Capua, with permission of the magistrates, under pretext of plundering the enemy's country, came to the Roman camp above Suessula. They told the guards outside who they were; that they wished to speak with the praetor. Gnaeus Fulvius was in command of the camp, and on being informed, he ordered that ten of their number be disarmed and brought to him. After he had heard their demands, and they made no other request than that upon the recovery of Capua their property should be restored to them, they were all taken under his protection.[6]

As the cement binding these politico-diplomatic dynamics, the general, helped by his *consilium*, played a crucial role in a complex ritual of audience.[7] As we have seen, one of the first stops when entering the camp was the guard post, which authorised or forbade entry. A request for an interview or audience was then communicated to the magistrate in command of the military compound. Once accepted, the meeting took place, either in the *praetorium*, that is, the courtyard (the *principia*) – the tribunal was also usually found in this space – or inside the general's tent.

A passage in Livy, referring to the reception in 168 BC of a Rhodian embassy coming from Rome, allows us to reconstruct another variation in the final stage of the protocol. The ambassadors, once they had entered the camp, were received by the camp council and the magistrate with *imperium* and tried to justify their attitude towards Macedonia.[8]

The topography of the camp compound itself, as well as the staging of the setting in which the audience took place – added to the active presence of the army – was an element that played an important role in diplomatic ceremony, on occasions organised as mechanisms of pressure and intimidation.[9] An illustrative example of this intimidation is Livy's narrative of the arrival in Amphipolis of the ten heads of each city summoned by Lucius Aemilius in 167 BC.[10] The passage narrates the events of the summit

---

[6] Livy 24.47.12–13, trans. F. Gardner Moore.
[7] The role of the *consilium* is recorded on the Alcántara Bronze, which intervenes directly in the resolution of the *deditio*. On the *consilium* as a permanent body in the Roman camp, see Johnston, 2008.
[8] ... *sub idem tempus Rhodii legati in castra venerunt ... multo iniquioribus animis a castrensi consilio auditi sunt* (Livy 44.35.4).
[9] On the internal layout of the camp, see in the first instance Polyb. 6.40–2, also Gilliver, 1993; on the archaeological remains: Dobson, 2008; 2013; Morillo Cerdán, 2008; Morillo Cerdán *et alii*, 2020.
[10] Livy 45.29.1–4.

in several acts. The Roman general took his seat in the tribunal alongside the ten members of the delegation.[11] The tribunal was situated in the *praetorium*, therefore occupying a privileged position, and raised above the crowd, acting to demarcate political *status*. The scene frightened not only defeated enemies, but also allies. The crowd of onlookers at the entrance, the solemnity of the herald and magistrate's assistant ... everything was set up as part of the ritual.[12] The intimidatory power of the ceremonial reached its climax when the *praeco* (herald) called for silence and the magistrate addressed the masses in the language of power.[13]

In parallel, the headquarters/camp was the centre that sent *legati* for the purpose of creating or re-establishing bonds of friendship.[14] It therefore appeared not as a passive subject, but rather as a political sphere that actively interacted with its surroundings, establishing bilaterality in diplomatic relations and a dual dynamic and direction of interaction, both centripetal and centrifugal.[15] We find an example of this dynamic in Scipio Africanus' dispatch of three centurions as emissaries to Syphax in 214 BC[16] in order to secure allies for the disembarkation in Carthage.

In the same way, emissaries with status gifts departed from the headquarters. Scipio should be mentioned again, who sent his colleague Laelius to Africa in 206 BC laden with presents to gain the friendship of Syphax.[17] Laelius returned not only with Syphax's acceptance; he did so with goods with which the latter had endowed him.[18]

---

[11] ... *cum decem legatis circumfusa omni multitudine Macedonum in tribunali consedit* (Livy 45.29.1).

[12] ... *adsuetis regio imperio tamen novi imperii formam terribilem praebuit tribunal, summoto aditus, praeco, accensus, insueta omnia oculis auribusque quae vel socios, nedum hostis victos, terrere possent* (Livy 45.29.2).

[13] ... *silentio per praeconem facto Paulus Latine ... ea Cn. Octavius praetor – nam et ipse aderat – interpretata sermone Graeco referebat* (Livy 45.29.3). Cf. with the study on the acoustics and perception of sound in a *contio* in Rome Kopij & Pilch, 2019. Also Morstein-Marx, 2004.

[14] See Burton, 2011 for relationships of friendship and diplomacy.

[15] See García Riaza, 2015.

[16] ... *ad eum centuriones tres legatos miserunt qui cum eo amicitiam societatemque facerent et pollicerentur* (Livy 24.48.3).

[17] An example of acting outside the *provincia* assigned by the senate, which had serious repercussions if the mission involved danger for the Republic or its armies, Sánchez, 2016.

[18] App. *Hisp.* 29.

The Importance of the Gift in the Camp Context

With relative frequency, political interaction in the camp included the presentation, receipt or exchange of goods with a diplomatic value.[19] The literary sources preserved do not always specify the nature of the goods presented as gifts. This is the case, for example, with the passage which refers to Scipio's dispatch of Laelius with gifts for Syphax. Neither Livy nor Appian specifies the type of gift with which the general hoped to attract the friendship of Numidia: *cum donis mittit*/δωρεὰς τε φέροντα.[20]

The evidence that does specify the contents of the gifts enables a preliminary distinction between the exchange of people and of objects. Within the first group are previously captured hostages and prisoners, used as a gift.[21] An example of this type of transaction comes with the arrival of Cato in the Iberian Peninsula in 195 BC.[22] After the Roman victory near Emporion and having dispatched various *legationes* who had come to the camp to surrender, he marched to Tarraco. In that city, the Hispanians presented themselves with their Roman and Latin ally prisoners who, for various reasons, had been seized on the peninsula and were brought to the consul as a gift.[23] The second group is of material offerings, which were given in the context of the headquarters. During 188 BC, in his winter camp in Asia, the proconsul Gnaeus Manlius received a large number of embassies from cities and towns to the west of the Taurus Mountains. They came to congratulate the Roman general on his victory over the Galatians, bringing golden wreaths as gifts, symbolising the magnitude of his victory, which was greater than that Antiochus won over them.[24] There is a third and final type: non-material gifts. These were the initiatives, decisions and

---

[19] There is an extensive bibliography on diplomatic gifts; see Grass, 2015; Satlow, 2013; Auliard, 2009.

[20] Livy 28.17.7; App. *Hisp.* 29. See Rosselló Calafell, 2023.

[21] On the classification of hostages and their politico-diplomatic implications in the Hispanian world and its interaction with Rome, see García Riaza, 1997; 2002; 2006; García Riaza & Sanz, 2019. Especially, on the release of hostages, note Álvarez Pérez-Sostoa, 2009; 2015: 113–14.

[22] For the Hispanian examples, see in this book the chapter by E. Sánchez Moreno & J. García Cardiel, especially, for our interest, the discussion about the return of prisoners and hostages as a *donum* to Alucius in the headquarters of Carthago Nova (Livy 26.50.6).

[23] ... *cum Tarraconem venit, iam omnis cis Hiberum Hispania perdomita erat, captivique et Romani et socium ac Latini nominis, variis casibus in Hispania oppressi, donum consuli a barbaris reducebantur* (Livy 34.16.7).

[24] ... *ad Cn. Manlium consulem primum, dein pro consule, hibernantem in Asia, legationes undique ex omnibus civitatibus ... pax Gallis domitis data esset, non*

prerogatives that brought a series of diplomatic, political and social implications. Their role was also to reward, and they found themselves bound by the physical conditions of the headquarters/Roman camp. Among them were the loan of services (escort, military training), as occurred for example with Masinissa's nephew, who was accompanied to a safe place;[25] hospitality (feasting, lodgings in the quarters of the camp itself), of which there are various examples, among them that of Indibilis and Mandonius;[26] even the possibility of enjoying free access to the general's *praetorium*, like the reward ordered by Marcellus for Lucius Bancio.[27]

Political Contexts of Gift-Bearing

With the gifts catalogued according to their typology, two political contexts have been established in which the exchange of presents took place. The first of those cemented the construction of new alliances, while the second involved the reaffirmation of existing bonds of friendship or the reward of specific attitudes and behaviours.[28]

New Alliances

On the one hand, there is a series of cases in which the goods exchanged were hostages and/or prisoners, within a protocol for their release; on the other, there are those episodes in which the alliance or agreement began with a series of typically diplomatic objects, such as golden wreaths.

Exchange of Hostages/Prisoners

The examples analysed below evolve in a very similar way, in a process of three consecutive stages that can be defined as a protocol of hostage/prisoner restoration. The protocol started with the arrival at the camp of those implicated in the restoration of hostages/prisoners.[29] They could go under their own initiative or at the request of the Roman general. The first step involved an interview, which probably took place in the *praetorium*,

---

gratulatum modo venerant sed coronas etiam aureas pro suis quaeque facultatibus attulerant (Livy 38.37.1–4).

[25] Livy 27.19.11–12.
[26] Livy 27.17.15–17.
[27] Livy 23.15.15.
[28] On alliances and interaction with Rome, see Balsdon, 1979; Braund 1984; García Riaza, 2011; Sánchez Moreno & García Riaza, 2019.
[29] Obtained by the general in chief by right of conquest.

during which both parties negotiated their petitions and claims for the alliance. Then followed the release of those people to their relatives and/or kin by the commander in chief, either directly (simultaneously) or through intermediaries (and therefore deferred). This initial gift could also be accompanied by another benefit.

The ritual continued with the signing of the agreement or alliance, which was carried out in the same headquarters. Finally, as a gift and accompaniment to the first phase, there was a banquet and/or lodging offered in the military compound, where the guests were welcomed in an environment of trust. The relationship built between the Roman general and the guests was asymmetrical, since the latter were indebted by the restoration of their relatives, as well as finding themselves in a compound with a strong symbolic and scenographic significance. The second and third stages were interchangeable in the sequence of the ceremony, which did not influence the outcome. The physical space in which the honoured guests' camps were situated is not clearly mentioned in the sources for our period of study. We do know, however, some Late Republican and Imperial cases that point to the use of the area adjoining the *praetorium* or of the *quaestorium* itself for that end.[30] It is therefore possible that these spaces were also used to accommodate guests in previous periods.

There are, finally, a series of cases which do not strictly follow the complete protocol of restoration discussed above, but which do show certain phases of it, such as the act of the establishment of alliances, and the hospitality. The first instance occurred after Scipio left Tarraco, where he wintered from 209 to 208 BC. In the course of his journey south, Indibilis and Mandonius appeared, who had already previously defected from the Punic side. During the encounter, Indibilis spoke for both of them, translating for the Roman general the reasons they felt obliged to abandon the Carthaginians and their recent interest in formalising an alliance with Rome. After the Iberian's statement, and with Scipio's inclination for reaching agreements, their wives and children, who had been in Roman hands since Carthago Nova,[31] were restored to them. Once their relatives were returned, they were offered hospitality that day in the camp as it travelled. The following day, the pledge was sealed with a treaty, and from that moment, the personal tents of Indibilis and Mandonius were set up in the same camp as the Romans. They then continued south together, and the

---

[30] *In quo maxime legati hostium et obsides; et, si qua praeda facta fuerit, in quaestorio ponitu* (Hyg. 18.3). Gilliver, 1993: 40; Campbell, 2018: 40.
[31] Livy 26.17.11.

Iberians served as guides, no doubt as part of that agreement or in gratitude for the restoration/hospitality.[32]

The second example relates to Edesco[33] or Edeco,[34] an Iberian chieftain[35] who until that point had collaborated closely with the Carthaginians. The fall of Carthago Nova, however, and the fact that Scipio had taken his wife and children as hostages/prisoners, pushed him to adopt a pro-Roman position. Edeco, who arrived at Tarraco after the Roman troops had quartered there for the winter (209/8 BC), was accompanied by his family and kinsfolk. He was admitted to the headquarters and had an interview with Scipio, in which he communicated his intention of handing himself over to the protection of Rome – not only himself, but also his friends and kinsfolk.[36] The agreement unleashed a wave of alliances with Iberians who wanted to recover their relatives.[37] When the Iberian finished his explanation, his wife and children were returned by the commander in chief, and he was also given the friendship he sought. During the time they were together, the Roman general delighted the Iberian by various means – probably with diplomatic and hospitality gifts – and with great hopes for future benefits for all who were with him, the commander in chief sent them back home.[38]

Various other evidence allows us to identify partially the protocol of restoration, testifying to some of its stages. The events following the Battle of Emporion, involving Cato and his troops (195 BC), include some of these stages of ceremony. After the Roman general's entry into Emporion – where he would establish his command post – the consul laid on a generous banquet in the headquarters for the individuals who had taken refuge in the Greek city. These were presumably pro-Roman leaders who had fled to Emporion after the start of the uprising.[39] Cato addressed them eulogistically before returning them safely to their cities. The Roman then left for Tarraco and was met on the road by different city *legationes* who wanted to surrender. When he arrived at his destination, the Iberians brought as a gift (*donum*) to the consul the imprisoned Romans and Latin allies who

---

[32] Livy 27.17.15–17.
[33] Livy 27.17.1–3.
[34] Polyb. 10.34–5.
[35] *dunatos dunastēs* is the Greek equivalent (Moret, 2002–3).
[36] For other examples of diplomatic practices in the context of surrender, see Sanz, 2015; García Riaza, 2021.
[37] See Hernández Prieto, 2019, and also the chapter by E. Sánchez Moreno & J. García Cardiel in this volume.
[38] Polyb. 10.35.2.
[39] Livy 34.16.5.

had been captured in Hispania during the uprising.[40] This passage unites all the components of the protocol, but carried out by different actors. The scenario includes, on the one hand, politico-diplomatic agreements such as the surrender of peoples to Rome; on the other hand, Cato's hospitality; and finally, the release of captured Romans and Latin allies by Iberian peoples from the pacified areas to the north of the Ebro River. This was the same modus operandi that we have seen in previous passages, with the one exception that it was not Rome returning prisoners.

There are other episodes in which the ritual of release does not take place completely. This is the case for the events of the winter of 209/8 BC in Tarraco, the city to which Scipio returned after taking Carthago Nova. On that occasion, the Roman general set about earning the goodwill of the Iberians by returning prisoners and hostages, and by offering gifts.[41] It is likewise mentioned in Livy, who gives us information about the gifts: 'At the beginning of the summer in which these events were taking place, after Publius Scipio in Spain had spent the entire winter in winning over the support of the barbarians, partly by gifts and partly by restoring their hostages and captives ...'[42]

Another case that involved the return of a captured relative thanks to a Roman victory occurred after the Battle of Baecula (208 BC) when Scipio returned Masinissa's nephew alongside a collection of diplomatic presents derived, probably, from the booty obtained after the battle.[43]

Concluding this section is one last passage which, although it does not specifically fit the protocol, includes the offer of hospitality after a *deditio*.[44] This example moves to another geopolitical context: the Illyrian War of 168 BC. The protagonist on this occasion is King Gentius, in Scodra. After the end of a three-day ceasefire which had been requested of the praetor Appius Claudius, and verifying that he had no allies with whom to confront Rome, Gentius sent messengers to the camp with a petition for an

---

[40] ... *confestim inde castra movit, et, quacumque incedebat agmen, legati dedentium civitates suas occurrebant, et, cum Tarraconem venit, iam omnis cis Hiberum Hispania perdomita erat, captivique et Romani et socium ac Latini nominis, variis casibus in Hispania oppressi, donum consuli a barbaris reducebantur* (Livy 34.16.6–7).

[41] Polyb. 10.34.1. See Hernández Prieto, 2019.

[42] Livy 27.17.1, trans. F. Gardner Moore.

[43] This episode is addressed in this volume in the chapters by E. Sánchez Moreno & J. García Cardiel and E. Sánchez Medina & G. Rosselló Calafell, respectively. For our particular interest, what again stands out is the resolution of the protocol in the camp, as well as the guard offered the young Numidian *iussisque prosequi, quoad vellet, equitibus dimisit*, Livy 27.19.12.

[44] On the mechanism of *deditio* see García Riaza & Sanz, 2019.

interview with the magistrate. This was accepted, and he came to the military compound, where he surrendered to Appius. Between the invitation to a banquet and its consumption in the camp itself, Gentius made a brief visit to the city, where he addressed his men to communicate to them the result of his interview.[45]

Exchange of Diplomatic Objects

The following examples pertain to the second section, where new alliances were affirmed through the bringing of gifts. Various cases have been identified in which the initiative was the responsibility of the different political entities who came to the headquarters to seek a treaty/alliance with Rome.

The first case to be analysed sits chronologically in 189 BC, the moment in which the city of Ambracia was being besieged by Fulvius Nobilior, who established the Roman camp outside its walls. This military compound played an important role as a politico-diplomatic centre, as a meeting place for the different *legationes* who at that time were moving around Greece.[46] There, the Aetolian ambassadors Phaeneas and Damoteles were presented, both with extensive powers conceded to them by popular decree.[47] To that same camp likewise arrived Athenian and Rhodian ambassadors, who came to intercede for the Aetolians.[48] The final spokesman to arrive was Amynander, King of the Athamanes, who was more concerned for the city under siege.[49] Under these circumstances, Amynander acted as mediator, addressing the leaders of Ambracia from outside the city wall, fruitlessly. He subsequently asked the consul permission to enter Ambracia, and managed to persuade them to surrender to the Romans. Once the departure of the Aetolian troops had been agreed, the Ambracians offered the consul a golden wreath of 150 pounds.[50]

A second piece of evidence for interaction within the camp took place during Nobilior's operations in 189 BC, with the reference, again, to the presentation of a golden crown as a diplomatic gift, this time by

[45] Livy 44.31.12–15.
[46] On Rome's interactions during her conquest of the Hellenic world, see Gruen, 1986; Eckstein, 2008; 2009.
[47] Livy 38.8.1.
[48] Livy 38.9.3.
[49] Livy 38.9.4.
[50] ... ἐδόθη δ᾽ αὐτῷ καὶ στέφανος ἀπὸ ταλάντων ἑκατὸν καὶ πεντήκοντα (Polyb. 21.30.10); ... *Ambracienses coronam auream consuli centum et quinquaginta pondo dederunt* (Livy 38.9.13). On embassies in the work of Polybius, see Zecchini, 2005.

Moagetes. The consul, mistrusting the intentions of the tyrant of Cibyra, sent a column headed by Gaius Helvius to enter his territory. He was offered a wreath of 15 talents by some of the tyrant's emissaries. After a series of requests, which included the petition that the land not be sacked, Helvius led them to the consul. The meeting took place in the marching camp. Before the magistrate, the emissaries made the same requests as they had to Helvius, but the Roman general mistrusted Moagetes' behaviour. They therefore only requested that Nobilior accept the wreath and allow the tyrant to present himself personally before him, and be given the opportunity to speak. The following day, Moagetes himself was admitted into the camp. Wearing modest clothes, he addressed the magistrate and tried to justify to the consul that, given the poverty of his resources and of the cities under his rule, he could not meet the tribute to Rome.[51] The tyrant of Cibyra had arrived with a small guard, unworthy of his status, to emphasise the delicate state of his power. Access was probably through the praetorian gate, which led most directly to the general's tent, beneath the intense scrutiny of the Roman troops, in the studied scenography of the Roman camp.

There is a case in which the initiative to travel was taken by Scipio, who – given the state of affairs in the theatre of operations – saw the need to open negotiations with Syphax. To do this, he sent Laelius *cum donis* from the headquarters in Tarraco.[52]

Gifts of Reward or Reaffirmation

This section is structured around two parts. The first examines those gifts authorised to reward services rendered to the Roman people in war. The second comprises those cases in which, through the exchange of prestige goods, a pre-existing relationship with Rome, which had continued for a greater or lesser period of time, was updated.

---

[51] ... πρὸς δὲ τὸν στρατηγὸν ἐκέλευσε πρεσβεύειν ὑπὲρ τῶν ὅλων (Polyb. 21.34.5); ... *quam ut coronam acciperet veniendique ad eum tyranno potestatem et copiam loquendi ac purgandi se faceret. permissu consulis postero die in castra tyrannus venit, vestitus comitatusque vix ad privati modice locupletis habitum, et oratio fuit summissa et infracta, extenuantis opes suas urbiumque suae dicionis egestatem querentis* (Livy 38.14.8–9). On crowns, see the chapter in this book by A. Erskine.

[52] Livy 28.17.7. This example is analysed in the chapter in this book by E. Sánchez Medina & G. Rosselló Calafell.

Reward Goods

These, which functioned to express gratitude to Rome, can be grouped into two strands. The first contains those that the general distributed in order to thank his officials and allies for military services rendered. The second includes the bringing of golden wreaths to thank the Roman general on campaign.

Among the cases of goods presented on Roman initiative, we can identify, firstly, that by Scipio after the conquest of Carthago Nova in 209 BC. During the *contio*, held in order to hand out awards, the elevation of Laelius, admiral of the fleet, and the treatment he received stands out. Scipio showered him with praise, as well as giving him equal status with himself, which we understand as a display of military recognition. He also gave him a golden wreath and thirty oxen.[53] Years later, in 203 BC, in a similar *contio* held to name Masinissa king, Scipio again bestowed a golden wreath upon Laelius.[54]

The most revealing evidence without doubt is that of the endowment of gifts upon Roman allies in the camp setting. In Hispania, specifically after the Battle of Baecula (208 BC), Scipio divided the booty among his troops in the occupied enemy camp. His next action was to proceed to distribute bounty among the Hispanian dignitaries who had participated in the conflict. In this context, the Roman general invited the Iberian chief Indibilis there so that he could pick from among the many captured horses 300 of his choosing.[55] A little later, in the north of Africa, after the Roman victory in Utica in 204 BC, Scipio likewise gave insignia and rewards to his officials, but above all to Masinissa.[56]

To conclude this classification, we again move to Hispania. In 133 BC, once Numantia was subdued, Scipio organised public commendations and generous gifts (*donatum atque laudatum*) for Jugurtha in a military assembly held in the camp.[57]

These five episodes share several features. They occurred after a Roman victory, structured around a public *contio–laudatio* held in the headquarters/camp. With the exception of Laelius, they were all Roman allies, who one way or another had to be rewarded for their commitment to the city of Latium. In Laelius' case, the commendations were more personal on the part of Scipio, but this did not stop him from presenting them publicly so

---

[53] ... *ante omnis C. Laelium praefectum classis et omni genere laudis sibimet ipse aequavit et corona aurea ac triginta bubus donavit* (Livy 26.48.14).
[54] ... *Laelium deinde et ipsum conlaudatum aurea corona donat* (Livy 30.15.11).
[55] Livy 27.19.7.
[56] Livy 29.35.3.
[57] Sall. *Iug.* 8.

that they received recognition from the troops who were there at each of the military assemblies. In the same way, the examples mentioned include both material and non-material gifts, which can be itemised as golden wreaths, bulls, horses, rewards, gifts, and military recognition and public prominence.

Confirmation of Friendship/Alliance with Rome

The Roman camp was also the scene for conducting private interviews in order to exchange gifts to guarantee and/or affirm friendship or alliance with Rome. The first example of the recovery of goodwill within our time frame is provided by Fabius Maximus in 217 BC. The events are transmitted by Plutarch. The Greek author records that the Roman general held a particular view on how to suppress defections and revolts by allies, preferring to use softer and more lenient measures. Upon discovering that a Marsian soldier was inciting desertion among soldiers in the Roman camp, he gave him a warhorse and other rewards relating to valour.[58] This gesture positioned the soldier as the most loyal and enthusiastic.[59]

The second passage occurs within the context of the dynamics of allegiance and defection that took place during Hannibal's expeditions through the Italian Peninsula, specifically in Campania during 216 BC. Nola provided the main stage, divided across the middle into two factions. On one side were those who wanted to remain loyal to the alliance with Rome – the senate and its most illustrious members; on the other side were the plebs, who, given the general state of panic and fear, were closer to the Punic faction. The senate, foreseeing the unsustainability of the situation, pretended to ponder defection in order to win time to send ambassadors to the Roman praetor Claudius Marcellus, who was with his army in Casilino: *ita spatio sumpto legatos propere ad praetorem Romanum Marcellum Claudium, qui Casilini cum exercitu erat.*[60] Once the city was controlled by Marcellus with the acquiescence of the senate and its leaders, danger emerged from the plebs, in the form of their leader Lucius Bancius. Having met Bancius in Cannae in a critical state of health, Hannibal not only let him return to his homeland, but also showered him with gifts. Given this history, it is not surprising that the Roman general questioned Bancius' goodwill. The praetor acted in the same way as the Carthaginian general, appealing to him with gifts to earn his goodwill. Camped next to the city, he sent for him to come

---

[58] In Frontinus 4.7.36 he calls him into his presence and gives him a horse and money; in contrast, in Val. Max. 7.3.7 he is honoured from the tribunal, but given no gift.
[59] Plut. *Fab. Max.* 20.2–3.
[60] Livy 23.14.10.

to the camp and, after offering him words of thanks and recalling his past acts to him, he gave him a horse, promises – understood to be *political commitments* – and the quaestor gave him 500 denarii. Marcellus also ordered his lictors that whenever he wished to see him, he should be allowed to.[61] The non-material aspect of the gifts was therefore the privilege of accessing the *praetorium* whenever he wanted, understood to be the tent of the commander himself. This permission should be judged as a social and military honour of great importance, since access to the tent was limited to the commander's *consilium* and his most immediate personal entourage.

Both the meeting with the Marsian soldier and the one with Lucius Bancius occurred in the headquarters. The commander in chief called them into his presence and after a praise-filled interview, offered them various material and non-material gifts. In both cases, the object is the recovery of their goodwill, in order to project a general image to a wider, expectant, public audience: their own troops and the city's representatives. We consequently have two cases which through their own traits could perfectly well be classified within the section on rewards. They are better understood, however, from the perspective of a reaffirmation of a previous status, since their most immediate implications were to strengthen the alliance with Rome.

A third example of the recovery of goodwill, with the camp as meeting space, is found in the North African campaign of 203 BC. The encounter occurred at a critical moment, after Syphax's capture and Sophonisba's death at Scipio's request. The Roman general feared that the young man, heartbroken by the events, might feel his loyalty to Rome compromised, so called a *contio* from the tribunal.[62] In this military assembly, he reaffirmed Masinissa's position through a collection of diplomatic gifts.[63] As well as the material, he was honoured with a public *laudatio* in which it was explained to him that, for the Romans, the most magnificent distinction was the triumph, and that for those who triumphed, there was no more splendid award than that of which the people judged Masinissa worthy.[64] The scene described by Livy had the tribunal as its epicentre. This was an elevated platform situated in the *praetorium*, the latter being the physical space which was also partially occupied by the general's tent. Given the public character of the act and its solemnity, the *praetorium* and

---

[61] Livy 23.15.15.
[62] See on the *contiones* Pina Polo, 1989, esp. 199–205; 1995. Also cf. with studies of the *contiones* in Rome Morstein-Marx, 2004.
[63] This episode is discussed in the chapter by E. Sánchez Medina & G. Rosselló Calafell in this volume.
[64] Livy 30.15.11.

its immediate surroundings (the *principia*) would have been occupied by legionaries and allies, thronging the centre of the camp.

Conclusions

The Roman camp played a crucial role in the development of diplomatic and political relationships in the Roman Republic. Its itinerant nature was not a handicap when it came to establishing itself as a politico-diplomatic centre in the *provincia* of the general who, assisted by his *consilium*, liaised between local interlocuters and Rome. The symbiosis between the formal and the scenographic modulated the camp as a space of pressure and intimidation, but also of negotiation and the strengthening of ties, both personal and institutional.

The study of the topographical dimension of the camp/headquarters reveals the existence of a series of quarters and spaces that directly contributed to the politico-diplomatic protocol. Firstly, the negotiators arrived at the guard post, where they identified themselves and outlined the object of their mission, requesting an audience with the Roman general, for example in the case of the nobles from Capua (*stationi militum qui essent dixerunt*).[65]

With permission given and passage granted to all or part of the delegation, the emissaries entered the camp unarmed. The route probably taken by those dignitaries, individual emissaries or *legationes* would have been along the *via praetoria*, which was the most direct access to the commander's quarters. Already knowing of the request for an audience, the general convened the *consilium* (or not) depending on the object of the mission, and received the ambassadors in the *praetorium*. There, in the magistrate's tent, the interview was held, which usually took place behind closed doors, in private. On occasion, members of the same group would be interviewed individually. This is how the meeting unfolded between Alucius and his fiancée's relatives, who were called before the general consecutively and 'addressed him in more studied language than he had used towards the parents'.[66] In this way, the commander ensured he achieved different agreements according to the political exigencies of the moment.

The reception of embassies with the presence of the *consilium* took place in political contexts with a greater need for decision-making. The *consilium* accompanied the magistrate in his tent or outside in the *praetorium*, on the tribunal itself.

---

[65] Livy 24.47.12–13.
[66] Livy 26.50.3, trans. F. Gardner Moore.

Beyond interviews with individuals or small *legatio*-type groups, the camp was also the scene of large meetings of leaders summoned by Rome: fora for coordination, like *concilia*, were held, uniting representatives of numerous provincial cities in the camp. These types of fora were conducted in the *praetorium*, continuing the policy of restricted access.

In terms of a physical place for guarding gifts which were exchanged in the camp, the *quaestorium* should be mentioned. The offerings which were put into circulation in the camp were probably guarded in this space, since captured booty was also deposited there.[67] On the other hand, Polybius,[68] in a vague reference, suggests that booty was deposited in the open spaces that existed between the tents and the *vallum*.

In regard to the strictly political role of the camp, the importance of the *contiones* should be highlighted. These military assemblies were held in open spaces, such as the *principia* or the *forum*, where the general would mount the tribunal to convene them (*in tribunal escendit et contionem advocari iussit*).[69] Around these squares the troops would congregate, expectant before the words of their general, in a solemn and ceremonial act. This kind of ceremony was designed to illustrate Roman power. When allies contributed, it entailed for them a staging with a marked performative component of the military life and ceremony which took place in the camp after a victory, although their participation was passive and asymmetrical.

The political-diplomatic interactions which took place in the camp/headquarters frequently provided for the exchange of prestige goods. In these transactions, the Roman general positioned himself as the main protagonist, both receiving and bestowing gifts. The offerings in circulation ranged from golden wreaths to horses, via *curule* chairs and unspecified goods. People who were returned to their relatives through the protocol of the release of hostages/prisoners in order to reach an alliance or friendship with Rome were likewise considered gifts (*dona*).

Beyond the gifts' material and physical manifestations, there was a non-material sphere in which the goods offered were a service. These contributions could occur both outside and within the camp. Within the military compound, hospitality/banqueting took place which, probably, based on examples from the Imperial period, would have used the *praetorium* for that end. It should also be borne in mind that staying in military compounds was exceptional. On the other hand, free access to the

---

[67] Hyg. 18, 42.
[68] Polyb. 6.31.13.
[69] Livy 30.15.11.

praetorium emerged as both a political and a military privilege, a sign of distinction that demonstrated who had been received by the *imperator* in his tent, but above all as an attractive gift to recover goodwill.

Outside the camp, on the other hand, services were offered, such as acting as a guide, understood as a provision offered by an ally who had incurred a debt to the commander in an exchange of gifts or having established an alliance. Another service, on this occasion offered by the Roman commander, was escorting. In cases such as that of Masinissa's nephew, this gift implied not only a service to the young man, but also a powerful message to Masinissa, an important ally for Rome, which was added to the offering of physical gifts.

It is noticeable that taken together, all the agreements, exchanges, ceremonies and meetings demonstrate the importance of the four spaces within

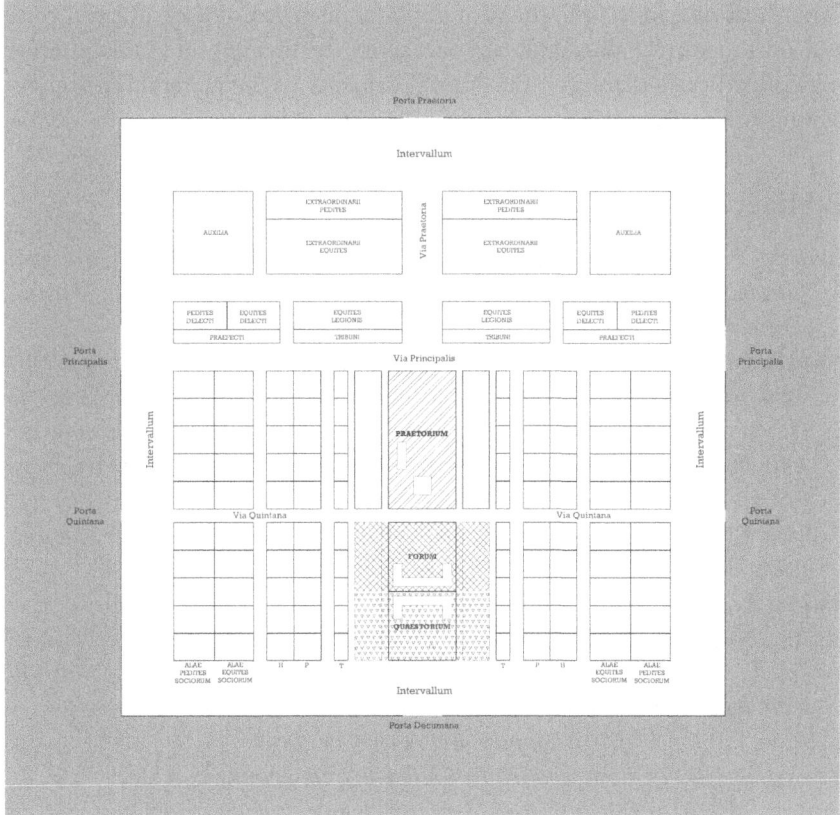

Figure 7.1 Diagram of the Roman Republican camp, based not only on archaeological evidence but also on literary sources, particularly Polybius, Livy and Appian (by the author).

the camp/headquarters that have been identified in this chapter – guard post, *praetorium, principia, forum* (Figure 7.1). These zones were structured as real stages where the progress of a function – in this case, politico-diplomatic – resulted in an alliance, a pact, a reward or an exchange of gifts; that is, a tangible result. The deployment of military spaces as hospitality for foreign leaders, as well as the deployment of military assemblies to reward allies, demonstrates the careful use of different spaces; their choice was neither random nor accidental, since the intention was to make an impression, to create a performance. The combination of private and public spaces by the commander in chief specifically for each of the ceremonies and meetings that took place in the camp demonstrates the multifunctionality of the military compound. It was not, however, only the material aspect that acquired a certain importance; as we have seen, the non-material was also revealed to be a unique characteristic within the camp/headquarters itself, functioning as an element of pressure and control on those new allies and, on occasions, reaffirming old collaborative networks. It also displayed the special capacity of the general for orchestrating and coordinating the political life of his *provincia*.

Bibliography

Álvarez Pérez-Sostoa, D. [2009]. *Los rehenes en la República romana: función social, política e ideológica (264–31)*. PhD dissertation, Vitoria-Gasteiz.

Álvarez Pérez-Sostoa, D. [2015]. '*Clementia* o "visión diplomática": devolución voluntaria de los cautivos en la República romana', in B. Grass & G. Stouder (eds), *La diplomatie romaine sous la République: réflexions sur une pratique. Actes des rencontres de Paris (21–22 juin 2013) et Genève (31 octobre–1er novembre 2013)*, Besançon, 107–26.

Auliard, C. [2009]. 'Cadeaux et marchandages diplomatiques à Rome jusqu'au debut de la conquête méditerranéenne', *Veleia*, 26, 63–73.

Austin, A. E. [1967]. *Scipio Aemilianus*, Oxford.

Austin, N. J. E. & Rankov, N. B. [2006]. *Exploratio: Military and Political Intelligence in the Roman World from the Second Punic War to the Battle of Adrianople*, London–New York.

Balsdon, J. P. V. D. [1979]. *Romans and Aliens*, London.

Braund, D. [1984]. *Rome and the Friendly King*, New York.

Burton, P. J. [2011]. *Friendship and Empire: Roman Diplomacy and Imperialism in the Middle Republic (353–146 BC)*, Cambridge.

Cadiou, F. [2008]. *Hibera in Terra Miles: les armées romaines et la conquête de l'Hispanie sous la République (218–45 av. J.-C.)*, Madrid.

Cadiou, F. & Moret, P. [2004]. 'Rome et la frontière hispanique à l'èpoque républicaine (IIe–Ier s. av. J.C.)', HAL Id: hal-00413651.

Campbell, D. B. [2018]. *Fortifying a Roman Camp: The Liber de munitionibus castrorum of Hyginus*, Glasgow.

Claudon, J.-F. [2015]. *Les ambassades des cités greques d'Asie Mineure auprès des autorités romaines: de la libération des Grecs à la fin du Haut-Empire (196 av. J.-C.–235 apr. J.-C.)*, PhD dissertation, École pratique des hautes études, Paris.

Díaz Fernández, A. [2015]. *Provincia et Imperium: el mando provincial en la República romana (227–44 a.C.)*, Seville.

Dobson, M. [2008]. *The Army of the Roman Republic: The Second Century BC, Polybius and the Camps at Numantia, Spain*, Oxford.

Dobson, M. [2013]. 'No Holiday Camp: The Roman Republican Army Camp as a Fine-Tuned Instrument of War', in J. DeRose Evans (ed.), *A Companion to the Archaeology of the Roman Republic*, Oxford, 214–34.

Eckstein, A. M. [2008]. *Rome Enters the Greek East: From Anarchy to Hierarchy in the Hellenistic Mediterranean, 230–170 BC*, Oxford.

Eckstein, A. M. [2009]. 'Ancient International Law, the Aetolian League, and the Ritual of Surrender during the Roman Republic: A Realist View', *International History Review*, 31 (2), 253–67.

García Riaza, E. [1997]. 'La función de los rehenes en la diplomacia hispano-romana', *Memorias de Historia Antigua*, 18, 81–107.

García Riaza, E. [2002]. *Celtíberos y Lusitanos frente a Roma: diplomacia y derecho de guerra*, Vitoria-Gasteiz.

García Riaza, E. [2006]. 'Rehenes y diplomacia en la Hispania romano-republicana', in G. Bravo & R. González Salinero (eds), *Minorías y sectas en el mundo romano: actas del III Coloquio de la Asociación Interdisciplinar de Estudios Romanos*, Madrid, 17–33.

García Riaza, E. (ed.) [2011]. *De fronteras a provincias: interacción e integración en Occidente (ss. III–I a.C.)*, Palma de Mallorca.

García Riaza, E. [2015]. 'Le protocole diplomatique entre particularisme romain et universalisme: quelques réflexions sur l'Occident républicain', in B. Grass & G. Stouder (eds), *La diplomatie romaine sous la République: réflexions sur une pratique*, Genoa, 15–41.

García Riaza, E. [2016]. 'Une institution politique dans le contexte de l'impérialisme romain: les *conuentus omnium sociorum* dans les références hispaniques de Tite-Live', *Ktéma* 41, 243–62.

García Riaza, E. [2020]. 'La supuesta contravención del *ius legationis* en el *bellum gallicum*', in E. Torregaray Pagola & J. Lanz Betelu (eds), *Algunas sombras en la diplomacia romana*, Vitoria-Gasteiz, 65–84.

García Riaza, E. [2021]. '*In conloqvivm venire*: Interviews between Roman Commanders and Western Leaders in the Age of Republican Expansion', in

A. Díaz Fernández (ed.), *Provinces and Provincial Command in Republican Rome: Genesis, Development and Governance*, Seville, 127–44.

García Riaza, E. & Sanz, A. M. (eds) [2019]. *In fidem venerunt: expresiones de sometimiento a la República Romana en Occidente*, Madrid.

Gilliver, C. M. [1993]. 'The *de munitionibus castrorum*: Text and Translation', *JRMES* 4, 33–48.

Grainger, J. D. [2017]. *Great Power Diplomacy in the Hellenistic World*, New York.

Grass, B. [2015]. 'Les présents diplomatiques à Rome (IIIe–Ier siècle av. J.-C.)', in B. Grass & G. Stouder (eds), *La diplomatie romaine sous la République: réflexions sur une pratique*, Genoa, 147–73.

Gruen, E. S. [1986]. *The Hellenistic World and the Coming of Rome*, Berkeley.

Hernández Prieto, E. [2019]. 'Las adhesiones hispanas a Escipión del 210–208 a.C. (Carthago Nova y Baecula)', in E. García Riaza & A.-M. Sanz (eds), *In fidem venerunt: expresiones de sometimiento a la República romana en Occidente*, Madrid, 27–57.

Hidalgo de la Vega, M. J. [1989]. 'El bronce de Lascuta: un balance historiográfico', *Studia historica: Historia Antigua*, 7, 59–66.

Johnston, P. D. [2008]. *The Military Consilium in Republican Rome*, Piscataway, NJ.

Kopij, K. & Pilch, A. [2019]. 'The Acoustics of *Contiones*, or How Many Romans Could Have Heard Speakers', *Open Archaeology*, 5, 340–9.

López Melero, R., García Jiménez Santiago, G. J. S. & Sánchez Abal, J. [1984]. 'El bronce de Alcántara: una *deditio* del 104 a.C.', *Gerión: Revista de Historia Antigua*, 2, 265–323.

Moret, P. [2002–3]. 'Los monarcas ibéricos en Polibio y Tito Livio', *CuPAUAM*, 28–9, 23–33.

Morillo Cerdán, A. [2008]. 'Criterios arqueológicos de identificación de los campamentos romanos en Hispania', *Saldvie* 8, 73–93.

Morillo Cerdán, A., Adroher, A., Dobson, M. & Martín Hernández, E. [2020]. 'Constructing the Archaeology of the Roman Conquest of Hispania: New Evidence, Perspectives and Challenges', *JRA*, 33, 36–52.

Morstein-Marx, R. [2004]. *Mass Oratory and Political Power in the Late Roman Republic*, Cambridge.

Nörr, D. [1989]. *Aspete des römischen Völkerrechts: die Bronzetafel von Alcántara*, Munich.

Pina Polo, F. [1989]. *Las contiones civiles y militares en Roma*, Zaragoza.

Pina Polo, F. [1995]. 'Procedures and Functions of Civil and Military *Contiones* in Rome', *Klio*, 77 (JG), 203–16.

Roselló Calafell, G. [2023]. *Relaciones exteriores y praxis diplomática cartaginesa: el período de las Guerras Púnicas* Saragossa/Seville.

Sánchez, P. [2016]. 'Quand Rome se cherchait de nouveaux alliés: les accords de coopération militaire négociés à l'initiative des Romains sur le théâtre des operations (IVe–IIIe s. av. n.è.)', *Ktéma*, 41, 165–90.

Sánchez Moreno, E. & García Riaza, E. (eds) [2019]. *Unidos en armas: coaliciones militares en el occidente antiguo*, Palma de Mallorca.

Sanz, A. M. [2015]. 'La *deditio*: un acte diplomatique au cœur de la conquête romaine', in B. Grass & G. Stouder (eds), *La diplomatie romaine sous la République: réflexions sur una pratique*, Genoa, 87–105.

Satlow, M. L. (ed.) [2013]. *The Gift in Antiquity*, Oxford.

Torregaray Pagola, E. [1998]. *La elaboración de la tradición sobre los Cornelii Scipiones: pasado histórico y conformación simbólica*, Zaragoza.

Torregaray Pagola, E. [2005]. 'Embajadas y embajadores entre Hispania y Roma en la obra de Tito Livio', in E. Torregary Pagola & J. Santos Yanguas (eds), *Diplomacia y autorepresentación en la Roma antigua*, Vitoria-Gasteiz, 25–62.

Torregaray Pagola, E. [2020]. 'Fracaso y oportunidad en la diplomacia de la República romana', in E. Torregary Pagola & J. Lanz Betelu (eds), *Algunas sombras en la diplomacia romana*, Vitoria-Gasteiz, 31–47.

Zecchini, G. [2005]. 'Ambasiate e ambasciatori in Polibio', in E. Torregary Pagola & J. Santos Yanguas (eds), *Diplomacia y autorepresentación en la Roma antigua*, Vitoria-Gasteiz, 11–23.

8

From Presents to Bribes
Symbolic and Political Evolution of the Diplomatic Gift in Relations between Romans and Numidians*

Esther Sánchez Medina and
Gabriel Roselló Calafell

Standing outside the North African context, the Romans did not perceive the political importance of the Numidian monarchs until 213 BC, when Livy reports the commission of an embassy of the Scipio brothers to Syphax, king of the Masaesylian Numidians.[1] Engulfed in the clamour of the Second Punic War in Hispania, the generals planned to destabilise the enemy by rocking the political chessboard and proposing an alliance to the king (*cum eo amicitiam societatemque facerent*).[2] Publius and Gnaeus hoped this manoeuvre would provide a robust counterweight to Carthaginian regional superiority.[3]

The Scipionic delegation constitutes the first known contact between Rome and the Numidians (*rex tres a Numidis legatos in Hispaniam misit ad accipiendam fidem*).[4] Livy claims that Syphax not only willingly accepted an alliance, but also persuaded one of the three centurions who led the delegation to agree to remain in his kingdom to train his soldiers in

---

* This work has been developed within the research project PGC2018-096415-B-C21 'La expresión diplomática en el Mediterráneo occidental bajo la expansión romana: el regalo en su contexto ideológico y cultural', funded by the State Research Agency, Ministry of Science and Innovation, Government of Spain (MCIN/AEI/10.13039/501100011033) and ERDF 'A way of making Europe'.
[1] Livy 24.48.1.
[2] It is not clear what initially induced the Roman commanders to involve themselves diplomatically with Numidia. Among the possible reasons are the intention of a future campaign in the territory, which their son and nephew would carry out years later; the destabilisation of the enemy's home environment; or the acquisition of military assistance as a counterbalance to the exhausting capability of the cavalry under the command of the enemy. Lancel, 1994: 357; Sanz, 2019: 60–2.
[3] Lancel, 1994: 357.
[4] Livy 24.48.1–10.

infantry tactics. The instruction of Quintus Statorius, the officer appointed to train the Africans, seems to have been among the conditions of the alliance, as Livy acknowledges (*ut pro bonis ac fidelibus sociis facerent*), but it is also arguably an offering made in the form of service. This may have been the first Roman diplomatic gift to a Numidian sovereign, a practice that would become common throughout the third and second centuries BC.

This first contact helped the high command of Rome to appreciate fully the importance of the Numidian kings in the competition with Carthage. As a result, from then onwards enticement of its kings became a specific diplomatic objective. In this sense, the Roman authorities sought to cultivate good institutional relations with the dual intention of destabilising the Carthaginian regions and obtaining profitable alliances for the provision of both military and frumentary resources.[5] These purposes would materialise through an indispensable tool: the diplomatic gift.

The collections of gifts presented to the Numidians between 210 and 148 BC suggest that Roman leaders planned their offers of gifts to the kings on the basis of certain tendencies. Firstly, and insofar as many of the gifts corresponded to objects of prestige within Roman society itself, they reveal the elite desire for self-representation. Togas, tunics, curule chairs[6] and gold rings were undoubtedly some of the distinctive features of the aristocracy.[7] Secondly, in the gift lots recorded in the literary sources, there are also allusions to the sovereignty of the monarchs (*apellatio regia*). Crowns and sceptres thus embodied the senate's recognition of the royal authority of both Syphax and Masinissa, who incorporated such symbols into their own iconography, as numismatics demonstrates.[8] Finally, the use of phalerated

---

[5] His *amicitia* with Rome prompted Masinissa to collaborate with the Romans on various occasions. In 200 BC, for example, coinciding with the Second Macedonian War, he sent 2,000 horsemen, of whom 1,000 were accepted, 200,000 *modii* of wheat and another 200,000 of barley (Livy 31.19.3–4). In 191, and in the context of the war against Antiochus, he offered 800,000 *modii* of wheat, 550,000 of barley, 500 horsemen and 20 elephants (Livy 36.4.8–9). Finally, his offering in the war against Perseus consisted of 1,000,000 *modii* of wheat, 1,200 horsemen and 15 elephants (Livy 43.6.13).

[6] Appian (*Pun.* 32) substitutes the curule chair for an ivory chariot in the gifts offered to Masinissa in 203 BC. This hypothesis is founded on a clarification by Aulus Gellius (*NA* 3.18.4): *Senatores enim dicit in veterum aetate, qui curulem magistratum gessissent, curru solitos honoris gratia in curiam vehi, in quo curru sella esset, superquam considerent, quae ob eam causam 'curulis' appellaretur.*

[7] Elliott, 2008: 182.

[8] Alexandropoulos, 2000.

horses, escorts and other military dignities suggests that Roman authority likewise sought to exalt the military nature of the Numidian kings.[9]

The first of the consignments of gifts designed to entice a Numidian sovereign travelled in 210 BC to Syphax, with the purpose of sanctioning the alliance inaugurated years earlier with the Scipiones (*ad commemorandam renovandamque amicitiam*). The conscript fathers presented the Masaesylian with a purple toga and tunic, an ivory chair and a five-pound gold *patera*.[10] Among other evidence, Dionysius of Halicarnassus[11] explains the symbolic value of such objects in the Roman imagination, in a text which enumerates the insignia of authority that Tarquin the Elder had adopted for the Etruscan monarchy, and which were later inherited by the rulers of the Republic.[12]

Among the gifts given to Syphax, the ivory chair, presumably to be identified with the curule chair, pointed to the *imperium* of the highest magistracies of Rome, while the *tunica purpurea* could have been the emblem of royalty, although not necessarily of Etruscan royalty. In this respect, it should be remembered that between the third and second centuries, the Romans assumed much of the symbolism displayed by the Hellenistic monarchies.[13] The purple, on the other hand, would also have fitted with the distinctive features of the Roman triumph (*ornamenta triumphalia*).[14]

The *dona* (gifts) conferred on Syphax therefore denoted a transfer of the 'language of power' by the Italian power to the African world. From the perspective of this chapter, in 210 BC the senate publicly recognised the sovereignty of the Masaesylian using a diplomatic gift, and it did so by wielding those distinctions that in Rome represented royalty and authority. To the *apellatio regia* can likewise be added the desire for self-representation of the elites themselves, who, by sending togas and curule chairs, were imposing their own codes on to those of the foreigners.

Roman affirmation of Syphax's sovereignty can also be inferred from other examples. It is striking, for example, that in the same passage Livy

[9] Roselló Calafell, 2021.
[10] Livy 27.4.8: *dona tulere togam et tunicam purpuream, sellam eburneam, pateram ex quinque pondo aurifactam*. The historical backdrop suggests relating this disbursement with Marcellus' pillaging of Syracuse only two years earlier. In this way, following the hypothesis proposed by Auliard (2009: 65–6) and Coudry (2009: 162–74), some of the booty obtained by the Roman generals could have been intended for the completion of strategic alliances.
[11] Dion. Hal. *Ant. Rom.* 3.61.1.
[12] That is, the gold crown, the ivory throne, the sceptre, purple and gold (Reinhold, 1971).
[13] Reinhold, 1969: 303.
[14] Abaecherly Boyce, 1942: 130; Lemcke, 2012.

notes that the *patres* dispatched in parallel a delegation of the highest level to Ptolemy IV and Cleopatra of Egypt,[15] aligning both monarchies on the same political horizon.[16] It does not seem trivial, in this respect, that the Egyptian sovereigns were also presented with an ivory chair and with purple: more than sufficient evidence to suspect that this represents a new *modus operandi* of Roman diplomacy, which from 210 BC arrogated to itself the power and privilege of presenting its 'international' recognition upon the legitimacy of foreign kings.[17]

This hypothesis is reinforced by the fact that Syphax himself seems to have assimilated into his iconography the profile of a Hellenistic monarch from his contacts with the Romans, as the numismatic record reflects. The Masaesylian issued different series in two periods, coinciding with the stages of his relationship with Rome.[18] The images of the first series of coins depict him without a diadem and as a military leader, a knight in battle. At a second point, nevertheless, with a *terminus post quem* of 213 BC, and

---

[15] Livy 27.4.5–10. As well as the value of the presents, the rank of the *legati* sent for this reason confirms this. Lucius Genucius, Publius Poetelius and Publius Popillius Laenas attended Syphax's kingdom. Greater dignity seems to have been given to the delegation sent to Alexandria, constituted by Marcus Atilius Regulus, praetor in 213 BC, and Manius Acilius Glabrio, possibly consul in 191 BC. Broughton, 1951–2: 283, supp. 1.

[16] Livy 27.4.8. The Egyptian rulers were rewarded with a toga, a purple tunic, an ivory chair, an embroidered *palla* and a purple cloak.

[17] It is important to note that there is no earlier record of the senate offering gifts of such quality to foreign kings. Until then, and with few exceptions, the gifts sent by the Romans had been of a religious nature, including in that same third century (Auliard, 2009: 64–6). It should therefore be asked what the reasons were that brought them to offer *dona* that were so generous and highly imbued with politico-diplomatic significance, and why this behaviour seems to have continued over time. One of the keys may be found in Rome's active participation in Greek affairs after the Pyrrhic War. In 280, Gaius Fabricius had already rejected – in Plutarch's opinion – the gift offered by the Epirote monarch as a symbol of friendship and hospitality: φιλίας δέ τι καὶ ξενίας ἐπονομάζων τοῦτο σύμβολον (Plut. *Pyrrh.* 20.1; App. *Sam.* 10.4). Seven years later, there were senators who refused to accept the offerings sent to Rome by Ptolemy II following their victory over Pyrrhus (Zonar. 8.6.11). The Hellenistic model brought to the senate's attention a system of external relationships in which exchanges of courtesy in order to consolidate alliances, strengthen connections or initiate close diplomatic ties were very important (Veyne, 1973: 834–5; Auliard, 2009: 64). Rome, therefore, would have started to associate closely the offering of presents with its diplomatic relationships of φιλία-*amicitia* with other states (Konstan, 1997: 122–4; Burton, 2003; 2011: ch. 4; Verboven, 2014: 150–1), strengthening bonds of hospitality inspired by ξενία (Mitchell, 1998; Herman, 2002; Burton, 2011: 164–72; Basile, 2016; Lenfant, 2017).

[18] Decret & Fantar, 1981: 83.

Figure 8.1 Coin attributed to Syphax, minted between 213 and 202 BC. Mazard's *CNNM*, n. 12.

therefore assimilable with the increasing closeness of his *amicitia* with the Scipiones, the sovereign appears already endowed with the insignia of power of the Hellenistic monarchies, the royal diadem being perfectly identifiable (Figure 8.1).[19] As Alexandropoulos has observed, there are solid arguments for claiming a relationship between Syphax's political evolution and coin typology.[20] In fact, the Masaesylian's evolution as a Hellenistic king seems to have been continued through his son Vermina. Syphax's death in Rome and the fall of Cirta to Masinissa at the end of the conflict with Hannibal did not, therefore, put an end to Syphax's line,[21] something that Appian confirms when he points out that the scion retained hegemony over a large part of his father's territory.[22]

The relative successes of the diplomatic strategy with Syphax and the economic solvency generated by the successful course of the Second Punic

---

[19] Müller, 1860: 32; *SNG* Cop 491–2; *CNNM* 12, Type Sear 6632; Gozalbes Cravioto, 2015: 83–4.

[20] Alexandropoulos, 2000. On Syphax's political evolution in relation to his ties with Rome: Sanz, 2019.

[21] Livy 30.12; Aragón Gómez, 2015: 72; Prados Martínez, 2015: 24.

[22] App. *Pun*. 73. In this respect, Vermina's negotiations with the senate in 200 BC (Livy 31.11.13–18, 31.19.4–6), seeking to obtain the status of *amicus*, bore fruit which allowed that monarch to enjoy a long reign. This fact is also corroborated by numismatics, which provides evidence for up to three periods of minting, two of them in silver, in contrast to his father's reign, for which only bronze has been identified. His coins also follow the same tendency as Syphax's, displaying use of the diadem (Gozalbes Cravioto, 2015: 86).

War led the Romans to follow the same path with other Numidian dignitaries.[23] It should be remembered that in the same year, 210 BC, *togae praetextae* and golden *paterae* were given to other regional *reguli*.[24] The diplomatic gift also played a critical role in closer ties with the Massilian kingdom in eastern Numidia. This would explain the value of the *dona* given by Scipio to Massiva in 208 BC, from the booty of the camp abandoned by Hasdrubal,[25] the purpose of which was not to secure the young man's affection, but rather the achievement of a coalition with his grandfather Gala, which would eventually materialise in the person of Masinissa.[26] Among the gifts, the golden ring can be related to aristocracy, while the harnessed horse and the escort, in addition to their obvious pragmatic character, perhaps expressed recognition of the bellicose nature of Numidian royalty.

Self-representation, *apellatio regia* and affirmation of the social values of the foreigner are seen more strongly in the relations between Rome and Masinissa. Syphax's flirtations with Carthage[27] and the burgeoning bonds of loyalty between Masinissa and Scipio in Hispania[28] eventually determined a marked preference for Masinissa when the latter claimed the right to Gala's throne in 205 BC. Such deductions are perfectly observable in the coronation ceremony that Africanus organised for the Numidian in 203, immediately after the fall of Syphax at the Battle of the Great Plains. Livy describes the *imperator* entertaining Masinissa in his camp from atop a tribunal during an assembly (*in tribunal escendit et contionem aduocari iussit*).[29] The solemnity was then ratified by the presentation of luxurious gifts: a golden wreath, a golden *patera*, a curule chair, an ivory

---

[23] In their behaviour with the foreign dignitaries, we witness a new scenario in which the Romans are the ones who give gifts, refusing to receive them reciprocally. This conduct may be understood within the belief that the gift is also a sign of status, conferring greater moral dignity upon the one who gives it: Reinhold, 1969; Muñiz Coello, 1998: 27; Verboven, 2002: 75–9; Auliard, 2009: 64.

[24] Livy 27.4.9.

[25] Livy 27.19.9; Val. Max. 5.1.7.

[26] Livy himself (27.19.12) recalls that the young man was the grandson of Gala and nephew of Masinissa.

[27] Livy 29.23. The king was finally constrained to embrace the alliance with the Carthaginians thanks to his engagement to Sophonisba, the daughter of Hasdrubal, son of Gisgo.

[28] Livy 28.35.1. The friendly relationship between Masinissa and the Scipiones would last until the king's death in 148. The Massilian, in fact, nominated Scipio Aemilianus as his executor, an honour that the young general accepted, dividing the kingdom and its riches between both legitimate and illegitimate sons (App. *Pun.* 106).

[29] Livy 30.15.11–14.

sceptre, a *toga picta* and a *tunica palmata*.³⁰ It cannot be coincidence that the senate revalidated the initiative of its general by dispatching a distinguished embassy bearing exquisite gifts to the Numidian king.³¹

In considering the possible significance of the *dona* given to Masinissa, it is noticeable that the Roman leaders acted according to the same predispositions as they had in the case of Syphax. In this case, moreover, they seem to have gone a step further by bestowing upon the Masaesylian a golden wreath³² and ivory sceptre, unmistakable representations of Hellenistic royalty. There is consequently no doubt that through gifts, Rome sought to legitimise local dynasts,³³ attempting to build a web of diplomatic relationships based on political dependence which would last over time.³⁴

The symbolic value and importance of the diplomatic gift dispensed to Masinissa is confirmed by the fact that he, like Syphax, seems to have designed his coins based around the dignities conceded by Rome. The coins attributed to his reign therefore represent him as a Hellenistic monarch,³⁵ with his head crowned in laurel and a sceptre in his hand,³⁶ perhaps representing the *eburnei Scipiones* that Africanus and the senate had given him.

---

³⁰ The *toga picta* and the *tunica palmata* were worn by the general in his triumph (Livy 10.7.9; Flor. 1.5.6).

³¹ Livy 30.17.13–14. The *legatio* consisted of two ex-praetors and an ex-consul: Gaius Terentius Varro (*cos.* 216; *praet.* 218), Spurius Lucretius (*praet.* 205) and Gnaeus Octavius (*praet.* 205). Broughton, 1951–2: 327.

³² Which in Livy's version was offered in 203 BC by Scipio, while the senate did so in Appian's.

³³ Something which is seen not only in their conduct towards Numidian royalty. In 172 the senate once again distinguished a foreign king, Eumenes of Pergamum, with royal insignia, offering the Attalid the most splendid presents, among them a curule chair and an ivory sceptre (Livy 42.14.10). Not long afterwards, in 160 BC, the conscript fathers showed their appreciation to Ariarathes, offering him an ivory throne (Polyb. 32.1.3). It is also reasonable to think that this praxis endured over time, as can be observed during Caesar's meeting with Ariovistus, when Caesar claimed that the concession of the title of king and friend, and the dispatch of splendid gifts, was a distinction assigned by the senate to very few deserving leaders, regardless of the real value that Rome and its magistrates gave to the content of this declaration of intentions in each situation.

³⁴ As is evidenced by the enduring nature of the alliance with Masinissa (Walsh, 1965: 161).

³⁵ An attitude that other documentary evidence echoes. Statues were erected in his honour in Delos (*IG* XI.4 1115–16); he established alliances with Rhodes, Nicomedes II Epiphanes and Ptolemy VIII Euergetes; his son, Mastanabal, participated in the Panathenaic Games (*IG* II.2 968.41–4), and both he and Micipsa studied Greek (Livy, *Per.* 50), the latter being a good student of philosophy (Diod. Sic. 34.5). Walsh, 1965: 155; Saumagne, 1966.

³⁶ Mazard, 1955: 30 n. 17, 31 n. 18.

Figure 8.2 Coin attributed to Masinissa, minted between 203 and 148 BC. Mazard's *CNNM*, n. 60.

Another coin series displays his head bearing a diadem on the obverse and a rampant horse in front of a palm on the reverse (Figure 8.2).[37] The diadem was an unmistakable symbol of the Hellenistic monarchs,[38] and the vegetal relief could have embodied the iconography of the *palmata tunica* worn by triumphing generals.[39]

The capture of Carthage in 146 BC marked a turning point in Rome's relationship with the African realms. Having eliminated its perennial Carthaginian enemy, Rome lost interest in Africa, including in that part which, having become a province that same year, remained at its disposal. This new scenario, however, did not involve total indifference towards the fate of the Numidians, as is demonstrated by the fact that Rome, through Scipio Aemilianus, was guarantor of Masinissa's will. Understanding the Roman Republic's diplomatic practices in the north of the continent of Africa during the second half of the second century necessarily implies a profound understanding of the power relationships that the Africans were developing in the area of what would later be the Roman provinces of

[37] The horse here would allude to the warlike character of the Numidian monarchy (Mazard, 1955: n. 60).
[38] Livy (27.31.4) emphasises this when he refers to Philip V in 214: *eo magis etiam quod populariter dempto capitis insigni purpuraque atque alio regio habitu aequaverat ceteris se in speciem*. For the relationship between the diadem and the crown as royal insignia: Suet. *Iul.* 79.1. In the case of *coronae*, the Roman biographer specifies, in an allusion to the ornamentation on a statue of Caesar, that for them to be considered royal insignia, they have to be tied with a white ribbon (*candida fascia praeligata*).
[39] Livy 30.15.11–12, 31.11.12.

Numidia and the *Mauretaniae*. For that reason, therefore, it is essential to analyse the evolution of the local powers and the various internal conflicts that affected their relationship with Rome. Without doubt, the integration of the Numidian, and later Mauretanian, powers was to a large extent due to their participation as troops in the Roman army. Relations, however, went further, since *amicitia*, through which a new political framework was established, also meant that Rome's various internal conflicts found expression in Africa. It may be said that the territorial problems that had gripped Numidia during the Second Punic War,[40] with Syphax and Masinissa as its main spatial defenders, cast a long shadow across the whole of the following century.[41]

Although little information has remained to us on the subject, the locals must have continued to seek Rome's approval in the period between wars. This can be deduced from Livy's account for 169 BC, in which animals from Africa – panthers, lions, elephants and ostriches – who knows whether as gifts? – were used in a *venatio* in the capital: in Gsell's words, 'un excellent moyen de se concilier la sympathie du peuple de Rome'.[42] Africa's main contribution, however, if not its most spectacular, was that of men, logistics and supplies for military contingents, necessary in the many wars that Rome waged across the Mediterranean at that time: Numidian cavalry, elephants and grain in the Second Macedonian War (200–197 BC) and in the war against Antiochus in 191 BC; cavalry and infantry, elephants and grain again in the Third Macedonian War; cavalry and elephants in the Celtiberian Wars; soldiers and elephants in the Third Punic War; elephants and cavalry against Viriathus in 141 BC; cavalry, infantry, elephants, archers and slingers in the war against Numantia in 134 BC.[43] This frequent military interaction necessarily involved continuity of diplomatic activity, which in the case of Africa, however, seems to fade for a few decades –

---

[40] In this respect, it is worth highlighting the attempt to usurp the Massilian throne in 206 BC (Thompson, 1981: 120–6).

[41] The Massilians had constituted an important support for Carthage during the Second Punic War, between 211 and 206 BC, under Masinissa and, especially in 208 BC, through the dispatch of Massiva and his men as Carthaginian reinforcements at the Battle of Baecula (Polyb. 3.33.15). All this was in the context of the unstoppable territorial expansion of Syphax, who, allied to Rome, represented a growing threat (Livy 24.48–9), which ultimately obliged the Massilians to change sides and ally with Rome in 206 BC (Sall. *Iug.* 5). From the beginning of the relationship with the Africans, the Massilians were considered changeable in their loyalties (Sall. *Iug.* 46.4: *genus Numidarum esse infidum, ingenio mobili, avidum rerum novarum*).

[42] Gsell, *HAAN* 3: 311–12; Livy 39.22 and 44.18; Plaut. *Persa* 199; *Poen.* 1011–12; this referred to the *venatio* offered by the aedile P. Cornelius Scipio Nasica Corculum.

[43] Bridoux, 2020: 156–7.

probably reflecting the state of our sources[44] – then to regain enormous importance at the end of the century and especially during the so-called Jugurthine War.

It seems clear that from the Second Punic War, Numidian royal authority had based its power and prestige on the network of diplomatic relations that it had managed to weave with the principal Mediterranean powers: Carthage and Rome. This had led, as has been demonstrated above, not only to close collaboration but also to the assumption of a series of external signs – coin iconography, royal building, titulatures etc. – that brought its image notably closer to that of the other Hellenistic monarchies that circled the eastern Mediterranean. This new system did not, therefore, imply only the provision of military support, but also the recognition of status. The dependence generated by the ties that the *amicitia* between the African dignitaries and the main military commanders sent by Rome required served in turn to reinforce personal power and, above all, the legitimisation of territorial interests.

Two pieces of evidence can illustrate this process of legitimisation. The first, in Appian,[45] describes Scipio overseeing the correct execution of Masinissa's will. Upon the death of the latter in 148, there was a profound transformation in the way Numidian power was transferred: the conventional agnatic formula was not used, but instead a mixed dynastic transmission was intended, which would bring notable consequences over the following decades. This also occurred upon the death of Micipsa, Masinissa's son, some decades later.[46] The new succession formula, alien to the Numidian world, must have been concocted by the senate to serve Roman interests, as it was as far removed from the traditional agnatic system as it was from primogeniture.[47] In order to purify the royal succession, Masinissa's illegitimate sons – born of concubines – were banished from the crown, after receiving considerable possessions from the hands of Scipio himself, while the three legitimate sons would reign together. The heirs did not receive specific territories, but rather different functions of

---

[44] The gap is especially obvious in the case of Mauretania, to the point of it being impossible to know even minimally about the evolution of African politics until the appearance of Bocchus I at the end of the second century, in the context of the Jugurthine War.
[45] App. *Pun.* 105.
[46] Lassère, 2010. We know this custom thanks to a text in Livy (29.29.6) in which he claims, in relation to Gala's succession in 206, that this was the custom among the Numidians. We also have evidence of events at the end of Masinissa's reign (Camps, 1960: 214–15).
[47] Camps, 1960: 232.

government: Micipsa was given the administration of Numidia and control of Cirta, its capital; Gulussa received *imperium* over the armies; and Mastanabal held the administration of justice. This experiment was short-lived, as the death of the two younger brothers made Micipsa sole ruler.[48]

The second piece of evidence is recorded by Sallust, on the disbanding of auxiliary troops after the Roman victory over the besieged Numantia in 133 BC. One of the Numidians who had supported Scipio, Jugurtha,[49] accepted numerous *dona* from the general, but above all received advice that would arguably mark his political development and, above all, his future disagreements with Rome: *secreto monuit ut potius publice quam privatim amicitiam populi Romani coleret neu quibus largiri insuesceret; periculose a paucis emi, quod multorum esset* ('In private he advised the young man to cultivate the friendship of the Roman people through official channels rather than through powerbrokers, and not to form the habit of bribery. It was dangerous, he said, to buy from a few what belonged to the many').[50]

It seems clear that Rome considered Jugurtha – as well as a military asset in his own right – a useful card in the power game that would break out in Numidia upon the death of Micipsa and therefore, perhaps, believed it necessary to recognise him beyond the private relationship that linked him to Scipio.[51] The letter the general sent to Micipsa seems to demonstrate this, in which he suggested to the monarch that he improve his nephew's position.[52] Jugurtha would achieve the status of heir and king after his uncle's death – although not alone, but alongside his cousins Hiempsal

---

[48] App. *Pun.* 502.

[49] Camps & Chaker, 2004. Jugurtha was the illegitimate son of one of Micipsa's younger brothers, the deceased Mastanabal.

[50] Sall. *Iug.* 8.2. Prior to his discharge, Jugurtha's mind had already been inflamed with the promise of rule by some nobles and *novi homines* (8.1: *fore uti solus imperi Numidae*). On the role of aristocratic *avaritia* and corruption, the works by Salinas de Frías, 2008 and 2010, are of particular interest. The frequent references to the venality of power cast a shadow of doubt over Aemilianus' staff, whose members Jugurtha must have befriended during the Numantine campaign (Salinas de Frías, 2010: 17–19).

[51] Sall. *Iug.* 7.6: *habere in amicis, magis magisque eum in dies amplecti, quippe cuius neque consilium neque inceptum ullum erat frustra.*

[52] Sall. *Iug.* 9. Jugurtha's consideration as the heir to the throne is somewhat controversial since, on the one hand, it seems to have been approved after Scipio's letter, but on the other, following the evidence of Sall. *Iug.* 11.6, it seems to have taken place in 121. It has been suggested that in 132 there was an adoption and recognition of Micipsa as heir, accommodating Rome's petition, while almost a decade later Jugurtha's right to the Numidian throne was recognised (Paul, 1984: 42).

and Adherbal, which would prove a significant obstacle to his ambitions. The assassination of the former and the flight of the latter to Africa and later to Rome left Jugurtha in a difficult position in relation to the senate, the favour of whose members he managed to win through bribery, something which was common throughout the conflict.[53] Adherbal, who recognised himself as a mere administrator of Numidia on behalf of Rome, found therein no guarantee at all of his rights, since Jugurtha, using his *privata amicitia*, managed to neutralise the punishment that should have been imposed upon him, given that the Republic was obliged to offer suitable protection for the Numidian prince. On the contrary, Jugurtha, in the immediate territorial distribution sanctioned by Rome, and again by bribing Lucius Opimius[54] and the ambassadors, achieved an advantageous outcome.[55] At this important political moment, when Rome had sent *legati* to Numidia – among them an ex-consul – we find none of the symbolic elements previously used to recognise Numidian power, nor even to display effective self-representation of the Roman elites in the African territories.

The division of Numidia only managed to stimulate Jugurtha's desire to possess the whole kingdom. In the face of his cousin's inaction, he therefore immediately besieged Cirta.[56] Given the city's importance in creating a legitimate image of his reign, as well as the difficulties of the siege, he had no qualms about trying to buy the goodwill of the Cirtans during the siege of the *urbs regia*.[57] Jugurtha's clear disregard for Rome's provisions – *legatorum verba*[58] – led Adherbal besieged in Cirta to request his liberation *per maiestatem imperi, per amicitiae fidem*,[59] via an embassy to Rome in which he called for protection for his legitimacy. The senate was not nonchalant about the Cirtan crisis, organising a new, higher-ranking embassy

---

[53] Sall. *Iug.* 13.6: *cum auro et argento multo Romam legatos mittit, quis praecipit, primum uti veteres amicos muneribus expleant, deinde novos adquirant, postremo quaecumque posiint largiundo parare ne cunctentur.*

[54] Consul in 121 BC, he was accused of accepting bribes and exiled to the Albanian Dyrrachium (Plut. *C. Gracch.* 18.1). Gsell (*HAAN* 7: 147) believes that the embassy took place in 117 and not in 116 as is generally believed.

[55] Sall. *Iug.* 16.1; 3–4. He also mentions the gifts (*munera*) given to the *legati* in 201 BC. In terms of the land distribution, Jugurtha received western Numidia – fertile and populated – while Adherbal received the east – ports and buildings – which undoubtedly was more useful to Rome and its commercial aspirations, being more urbanised and possessing the principle commercial centres.

[56] Cirta's importance in the construction of the Numidian monarchs' legitimacy has already been demonstrated by Bridoux (2020: 121).

[57] Sall. *Iug.* 23.1: *praemia*.

[58] Sall. *Iug.* 24.7.

[59] Sall. *Iug.* 24.10.

under Aemilius Scaurus,⁶⁰ ex-consul and *princeps senatus*, who sent for Jugurtha *in provinciam*,⁶¹ clearly marking his status and the Numidian's obligations to Rome. At this point, the diplomatic language rose and the gravity of the conflict demanded a direct dialogue on Roman territory. This was also supported by the simultaneous embassy of Jugurtha's son to Rome, with the motto *omnis mortales pecunia aggrediantur* ('To go on the offensive with money against every mortal'),⁶² which, however, reaped terrible failure, as the legates were expelled from Italy by order of the senate. Neither the emissaries sent with money to Bestia, nor the large sum given to Scaurus, nor indeed the actions carried out in the Italian capital through *pretio et gratia* (payment or favour) seemed to have obtained any result.⁶³ Jugurtha was even forced to hand over a quantity of wheat, as well as thirty elephants,⁶⁴ cattle, many horses and a small amount of money to buy a truce that would win him some time.⁶⁵ In the end, the Numidian achieved an advantageous capitulation thanks to the numerous bribes given to the Romans and the fact that Bestia left Africa to prepare elections in Rome.⁶⁶

With stalemate in the war, Sallust's account introduces new agents into the conflict's diplomatic game, with other candidates to the Numidian throne trying to assert their lineage. Massiva,⁶⁷ son of Gulussa and grandson

---

⁶⁰ According to Aur. Vict. *De vir. ill.* 72.4, he had resisted Jugurtha's pretensions to the Numidian throne, although later he too was corrupted by bribery: *praetor adversus Iugurtham, tamen eius pecunia victus*.

⁶¹ Sall. *Iug.* 25.10.

⁶² Sall. *Iug.* 28.1.

⁶³ Sall. *Iug.* 29.

⁶⁴ Those elephants were sold back to Jugurtha, Sallust relates (*Iug.* 32.3).

⁶⁵ The payment of bribes was not only made to generals, but also attempted with centurions and squadron leaders, as can be gathered from some Sallustian references (*Iug.* 38.3 and with greater detail 38.6: a cohort of Ligurians as well as two squadrons of Thracians and a few private soldiers defected to the king, and the chief centurion of the third legion allowed the enemy to penetrate the fortification that he had been appointed to defend). On the Ligurian participation in the war, Frasson, 2012, esp. 1353. It is likely that those corrupt Ligurians who had facilitated the Numidian victory can be identified as the deserters from Aulus' army – Ligurians and Thracians – who were handed over to Metellus in 108 and whose bloody end is related by Appian (*Num.* 3).

⁶⁶ Sall. *Iug.* 27–9, 32.2, 85.16; Livy, *Per.* 64; Plut. *Mar.* 9.3; Flor. 1.36.7; Eutr. 4.26.1; Oros. 5.15.4.

⁶⁷ He had sought refuge in Rome after Cirta's submission and Adherbal's death. Spurius Postumius Albinus, consul in 110 BC, and by then holding command over Africa, seems to have persuaded Massiva to request before the senate that the kingdom of Numidia be handed over. Flor. 1.36.8; Diod. Sic. *FHG* II, pp. xxii, xxviii considers Massiva a 'second Jugurtha' and claims that his demand was very well received in

of Masinissa, and, later, Gauda, son of Mastanabal and second heir in Micipsa's will, and finally Dabar, son of Masugrada, also of Masinissa's line, thus actively sought support from Rome that could help them to attain the Numidian throne or, at least, some kind of political recognition.

Although it is not the most representative case for analysis of the diplomatic gift in the context studied, perhaps Massiva's is the clearest example of a threat to Jugurtha's legitimacy, as he is the only one of the three candidates who provoked direct and immediate intervention by Jugurtha, who ordered his assassination. This conflict must have been an old one and perhaps entailed a greater threat than historiography has hitherto considered. The abovementioned *dissensio*, to which Sallust alludes,[68] did not pertain only between Micipsa's three recognised heirs, but also between other candidates, as demonstrated by the overlooked datum about the existence of 'second heirs' (such as Gauda) in the king's will. On the other hand, the mere fact of Jugurtha being in Rome again at the moment when Massiva's rights were vindicated – in 111 BC – is evidence of the vicissitudes his position must have been suffering and his need to earn the support of the senate, which was still not certain despite the constant bribes. Jugurtha's weakness increased decisively following the emergence of the new candidate, since his emissaries no longer appeared as ambassadors before Metellus, the new general in charge of the war in Africa, but as supplicants in a constant game of promises and counter-promises that seemed to herald the final negotiation and Jugurtha's submission to Rome.[69] From this point on, diplomatic relations seem to have evolved on two different levels even more indisputably. On the one hand, they continued to be held in the usual space for public dialogue, while at the same time, private negotiations – what was promised to the emissaries individually and secretly – gained in importance.

Massiva's assassination on the orders of Bomilcar, Jugurtha's right-hand man, seems to have blown the Numidian's position out of the water in Rome, a city from which he was expelled, for although his action was not precisely against the *ius gentium*, it did violate Roman morality and

---

Rome. On the other hand, it should be pointed out that his original name (*MSWi*) probably indicates a function (of government), according to Chaker, 1986: 552 and also Galand, 1997: 59.

[68] Sall. *Iug.* 12.1.
[69] Sall. *Iug.* 46.2 and 4. Similarly, there were also movements reversing the *fides* owed to Jugurtha, since various prefects of Numidia, of cities and *mapalibus* – a clear allusion to tribal structures – revealed themselves to be favourable towards Metellus, to whom they offered grain and provisions (46.5; 54.6 also includes the surrender of hostages).

justice.⁷⁰ Against this immorality, Metellus offered Bomilcar impunity, but no recognition beyond the maintenance of his property, and all that so long as he betrayed Jugurtha.⁷¹ At the same time, the general terms of surrender were also publicly negotiated with Jugurtha himself: 200,000 pounds of silver, all the elephants, horses and arms.⁷²

With Massiva eliminated, there remained two opponents to Jugurtha's power, Gauda and Dabar.⁷³ The first of these is really the one who offers the most interesting information in relation to the subject of analysis proposed in these pages. Gauda was the son of Mastanaba, the Mastanabal of the Latin sources, and therefore the grandson of Masinissa, as well as half-brother of Jugurtha, with whom he struggled for power. Although he was not included in the shortlist of three chosen by Micipsa to rule after his death, Gauda had been recognised as a crown prince, perhaps to rule after the three appointed kings or in case any of them disappeared (it should be noted that by this time Hiempsal and Adherbal had already been assassinated). Removed from power due to health problems and, according to Sallust, low intelligence, he found himself in the service of the Republic, as Jugurtha had been some time before.

The aspirant took into consideration the diplomatic language that Rome had imposed during the second century, which led him to solicit from Metellus the concession of an important honour: to take a seat (*sella*) next to the general – a position of the highest prestige – as well as to receive an escort, made up of a unit of citizen cavalry (*turma equitum romanorum*).⁷⁴ This evidence, which has passed largely unnoticed by scholars, seems to offer the interpretative key to what the real Numidian conflict must have

---

⁷⁰ Sall. *Iug.* 35.9–10.
⁷¹ Sall. *Iug.* 61.4. There is another case in which Metellus seems to have negotiated a reward personally, but secretively: Nabdalsa, Jugurtha's secretary, was bribed with *praemia Metelli* (Sall. *Iug.* 70.5).
⁷² Those charged with studying the proposal were the members of the senate who belonged to the provincial *consilium*, as well as *aliorum, quos ducebat idoneos* (Sall. *Iug.* 62.4).
⁷³ Very little information survives about this person. He was considered of a lower status because his father was born to a concubine. He was sent as Bocchus' ambassador to Sulla to demonstrate his conformity to the will of the Roman people. His supposed intermediation (*internuntius vir sanctus et ex sententia ambobus*) could also have included a veiled proposal for a new candidate for the eastern Numidian throne, once Jugurtha was defeated. The respect shown by Bocchus towards the pre-existing pact with Micipsa, through which he recovered the pre-war territorial status quo, was in fact sanctioned in the presence of Dabar at the time the agreement with the *mauri* was ratified with Sulla.
⁷⁴ Sall. *Iug.* 65.1.

been, especially if we consider Metellus' refusal to Gauda: *honorem, quod, eorum modo foret, quos populus Romanus reges appellavisset* ('[he denied] the honour on the ground that by custom it belonged only to those who had been formally recognised as kings by the Romans').[75] The general's reply, besides being humiliating, must have provoked what was undoubtedly a very intelligent reaction on the part of Gauda, who took refuge in a new pact with Marius, then legate in Africa but later consul charged with the conflict. Finally, in 105 BC, when the war with Jugurtha was over, Gauda was recognised as monarch of the Numidians by senatorial sanction, as a reward for his loyalty to Rome, as he had been promised by the *popularis*.[76] It seems clear that Metellus and Marius did not share the same plans for the government of post-Jugurthine Numidia.

With regard to Gauda's request, it is perhaps essential to consider the importance of the honours requested and their relationship with the legitimacy they could confer on him. The first of these, the *sella* and with it the proximity to Roman power embodied in the general,[77] bore a clear correspondence with the recognition of his status as king (*more regum*), something we know not only from Metellus' brusque response, but also from the concession made to Masinissa in 203 BC, a time when Rome gave him not only the curule chair but also a set of objects including a golden crown, an ivory sceptre etc.[78] It is clear that the gifts had an intrinsic significance (material, social and symbolic) and an extrinsic one, especially symbolic, as they functioned within certain sets, as seems to be the case here.[79] This was not a mere juxtaposition of objects/honours, but a semantic conjunction

---

[75] Sall. *Iug.* 65.2.
[76] Sall. *Iug.* 65.3: *illum regem, ingentem virum, Masinissae nepotem esse; si Iugurtha captus aut occisus foret, imperium Numidiae sine mora habiturum*. Gauda's reign was long, as it must have continued until 88, when the reign of his son, Hiempsal II, is recorded in Plut. *Mar.* 40.
[77] Gell. *NA* 3.18.4.
[78] The set of gifts offered to Masinissa is the most complete of those we know: golden crown, golden *patera*, ivory sceptre, embroidered toga, tunic decorated with palms, purple cloaks, gold *fibulae*, purple-bordered tunics, horses decorated with *phalerae*, equestrian armour with cuirasses, military tents, military equipment (Livy 30.15.11–12 and 17.13–14; App. *Pun.* 32). Barely a decade earlier, Syphax had also received an ivory chair, among other gifts (Livy 27.4.8–9). Vermina's request for the throne of his father, Syphax, after his capture and imprisonment in Italy seems to confirm the royal status of the gifts the latter had previously received (Livy 31.11.13).
[79] We have other evidence that horses were given without any appreciable relationship with the recognition of royalty (in 208, to Massiva, nephew of Masinissa, Livy 27.19.12; in 170 to Masinissa's ambassadors, Livy 43.6.13; in 168 to Masinissa's sons, Livy 45.13.13 and 17).

that has not always been evaluated in its proper importance. On the other hand, as previously articulated, the use of escorts or other military dignities suggests the recognition of the political importance of Numidian power, and in some cases these honours could be considered gifts made in the form of service.[80] The fact that no such significant gifts appeared either for other members of the Numidian royal families,[81] or for other African *reguli*,[82] or unidentified ambassadors – perhaps because they did not belong to the royal family[83] – is highly significant. Jugurtha, of course, does not seem to have received any of these gifts. It is also very revealing that the Numidian, in addition to not receiving any of the gifts that could have implied a sanction of his power as king, also did not issue coinage. This absence of coinage may well have been related to his lack of control over the big coastal cities, where the great financial activities were carried out,[84] but also with the lack of sanction from Rome, the real introducer of the practice and form of representation of Numidian kingship according to Hellenistic models. It is therefore not surprising that his successor, the candidate supported by Marius, Gauda, did have his own coinage,[85] and, moreover, some epigraphic evidence in which he is considered *rex*.[86]

The Second Punic War had obliged Rome to seek, through intense diplomatic activity, the collaboration of the autochthonous African powers in its fight against the Punic enemy, and this entailed as a counterpart the indispensable sanction of these powers in their territorial and symbolic domination of the African space. Later, the fall of Carthage created a new political situation in which diplomatic relations became increasingly numb. Rome now owned Africa, and the Numidian kings only had to administer their former properties in the name of the Republic. The imposition of a system of exogenous succession during the second century, however, led to a series of internal conflicts after the death of Micipsa, which by no means served Rome's economic interests in the prosperous coastal cities of Numidia. During the Jugurthine War, it can be clearly seen how the diplomatic gift practically disappeared, in what could be read as clear senatorial opposition

---

[80] In this respect the possibility should also be borne in mind that this is a literary *topos*, since the Numidians appear both barbaric and bellicose, etc.
[81] Massiva in 208 and Masgaba and Misagenes in 168, who formed part of a Numidian royal embassy to Rome.
[82] Livy 27.4.8–9.
[83] App. *Pun.* 32.
[84] Alexandropoulos, 2000: 156.
[85] Although Mazard considered that they could have been Gulussa's (1955: 37–9).
[86] *CIL* II 3417 from Cartagena and *ILAlg.* I 1242 from Khamissa, ancient *Thubursicu Numidarum*.

to Jugurtha's government, which, deprived of any legitimacy, was obliged in contrast to pay constant bribes to maintain its position against other candidates who might have had more support. This seems to have been the case with Massiva, supported by the consul Spurius Postumius Albinus, or Gauda himself, supported by Marius and finally victorious.

The Numidian monarchs of the third and second centuries, at the head of tribal confederations supported by a tricky balance of personal forces, achieved a progressive entrenchment of their authority through the prestige with which their relations with Rome furnished them, of which the diplomatic gift was the most perfect expression. Jugurtha, however, little disposed to being a mere administrator for Rome, saw his legitimacy constantly questioned, as can be gathered from his long confrontation with the senate and his inability to achieve any of the recognition that Syphax or Masinissa had received years earlier. On the contrary, indeed, Jugurtha was obliged to move on a subordinate plane in which, in the face of other options, he barely managed to maintain his position by means of bribery (another form of diplomacy). This bribery was clearly linked to the internal strains of the Late Republic themselves, in which *amicitia* relationships provided a new relational and political system between Roman military leaders and high-ranking African figures who sought to reinforce their personal power and protect their territorial interests.

Bibliography

Abaecherly Boyce, A. [1942]. 'The Origin of *Ornamenta Triumphalia*', *CJ*, 37 (2), 130–41.

Alexandropoulos, J. [2000]. *Les monnaies de l'Afrique antique: 400 av. J.-C.–40 ap. J.-C.*, Toulouse.

Aragón Gómez, M. [2015]. 'Sífax: el rey númida masaesilio en los pasajes de Tito Livio', *Aldaba*, 40, 57–76.

Auliard, C. [2009]. 'Cadeaux et marchandages diplomatiques à Rome jusqu'au début de la conquête méditerranéenne', *Veleia*, 26, 63–73.

Basile G. J. [2016]. 'Xenía: la amistad-ritualizada de Homero a Heródoto', *Emerita*, 84 (2), 229–50.

Bridoux, V. [2020]. *Les royaumes d'Afrique du Nord: émergence, consolidation et insertion dans les aires d'influences méditerranéennes (201–33 av. J.-C.)*, Rome.

Broughton, T. S. S. [1951–2]. *The Magistrates of the Roman Republic*, New York.

Burton, P. J. [2003]. '*Clientela* or *Amicitia*? Modelling Roman International Behaviour in the Middle Republic (264–146 B.C.)', *Klio*, 83, 333–69.

Burton, P. J. [2011]. *Friendship and Empire: Roman Diplomacy and Imperialism in the Middle Republic (353–146 BC)*, Cambridge.
Camps, G. [1960]. *Aux origines de la Berbérie: Masinissa ou les débuts de l'histoire*, Paris.
Camps, G. & Chaker, S. [2004]. 'Jugurtha', *Encyclopédie berbère*, 26, 2004, http://journals.openedition.org/encyclopedieberbere/1377.
Chaker, S. [1986]. 'À propos de la terminologie libyque des titres et fonctions', *Annali dell'Università degli studi di Napoli 'L'Orientale': Rivista del Dipartimento di Studi Asiatici e del Dipartimento di Studi e Ricerche su Africa e Paesi Arabi*, 46 (4), 541–62.
Coudry, M. [2009]. 'Les origines républicaines de l'or coronaire', in M. Coudry & M. Humm (eds), *'Praeda': butin de guerre et société dans la Rome républicaine/Kriegsbeute und Gesellschaft im republikanischen Rom*, Stuttgart, 153–85.
Decret, F. & Fantar, M. [1981]. *Afrique du Nord dans l'Antiquité: des origines au Ve siècle*, Paris.
Elliott, C. [2008]. 'Purple Pasts: Colour Codification in the Ancient World', *Law & Social Inquiry*, 33 (1), 173–94.
Frasson, F. [2012]. 'Numidi in Liguria, Liguri in Numidia: a proposito di alcuni episodi bellici del II secolo a.C.', in M. Bastiana Cocco, A. Gavini & A. Ibba (eds), *L'Africa romana XIX, Sassari 2010*, Rome, 1343–62.
Galand, L. [1997]. 'Inscriptions libyques du Constantinois', *Hommages G. Souville, Antiquités Africaines*, 33, 49–65.
Gozalbes Cravioto, E. [2015]. 'Sobre el rey Syfax de Numidia', *SHHA*, 33, 69–96.
HAAN = Gsell, S. [1913–30]. *Histoire ancienne de l'Afrique du Nord*, Paris.
Herman, G. [2002]. *Ritualised Friendship and the Greek City*, Cambridge.
Konstan, D. [1997]. *Friendship in the Classical World*, Cambridge.
Lancel, S. [1994]. *Cartago*, Barcelona.
Lassère, J.-M. [2010]. 'Masinissa', *Encyclopédie berbère*, 30, 2010, http://journals.openedition.org/encyclopedieberbere/493.
Lemcke, L. [2012]. 'Status Identification on the Road: Requisitioning of Travel Resources by Senators, Equestrians, and Centurions without *Diplomata*: A Note on the Sagalassus Inscription (SEG XXVI 1392)', *GEPHYRA*, 9, 128–42.
Lenfant, D. [2017]. 'Liens personnels, pots-de-vin ou protocole? Les dons du roi de Perse aux ambassadeurs grecs', in G. Cuniberti (ed.), *Dono, controdono e corruzione: ricerche storiche e dialogo interdisciplinare*, Alessandria.
Mazard, J. [1955]. *Corpus nummorum Numidiae Mauretaniaeque*, Paris.
Mitchell, L. G. [1998]. *The Public Use of Private Relationships in the Greek World, 435–323 B.C.*, Cambridge.
Müller, L. [1860]. *Numismatique de l'ancienne Afrique*, Copenhagen.

Muñiz Coello, J. [1998]. 'Riqueza y pobreza en la España prerromana: notas sobre la función de los objetos suntuarios', *Habis*, 29, 23–36.
Paul, G. M. [1984]. *A Historical Commentary on Sallust's 'Bellum Iugurthinum'*, Liverpool.
Prados Martínez, F. [2015]. 'Masinisa y el Reino númida', *DF*, 31, 20–5.
Reinhold, M. [1969]. 'On Status Symbols in the Ancient World', *CJ*, 64 (7), 300–4.
Reinhold, M. [1971]. *History of Purple as a Status Symbol in Antiquity*, Brussels.
Rosselló Calafell, G. [2021]. 'El regalo diplomático entre Roma y los númidas entre los siglos III y II a.C.', *Habis*, 52, 31–55.
Salinas de Frías, M. [2008]. '*Urbem venalem!* Provincias y corrupción política en la obra de Salustio', in G. Bravo Castañeda & R. González Salinero (eds), *La corrupción en el mundo romano: actas del V Coloquio de la Asociación Interdisciplinar de Estudios Romanos (AIER)*, Madrid, 43–52.
Salinas de Frías, M. [2010]. '*In castreis Scipionis*: ejército y política en Roma durante el siglo II a.C.', in J. J. Palao Vicente (ed.), *Militares y civiles en la antigua Roma*, Salamanca, 15–30.
Sanz, A.-M. [2019]. 'L'alliance militaire entre Syphax et Rome', *Le royaume des Massaesyles: Syphax et la rencontre de Siga, 206 av. J.-C.: actes du Colloque international organisé par le Haut Commissariat à l'Amazighité, Aïn Témouchent, 22–24 sept. 2018*, Algiers, 67–93.
Saumagne, C. [1966]. *La Numidia et Rome: Masinissa et Jugurtha*, Paris.
Thompson, L. A. [1981]. 'Carthage and the Massylian "Coup d'État" of 206 B.C.', *Historia: Zeitschrift für alte Geschichte*, 30 (1), 120–6.
Verboven, K. [2002]. *The Economy of Friends: Economic Aspects of 'Amicitia' and Patronage in the Late Republic*, Brussels.
Verboven, K. [2014]. 'Like Bait on a Hook: Ethics, Etics and Emics of Gift-Exchange in the Roman World', in F. Carlà & M. Gori (eds), *Gift Giving and the 'Embedded' Economy in the Ancient World*, 135–55.
Veyne, P. [1973]. 'Y-a-t-il eu un impérialisme romain?', *MEFRA*, 87, 793–855.
Walsh, P. G. [1965]. 'Masinissa', *JRS*, 55 (1–2), 149–60.

9

Torques, Horses and Gold
Approaching Diplomatic Gifts in Gaul*

Alberto Pérez Rubio

The giving of diplomatic gifts, understood as offerings imbued with political significance, enters a scheme of gift and counter-gift, widely studied since the seminal work by Mauss,[1] and has generated abundant debate and scientific literature.[2] Mauss himself postulated that Celtic communities had functioned as 'potlatch' societies, in the image of indigenous societies of North-western America, with a gift exchange that reached paroxysmal levels – 'prestations totales à type agonistique', from the example related by Posidonius of suicide in exchange for gold, silver or amphorae of wine[3] – and that structured them hierarchically.[4] Hubert argued along these same lines, finding support both in the texts of the insular literature of the early Middle Ages and also in the anthropological work on the American 'potlatch', to maintain that among Celts, the gift was characterised by entailing a counterpart, by having to be proportional to the status of the recipient or even greater, by the sanction that it would involve an obligation, and

---

* This work has been developed within the research project PGC2018-096415-B-C21 'La expresión diplomática en el Mediterráneo occidental bajo la expansión romana: el regalo en su contexto ideológico y cultural', funded by the State Research Agency, Ministry of Science and Innovation, Government of Spain (MCIN/AEI/10.13039/501100011033) and ERDF 'A way of making Europe'.
[1] Mauss, 1924; 1925; Lewuillon, 1990: 317–18; Baray, 2007: 30–5.
[2] Among the most recent work on the subject, see Godelier, 1996; James & Allen, 1998; Osteed, 2002; Sykes, 2005; Gregory, 2015; Cuniberti, 2017. For the ancient world in particular, see Satlow, 2013; Carlà-Uhink & Gori, 2014.
[3] Posidonius, fr. 23, *ap*. Athen. 4.154f.
[4] Mauss, 1925.

by generating a bond of dependence.[5] Lewuillon in turn criticised Mauss's perspective, rejecting the existence of a 'potlatch' in Gaul:[6] for him, giving gifts did not correspond to dynamics of circulation or redistribution of goods, but instead was a mechanism 'parfaitement adapté à la production d'une véritable plus-value, entre autres fins économiques'.[7] More recently, Baray has revised the topic: like Lewuillon, he rejects the existence of a 'potlatch', but thinks that 'le don est bel et bien central dans les sociétés celtiques'.[8] That author believes that institutions such as communal banquets, hospitality bonds, war and client relationships should be understood along the axis that marks the giving of gifts, whether that was the offering of food and drink at feasts, the exchange of gifts between aristocrats, the distribution of booty or the protection offered to clients. Baray thus maintains that social hierarchy and power relationships were defined and understood in relation to gifts.[9]

Without judging this centrality of the gift as a creator of social structure, it is worth affirming its importance in the establishment of relations, not only within Gallic societies, but also among different political actors. The Graeco-Roman written sources provide some examples of the diplomatic gift in the Gallic context, among which stand out elements like torques – ornaments with a strong symbolic significance – horses and money. The identification of diplomatic gifts in the archaeological record is highly problematic, although certain objects, such as some particularly luxurious *fibulae*, may be considered – always with caution – within this category, because of their parallels with those we know in written sources, their luxurious or exotic nature, or their presumed life histories. The exchange of these gifts among the Celtic elites or their provision by representatives from powers such as Rome and Carthage should be understood as a mark of prestige and recognition, constituting in this way an important mechanism for the establishment and maintenance of diplomatic relations. On occasions the character of these gifts is unclear, since the line that separates the gift from compensation, payment or bribery can be, as we will see, deeply blurred.

[5] Hubert, 1932: 236–7. Being conscious of the problems posed by using early medieval Irish literature to reflect on the Iron Age, it should be indicated that in it, trade does not appear as an impersonal exchange, but always generated a personal bond of mutual obligation that honoured both parties (Koch, 2007: 278–9).
[6] Lewuillon, 1990; 1992; 1999.
[7] '... perfectly suited to the production of a genuine surplus value, among other economic purposes'; Lewuillon, 1992: 151.
[8] 'The gift is central to Celtic societies'; Baray, 2007: 68.
[9] Baray, 2007: 69.

We have a possible example of a diplomatic gift in 218 BC, when, on his path to Italy, Hannibal had to negotiate with the leaders of a coalition of various communities from southern Gaul who had met in Ruscino (Perpignan) to confront him. The episode is narrated by Livy, with a briefer version in Polybius. The latter limits himself to stating laconically that 'Hannibal, however, ... had bribed some of the Celts and forced others to give him passage.'[10] Livy, by contrast, gives many more details. Initially, while his army crossed the Ebro River, the Carthaginian general sent emissaries to Gaul to win over those whose territories he had to cross, and to reconnoitre the alpine passes.[11] Once the Pyrenees were crossed, however, a coalition of Gallic *populi* assembled troops in Ruscino to oppose him, afraid of being subjugated, as had happened with many communities on the Iberian Peninsula. Hannibal sent emissaries – *nuntii* – to their leaders, whom Livy categories as *reguli*, to offer them an interview in person either in Ruscino or at his camp in Iliberris (Elna), to try to dissipate their fears. The Gallic leaders moved their camp close to Iliberris, and the Carthaginian won them over with gifts – *dona*, without further detail – so that they facilitated the peaceful passage of the Punic army through their territories.[12]

There are many mentions of the giving of precious metal to seal alliances, which in some cases may be considered diplomatic gifts and in others would have been, plainly and simply, payment for a mercenary service or bribes, although it is not easy to distinguish between them. In fact, among the many functions suggested for the first Gallic coinage – maintenance of clients, provision of a dowry, payment of taxes, as a 'wergeld' etc. – one would be the diplomatic gift as a mechanism to establish alliances. In this respect, we know that the Cisalpine communities of Insubres and Boii offered the kings of the Gaesatae, Concolitanus and Aneroestes, a large quantity of gold to win them over in their war against Rome[13] – although since 'Gaesatae' came to mean 'mercenaries,'[14] this suggests that

---

[10] Ἀννίβας δὲ παραδόξως τοὺς μὲν χρήμασι πείσας τῶν Κελτῶν τοὺς δὲ βιασάμενος ἧκε μετὰ τῶν δυνάμεων, δεξιὸν ἔχων τὸ Σαρδόνιον πέλαγος, ἐπὶ τὴν τοῦ Ῥοδανοῦ διάβασιν (Polyb. 3.41.7), trans. W. R. Paton.

[11] *Hoc visu laetus tripertito Hiberum copias traiecit, praemissis qui Gallorum animos, qua traducendus exercitus erat, donis conciliarent Alpiumque transitus specularentur* (Livy 21.23.1).

[12] *Et per nuntios quidem haec; ut vero reguli Gallorum castris ad Iliberrim extemplo motis haud gravate ad Poenum venerunt, capti donis cum bona pace exercitum per fines suos praeter Ruscinonem oppidum transmiserunt* (Livy 21.24.5).

[13] ὧν τοῖς βασιλεῦσι Κογκολιτάνῳ καὶ Ἀνηροέστῳ παραυτίκα μὲν χρυσίου προτείναντες πλῆθος (Polyb. 2.22.1).

[14] Polyb. 2.22. Orosius (4.13.5) emphasises that the term was not an ethnonym, but that it meant 'mercenaries' – *Gaesatorum, quod nomen non gentis sed mercennariorum*

this is, simply, a case of payment for services. In the winter of 54/3 BC the Treverian leader Induciomarus offered the Transrhenane Germani *pecunia* to win them over,[15] and the Treveri renewed the promise after his death, handing over hostages as a guarantee of payment.[16] In 52 BC, the Arverni bribed the *vergobret* (chief magistrate) of the Aedui, Convictolitavis, who shared the money with some *adulescentes* of the elite of the Aedui so that their *civitas* would switch sides,[17] and Vercingetorix promised money to the Allobrogian *principes* to tempt them and so that they defected from Rome.[18] The discovery of hoards of coins with foreign money, often interpreted as possible payments to mercenaries, could also have functioned as a sort of diplomatic gift, for example, in order to buy the passage of troops through a territory, perhaps like the Aquitanian coinage found in mixed hoards in the southern Meseta region of the Iberian Peninsula around the time of the Second Punic War.[19]

Gallorum est – although Strabo (5.1.6) considers them an ἔθνος of Cisalpine Gaul, erroneously since through Polybius we know that the Gaesatae came from the other side of the Alps. Γαισάται/*Gaesatae* would come from the Celtic term 'lance', 'spear' (Delamarre, 2003: 173–4; Matasovic, 2009: 155; Hyllested, 2010: 114; Gleser, 2020: 307). On the Gaesatae, see Lucas, 2009; Péré-Noguès, 2014; Almagro-Gorbea, 2016: 147.

[15] *Trans Rhenum legatos mitterent, civitates sollicitarent, pecunias pollicerentur* (Caes. *BGall.* 5.55.1).

[16] *Illi finitimos Germanos sollicitare et pecuniam polliceri non desistunt* (Caes. *BGall.* 6.2.1).

[17] *Dum haec ad Gergoviam geruntur, Convictolitavis Aeduus ... sollicitatus ab Arvernis pecunia cum quibusdam adulescentibus colloquitur; quorum erat princeps Litaviccus atque eius fratres, amplissima familia nati adulescentes. cum his praemium communicat hortaturque* (Caes. *BGall.* 7.37.1–2). *celeriter adulescentibus et oratione magistratus et praemio deductis* (Caes. *BGall.* 7.37.6).

[18] *Horum principibus pecunias, civitati autem imperium totius provinciae pollicetur* (Caes. *BGall.* 7.64.8).

[19] Examples of *à la croix* and Aquitane coinage – series sotiate *au cheval* and *aux protubérances* – have appeared in mixed hoards found in the Iberian Peninsula, in the zones of the Celtiberians and Carpetani: hoard X4, Armuña de Tajuña (Guadalajara), Los Villares (Caudete de las Fuentes, Valencia), Valeria (Cuenca), Boos (Valdenebro, Soria) and Driebes (Guadalajara) (Hébert, 1998; Villaronga Garriga, 2000; Callegarin, 2009: 24–5; 2011: 322–3; Callegarin *et alii*, 2013: 190–3; Callegarin & García-Bellido, 2012: 131). These small treasures would have been hidden during the Second Punic War or in the years immediately after the conflict (Villaronga Garriga, 1993: 28–31; 2000; Ripollès Alegre *et alii*, 2009: 164, 171; Rodríguez Casanova, 2014: 99–100; Hiriart, 2016: 188) or during the campaigns of 185 BC by Gaius Calpurnius Piso and Lucius Quinctius Crispinus in Carpetania against a coalition of Hispani mentioned by Livy (39.30-1) (García-Bellido, 2007: 217–21; Rodríguez Casanova & Canto García, 2011: 249, 263; Chaves Tristán, 2012: 171–80). In any case, their heterogeneous composition undoubtedly seems connected with the necessities of conflict,

Rome would also use gifts in its diplomatic dealings with Gallic leaders. When Caesar, for example, met Ariovistus in 58 BC, he recorded the 'splendid gifts' – *munera amplissima* – that the senate had bestowed upon the Suebian, alongside the titles of *rex* and *amicus*.[20] We do not know of what nature these *munera* might have been. Perhaps gifts that recognised Ariovistus' royalty, like those that Scipio offered the Numidian Masinissa when he addressed him as *rex*, which were 'a golden wreath, a golden *patera*, a curule chair and ivory sceptre, an embroidered toga and a tunic adorned with palms'?[21] When the senate ratified this acknowledgement, it sent Masinissa's ambassadors with additional presents: 'two purple military cloaks, each with a golden brooch [*fibula*], and tunics having the broad stripe, two horses with their trappings, two sets of arms with cuirasses for a horseman, and tents and field furniture such as were customarily furnished to a consul'.[22]

We know in detail, thanks to Livy, the gifts with which in 179 and 169 BC the Roman senate honoured the *reges Gallorum* Cincibilus and Balanos.[23] In 170 BC, the Gallic king Cincibilus sent ambassadors, among them his brother, to complain to the senate about the depredations committed

particularly the payment of soldiers (Ripollès Alegre *et alii*, 2009: 164; Callegarin & García-Bellido, 2012: 132).

[20] *Ubi eo ventum est, Caesar initio orationis sua senatusque in eum beneficia commemoravit, quod rex appellatus esset a senatu, quod amicus, quod munera amplissime missa; quam rem et paucis contigisse et pro magnis hominum officiis consuesse tribui docebat* (Caes. BGall. 1.43.4–5).

[21] *... ibi Masinissam, primum regem appellatum eximiisque ornatum laudibus, aurea corona aurea patera sella curuli et scipione eburneo toga picta et palmata tunica donat* (Livy 30.15.11), trans. F. G. Moore.

[22] *... munera quoque quae legati ferrent regi decreverunt, sagula purpurea duo cum fibulis aureis singulis et lato clavo tunicis, equos duo phaleratos, bina equestria arma cum loricis, et tabernacula militaremque supellectilem qualem praeberi consuli mos esset* (Livy 30.17.13). Cf. Rosselló Calafell, 2021, and in this volume the chapter by E. Sánchez Medina & G. Rosselló Calafell.

[23] Although these two Gallic leaders are usually situated among the Celtic communities of the east of the Alps (Dobesch, 1980: 108–65), Raydon (2014) suggests placing them in Transalpine Gaul, since Livy uses the expression *trans Alpis/Transalpini*. For Hostein (2012: 351 n. 22), the name of Balanos could be related to the BELINO/BEINO/BIENOS that appears in the legend of a series of silver quinarii (*RIG* IV 132–5; DT 2658–61) the minting of which has been attributed to one of the peoples of central Gaul – Arverni, Aulerci, Carnutes ...? – thus giving a clue to the community of origin of the embassy to Rome in 169 BC. It is, however, worth bearing in mind that those quinarii are late, and their discovery in Roman camps to the north of the Loire could be related to the payment of auxiliaries (Delestrée & Tache, 2004: 145–6), and that, moreover, the anthroponym Belinus is very common throughout the Celtic linguistic sphere (Prósper Pérez, 2017), making this argument difficult.

by the military tribune Gaius Cassius Longinus among his Alpine allies (*socii*).²⁴ The senate promised to address the problem when the tribune returned and to send two *legati* to make its decision known to Cincibilus, and furthermore gave the king's ambassadors 2000 *asses*, and the king and his brother 'two twisted necklaces [*torques*] made of five pounds of gold and five silver vessels of twenty pounds, and two horses with trappings for head and chest, along with their grooms, and cavalry weapons and military cloaks, and to the princes' attendants, both free and slave, garments'.²⁵ They also obtained permission to buy ten horses and were authorised to remove them from Italy.²⁶ In this instance, we see that they offered gifts to the ambassadors, something the senate had done for example with the *legati* sent by Masinissa in the abovementioned recognition, whom they gave 'not less than five thousand asses for each of them, for their attendants one thousand each; and two garments apiece for the envoys, one each for their attendants'.²⁷ The following year, the Gallic leader – *regulus Gallorum* – Balanos sent ambassadors to Rome to offer help in the war that was being fought against Perseus: 'Thanks were expressed by the senate and gifts sent the envoys, a twisted necklace [*torques*] of two pounds of gold and golden bowls of four pounds, a horse with ornamental trappings, and cavalry weapons.'²⁸ In both cases, we see how the senate offered similar gifts: gold torques, *paterae* and cups, and a panoply for cavalry, including

---

²⁴ Livy 43.5.1–9. Against Raydon's hypothesis of a western origin of Cincibilus is Livy's indication in the same passage that in this same period ambassadors arrived from the Carni, Histri and Iapydes to complain about Cassius' depredations in their territories.

²⁵ *Duobus fratribus regulis haec praecipua, torques duo ex quinque pondo auri facti et vasa argentea quinque ex viginti pondo et duo equi phalerati cum agasonibus et equestria arma ac sagula, et comitibus eorum vestimenta, liberis servisque* (Livy 43.5.8), trans. A. C. Schlesinger.

²⁶ *Munera mitti legatis ex binis milibus aeris censuerunt; fratri reguli haec praecipua, torques duo ex quinque pondo auri facti et vasa argentea quinque ex viginti pondo et duo equi phalerati cum agasonibus et equestria arma ac sagula, et comitibus eorum vestimenta, liberis servisque. haec missa; illa petentibus data, ut denorum equorum iis commercium esset educendique ex Italia potestas fieret* (Livy 43.5.8–9); *gratiae ab senatu actae muneraque missa, torquis aureus duo pondo et paterae aureae quattuor pondo, equus phaleratus armaque equestria* (Livy 44.14.2).

²⁷ *Legatis in singulos dona ne minus quinum milium, comitibus eorum milium aeris, et vestimenta bina legatis, singula comitibus* (Livy 30.17.14), trans. F. G. Moore.

²⁸ *Dum bellum in Macedonia geritur, legati Transalpini ab regulo Gallorum – Balanus ipsius traditur nomen; gentis ex qua fuerit, non traditur – Romam venerunt pollicentes ad Macedonicum bellum auxilia. gratiae ab senatu actae muneraque missa, torquis aureus duo pondo et paterae aureae quattuor pondo, equus phaleratus armaque equestria* (Livy 44.14.1–2), trans. A. C. Schlesinger.

a harnessed mount. Raydon understands this triad of *munera* as typical of Roman diplomatic practice, reminiscent of trifunctionality in the Indo-European conception of sovereignty, although in this respect it would also fit in with the Celtic conception of the *rix*.[29] The torque may be understood as a translation of the gold crown with which the senate recognised the sovereignty of representatives in other spheres, as in the aforementioned case of Masinissa, which would indicate a certain Roman familiarity with the Gallic symbolic universe.

Similar presents were offered by the Macedonian king, Perseus, to the leaders of an army of 10,000 Gallic cavalry and 10,000 Gallic infantry,[30] recruited through the Illyrian king, Gentius. Perseus had promised a stipend to these mercenaries of 5 gold Philippics to each infantryman, 10 to each horseman, and 1,000 to their *dux* Clondicus. Perseus went out to meet them and bestowed upon their *principes* horses, *phalerae*, cloaks and a small quantity of gold,[31] although he later refused to pay them as agreed. Despite his promises – which again included clothing, money and horses[32] – and his counteroffer to contract only 5,000 horsemen, the Gauls decided to return to their homes by the Danube.

In these three examples, the horses appeared pre-eminently as a diplomatic gift, something also known, for example, in Hispania. After the Battle of Baecula, among the gifts that Scipio offered the Hispanian *reguli* and *principes* were the 300 horses that he allowed Indibilis, leader of the Ilergetes, to choose.[33] A harnessed horse was also given, along with other gifts, to the Numidian prince Massiva. The presentation of horses as a diplomatic gift fits perfectly with the progressive importance that cavalry gained in Celtic warfare from the last quarter of the third century BC, and with the abundant

---

[29] Raydon, 2014: 67 n. 33.

[30] Livy makes very interesting mention of how the infantry kept pace with the horsemen, and mounted their horse if they fell – *veniebant decem milia equitum, par numerus peditum et ipsorum iungentium cursum equis et in vicem prolapsorum equitum vacuos capientium ad pugnam equos* (Livy 44.26.3) – which recalls the *trimarkisia* described by Pausanias (10.19.9–11) and the numerous instances known in which the Gallic cavalry and infantry were mixed when they fought (Pérez Rubio, 2012: 18; 2015).

[31] Livy 44.26.6.

[32] Livy 44.26.9. On this episode see the chapter by M. Esteban Payno and G. Ventós Rodríguez in this volume.

[33] πλὴν τότε γε διαλέξας ἐκ τῶν αἰχμαλώτων τοὺς Ἴβηρας, τούτους μὲν ἀπέλυσε χωρὶς λύτρων πάντας εἰς τὰς ἑαυτῶν πατρίδας, τῶν δ' ἵππων τριακοσίους κελεύσας ἐκλέξαι τοῖς περὶ τὸν Ἀνδοβάλην τοὺς λοιποὺς διέδωκε τοῖς ἀνίπποις (Polyb. 10.40.10); *dona inde regulis principibusque Hispanorum divisa, et ex magna copia captorum equorum trecentos quos vellet eligere Indibilem iussit* (Livy 27.19.7).

reports of mounted retinues in the Gallic world, which research has come to call *comitatus*, following Tacitus.³⁴ In the last quarter of the third century BC – the transition between La Tène C1 and C2 – there were changes in the panoply in Continental Europe that were related to the increasingly important role of cavalry, as we know from the written sources.³⁵ We thus find swords in two models of different lengths, probably for cavalry and infantry; spearheads hypertrophied; the size of the *umbones* (central metal part of the shields) increased;³⁶ and chain belts disappearing for infantrymen who did not need their stabilisation, as by then they fought more statically, since their mobility had been inherited by the cavalry. This evolution of the cavalry was related to the internal changes in Celtic societies, which underwent processes of growing political structuring that entailed the birth of the *civitates* that we know from the Classical sources,³⁷ but also intensified thanks to the conflicts that implicated Celtic groups at the end of the third century BC, whether as auxiliaries, allies or mercenaries. Already from the end of the fourth century BC scabbards decorated with dragons and griffins suggest a tactical differentiation among the combatants while in the expedition against Delphi in 279 BC cavalry are reported as playing an important role.³⁸ But it would be the agricultural advances in Continental Europe during the third century BC which allowed for the breeding and maintenance of a larger equine population suitable for the needs of warfare. As Baray has correctly noted, the invention of the scythe could have been related to the need for fodder, and carpological analyses carried out in around twenty sites from La Tène C1a–D1a indicate an absence of hay, gathered to feed a herd that would include horses.³⁹ There are several examples of cohorts of mounted warriors gathered around a leader for the first century BC: the large number of *equites* maintained by Dumnorix,⁴⁰ the escort of Ariovistus,⁴¹ the *comitatus* of Commius⁴² and Ambiorix,⁴³ and, probably, some of the *equites* that accompanied Teutomatus when he joined Vercingetorix.⁴⁴ It is worth also considering

---

³⁴ Tac. *Germ.* 13.3–4. Cf. Creighton, 2000: 11–15; Roymans, 2004: 19; Roymans & Scheers, 2012: 27–8.
³⁵ Pérez Rubio, 2012.
³⁶ Vitali, 2002; García-Jiménez, 2020: 50.
³⁷ Pérez Rubio, 2022.
³⁸ Paus. 10.19.9–11.
³⁹ Baray, 2016: 247–8.
⁴⁰ *Magnum numerum equitatus suo sumptu semper alere et circum se habere* (Caes. *BGall.* 1.18.5).
⁴¹ Caes. *BGall.* 1.43.2–3.
⁴² Caes. *BGall.* 6.6.4.
⁴³ Caes. *BGall.* 6.301–4, 43.6.
⁴⁴ Caes. *BGall.* 7.30.5.

through this prism Caesar's 400 *Germani*,[45] the approximately one thousand Gallic cavalry who shared Publius Licinius Crassus' doom in Carrhae,[46] and the Gallic and Germanic horsemen who fought alongside Titus Labienus in the Civil War.[47] A passage from the *Bellum Gallicum* indicates how prized horses were by the Gauls, who paid any price for them, in contrast with the Germans, who used 'small and deformed' native horses for the war.[48] Osteological studies of equine remains found in settlements in Gaul reveal a progressive increase in height, which in the local animals reached a limit of 1.40 m at the top of the withers, with other larger examples, a consequence of cross-breeding with imported animals.[49] The permission that the senate gave to Cincibulus and his brother to export horses from Italy involves an exceptional trade, of a luxury good. The bestowal of horses as a gift to a Gallic leader and the permission to trade them enabled him in turn to distribute them among the members of his *comitatus*, increasing his prestige and lubricating the balance of loyalty and service in exchange for gifts that this institution articulated, or to give them to other leaders as a further element in the web of alliances that criss-crossed the Celtic world.

Torques as Diplomatic Gifts

The torque, a rigid necklace of metal – gold,[50] silver or bronze – with a range of stylistic variations, constituted an ornament that was characteristic of (but not exclusive to) the Celtic world, to the point of being one of the markers of identity that Graeco-Roman art used to represent the 'Celt'. It was an object imbued with different meanings:[51] it appears decorating the figurations of heroes and

---

[45] Caes. *BGall.* 7.13.1. On Caesar's 'Germanic' *equites* see Tausend, 1988.

[46] Plut. *Crass.* 17.4, 25.

[47] Caes. *BAfr.* 40. These Gaulish and 'Germanic' horsemen had accompanied Labienus from Gaul because of his *auctoritas*, or had been attracted through rewards and promises: *qui partim eius auctoritatem erant ex Gallia secuti, partim pretio pollicitationibusque adducti ad eum se contulerant.*

[48] *Quin etiam iumentis, quibus maxime Galli delectantur quaeque impenso parant pretio, Germani importatis non utuntur, sed quae sunt apud eos nata, parva atque deformia, haec cotidiana exercitatione summi ut sint laboris efficiunt* (Caes. *BGall.* 4.2.2). The term Caesar uses, *iumentum*, is usually used for beasts of burden, but given the paragraph in which it appears, which speaks about the Germanic cavalry, we can infer that it indicates warhorses.

[49] Méniel, 1996; 2013: 561; Buchsenschutz, 2004: 341.

[50] Eluère, 1987; Hautenauve, 2005. A recent multidisciplinary approach to gold torques in the western sphere of the La Tène culture in Armbruster *et alii*, 2019.

[51] Hautenauve, 2005.

deities;[52] in the grave goods of women in some Gallic communities, such as the Senones, where between the mid-fourth and early third centuries BC torques with ternary decoration and decoration in an arch perhaps served to identify women of two *pagi*[53] or two clans;[54] or on the necks of warriors, such as the *promachoi* that Polybius describes in the Battle of Telamon – 'all in the leading companies richly adorned with gold torques and armlets'[55] – and thence the recurrent presence of torques in the booty taken by the Romans from the Gauls and their display in triumphs,[56] and later their incorporation as *dona militaria*, as military decoration.[57] Torques often appear in small hoards associated with coins,[58] and frequently broken, as we also see in other objects like weapons in sanctuaries, which could indicate a votive character.[59] We know that an Insubrian leader, Ariovistus, promised to dedicate to his god of war a torque made with the booty taken from Roman soldiers – although it was later the consul C. Flaminius who dedicated a golden trophy to Jupiter made of captured torques.[60] From the third century BC, the torque would above all be a symbol of power that the gods conferred on warriors to achieve victory.[61] Pion has linked the first Gallic coin issues with gold torques, given their frequent association in hoards and the presence of torques in the iconographic repertoire of coins. In his hypothesis, both had a sacred character – symbolised by their material, gold[62] – with coins used in treaties among humans and torques in treaties with the divine, but both constituting instruments for the perpetuation of the status quo: the torque, indivisible and unique, was used in exchanges of prestige and treaties with the gods, assuring the ideal reproduction of society, while coins, divisible and transportable, were used for military mobilisation, which assured the immediate, real, reproduction of society.[63]

---

[52] Chassaing, 1963; Schomas, 2011: 159; Poitrenaud, 2014.
[53] Baray, 2018a: 320.
[54] Baray, 2018b: 322. From La Tène B2 torques disappear from women's graves (Marion, 2018: 265).
[55] πάντες δ᾽ οἱ τὰς πρώτας κατέχοντες σπείρας χρυσοῖς μανιάκαις καὶ περιχείροις ἦσαν κατακεκοσμημένοι (Polyb. 2.29.8), trans. W. R. Paton. Other mentions of Gallic warriors wearing torques in combat in Strab. 4.4.5; Prop. 4.10.43–4; Plin. *NH* 33.5.15; Livy 7.9.6–7.10.14.
[56] Ostenberg, 2009: 108–11.
[57] Maxfield, 1981: 86–8; Linderski, 2001. On the meanings of the torque in the Roman sphere and its impact on coin iconography, see Rowan & Swan, 2015.
[58] Fitzpatrick, 2005; Gruel & Hiriart, 2018: 61.
[59] Fitzpatrick, 2005.
[60] Flor. 1.20.4–5.
[61] Brunaux, 1996: 98–9, 145–6; Lamoine, 2012: 174.
[62] Cf. Fitzpatrick, 2005.
[63] Pion, 2012. Cf. Wigg-Wolf, 2010: 306; Gruel & Hiriart, 2018: 61.

One of the most conspicuous meanings of the torque is that of sovereignty and authority, within the set of symbols common to all Gallic aristocracy and royalty, which invokes a heroic universe in which martial virtues played a primordial role, as Lamoine has indicated (Figures 9.1 and 9.2).[64] According to Dio Cassius, Boudicca wore a gold torque – στρεπτός.[65] The Roman senate's gift of torques to the ambassadors sent by two Gallic *reges* has already been mentioned, which may be understood as recognition of their sovereignty. Conversely, we know that the Gauls bestowed a gold torque upon Augustus which weighed 100 pounds.[66] Although in a very different sphere, the reliefs on the north stairs of the Apadana in Persepolis should be mentioned, in which Scythian ambassadors appear carrying

Figure 9.1 Statue known as the 'Warrior of Vachères', representation of a Gallic auxiliary from the Province c. 50–30 BC, in which the thick torque that decorates his neck stands out (Barruol, 1996; Pernet & Rouzeau, 2013) (Musée Calvet, Avignon; © Radu Oltean).

---

[64] Lamoine, 2009: 138–65; 2012: 174. Cf. Schomas, 2011: 160.
[65] Cass. Dio 62.2.4.
[66] Quint. *Inst.* 6.3.79–80.

Figure 9.2 Statue known as the 'Warrior of Mondragon', representation of a Gallic aristocrat from the Province at the end of the second century BC or first half of the first century BC, who supports himself on his shield and shows a torque with his right hand (Cavalier & Baudrand, 2018) (Musée Calvet, Avignon; © Radu Oltean).

torques for the Great King.[67] The Achaemenid sovereign used to present ambassadors with lavish gifts that included a torque – στρεπτός – worth 1,000 darics, in addition to a Babylonian talent of silver, two silver cups weighing one talent, an akinakes worth 1,000 darics, and Median apparel.[68]

The dimension of torques as diplomatic gifts perhaps finds a material example in the gold torque found fortuitously and without archaeological context in Mailly-le-Camp (Aube) in 1965,[69] whose typology corresponds with a type that appears in Britannia, Gallia Belgica and the east of Gaul,[70] and which can be dated around the middle of the first century BC.[71]

[67] The torque in the Achaemenid world could only be worn with the express permission of the Great King (Xen. *Cyr.* 8.2.8).
[68] Ael. *VH* 1.22.
[69] Joffroy, 1967; 1969; Duval, 1994.
[70] Duval, 1994.
[71] Joffroy, 1969: 56–8; *RIG* I, G-275 a 278.

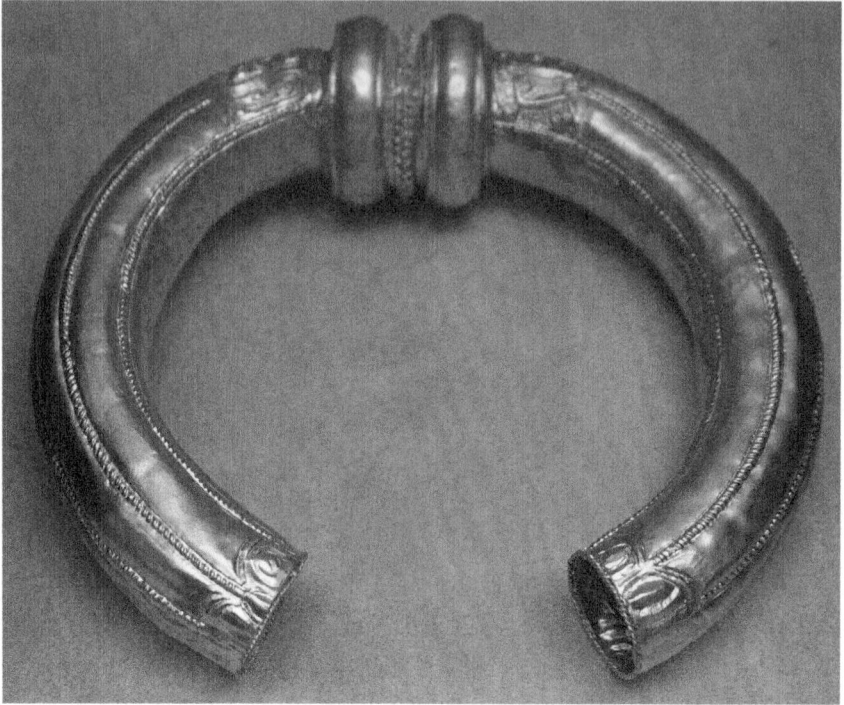

Figure 9.3 Torque from Mailly-le-Camp (Musée d'Archéologie Nationale; Wikimedia Commons/ Gérald Garitan).

Metal analysis seems to indicate Rhenish gold (Figure 9.3).[72] What is really interesting is that the piece displays in the inner part a series of graffiti in Greek characters, which according to Lejeune are independent, successive – two of them overlap, incised by different hands and surrounded by symbols, which this author interprets as numbers.[73] The first graffito (G-278) can be read as κιντουλλος; the second (G-276), as ταουτανοι; the third (G-275), as νιτιοβρογεις; the fourth (G-275), as νιτιοβρο; the fifth (G-277), as αυραππιιος; and the sixth (G-275), as νιτιοβρογεις. Graffiti 1 and 5 are anthroponyms in the nominative, while those numbered 3, 4 and 6 – νιτιοβρογεις, νιτιοβρο and νιτιοβρογεις – record the ethnonym Nitiobroges in nominative plural, *nitiobrogeis* (Figure 9.4).[74] The second,

---

[72] Joffroy, 1969: 58.
[73] Lejeune, 1969; *RIG* I, G-275 a 278.
[74] The discovery has served to determine the correct form of the ethnonym for the Nitiobroges/Nitiobriges, which appears in both ways in the Latin manuscripts – βριγ in almost all the Greek ones – probably out of confusion, since there are Gallic

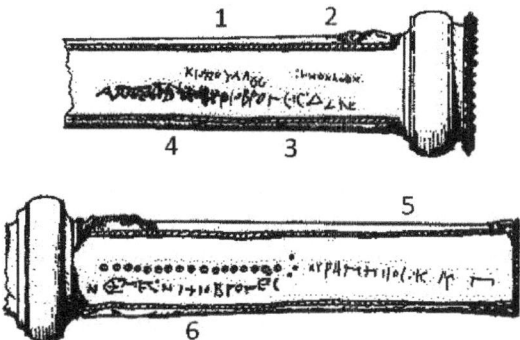

Figure 9.4 Graffiti on the Mailly-le-Camp torque: 1 – κιντουλλος; 2 – ταουτανοι; 3 – νιτιοβρογεις; 4 – νιτιοβρο; 5 – αυραππιιος; 6 – νιτιοβρογεις (Lejeune, 1969).

ταουτανοι – *tautanoi* – is nominative plural of *touta/teuta*, an 'Aquitanism' which mentions the 'citizens', the 'members', of the Nitiobroges who would have made the offering or gift of the object.[75] Lejeune interprets the torque as a sort of accounting record of a treasure of the *civitas* of the Nitiobroges: the object would have been offered to a divinity or a leader, and then successive contributions to this treasure, individual or collective, would have been reflected in the successive graffiti.[76] Its discovery in the north of Gaul could be the consequence of pillaging.[77] Goudineau, in turn, accepting that the torque would have constituted part of a religious treasure belonging to the Nitiobroges, suggests an offering/accounting record of theirs in an unknown sanctuary in Champagne since, in his opinion, if the offering had been made in Nitiobrogan territory, there would be no need to specify the people.[78] Lastly, Duval indicates that the torque belongs to a type that, although appearing in the north-east of Gaul, is absent in Aquitania. He joins this with the mention of some Nitiobroges in Champagne in the *Tabula Peutingeriana*, situated between the Remi and Tricasses. He adds that the meaning of their ethnonym, 'those of the country', 'the natives',[79] suggests the existence there of a fraction of that *civitas* or of an unidentified *pagus* – in Garonne the Celtic Nitiobroges were on the frontier with Aquitania, and those supposed northern Nitiobroges would have

---

ethnonyms constructed from the two terms; Nitiobroges would therefore be the correct appellation (Lejeune, 1969: 11).
[75] Lejeune, 1969: 66–7; *RIG* I, G-276.
[76] Lejeune, 1969: 76; *RIG* I: 406.
[77] Lejeune, 1969: 75.
[78] Goudineau, 1989; 1991; De Hoz Bravo, 2015: 508.
[79] Lejeune, 1969: 71–3; Delamarre, 2003: 235.

been on the frontier between Gallia Celtica and Belgica – although the *Peutingeriana* does not record the name of any *pagus*.[80] Although this is an appealing hypothesis, the Aquitanism of *tautanoi* arguably encourages the idea that the mention of certain Nitiobroges would refer to the community located in the middle Garonne basin.

We would like to propose a different hypothesis. We know that torques were given as diplomatic offerings, and we also know of their deposition in sacred spaces, given their special significance. Perhaps the Mailly-le-Camp torque was dedicated in an undiscovered sanctuary in Champagne by Nitiobrogan 'citizens' – ταουτανοι – as a validation of a pact between them and some northern community such as the Remi or Tricasses; the successive graffiti mentioning the νιτιοβρογεις could indicate the periodic renewal of that pact, and the anthroponyms could reflect the names of the Nitiobrogan leaders – although they do not correspond with the Olloviconus and his son Teutomatus, *rex* in 52 BC whom we know from the *Bellum Gallicum*[81] – or of the magistrates delegated to reconfirm the alliance.

The identification of diplomatic gifts in the archaeological record is highly conjectural, as is patently clear in the example just discussed. Advancing another hypothesis, if the Roman senate gave King Balanus golden *paterae*, it may be proposed that the two silver *paterae* found in the tumulus at Vieille Aubagnan (Landas), with Iberian inscriptions and probably from a workshop in the lower Ebro,[82] could be diplomatic gifts received by an Aquitanian leader who perhaps participated as a mercenary in the Second Punic War south of the Pyrenees – although they could also have arrived in western Aquitania as booty, soldiers' pay or aristocratic exchange.[83] It remains a plausible conjecture, like the idea that some of the thousands of wine amphorae that circulated in Gaul could have been brought as gifts with diplomatic objectives as well as commercial ones. A possible example of coins as a material object capable of symbolising an alliance and preserving its memory through time would be the preservation of a semi-uncial of *aes grave* minted in the mid-third century BC but which appeared in a level from La Tène D2a at the *oppidum* of Bibracte, perhaps a record of the alliance between the Aedui and their Latian *fratres*.[84]

As well as torques, other objects of attire seem to have been used as diplomatic gifts. Poux indicates that *fibulae* in precious metals could have

---

[80] Duval, 1994.
[81] Caes. *BGall*. 7.1.2.
[82] Hébert, 1990; Gorgues, 2013: 549–50.
[83] Gorgues, 2013: 550; Pérez Rubio, 2022: 385.
[84] Gruel & Popovitch, 2007: 48; Martin, 2015: 47–8; Pérez Rubio, 2022: 181.

been used as gifts by Rome to Gallic leaders or given to chiefs of auxiliary contingents as status symbols or *dona militaria*, despite being absent in descriptions of Celtic dress that for example occur in Strabo[85] and Diodorus[86] and not appearing conspicuously in artistic representations of Celts in the Mediterranean world.[87] Although there is no reference for the Gallic sphere, we do know them from other contexts: for example, in 208 BC, Publius Cornelius Scipio offered the abovementioned Massiva, nephew of the Numidian king Masinissa, captured in Baecula, 'a gold ring, a *tunica laticlavia*, a *sagum*, a gold fibula and a harnessed horse' (Figure 9.5),[88] and handed him to his uncle hoping to win him over. The *fibulae* of the Almgren 65 type, such as those found in Corent,[89] have been interpreted in this way, as well as the *fibula* that is represented on the reverse of the CRICIRV staters (Figure 9.5),[90] which recalls the 'Ravenna' *fibula* preserved in the British Museum. It should be pointed out that the *fibula* appears in these coins associated with horses, torques and small wheels – a civic symbol? a ballot? – as insignia of power, which we can conjecture figured among the gifts offered by Rome to her allies,[91] perhaps in this case signalling the leader of the Suessiones supported by Rome after their defeat in 57 BC. We also find a large *fibula*, in this case an elbow *fibula*, associated with a torque, in the bust on the obverse of a class of Carnutian bronzes of PIXTILOS (DT 2473) (Figure 9.6),[92] and also on the reverse of the *potin* of the Remi *au personnage dansant* (Figure 9.7).

The objects used as diplomatic gifts were chosen depending on their recipient, his power, his status and his importance to the interests of the sender, and served as a medium both to emphasise the messages that they wanted to communicate as well as to grade the recognition offered. They also constituted a material and tangible symbol, and a record, of alliances and pacts. In the Gallic milieu, we find objects that served as presents and that clearly fit within the Celtic cosmovision, such as the torque, but also others that functioned throughout the length and breadth of the Mediterranean, diplomatic 'universals' as it were, which constituted common codes which were the fruit of increasingly intense interactions – in the military and political sphere but also in economic and cultural ones,

[85] Strabo 4.4.5.
[86] Diod. Sic. 5–27.
[87] Poux, 2007: 210–12.
[88] *Tum puero anulum aureum, tunicam lato clavo cum Hispano sagulo et aurea fibula equumque ornatum donat* (Livy 27.19.12). Cf. Livy, *Per.* 27.12; Val. Max. 5.7.
[89] Poux, 2007.
[90] Scheers 27.I–II, DT 547–51.
[91] Poux, 2007: 215–16.
[92] Poux, 2007: 216.

Figure 9.5 Stater minted in the territory of the Suessiones with the legend CRICIRV, and a horse, torque, small wheel and *fibula* on the reverse (Bibliothèque nationale de France).

Figure 9.6 Bronze of the Carnutes with the legend PIXTILOS. Obverse, a male bust with *fibula* and torque (Bibliothèque nationale de France).

forging what we can call a *Hellenistic West*.[93] To receive a harnessed horse, a valuable fibula, rich attire or, directly, minted metal, sent messages that were understood and shared by a Numidian prince, a Roman consul and a Gaulish *rix*: *a common world in the making*.

---

[93] Prag & Quinn, 2013.

Figure 9.7 *Potin* minted by the Remi *au personnage dansant*. Obverse, a figure holding a torque; reverse, *fibula* on a quadruped (Bibliothèque nationale de France).

Bibliography

Almagro-Gorbea, M. [2016]. '*Lancea*, palabra lusitana, y la etnogénesis de los *Lancienses*', *Complutum*, 27 (1), 131–68.

Armbruster, B., Nordez, M., Blet-Lemarquand, M., Fürst, S., Lockhoff, N., Milcent, P.-Y., Nieto-Pelletier, S., Schönfelder, M. & Schwab, R. [2019]. 'Celtic Gold Torcs – An Interdisciplinary and Diachronic Perspective', in B. Török & A. Giumlia-Mair (eds), *Proceedings of the 5th International Conference 'Archaeometallurgy in Europe', 19–21 June 2019, Miskolc, Hungary*, Drémil-Lafage, 417–32.

Baray, L. [2007]. 'La question du don dans les sociétés celtiques', in E. Magnani (ed.), *Don et sciences sociales: théories et pratiques croisées*, Dijon, 29–70.

Baray, L. [2016]. *Sociétés celtiques et mercenaires (VIIe–I^e siècle av. J.-C.)*, Paris.

Baray, L. [2018a]. 'Parures, costumes funéraires et identité ethnique', in L. Baray (ed.), *Les Sénons: archéologie et histoire d'un peuple gaulois*, Gent, 316–20.

Baray, L. [2018b]. 'Les torques ternaires et à arceux comme marqueurs identitaires', in L. Baray (ed.), *Les Sénons: archéologie et histoire d'un peuple gaulois*, Gent, 321–3.

Barruol, G. [1996]. 'La statue du guerrier de Vachères (Alpes-de-Haute-Provence)', *Revue archéologique de Narbonnaise*, 29, 1–12.

Brunaux, J.-L. [1996]. *Les religions gauloises: rituels celtiques de la Gaule indépendante*, Paris.

Buchsenschutz, O. [2004]. 'Les Celtes et la formation de l'Empire romain', *Annales (ESC)*, 59 (2), 337–61.

Callegarin, L. [2009]. 'Les monnaies des peuples aquitains', *Aquitania*, 25, 21–48.
Callegarin, L. [2011]. 'Sociétés et pratiques monétaires dans l'espace pyrénéen occidental au second âge du Fer', in M. P. García-Bellido, L. Callegarin & A. Jiménez Díez (eds), *Barter, Money and Coinage in the Ancient Mediterranean (10th–1st Centuries BC)*, Madrid, 315–34.
Callegarin, L. & García-Bellido, M. P. [2012]. 'Métal, objets d'échanges et systèmes pondéraux en péninsule Ibérique et dans le sud-ouest de la Gaule durant l'Antiquité', in P. Pion & B. Formoso (eds), *Monnaie antique, monnaie moderne, monnaie d'ailleurs: métissages et hybridations*, Paris, 116–39.
Callegarin, L., Geneviève, V. & Hiriart, E. [2013]. 'Production et circulation monétaire dans le sud-ouest de la Gaule à l'âge du Fer (IIIe–Ier s. a.C.)', in A. Colin & F. Verdin (eds), *L'âge du Fer en Aquitaine et sur ses marges: mobilité des hommes, diffusion des idées, circulation des biens dans l'espace européen à l'âge du Fer. Actes du XXXVe Colloque international de l'Association française pour l'étude de l'âge du Fer (Bourdeaux 2–5 juin 2011)*, Bourdeaux, 185–217.
Carlà-Uhink, F. & Gori, M. (eds) [2014]. *Gift Giving and the 'Embedded' Economy in the Ancient World*, Heidelberg.
Cavalier, O. & Baudrand, M.-N. (eds) [2018]. *Le guerrier de Mondragon: recherches sur une sculpture celtique de la fin de l'âge du Fer*, Milan.
Chassaing, M. [1963]. 'Le *torques* attribut divin', *Bulletin de la Société préhistorique de France*, 60 (11/12), 865–74.
Chaves Tristán, F. [2012]. 'Plata, guerra y sociedad: Iberia, finales del siglo III a.C.–inicios II a.C.', in M. Asolati & G. Gorini (eds), *I ritovamenti monetali e i processi storico-economici nel mondo antico*, Padua, 151–89.
Creighton, J. [2000]. *Coins and Power in Late Iron Age Britain*, Cambridge.
Cuniberti, G. (ed.) [2017]. *Dono, controdono e corruzione: ricerche storiche e dialogo interdisciplinare*, Alessandria.
De Hoz Bravo, J. [2015]. 'L'écriture aprés l'économie? Peuples et réponses', in R. Roure (ed.), *Contacts et acculturations en Méditerranée occidentale: hommages à Michel Bats (Études Massaliètes 12)*, Paris–Aix-en-Provence, 501–10.
Delamarre, X. [2003]. *Dictionnaire de la langue gauloise: une approche linguistique du vieux-celtique continental*, Paris.
Delestrèe, L.-P. & Tache, M. [2004]. *Nouvel atlas des monnaies gauloises*, Vol. 2: *De la Seine à la Loire moyenne*, St.-Germain-en-Laye.
Dobesch, G. [1980]. *Die Kelten in Österreich nach den ältesten Berichten der Antike: das norische Königreich und seine Beziehungen zu Rom im 2. Jahrhundert v. Chr.*, Vienna.

Duval, A. [1994]. 'Le torque de Mailly-le-Camp (Aube) et les Nitiobroges: une coïncidence troublante', in R. Boudet (ed.), *L'âge du Fer en Europe sud-occidentale: actes du XVIᵉ Colloque de l'Association française pour l'étude de l'âge du Fer (AFEAF), 8–31 mai 1992, Agen*, Bordeaux, 203–11.

Eluère, C. [1987]. 'Celtic Gold Torcs', *Gold Bulletin*, 20, 22–37.

Fitzpatrick, A. P. [2005]. 'Gifts for the Golden Gods: Iron Age Hoards of Torques and Coins', in C. Haselgrove & D. Wigg-Wolf (eds), *Iron Age Coinage and Ritual Practices*, Mainz, 157–82.

García-Bellido, M. P. [2007]. 'Numismática y territorios étnicos en la Meseta meridional', in G. Carrasco Serrano (ed.), *Los pueblos prerromanos en Castilla-La Mancha*, Cuenca, 199–226.

García-Jiménez, G. [2020]. 'A hierro desnudo: el armamento céltico al sur de los Alpes', *Desperta Ferro Antigua y Medieval*, 59, 44–50.

Gleser, R. [2020]. '*Treveri* and *Mediomatrici*: Spatial Delimitation, Group Identities and the Question of Definition as Regional Archaeological Cultures', in G. Pierrevelcin, J. Kysela, S. Fichtl (eds), *Unité et diversité du monde celtique: actes du XLIIᵉ Colloque international de l'Association française pour l'étude de l'âge du Fer (AFEAF), mai 2013, Prague*, Paris–Prague, 301–10.

Godelier, M. [1996]. *L'énigme du don*, Paris.

Gorgues, A. [2013]. 'Une communauté de marchands méditerranéens à Tolosa au IIᵉ s. a.C.', in A. Colin & F. Verdin (eds), *L'âge du Fer en Aquitaine et sur ses marges: mobilité des hommes, diffusion des idées, circulation des biens dans l'espace européen à l'âge du Fer. Actes du XXXVᵉ Colloque international de l'Association française pour l'étude de l'âge du Fer (Bourdeaux 2–5 juin 2011)*, Bourdeaux, 737–45.

Goudineau, C. [1989]. 'L'apparition de l'écriture en Gaule', in J.-P. Mohen (ed.), *Le temps de la Préhistoire*, Paris, 236–8.

Goudineau, C. [1991]. 'Les sanctuaires gaulois: relectures d'inscriptions et de textes', in J.-L. Brunaux (eds), *Les sanctuaires celtiques et leurs rapports avec le monde méditerranéen: actes du Colloque de Saint-Riquier, 8 au 11 novembre 1990*, Paris, 250–6.

Gregory, C. A. [2015]. *Gifts and Commodities*, Chicago [1st edition 1982].

Gruel, K. & Hiriart, E. [2018]. 'Les élites celtiques: le témoignage des monnaies', *L'Archéologue*, 146, 58–71.

Gruel, K. & Popovitch, L. [2007]. *Les monnaies gauloises et romaines de l'oppidum de Bibracte* (Bibracte 13), Glux-en-Glenne.

Hautenauve, H. [2005]. *Les torques d'or du second âge du Fer en Europe: techniques, typologie et symbolique*, Rennes.

Hébert, J.-C. [1990]. 'Les deux phiales à inscriptions ibériques du tumulus n III de la lande "Mesplede", a Vielle-Aubagnan (Landes)', *Bulletin de la Société de Borda-Dax*, 115, 1–40.

Hébert, J.-C. [1998]. 'La datation haute des monnaies aux types de Béziers, Moussan, et Bridiers, d'après les monnaies de ces types trouvées dans quatre trésors espagnols', *Acta Numismatica*, 28, 79–126.

Hiriart, E. [2016]. 'Les monnaies "à la croix": retour sur l'un des principaux monnayages de la Gaule méridionale', *Revue belge de numismatique et de sigillographie*, 162, 179–98.

Hostein, A. [2012]. *La cité et l'empereur: les Éduens dans l'Empire romain d'après les Panégyriques latins*, Paris.

Hubert, H. [1932]. *Les Celtes depuis l'époque de La Tène et la civilisation celtique*, Paris.

Hyllested, A. [2010]. 'The Precursors of Celtic and Germanic', in S. W. Jamison, H. C. Melchert & B. Vine (eds), *Proceedings of the Twenty-First Annual UCLA Indo-European Conference, Los Angeles, October 30th and 31st, 2009*, Bremen, 107–28.

James, W. & Allen, N. J. (eds) [1998]. *Marcel Mauss: A Centenary Tribute. Methodology and History in Anthropology*, Vol. 1, Oxford.

Joffroy, R. [1967]. 'Un torque d'or de La Tène III dècouvert en Champagne', *CRAI*, 111 (3), 479–84.

Joffroy, R. [1969]. 'Le torque de Mailly-le-Camp (Aube)', *MMAI*, 56, 45–59.

Koch, J. T. [2007]. 'Mapping Celticity', in C. Gosden, H. Hamerow, P. de Jersey & G. Lock (eds), *Communities and Connections: Essays in Honour of Barry Cunliffe*, Oxford, 263–86.

Lamoine, L. [2009]. *Le pouvoir local en Gaule romaine*, Clermont-Ferrand.

Lamoine, L. [2012]. 'Représentations et attributs des rois gaulois de la Gaule Chevelue', in E. Santinelli & C.-G. Schwentzel (eds), *La puissance royale: image et pouvoir de l'Antiquité au Moyen Âge*, Rennes, 163–82.

Lejeune, M. [1969]. 'Les graffites gallo-grecs du torque de Mailly-le-Camp (Aube)', *MMAI*, 56, 61–76.

Lewuillon, S. [1990]. 'Affinités, parentés et territoires en Gaule indépendante: fragments d'anthropologie', *DHA*, 16 (1), 283–358.

Lewuillon, S. [1992]. 'Contre le don: remarques sur le sens de la réciprocité et de la compensation sociale en Gaule', *DHA*, 18 (1), 105–56.

Lewuillon, S. [1999]. 'Le pesant d'or: dépôts fastueux et trafics barbares', in A. Villes & A. Bataille-Melkon (eds), *Fastes des Celtes entre Champagne et Bourgogne aux VIIe–IIIe siècles avant notre ère: actes du colloque de l'Association française pour l'étude de l'âge du Fer (AFEAF) tenu a Troyes en 1995*, Reims, 427–46.

Linderski, J. [2001]. 'Silver and Gold of Valor: The Award of Armillae and Torques', *Latomus*, 60, 3–15.

Lucas, G. [2009]. 'Gésates et *gaesum* dans les sources littéraires gréco-latines', in M.-J. Roulière-Lambert, A. Daubigney, P.-Y. Milcent, M. Talon & J. Vital (eds), *De l'âge du Bronze à l'âge du Fer en France et en Europe occidentale (X^e–VIIe siècle av. J.-C.): la moyenne vallée du Rhône aux âges du Fer. Actes du XXXe Colloque international de l'Association française pour l'étude de l'âge du Fer (AFEAF), mai 2006, Saint-Romain-en-Gal*, Dijon, 11–25.

Marion, S. [2018]. 'Ce fut comme une apparition: sanctuaire et monnaie à l'aube du IIIe s. av. n. è.', in E. Hiriart, J. Genechesi, V. Cicolani, S. Martin, S. Nieto-Pelletier & F. Olmer (eds), *Monnaies et archéologie en Europe celtique: mélanges en l'honneur de Katherine Gruel* (Bibracte 29), Glux-en-Glenne, 263–6.

Martin, S. [2015]. *Du statère au sesterce: monnaie et romanisation dans la Gaule du Nord et de l'Est (IIIe s. a.C./Ier s. p.C.)*, Pessac.

Matasovic, R. [2009]. *Etymological Dictionary of Proto-Celtic*, Leiden.

Mauss, M. [1924]. 'Essai sur le don: forme et raison de l'échange dans les sociétés archaïques', *L'Année Sociologique*, 1923/4, 2 (2).

Mauss, M. [1925]. 'Sur un texte de Posidonius: le suicide, contre-prestation suprême', *Revue Celtique*, 42 (1–2), 324–9.

Maxfield, V. A. [1981]. *The Military Decorations of the Roman Army*, London.

Méniel, P. [1996]. 'Importation des grands animaux romains et amélioration du cheptel à la fin de l'âge du Fer en Gaule Belgique', *RAPic*, 3/4, 113–22.

Meniel, P. [2013]. 'Circulation d'animaux et difusión d'innovations zootechniques à l'âge du Fer', in A. Colin and F. Verdin (eds), *L'âge du Fer en Aquitaine et sur ses marges: mobilité des hommes, diffusion des idées, circulation des biens dans l'espace européen à l'âge du Fer. Actes du XXXVe Colloque international de l'Association française pour l'étude de l'âge du Fer (Bourdeaux 2–5 juin 2011)*, Bourdeaux, 555–62.

Osteed, M. (ed.) [2002]. *The Question of the Gift: Essays across Disciplines*, London–New York.

Ostenberg, I. [2009]. *Staging the World: Spoils, Captives, and Representations in the Roman Triumphal Procession*, Oxford.

Péré-Noguès, S. [2014]. 'L'arrivée des Celtes en Italie du Nord à travers les lectures historiographiques grecques et romaines', in P. Barral, J.-P. Guillaumet, M.-J. Roulière-Lambert, M. Saracino & D. Vitali (eds), *Les Celtes et le Nord de l'Italie/I Celti e l'Italia del Nord: actes du XXXVIe Colloque international de l'Association française pour l'étude de l'âge du Fer (Vérone, 17–20 mai 2012)*, Dijon, 145–50.

Pérez Rubio, A. [2012]. 'Making Epona Proud: Celtic Cavalry at War', *Ancient Warfare*, 6 (3), 15–19.

Pérez Rubio, A. [2015]. 'Trouble Comes in Threes: From Chariot to Cavalry in the "Celtic" World', in G. Lee, H. Whittaker, G. Wrighston (eds), *Ancient Warfare*, Vol. 1: *Introducing Current Research*, Cambridge, 172–90.

Pérez Rubio, A. [2022]. *Coaliciones, diplomacia y conectividad en la Galia ca. 150–50 a.C.: una Segunda Edad de Hierro en red*. PhD dissertation, Universidad Autónoma de Madrid.

Pernet, L. & Rouzeau, N. [2013]. 'La statue de guerrier de Vachères (Alpes-de-Haute-Provence)', in B. Girard (ed.) *Au fil de l'épée: armes et guerriers en pays celte méditerranéen*, Nîmes, 393–7.

Pion, P. [2012]. 'La monnaie mercenaire: une approche anthropologique des premiers monnayages celtiques au nord-ouest du complexe Nord-alpin (IIIe siècle av. J.-C.)', in P. Pion, B. Formoso & E. Roland (eds), *Monnaie antique, monnaie moderne, monnaies d'ailleurs: métissages et hybridations*, Paris, 151–64.

Poitrenaud, G. [2014]. *Cycle et métamorphoses du dieu Cerf*, Toulouse.

Poux, M. [2007]. 'Paire de fibules en or du Ier s. av. J.-C.: autour d'une découverte de l'oppidum de Corent (Puy-de-Dôme)', *Gallia*, 64, 191–225.

Prag, J. & Quinn, J. C. [2013]. *The Hellenistic West: Rethinking the Ancient Mediterranean*, Cambridge–New York.

Prósper Pérez, B.-M. [2017]. 'The Irreducible Gauls Used to Swear by Belenos. Or Did They? Celtic Religion, Henbane and Historical Misapprehensions', *Zeitschrift für celtische Philologie*, 64, 255–97.

Raydon, V. [2014]. 'Deux triades trifonctionnelles de cadeaux diplomatiques offertes par Rome à des roitelets gaulois de La Tène C2 (Tite-Live XLIII,5,1–9 et XLIV,14,1–2)', *RBPh*, 92 (1), 57–70.

Ripollès Alegre, P. P., Cores Urias, G. & Gozalbes, M. [2009]. 'El tesoro de Armuña de Tajuña (Guadalajara)', in A. Arévalo (ed.), *Moneda y arqueología: XIII Congreso Nacional de Numismática (22–24 de octubre 2007, Cádiz)*, Vol. 1, Madrid–Cádiz, 163–82.

Rodríguez Casanova, I. [2014]. 'El tesoro de Valeria: nuevas aportaciones sesenta años después', in E. Gozalbes & J. A. Almonacid (eds), *Cuenca: la historia en sus monedas*, Cuenca, 85–106.

Rodríguez Casanova, I. & Canto García, A. [2001]. 'Alteraciones en moneda hispánica: algunas reflexiones sobre la moneda cizallada', in M. P. García-Bellido, L. Callegarin & A. Jiménez Díez (eds), *Barter, Money and Coinage in the Ancient Mediterranean (10th–1st Centuries BC)*, Madrid, 247–66.

Rosselló Calafell, G. [2021]. 'El regalo diplomático entre Roma y los númidas durante los siglos III y II a.C.', *Habis*, 52, 31–50.

Rowan, C. & Swan, D. [2015]. 'Victory, Torcs and Iconology in Rome and Britain', *Journal of the Numismatic Association of Australia*, 26, 71–90.

Roymans, N. [2004]. *Ethnic Identity and Imperial Power: The Batavians in the Early Roman Empire*, Amsterdam.

Roymans, N. & Scheers, S. [2012]. 'Eight Gold Hoards from the Low Countries: A Synthesis', in N. Roymans, G. Creemers & S. Scheers (eds), *Late Iron*

Age Gold Hoards from the Low Countries and the Caesarian Conquest of Northern Gaul, Amsterdam, 1–46.

Satlow, M. (ed.) [2013]. *The Gift in Antiquity*, Oxford.

Schomas, H. [2011]. *Les images monétaires des peuples gaulois: figures primitives ou expressions d'une société en mutation? L'exemple des Arvernes, Bituriges, Carnutes, Eduens, Lingons, Meldes, Parisii, Sénons et Séquanes.* PhD dissertation, Université de Bourgogne.

Sykes, K. [2005]. *Arguing with Anthropology: An Introduction to Critical Theories of the Gift*, London–New York.

Tausend, K. [1988]. 'Caesars germanische Reiter', *Historia: Zeitschrift für alte Geschichte*, 37 (4), 491–7.

Villaronga Garriga, L. [1993]. *Tresors monetaris de la Península Ibèrica anteriors a August: repertori i anàlisi*, Barcelona.

Villaronga Garriga, L. [2000]. 'Les monedes à la croix trobades a la Peninsula Ibérica', *Acta Numismàtica*, 30, 19–31.

Vitali, D. [2002]. 'L'armamento dei celti nel periodo della battaglia del Metauro', in M. Luni (ed.), *La battaglia del Metauro: tradizione e studi*, Urbino, 103–34.

Wigg-Wolf, D. [2010]. 'The Function of Celtic Coinages in Northern Gaul', in M. P. García-Bellido, L. Callegarin & A. Jiménez Díez (eds), *Barter, Money and Coinage in the Ancient Mediterranean (10th–1st Centuries BC)*, Madrid, 301–14.

10

Do ut des
Liberating Hostages and Offering Gifts on the Hispanian Front in the Second Punic War*

Eduardo Sánchez Moreno and Jorge García Cardiel

Traditionally, the Second Punic War has been conceptualised as the predictable collision between the two great powers of the Central Mediterranean, Rome and Carthage, whose competition for the same resources sucked them into escalating confrontations which would ultimately result in the disappearance of Carthage. There has therefore been a tendency to think in terms of a bipolar world, in which other local communities passively witnessed the conflagration between the two powers, 'an outside war' in which they found themselves 'implicated more or less forcibly'.[1]

In the last two decades, however, the development of postcolonial theory, firstly, and later the application to Ancient History of the theoretical paradigms of International Relations, have made it clear that the Mediterranean world of the time was a multipolar space, in which a myriad of political actors (state, but also individual) battled to pursue their own agendas. The confluence of some of these actors into the orbit of one or the other great power was what determined the balance of regional power. Hellenistic war, in fact, tended to have as an objective the erosion of the enemy power's network of alliances and the conversion, as far as possible, of some of the

---

* This work has been developed within the research project PGC2018-096415-B-C21 'La expresión diplomática en el Mediterráneo occidental bajo la expansión romana: el regalo en su contexto ideológico y cultural', funded by the State Research Agency, Ministry of Science and Innovation, Government of Spain (MCIN/AEI/10.13039/501100011033) and ERDF 'A way of making Europe'.
[1] Barceló Batiste, 2014: 83.

adversary's old allies into one's own.² In this respect, the Second Punic War was no exception.³

Beyond armed conflict per se, however, and on many occasions parallel to it, the abovementioned plurality of agents always endeavoured to maintain channels of communication based on shared codes around which to construct confluences of interests.⁴ The analysis of ancient diplomacy, of its mechanisms, channels and intervening actors, thus reveals its full significance. Based on these hypotheses, the objective of this chapter is specifically to investigate more deeply the diplomatic discourses undertaken along the Hispanian front of the Second Punic War, by virtue of which the plurality of local actors positioned themselves in each moment on the side of one or the other great power.⁵ This will be done by focusing on the recurring significance of one of those discourses, repeated at least three times throughout the war: the liberation of hostages in contexts of the exchange of diplomatic gifts between political interlocutors.

Saguntum, 217 BC

The first episode to analyse more deeply fell during the early stages of the conflict. Gnaeus Cornelius Scipio, recently landed in Hispania to cut Hannibal's supply lines and subvert the network of alliances that the Carthaginians had established in the peninsula, had taken control of the coastal territories north of the Ebro River.⁶ With such an audacious operation, symmetrical to the one Hannibal had led in Italy, the Roman became the hegemonic force in the region, which precipitated a cascade of *deditiones* (surrenders, affirmed with the consequent handing over of hostages) of up to 120 local communities, as well as the arrival of ambassadors from the most far-flung corners of the peninsula.⁷

---

² Eckstein, 2006: 118–80.
³ Italy: Fronda, 2010; Fronda & Gauthier, 2018. Africa: Rawlings, 2017. Greece: Eckstein, 2002.
⁴ Burton, 2011.
⁵ García Riaza, 1997–8; Sánchez Moreno & García Riaza, 2012; Bendala Galán, 2013; Hernández Prieto, 2014a; 2019; García Cardiel, 2019; 2021; García Cardiel & Sánchez Moreno, 2022.
⁶ Polyb. 3.76, 3.95–6; Livy 21.60–1 and 22.19–21. For the historical and archaeological context of the Second Punic War on the Hispanian front, cf. in the last two decades Barceló Batiste, 2000; Costa Riba & Fernández Gómez, 2000; Hoyos, 2001; Levene, 2010; Edwell, 2011; Remedios Sánchez *et alii*, 2012; Bendala Galán, 2013; 2015a; 2015b; Noguera Guillén *et alii*, 2013; Hernández Prieto, 2014a; Chaves Tristán & Pliego Vázquez, 2015; Bellón Ruiz *et alii*, 2015.
⁷ Livy 22.20.11–12.

Early the following year, a new army commanded by the proconsul Publius Cornelius Scipio disembarked in Tarraco. Immediately, the Romans crossed the Ebro, in this case moving their field of operations – and the resulting instability – south of the river.[8] Once there, and after 'intimidating' the local populations[9] (that is, after receiving their *deditio* without a fight, as can apparently also be deduced from Livy),[10] they continued their march to Saguntum. This was the place where Bostar, the Carthaginian official who had been entrusted the defence of the Ebro by a Hamilcar mired in the fight against the Celtiberians, had taken refuge, and, having apparently failed in his mission, he had retired to the vicinity of the Iberian city without putting up a fight.[11]

While the Scipiones entrenched themselves in the city's surroundings, conversations took place in the Punic camp that, in some ways, marked the fate of this first phase of the war. Behind the walls of Saguntum, our sources claim, Hannibal detained sons of all his Hispanian allies whose loyalty he mistrusted.[12] This concentration of hostages in a place with the symbolic significance of Saguntum, as well as their later liberation, has been contemplated with scepticism by a section of modern historiography, which has tended to consider them a mere literary construction reflecting the famous event that occurred after the fall of Carthago Nova, which will be discussed later. The parallels between the two events are certainly notable, and various authors have indicated with distrust the suspicious profusion of details offered by our sources, the unjustified risk of grouping hostages from across Hispania in so northern an enclave as Saguntum, and the naïve character of the stratagem that precipitated their liberation.[13] None of these arguments, however, are sufficiently convincing. It is probable that all these hostages, offspring of 'allies of doubtful loyalty', came from the communities of the north-eastern peninsula recently controlled by Carthage.[14] It would make sense, in this case, to keep them under guard behind the walls of Saguntum, where, apparently, Bostar, the official in command of this front in the war, had his operational base.[15] The degree of detail in the narrative, in turn, does not reveal its falseness but rather the contrary, especially

[8] Richardson, 1986: 37–8; Hoyos, 2001: 74.
[9] Polyb. 3.97.6.
[10] Livy 22.22.4.
[11] Polyb. 3.98.5.
[12] Polyb. 3.97–8; Livy 22.22.5; Zonar. 9.1.3.
[13] Beloch, 1915: 361; De Sanctis, 1917: 174 and 244 n. 45; Rodríguez Adrados, 1946: 146–7; Walbank, 1957, 1: 432.
[14] Hoyos, 2001: 74.
[15] This is what Polybius implies (3.98.1).

when we know that Polybius used Carthaginian sources first-hand,[16] and when the progress of research is gradually demonstrating the plausibility of many of the details mentioned.[17] Perhaps the most definitive argument, however, is that, despite the apparent similarities between this episode and that of Carthago Nova, there is a fundamental difference between them, sufficiently salient in the Graeco-Roman sources that we cannot consider it anecdote: unlike in the events of 209 BC, in 217 BC the Scipio brothers played a passive role,[18] insofar as the initiative for liberating the hostages and its implementation fell entirely upon an Hispanian.[19]

This was one Abilyx (or Abelux in alternative transcriptions), a Hispanian dignitary who at that time was in Saguntum collaborating with Bostar, and whose mind forged the idea of betraying the commander, tricking him into freeing the hostages held at Saguntum and passing the act off as a favour granted by the Romans. Our sources emphasise his high status: he was a 'noble Spaniard',[20] who 'enjoyed the highest character and reputation with his countrymen'[21] and who until that point had stood out for his unshakeable loyalty to the Carthaginian side.[22] On the other hand, they omit his specific origin, since it was enough for them to affirm his Iberian nature to explain, in some way, his lack of *fides*: his strategy was typical of an Iberian and a barbarian.[23] In Polybius, after all, the παρανομία of barbarians,[24] their natural tendency to contravene human and divine laws, is a recurrent and self-explanatory *topos*;[25] a defect, in fact, all the more pronounced (and pointed out) when referring to Hispanians, one of whose defining traits it became for many authors.[26] With his betrayal, Abilyx attempted to ensure a prominent position for himself in the new scenario generated if the Romans won the conflict, something that, according to our sources, the Hispanian believed to be imminent.[27] His action should therefore be contextualised in

---

[16] Cruz Andreotti, 2003: 193–4; Hernández Prieto, 2019: 34 n. 49 and 38 n. 79.
[17] García Cardiel & Sánchez Moreno, 2022.
[18] Lazenby, 1978: 128; Walker, 1980: 128; Richardson, 1986: 37 n. 28; Eckstein, 1987: 200 n. 50.
[19] This is what Polybius' narrative suggests (3.99.9), judging that the Scipiones had a real stroke of luck in Saguntum.
[20] Livy 22.22.6.
[21] Polyb. 3.98.2.
[22] Polyb. 3.98.2; Livy 22.22.6; Zonar. 9.1.3.
[23] Polyb. 3.98.3; Livy 22.22.6.
[24] Polyb. 3.3.5, 21.41.2.
[25] Eckstein, 1995: 122.
[26] Mayorgas Rodríguez, 2014; Aguilera Durán, 2012; 2018: 513–29; Padín Portela, 2017.
[27] Polyb. 3.98.4; Livy 22.22.7.

the many changes of side that other Hispanian leaders tried out with the many twists and turns of the war, and also within the internal disputes that existed in the heart of Saguntum itself, as surely happened in the majority of other Hispanian cities, between a pro-Roman faction and a pro-Carthaginian one, even before the outbreak of war.[28]

Abilyx's interlocutor in Saguntum was, as stated above, Bostar, the Carthaginian official commanding this front. In this case, Polybius describes the soldier through the eyes of his Hispanian counterpart, who considered him harmless and naïve,[29] lacking the astuteness characteristic of his people (*Punica ingenia*),[30] although not, it appears, the Carthaginians' proverbial avarice, since the argument that ended up persuading Bostar was none other than the huge number of presents with which the Hispanian communities would shower him if he agreed to the liberation of hostages.[31] Before arriving at this point, however, Abilyx spoke to him of the abovementioned turn of events in the war, in a true exercise of realist international politics: given that the Romans had crossed the Ebro unopposed, they had become the hegemonic power in the region, for which reason the local communities would naturally look to break their alliances with Carthage to throw themselves into the arms of the Scipiones.[32] The only thing that could prevent this unfolding of events was a great gesture of magnanimity by the Carthaginians: the unilateral and voluntary liberation of the hostages who until then had guaranteed the loyalty of their respective communities, and their return to them, something that Abilyx himself offered to undertake personally.[33] Once he had overcome his initial reticence, Bostar apparently agreed to the idea, falling into a trap which was unbefitting his age.[34]

Abilyx, instead to limiting himself to undertaking the liberation of the hostages agreed with the Carthaginian official, that night slipped off secretly to the Roman camp, where, through the intermediation of some Hispanian auxiliary soldiers,[35] he was led before Scipio himself to explain his plan to him: once in possession of the hostages, he would pass them into Roman hands so that it was they, and not the Carthaginians, who

---

[28] Polyb. 3.15.7, 3.30.1. Cf. Domínguez Monedero, 2011–12.
[29] Polyb. 3.98.5.
[30] Livy 22.22.15.
[31] Polyb. 3.98.10.
[32] Polyb. 3.98.6; Livy 22.22.10–11.
[33] Polyb. 98.7–9; Livy 22.22.10.14.
[34] Polyb. 3.99.8.
[35] Polyb. 3.99.2; Livy 22.22.15.

ultimately liberated them, charging Abilyx himself to accompany them to their communities to divulge the benevolence of Rome.[36]

Firstly, we should note that the Hispanian auxiliaries had to intervene for Abilyx to be admitted to the camp. In this episode, the Romans maintained at all times a passive role, limiting themselves to receiving the proposal enthusiastically and promising great gifts for his services.[37] They also perhaps proposed that the negotiations take place in the Sanctuary of Aphrodite next to the camp,[38] as Scipio Africanus the Younger did years later in another similar meeting, availing himself of the goddess' virtues as a bridge for transcultural communication.[39] For the Romans, Saguntum constituted an enclave of key symbolic importance,[40] and the liberation of the hostages held there could earn them – as it in fact did – the grateful support of the hostages' communities. The Scipiones, however, unlike in the situation for the future Africanus in 209 BC, were not in a position to demand that support, so they had to leave it to the chance of moral obligations and anxieties experienced (or not) by their Hispanian counterparts, in the hope that the articulate Abilyx would this time honour his word and speak in their favour to the local elites.

In this respect, Abilyx's effort was apparently impeccable. His plan went as expected, and the hostages were liberated first by the Carthaginians, followed by the Romans, to be distributed finally among their respective communities by the Hispanian and his collaborators. The propaganda this created could not have been more effective, since the communities of the north-eastern peninsula felt so grateful[41] that they remained thereafter loyal to Rome. As Zonaras indicates with a certain cynicism, 'in this way the Romans obtained possession of these men and won over their native states by restoring them to their homes'.[42] In a cunning game of mirrors, Abilyx – the same man who had betrayed the 'loyal' and 'naturally benevolent' Bostar[43] with Rome's acquiescence – managed to get his compatriots to believe in the 'disloyalty' and 'severity'[44] of the

---

[36] Polyb. 3.99.2–3.
[37] Polyb. 3.99.4.
[38] Polyb. 3.97.6.
[39] García Cardiel & Sánchez Moreno, 2022.
[40] The recollection continued to be used years later as an argument for maintaining the pacts (Livy 31.7.6–7). See Burton, 2011: 241.
[41] Polyb. 3.99.6; Livy 22.22.19–21.
[42] Zonar. 9.1.3.
[43] Polyb. 3.98.5–6.
[44] Polyb. 3.99.7.

Carthaginians, contrasting that with the 'goodness' and 'magnanimity' of the Romans.[45]

If the ruse was successful, in any case, it was because the different agents implicated agreed to participate in a diplomatic exchange with many groups, enabled as usual with gifts, with the rules of which everyone was familiar. The practice of offering hostages as a token of loyalty was, of course, spread widely throughout the Mediterranean during the latter centuries of the Republic,[46] to the point that it was likely that the Hispanians themselves exchanged hostages amongst themselves to consolidate alliances or as a symbolic expression of submission.[47] Their surrender to Carthage, in any case, had no other end than to guarantee the communities' loyalty, according to the custom of the day. It was not, therefore, outlandish of Abilyx to reason that Bostar's unilateral and magnanimous decision to free the hostages would sublimate the gratitude of their respective communities, since, as Livy specifically indicates, 'confide in people, and almost always you confirm their confidence in you.'[48] To put it another way, the unexpected gift (*subitum tantae rei donum*)[49] would generate in the recipient the necessity of responding with loyalty (to the Carthaginian state) and with new gifts (to Bostar himself). The terms of the expected exchange were disrupted when, thanks to Abilyx's Machiavellianism, the Romans captured the Hispanian hostages before they could be returned to their communities, turning them thereby into prisoners of war.[50] Given that the status of prisoners of war was much more precarious than that of hostages, their magnanimous and unilateral liberation by the Romans was considered an even greater gift than the one the Carthaginians could have given; the origin communities' gratitude towards the Romans, and ultimately their need to respond in turn with gifts, was thus greater.[51]

What role did Abilyx play in all these successive gift exchanges designed by him? Both the local communities and the Roman cause benefited directly from the exchange, and the same would have been true for the Punic side had the plan been undertaken that was detailed to Bostar, who had also hoped to enrich himself personally from the Hispanian gifts. In neither of the two cases, however, in either the spurious exchange with

[45] Pitcher, 2017: 193–4.
[46] Álvarez Pérez-Sostoa, 2009.
[47] García Riaza, 1997: 85; 2006: 18. For the Celtiberian world, cf. Esteban Payno, 2021: 414–32.
[48] Livy 22.22.14.
[49] Livy 22.22.12.
[50] García Riaza, 2006: 28–9.
[51] Livy 22.22.18.

which the Carthaginians were tricked, or in that which ultimately benefited the Romans, did Abilyx ask for anything for himself. The Scipiones, nevertheless, knew to reward his services with munificent gifts,[52] which would be no less than a token of the *amicitia* established between Rome and this local grandee. We have yet to establish, nonetheless, how the local communities compensated the 'gift' that Abilyx gave them in orchestrating the liberation of their sons. Polybius and Livy, uninterested in entirely Hispanian matters, rob us of the data, but Abilyx's interest in personally overseeing the return of the hostages should, at the very least, make us suspect the benefit (material and, above all, symbolic) that he himself hoped to obtain from the deal. The grandee, as our sources recognise,[53] sought to consolidate his position in the changing Hispanian political landscape.[54]

Carthago Nova, 209 BC

The second episode on which this chapter focuses took place in Carthago Nova immediately after the city's capture by the future Scipio Africanus in 209 BC. A year before, Publius Cornelius Scipio, son and nephew of the generals who had been defeated – and met their deaths – at the hands of the Carthaginians in the Saltus Castulonensis, received from the senate an extraordinary *imperium* to take charge of what remained of the armies stationed in Hispania, who had retreated to the Ebro line after the Scipionic disaster of 211 BC. From Tarraco, and after dedicating some time to re-establishing alliances with local populations, Scipio undertook an audacious march that in a few days brought him to Carthago Nova.[55] The surprise

---

[52] Polyb. 3.99.4.
[53] Polyb. 3.98.3; Livy 22.22.6–7.
[54] Abilyx's capable diplomatic performance in front of the Scipiones, staged as a spontaneous exchange of gifts, demonstrates the fluency with which even in these early moments the Saguntine nobles were able to participate in the language of diplomatic gift exchange. This circumstance explains the presence of a Saguntine delegation in Rome in 206 BC to offer a gold crown to Jupiter Optimus Maximus in thanks for Roman *amicitia*, a gesture that was in turn recognised by the senate with a gift of 10,000 *asses* to each *legatus* (Livy 28.39.15). It also explains the arrival in Rome three years later of a new Saguntine embassy to hand over to the senate some Carthaginian recruiters that the Saguntines had captured along with the treasure they were transporting, a gesture that was a priori altruistic which the senate rewarded by giving gifts (*munera*) to the ambassadors, returning to them the gold confiscated from the recruiters and providing them with ships for their return (Livy 30.21.5). See Torregaray Pagola, 2005; Ito, 2015: 33–4.
[55] A narrative of the events in Polyb. 10.2–15 and Livy 26.17–20 and 41–8. Cf. Richardson, 1986: 43–9; Eckstein, 1987: 210–15; Zimmermann, 2011: 291–2; Edwell,

capture of the city shattered Carthaginian control over the south-eastern and eastern peninsula, which in turn precipitated a large number of Iberian communities in these territories to abandon the Punic cause in favour of the Roman. It marked, in summary, a turning point in the progress of the war. This, according to our sources, had a lot to do with Scipio's treatment of the Hispanian hostages taken by the Carthaginians.

In the city, over 300 hostages were held who belonged to the circles of power (among them wives, mothers and children of dignitaries) of communities who had signed an alliance with the Carthaginians.[56] As victorious *imperator*, Scipio disposed of this valuable human capital as booty captured from the Carthaginians, alongside prisoners, riches, the arsenal, the navy and the city's treasury. Although the voluntary return of the hostages to their communities and the liberation of some of the prisoners[57] are presented in the sources as acts of the magnanimity and clemency that Scipio would demonstrate,[58] there is arguably no doubt of the instrumentality that this select contingent of booty brought to the interests of a strategist like Africanus.[59] As we will see shortly, moreover, the pragmatism with which Scipio conducted himself in this area is revealed by the control of the timing and scenarios in the restitution process, combining immediate returns with others subject to the progression of events, and the deliberate choice of gifts to ingratiate both the hostages and, above all, their families and communities, taking into account the rank, age and gender[60] as well as the origin of those to be released. The scale of these human and material redistributions should be measured, however, beyond a precise

2011: 323; Olcina Doménech *et alii*, 2016. Scipio's diplomatic endeavours between 210 and 208 BC have been evaluated by Hernández Prieto (2019).

[56] Polyb. 10.18.3. Livy (26.49.1) situates the number of hostages between 300 and 3,724 depending on the different sources he consults. A rhetorical *summum* on the importance of the hostages in the oration that Scipio – via Livy – addressed to the military assembly before besieging the city: 'Here are the hostages of all the important kings and peoples (*Hic sunt obsides omnium nobelium regum populorumque*); and once they are in your power, they will immediately surrender all that is now subject to the Carthaginians' (Livy 26.43.3–4).

[57] Polyb. 10.17.7–14; Livy 26.47.1–2. On the differences of treatment, function and status between prisoners of war (*captivi*) and hostages (*obsides*): Ndiaye, 1995: 151; García Riaza, 2006: 28–9; Allen, 2006: 13–22; Álvarez Pérez-Sostoa, 2009: 154–5; Gueye, 2013: 23–47.

[58] A *topos* within a historiographical tradition (the Polybian–Livian one) exulting the *gens Cornelia*: Torregaray Pagola, 1998; 2017; Zecchini, 2002.

[59] The use Scipio made of the hostages corresponds to a clear political calculation: García Riaza, 2006: 28–9; Collas-Heddeland, 2009: 228; Álvarez Pérez-Sostoa, 2015: 113–15; Hernández Prieto, 2019: 34–9.

[60] Alvar Ezquerra, 2000: 374–5.

time and place, beyond Scipio's hyperbolic protagonism, acquiring their full meaning in the context of the construction and deepening of alliances as fragile as they were necessary for the actors in the struggle.

When the hostages were led into his presence, Scipio first addressed the children, whom he calmed by communicating that they would soon be returned to their homes and upon whom he bestowed gifts taken from the city's booty. He thus offered earrings and bracelets (κόνους καὶ ψέλλια) to the girls and daggers and swords (ῥαμφὰς καὶ μαχαίρας) to the boys.[61] There are implicit messages associated with these gifts: that the young recipients of the gifts were considered aristocratic and, significantly, the future political and military capital of the boys as leaders of their communities. From Polybius' account can also be extrapolated Scipio's interest in establishing contact with the citizens from whom the hostages were drawn; it is for this reason that he urged them to write to their families to communicate that they were safe and let them know – and this is his motive – that 'the Romans were willing to restore them all in safety to their homes *if* their relatives chose to become allies of Rome'.[62] It is probable that a considerable number of hostages – among them the younger ones[63] – were freed a little after the city was taken; Livy indicates that this was the fortune of those hostages who had representatives of their cities in Carthago Nova, who acted as emissaries and escorts of the freed nobles.[64] Another unspecified number of hostages were put under the guard of the quaestor Gaius Flaminius and taken to Tarraco, where the *imperator* withdrew after completing the campaign.

In the case of this latter group, their release, staggered over time, was in line with the negotiation processes with the representatives of the communities that turned their eyes towards an elevated Scipio. Indeed, the establishment of agreements of cooperation would have been an indispensable prerequisite for the transfer of hostages to take place.[65] During the winter

---

[61] Polyb. 10.18.6. Note, from the Greek historian's perspective, Scipio's paternal and affectionate treatment of the young Hispanians, in line with the decorum that he displayed towards the wife and daughters of Indibilis and Mandonius (Polyb. 10.18.7–14; cf. Livy 26.49.11–16); the Roman's benevolence is the antithesis of the cruelty of the Carthaginians towards their hostages, which Polybius denounces through the mouth of Indibilis (Polyb. 10.37.7–10; Livy 27.17.13. Cf. Erskine, 2005: 230–4).

[62] Polyb. 10.18.4–6; cf. Livy 26.49.9.

[63] Eckstein (1987: 212) considers that the children were returned to their homelands unconditionally, but the passage in Polybius (10.18.3–6), in our opinion, does not confirm that.

[64] Livy 26.49.10.

[65] García Riaza, 1997: 86; 2015: 133–4; Hernández Prieto, 2019: 38–9.

of 209 BC, Scipio received various Hispanian delegations in Tarraco with the dual purpose of renewing alliances and winning new loyalty, sanctioned with the return of relatives of kings and dignitaries among other prerogatives.[66] On occasion the initiative came from local leaders who went out to meet Scipio, such as the retinue led by the *regulus* Edecon, who intended to offer his *amicitia* to the Romans in the knowledge that among the hostages held were his wife and children.[67] The alignment with the Romans by the Ilergetes, Indibilis and Mandonius, likewise led to the recovery of their female relatives,[68] also hostages of the Carthaginians, whom Scipio would have treated scrupulously.[69] In any case, the situation of the hostages from Carthago Nova was critical since, with Carthaginian power annulled, their legal protection no longer had meaning, as it did not apply to the Roman state, converting them de facto into prisoners in the hands of the military magistrate.[70]

From the scenes of liberation that took place in Carthago Nova, however, perhaps the most substantial episode is that of the restitution of the captive promised to a Celtiberian noble. It is not for nothing that this anecdote has fed one of the most popular *exempla* in literature and painting since the Renaissance: Scipio's continence (Figure 10.1).[71] From Livy's account, which is more elaborate than Polybius',[72] up to five phases of diplomatic exchange can be inferred which conform to what Burton, in an astute processual analysis of *amicitia*, has called the 'dynamic model of friendship interaction'.[73] Let us review it briefly. The first level is represented by the Roman

[66] Livy 26.51.9–11. According to the Patavian, Scipio 'had spent the entire winter in winning over the support of the barbarians, partly by gifts and partly by restoring their hostages and captives (*reconciliandis barbarorum partim donis, partim remissione obsidum captivorumque*)' (Livy 27.17.1.).
[67] Polyb. 10.34.1–11 and 35.1–3; Livy 27.17.1–2.
[68] Polyb. 10.35.6–8 and 38.1–6; Livy 27.17.8–17.
[69] Polyb. 10.18.7–14 and 38.1–2; Livy 26.49.11–16. The prostration of Mandonius' wife before Scipio, imploring a decorous treatment for the Iberian princesses, draws from the Alexandrian model (the parallel with the scene in which the mother and daughters of Darius III commend themselves to a triumphant Alexander is notorious), which inspires the image of the Roman general (Romilly, 1988: 12–14; Torregaray Pagola, 2003: 161–2; François, 2006; Levene, 2010: 120; Gueye, 2013: 165–7).
[70] García Riaza, 2007: 26; 2015: 134; Hernández Prieto, 2014b: 384.
[71] Herreros González, 2002; Keulen, 2019; Taylor, 2022: 128–34.
[72] Livy 26.50.1–14; Polyb. 10.19.3–7. See also Val. Max. 4.3.1; Sil. *Pun.* 15.263–73; Frontin. *Str.* 2.11.5; Gell. *NA* 7.8; Flor. 1.22.39–40; Polyaenus, *Strat.* 8.16.6; Cass. Dio 16.43; Aur. Vict. *De vir. ill.* 49.7–8; Zonar. 9.8.5.
[73] Burton, 2000: 1–17; 2011: 25, *passim*. For this author, 'friendship is an asymmetrical gift-exchange-based relationship, … a zero-sum competition for status' (Burton, 2011: 66). In the construction of bonds of *amicitia*, both private (between individuals)

Figure 10.1 *The Continence of Scipio*, by Federico de Madrazo y Kuntz, 1831 (© Real Academia de Bellas Artes de San Fernando, Madrid).

soldiers offering Scipio a singularly beautiful young Hispanian woman who was captured in the siege of the city:[74] a 'gift' that operates in the distributive context of war booty and seeks the gratification of the military elite. This is not to diminish the moralising tone of the sources, which focus their attention on the Roman's exemplary respect for the maiden's integrity: his famous *continentia*. The next level transcends the exclusively Roman interlocution to implicate tertiary Hispanian actors, in the way, informed that the maiden in question was engaged to a Celtiberian *princeps* – Livy records his name, Alucius[75] – Scipio turns the young woman into a diplomatic instrument, elevating her status from prisoner to hostage through a dual restitution of high gesture: her return to her betrothed, on the one hand, and to her parents and kin on the other, after summoning them all to the camp where a three-way negotiation was taking place.[76]

The asymmetrical reciprocity of diplomatic materiality is revealed in the third level of the interaction, with an unusual insight into the locals' responses by Livy. The young woman's parents, feeling themselves deeply indebted to Scipio, begged him to accept the gold they had intended to use for their daughter's release.[77] The wealth of these aristocrats serves ambivalently as tribute – what else would it have been but ransom money? – and compensation to the Roman authority. There yet remains, however, space for a further metamorphosis of the gift. In the fourth level of the interaction, the gold offered to Scipio, which is finally accepted in the face of her grateful parents' insistence,[78] became in the *imperator*'s hands a wedding

---

and public or diplomatic (between states), Burton emphasises, primary importance was accorded to gestures, protocols, attitudes, emotions and, significantly, the language of communication.

[74] Livy 26.50.1.

[75] An anthroponym of Palaeo-Hispanic origin epigraphically attested with the Latin variants *Allucquius* and *Alluquius* (Vallejo Ruiz, 2016: 253), which fits ill with the idea that Livy or his sources invented the character (see below, n. 85). Alucius is identified only in Livy (26.50.2) and Dio Cassius (16.43). In terms of his geographical *origo*, a southerly area not far from Carthago Nova has been suggested, around the territories of the Oretani and Bastetani (Capalvo Liesa, 1996: 133–4).

[76] Livy 25.50.2–9. Behind the triangle created by Scipio, the parents of the young woman, and Alucius, it is possible to intuit a political dialogue between three communities: the Roman state represented by the *imperator*, and the Hispanian cities to which belonged the bride's family on the one hand, and the Celtiberian prince on the other, connected ultimately by the exogamy established between them (Sánchez Moreno, 1997: 292–3).

[77] Livy 26.50.10–11. The gold, as neither ransom nor dowry, is present in Polybius.

[78] The unpayable debt to Scipio translated into 'dynamics of anxiety' (Burton, 2011: 74–5).

dowry with which to gratify Alucius.⁷⁹ This is a double reward: Scipio offers the Celtiberian chief not only his liberated betrothed but also a part of the dowry (in gold), acting as a *paterfamilias* complementing, if not supplanting, the parents of the young Hispanian woman.⁸⁰ Once again, the paternalism and *liberalitas* with which Scipio is painted camouflage a complex multilateral dialogue around the movement of goods and services. The fifth level of interaction closes the cycle and endows the diplomatic sequence with a political meaning. Moved by Scipio's gesture, Alucius responds with *fides* and subsequent military support which offered the 1,400 horseman he recruited from his domains and which he soon put at Scipio's disposal.⁸¹ Such was the response to the not-very-veiled condition that the Roman had imposed on the Celtiberian for the return of his betrothed. To quote the words that Livy puts in Scipio's mouth, 'in return for that gift I ask this one recompense: that you be a friend of the Roman people.'⁸²

There is a final substantial detail to be added in the area of Alucius' reciprocity with Scipio. This is the Celtiberian's central communicative function in proclaiming among his people – while he gathered the contribution of the horsemen – the benevolence of the Roman general, with whom he had just bonded himself in *amicitia*. Livy thus details it: '[Alucius] filled the ears of his countrymen with well-deserved eulogies of Scipio. A young man had come who was very much like the gods, he said, a man victorious everywhere thanks to his generosity and kindness as well as his military prowess.'⁸³ Behind the rhetoric, the allies' propaganda. A similar role to that played by the *princeps* Alucius as a new philo-Roman agent can be seen, *mutatis mutandis*, in some of the hostages returned by Scipio to their cities, because they – gratified with gifts that offered dignity and power, and more or less educated about (or convinced of) the benefits of a collaboration with Rome – transmitted these ideals (or practical advantages) among their own, from their triple profile of emissaries and mediators with Roman power and aristocratic elite from their communities of origin.⁸⁴

It is difficult to discern whether the history of the captured beauty liberated by Scipio is a fiction invented by Livy or one of his sources, or

---

⁷⁹ Livy 26.50.12. Thanks to Scipio, the gold travels as goods from the property of the young woman's clan to Alucius', with a parade in the Roman camp: a metaphor for the reorganisation of the Iberian political space, of the framework of regional alignments, as an effect of the initial Roman interventionism.
⁸⁰ Allen, 2006: 134–5; Burton, 2011: 75.
⁸¹ Livy 26.50.13–14.
⁸² Livy 26.50.7–9.
⁸³ Livy 26.50.13; trans. F. Gardner Moore.
⁸⁴ García Riaza, 2006: 33; Álvarez Pérez-Sostoa, 2015: 109–10, 121.

whether it could contain traces of reality.⁸⁵ This is perhaps not the principal question. The value of this story, measured not in isolation but together with all the hostage liberations that we are examining, arguably lies in two aspects that benefit historical analysis. On the one hand is the consideration of the active role in diplomatic, multilinear and plastic interaction deployed during the Second Punic War by the local actors (symbolised in the relatives of the maiden and the *princeps Celtiberorum*: aristocratic and, in the case of Alucius, also military powers in their communities). On the other is the recourse to the use of gifts – of which the liberation of hostages is a further variable – as a language of communication, rapprochement and hierarchical bond shared by Romans, Carthaginians and the Hispanian political entities.⁸⁶

What objects were used with diplomatic ends? The literary record demonstrates that, in contexts of war such as the one discussed, they were above all elements of wealth confiscated from conquered populations: arms, horses, jewellery and personal ornaments, sumptuary vessels ... as well as coins and metal by weight. Booty (*praeda*) became the treasure used by the *imperator* to hand out rewards and bounty selectively,⁸⁷ in the first instance within the army, to reward officers and soldiers, and additionally to foreign interlocutors: old friends and potential, new allies. It is here that the return of hostages, anticipated or satisfied with promises and gifts, and loudly proclaimed, became meaningful.

Livy's quantification of the riches confiscated in Carthago Nova gives a good account of the gains made by the Romans after the fall of the city. Specifically, the Roman historian claims, 'there were 276 golden dishes (*paterae aurae*), nearly all a pound in weight; there were 18,300 pounds of silver in bullion and coin (*argenti infecti signatique*), and a large number of silver vessels (*vasorum argentorum*)'.⁸⁸ In particular, the items of precious metalware would add to their intrinsic and metrological value a symbolic capital that would make them, arguably, prestige goods that were singularly useful in diplomatic interaction. The aristocratic essence of those pieces –

---

[85] The predominant historiographical opinion doubts or denies the historicity of this episode. Thus: Scullard 1930: 93; Walbank, 1967: 219; Eckstein, 1987: 213 n. 101; Allen, 2006: 135; García Riaza, 2007: 26; 2015: 132; Salinas de Frías, 2011: 106; Hernández Prieto, 2019: 37.

[86] Burton, 2011: 260–1. Cf. Sánchez Moreno, 2011; Sánchez Moreno & Aguilera Durán, 2013: 230–7.

[87] On the administration of war booty in the Roman Republic and the implicit terminological debate (*praeda, spolia, manubiae* ...): Churchill, 1999; Rivero Gracia, 2006: 129–33; Coudry & Humm, 2009; Helm & Roselaar, 2023.

[88] Livy 26.47.7.

Figure 10.2 Silver *paterae*, vases and jewellery from El Castellet de Banyoles, Tivissa, Tarragona (© Museu d'Arqueologia de Catalunya, Barcelona).

sometimes exogenous goods of accumulated antiquity, careful manufacture and detailed decoration – their association with commensality and hospitality, as well as their malleability and easy transportation, reinforced their sociopolitical agency. From this perspective we should consider the reading of coin hoards with silver objects that are recognised in Iberian and Celtiberian areas at the end of the third century BC,[89] and significantly, the distribution of *paterae* and *phiales* as representative as those found in Castellet de Banyoles, Tivissa (Tarragona) (Figure 10.2), Santiesteban del Puerto (Jaén) and Titulcia (Madrid),[90] with chronologies of manufacture or concealment (in those cases where these can be estimated archaeologically) close to the Second Punic War.

---

[89] Chaves Tristán, 2012; Chaves Tristán & Pliego Vázquez, 2015.
[90] Raddatz, 1969: 68–102; Olmos Romera, 1997; Jaeggi, 2004; Valenciano Prieto & Polo López, 2017. Cf. Chapa Brunet & Pereira Sieso, 1991; Olmos Romera, 2004: 3. To the list of examples can be added the group of silver plates from Abengibre (Albacete) (Olmos Romera & Perea Cavea, 2004).

Baecula, 208 BC

The third episode to examine more deeply took place the following year, in 208 BC. As spring dawned, Scipio abandoned Tarraco for the south, intending to inflict a new blow upon the Carthaginians, withdrawn at that point to the Guadalquivir Valley and the south-western quadrant of the peninsula. On the road, however, he was approached by Indibilis and Mandonius, who, together with their men, showed that they desired to change sides and embrace the Roman cause, arguing that they had been pushed into it by the snubs they had received from the Carthaginians in the recent past.[91] The growing Roman hegemony over the north-east of Iberia[92] no doubt also weighed in the decision, as well, as we have just seen, as the policy of conditional return of hostages pursued by Scipio. In any case, the *amicitia* between Romans and Ilergetes was sanctioned on the spot by the return of Mandonius' wife and Indibilis' daughters,[93] in a new 'spontaneous' exchange of diplomatic gifts.

The Romans and their allies continued their advance, resupplying in Carthago Nova, and eventually caught up with Hasdrubal's Carthaginian army near Baecula.[94] Once the conflict was over, Scipio shared part of the spoils among his men, but reserved for himself the 12,000 prisoners caught.[95] His next act was to order the quaestor to sell into slavery all the captives of African origin, but to allow those of Hispanian origin to return to their houses without demanding either ransom or any other kind of commitment on their part.[96] With this policy of double standards, Scipio was imitating what he had already done at Carthago Nova, but, above all, what Hannibal had spent years doing in Italy to win the allegiance of Rome's allies.[97]

Undoubtedly, as had already occurred before in Saguntum and Carthago Nova, the gesture constituted an unbeatable first step towards building

---

[91] Polyb. 10.37.7–10; Livy 27.17.13. Hasdrubal Gisco mistreated his former Ilergetan allies: Polyb. 9.11.3.

[92] Quesada Sanz, 2005: 147; Riera Vargas & Principal Ponce, 2015: 65.

[93] Polyb. 10.38.1; Livy 27.17.17.

[94] For the identification of Baecula with the Cerro de las Albahacas (Santo Tomé, Jaén), cf. Bellón Ruiz *et alii*, 2015: 386.

[95] Polyb. 10.40.1; Livy 27.19.2.

[96] Polyb. 10.40.10; Livy 27.19.2.

[97] After the successive battles, Hannibal retained the captured Romans as prisoners of war, but freed the *socii* unconditionally; Ticinus: Polyb. 3.67.4; Trebia: Polyb. 3.69; Trasimene: 3.85.1–4; Livy 22.7.5; App. *Hann.* 11; Zonar. 8.25.8; Cannae: Polyb. 6.58; Livy 22.58.2–4. Hannibal recalled his generosity when he negotiated with the local populations: Livy 25.10.8–9. Cf. Álvarez Pérez-Sostoa, 2015: 111–12.

diplomatic bridges with Hispanian communities with whose elites Rome wanted to create new alliances. The representatives of the communities benefiting arrived at the Roman camp to renounce their previous links with the Carthaginian power and 'submitted to the Roman obedience',[98] that is, sought a *deditio in fidem* around which to construct asymmetrical relationships with the new Roman hegemonic power.[99]

Not only this: the Iberian leaders abased themselves before the Roman general and called him 'king', a title that Scipio swiftly rejected.[100] The attribution of the title, in any case, should in this instance arguably also be read through a diplomatic lens: if we follow Livy's version, the Iberian communities, anxious to respond to the gift that Scipio had given them with the liberation of the captives, not only lent themselves to collaborate with the Roman state henceforth, but also personally repaid the consul by paying him homage that would reinforce his position in the eyes of his own soldiers and in the face of his political rivals in Rome.[101] Perhaps, however, it was the reverse, as Polybius maintains: Scipio, moved by the tribute that the local communities has spontaneously paid him, hurried to respond to them by sending the captives home.[102] The unilateral liberation, voluntary and apparently philanthropic, of the prisoners, in any case, again reveals itself to be a real diplomatic gift, mobilised to lay out a line of communication around which to orchestrate alliances.[103]

Far from contenting himself with that, nevertheless, Scipio wanted to single out the collaboration of the Ilergetes who, as seen above, had joined the Roman column on the road to Baecula. He thus ordered the 300 best horses among those captured to be selected and sent to Indibilis for him to distribute among his men.[104] This is no mere reward or payment promised to a mercenary contingent,[105] but rather a diplomatic present whose symbolic value much outweighed the pecuniary. Three hundred was the number of horsemen Indibilis had ceded to Hannibal in the role of hostages as thanks for having elevated him to the Ilergetan throne ten years

---

[98] Polyb. 10.40.2.
[99] On the expedient of *deditio in fidem*: García Riaza, 2012: 163–6.
[100] Polyb. 10.40.3–9; Livy 17.19.3.5.
[101] On the relationship between the royal proclamation after Baecula and the existence of an anti-Scipio political current in Rome, see Hernández Prieto, 2019: 43, with previous bibliography.
[102] Polyb. 10.40.10. Cf. Richardson, 1986: 49, who assumes this second reading.
[103] Álvarez Pérez-Sostoa, 2015: 109–10.
[104] Polyb. 10.40.10; Livy 27.19.7.
[105] Hernández Prieto, 2014b: 382–3.

before,[106] and 300 was also the number of Roman *equites* who, according to tradition, Romulus had designated to form his personal guard at the dawn of the Roman state.[107] It therefore seemed appropriate to give Indibilis 300 horses to compensate him for the hostages given to Hannibal as a guarantee of defrauded loyalty, but also to recognise his status as king, which appears to have been fiercely disputed at the heart of his community,[108] and which was reinforced by the possibility of redistributing mounts among his most loyal clients.[109]

It is also arguable that Indibilis was not just another ally for Scipio. Our sources indicate that, in the final throes of the war, the Ilergetes were capable of mobilising 20,000 infantry and 2,500 cavalry.[110] More than that, however, was that their leader was used to the Mediterranean diplomatic game and practised it with fluency, ceding hostages to the Carthaginians when he considered it opportune, denying them when the hegemony of the power demanding them was in dispute, operating on the interstate limits as a warlord each time he was deposed from the Ilergetan throne, and offering his services to one power and then the other in the best style of Hellenistic realpolitik. The sources let us glimpse it when they claim that Indibilis spoke before Scipio 'not at all boorishly or carelessly, as one might expect of a barbarian, but rather with modesty and dignity',[111] not trivial praise in the words of a historian as attached to the pro-Scipionic tradition as Livy. It should not be forgotten that the diplomatic exchange between Scipio and Indibilis had been fluent since before Baecula: the Ilergetan had taken the initiative, approaching Scipio and offering to switch to the Roman side due to the poor treatment dispensed by the Carthaginians; Scipio had responded by recognising Indibilis' motives as legitimate, returning his family to him and accepting his collaboration; then the Ilergetan (himself a reigning monarch, after all) had encouraged all the Hispanians present

---

[106] Riera Vargas & Principal Ponce, 2015: 57 and 64, based on Polyb. 3.33.15 (in Livy 21.22.3 the Ilergetan horsemen were 200 in number). For the consideration of those horsemen as hostages, see Moret, 1997: 148. On the abundance of Carthaginian coins in Ilergetan territory during the Second Punic War, see Giral Royo, 2015.

[107] Dion. Hal. 2.13.1; Plut. *Rom.* 26.2; Livy 1.13.8, 1.36.3, 1.43.9; Varro, *Ling.* 89–91; Cass. Dio, fr. 5.8.

[108] Rodríguez Adrados, 1950; Riera Vargas & Principal Ponce, 2015.

[109] Sánchez Moreno, 2005: 239.

[110] Livy 28.31.7. In a later passage, Livy (29.1.26) increases the figure to 30,000 infantry and 4,000 cavalry.

[111] Livy 27.17.10; trans. F. Gardner Moore.

to recognise Scipio as king,[112] an act the proconsul gratified by offering Indibilis his hospitality[113] and, the next day, a *foedus*.[114]

Finally, let us focus on the symbolic connotations that this distribution of horses had for its recipients.[115] Equidae constituted a powerful signal of aristocratic status in the Hispania of the Second Iron Age: that is demonstrated by the abundant representations of horsemen and horses documented in statuary, decorations on vessels, gold and silver work and other metalwork.[116] We also know, moreover, that sacrifices of horses acquired a special resonance for the Hispanian populations.[117] The frequency with which horsemen were represented in coinage from Hispania Citerior is well known,[118] which is seen in the special social, political and ideological consideration of the horse, also useful for constructing shared memories and identities.

Despite the fragmentary and confusing nature of the record, it can be postulated that the Ilergetes put an even greater emphasis on the symbolic importance of horses.[119] In the settlement of Els Vilars (Arberca, Lleida), up to fifteen horse foetuses have been documented buried as votive deposits beneath houses, while in the necropolis of La Pedrera (Vallfogona de Balaguer, Lleida) there are three tombs beneath a fourth-century BC tumulus in which, alongside the funerary urn, three complete horses were buried. Horses are likewise represented on the late stele from Vispesa (Tamarite de Litera, Huesca) demonstrating that among the Ilergetes, horses added a certain funerary component to their aristocratic and warlike connotations. For the Ilergetes, in short, horses were not only mounts, for which reason the gift that Scipio knew to choose for Indibilis tied his grateful ally with a symbolic (but very real) gift that he would not be able to repay throughout what remained of the war.

---

[112] Polyb. 10.37.7–10.38.3.
[113] Polyb. 10.38.3; Livy 27.17.17.
[114] Polyb. 10.38.4; Livy 27.17.17. See Hernández Prieto, 2019: 39.
[115] But certainly also for the Romans themselves. The parallel between the words of Polybius, who juxtaposes the liberation of hostages and the distribution of horses, and the dedication formula on the *tabula* from Alcántara (*AE* 1984, 495), which demands as a prior condition that the conquered return the prisoners and horses, is intriguing.
[116] Blázquez Martínez, 1954; Quesada Sanz & Zamora Merchán, 2003; Lillo Carpio *et alii*, 2004; Barril Vicente & Quesada Sanz, 2005; Almagro Gorbea & Lorrio Alvarado, 2011.
[117] Quesada Sanz, 2012.
[118] Arévalo González, 2003.
[119] Garcés Estalló, 2007.

The gifts that Scipio distributed after the Battle of Baecula did not stop there. According to some information surprisingly omitted by Polybius but included by Valerius Maximus and Livy, when Scipio's quaestor prepared to sell the Africans captured in Baecula into slavery, he noticed that one of them was of royal lineage, so brought him before Scipio. This was Massiva, one of the grandchildren of the Massilian king Gala, who had sent him to Hispania with his uncle Masinissa to harden him on the front. Ignoring the orders of Masinissa, however, who considered him too young to fight, Massiva had thrown himself into the skirmish, ending up captured. Scipio valued this act of bravery and decided to free the young man unconditionally so that he could return with his uncle. Not only this, he also granted him an escort and gave him a gold ring, a *tunica laticlavia*, a Hispanian cloak, a gold fibula and a new horse with trappings.[120]

From our perspective, in this passage Scipio is offering diplomatic gifts on two levels simultaneously. Firstly, he offers an ostentatious group of gifts to Massiva, corresponding *grosso modo* with the attributes that in the Rome of the time were considered appropriate for an aristocratic *eques*: the *anulus aureus*, the *tunica laticlavia* and the harnessed horse.[121] The choice of gifts, evidently, was not accidental. Note, for example, that two years earlier, Scipio himself had sent Syphax, King of the Masaesylians, a toga, a purple tunic, an ivory throne and a gold *patera*, and to King Ptolemy IV of Alexandria a toga, a purple tunic and an ivory throne:[122] in both cases, groups of gifts that were considered royal, qualitatively superior to those that Massiva received – just as the gifts that Massiva received were, of course, qualitatively superior to those that Scipio gave the Iberian *reguli* who followed him. The *imperator*, in short, made use of gifts to construct a space for the negotiation (and recognition) of power and hierarchy between his interlocutors and himself. The logic of diplomatic presents itself demanded that they be made according to the status of the recipient. Let us recall, for example, that during the Principate the allied kings regularly received groups of gifts explicitly ordered hierarchically in accordance with Rome's highest magistracies, whose giving served to make explicit and negotiate the role of each one in the Roman international system.[123] By giving those gifts to Massiva, Scipio tacitly acknowledged his social pre-eminence and that of his lineage. In the process, he built a bridge

---

[120] Livy 27.19.8–12 and *Per.* 27.12; Val. Max. 5.1.7.
[121] Ritter, 1987: 38. On the gradual consolidation of attributes for an equestrian status in the Republican period, see Davenport, 2019: 48–9.
[122] Livy 27.4.5–10.
[123] Braund, 1984: 29.

of communication with the Massilians, which in future would prove to be decisive in the outcome of the war.

This latter consideration in fact leads to the second level of meaning of the Scipionic gifts to Massiva. The young Numidian, let us recall, had been captured and was included among the African prisoners of war that Scipio had decided to sell as slaves. This initiative was protected by the right of war, socially accepted by all the agents implicated in the conflict. Not even the high status of the young man necessarily provided a safeguard: during the subsequent Seleucid War, for example, the son of Scipio Africanus was captured by Antiochus III, who detained him for a while to try to blackmail his father, without success.[124] Scipio, in contrast, by returning the orphan Massiva to his uncle Masinissa immediately, is sending the latter a diplomatic gift: a unilateral gift, generous and apparently disinterested,[125] which aspired to nothing other than opening a channel of communication with the Massilian prince.

The generous liberation of Massiva should be related to the Roman quest for new collaborators in North Africa and, more generally, with the turbulent North African geopolitical landscape.[126] The Scipionic policy of diversification of allies in Numidian territories would not, in fact, be long in yielding results.

A Final Reflection

Analysis of the examples discussed here results in a clear association: the liberation of hostages, and on occasion of prisoners, was often accompanied by the gift of material offerings. They constitute, in reality, two sides of the same coin, since the practice of giving gifts was manifested in multiple and supplementary forms, as a discourse or representation that could be modelled to a variety of cultural and historical contexts.[127] Gifts did not only question the recipient but rather, within the ritual in which they were deployed, acted moreover as a medium for the giver to express himself, as a tool of symbolic communication in the projection of messages and values –

---

[124] Livy 37.34–7.
[125] The gift was, indeed, explicitly disinterested: Scipio not only liberated Massiva, but also bestowed upon him a mount for him to continue fighting alongside his uncle, who at that point fought on the Carthaginian side and had just received the command to lead the Punic cavalry (Livy 27.20.8).
[126] Storm, 2001: 31–2; Rawlings, 2017: 175. Additionally, see the chapter by E. Sánchez Medina & G. Rosselló Calafell in this volume.
[127] Silber has emphasised the diversity and contextualisation of the phenomenon, developing the concept of 'le repertoire du don' (Silber, 2007: 134–8, 143).

specifically, in the Scipionic examples analysed here, the calculating or manipulative generosity of the giver – which surpassed the (direct) recipient of the present (which acquired the form of hostages, objects, promises) to involve other audiences. It would be a simplification to assume a merely receptive or passive role in such audiences (the Hispanian communities, in the cases discussed here); on the contrary, at the point of reciprocating, of responding with services and favours to those gifts received, these audiences also acted as issuing agents of gifts and speeches, and with them of strategies of cooperation, threat or domination over successive actors and spheres of influence. The gift, in essence, transmitted and substantiated power in the theatre of interaction. Like the circular journey of the riches from the spoils of war obtained in Saguntum, Carthago Nova and Baecula – which passed from Punic and Hispanian hands to Roman ones, from Roman to Hispanian … – the dance of the gifts transcended the dancers and ballrooms. Diplomatic materiality is the correlate, the other history, of Hannibal's War in Hispania.

Bibliography

Aguilera Durán, T. [2012]. 'Héroes huidizos y traicioneros: los hispanos de la Segunda Guerra Púnica en el imaginario nacionalista', in J. M. Aldea Celada, P. Ortega Martínez, I. Pérez Miranda and M. de los Reyes de Soto García (eds), *Historia, identidad y alteridad*, Salamanca, 437–61.

Aguilera Durán, T. [2018]. *Barbaros y heroes: recepción de la Iberia prerromana en la España moderna*, PhD dissertation, Universidad Autónoma de Madrid.

Allen, J. [2006]. *Hostages and Hostage-Taking in the Roman Empire*, Cambridge.

Almagro Gorbea, M. & Lorrio Alvarado, A. J. [2011]. *Teutates, el héroe fundador y el culto al antepasado en Hispania y en la Keltiké*, Madrid.

Alvar Ezquerra, J. [2000]. 'El sexo y la edad en la derrota: los romanos en Hispania', in M. M. Myro, J. M. Casillas & D. Plácido (eds), *Las edades de la dependencia durante la Antigüedad*, Madrid, 363–84.

Álvarez Pérez-Sostoa, D. [2009]. 'El confinamiento de los prisioneros de guerra y rehenes en la Roma republicana', *Veleia*, 26, 53–171.

Álvarez Pérez-Sostoa, D. [2015]. '*Clementia* o "visión diplomática": devolución voluntaria de los cautivos en la República romana', in B. Grass & G. Stouder (eds), *La diplomatie romaine sous la République: réflexions sur une pratique*, Besançon, 107–26.

Arévalo González, A. [2003]. 'La moneda hispánica del jinete ibérico: estado de la cuestión', in F. Quesada & M. Zamora (eds), *El caballo en la Antigua Iberia*, Madrid, 63–74.

Barceló Batiste, P. [2000]. *Aníbal de Cartago: un proyecto alternativo a la formación del Imperio Romano*, Madrid.

Barceló Batiste, P. [2014]. 'El final del dominio cartaginés en Occidente', in C. Fernández & B. Costa (eds), *In amicitia: miscellania d'estudis en homenatge a Jordi H. Fernández*, Eivissa, 75–86.

Barril Vicente, M. & Quesada Sanz, F. (eds) [2005]. *El caballo en el mundo prerromano*, Madrid.

Beloch, K. J. [1915]. 'Polybios' Quellen im Dritten Buche', *Hermes*, 50 (3), 357–72.

Bellón Ruiz, J. P., Ruiz Rodríguez, A., Molinos Molinos, M., Rueda Galán, C., Gómez Cabeza, F. & Quesada Sanz, F. [2015]. 'Conclusiones y propuestas sobre el desarrollo de la batalla de *Baecula*', in J. P. Bellón Ruiz, A. Ruiz Rodríguez, M. Molinos Molinos, C. Rueda Galán & F. Gómez Cabeza (eds), *La Segunda Guerra Púnica en la Península Ibérica: Baecula, arqueología de una batalla*, Jaén, 537–99.

Bendala Galán, M. [2013]. 'Aníbal y los Barca: el proyecto político cartaginés de Hispania', in M. Bendala Galán (ed.), *Fragor Hannibalis: Aníbal en Hispania*, Madrid, 46–81.

Bendala Galán, M. [2015a]. *Hijos del Rayo: los Barca y el dominio cartaginés en Hispania*, Madrid.

Bendala Galán, M. (ed.) [2015b]. *Los Escipiones: Roma conquista Hispania*, Madrid.

Blázquez Martínez, J. M. [1954]. 'Dioses y caballos en el mundo ibérico', *Zephyrus*, 5, 193–212.

Braund, D. [1984]. *Rome and the Friendly King: The Character of Client Kingship*, London.

Burton, P. J. [2000]. *Amicitia in Roman Social and International Relations (350–146 B.C.)*, PhD dissertation, University of Maryland, Ann Arbor.

Burton, P. J. [2011]. *Friendship and Empire: Roman Diplomacy and Imperialism in the Middle Republic (353–146 BC)*, Cambridge.

Capalvo Liesa, A. [1996]. *Celtiberia: un estudio de fuentes literarias antiguas*, Zaragoza.

Chapa Brunet, T. & Pereira Sieso, J. [1991]. 'El oro como elemento de prestigio social en época ibérica', *AEA*, 64, 23–5.

Chaves Tristán, F. [2012]. 'Plata, guerra y sociedad: Iberia, finales del siglo III a.C.–inicios II a.C.', in M. Asolati & G. Gorini (eds), *I ritrovamenti monetali e i processi storico-economici nel mondo antico*, Padua, 151–90.

Chaves Tristán, F. & Pliego Vázquez, R. [2015]. *Bellvm et argentvm: la Segunda Guerra Púnica en Iberia y el conjunto de monedas y plata de Villarrubia de los Ojos (Ciudad Real)*, Seville.

Churchill, J. B. [1999]. '*Ex qua quod vellent facererunt*: Roman Magistrates' Authority over *Praeda* and *Manubiae*', *TAPhA*, 129, 85–116.

Collas-Heddeland, E. [2009]. 'Faut-il libérer les prisonniers de guerre? Pratiques grecques et pratiques romaines', in M. Coudry & M. Humm (eds), *Praeda: butin de guerre et société dans la Rome républicaine/Kriegsbeute und Gesellschaft im republikanischen Rom*, Stuttgart, 223–46.

Costa Riba, B. & Fernández Gómez, J. H. (eds) [2000]. *La Segunda Guerra Púnica en Iberia*, Ibiza.

Coudry, M. & Humm, M. (eds) [2009]. *Praeda: butin de guerre et société dans la Rome républicaine/Kriegsbeute und Gesellschaft im republikanischen Rom*, Stuttgart.

Cruz Andreotti, G. [2003]. 'Polibio y la geografía de la Península Ibérica: la construcción de un espacio político', in J. Santos & E. Torregaray (eds), *Polibio y la Península Ibérica*, Vitoria, 185–227.

Davenport, C. [2019]. *A History of the Roman Equestrian Order*, Cambridge.

De Sanctis, G. [1917]. *Storia dei Romani III.2: l'età delle Guerre Puniche*, Turin.

Domínguez Monedero, A. J. [2011–12]: 'Saguntum, el *emporion* de *Arse*, punto de fricción entre las políticas de Roma y Cartago en la Península Ibérica', in *Homenaje al profesor Manuel Bendala Galán: Cuadernos de Prehistoria y Arqueología de la UAM*, 37–8 (2), 395–417.

Eckstein, A. M. [1987]. *Senate and General: Individual Decision-Making and Roman Foreign Relations, 264–194 BC*, Berkeley.

Eckstein, A. M. [1995]. *Moral Vision in the Histories of Polybius*, Berkeley.

Eckstein, A. M. [2002]. 'Greek Mediation in the First Macedonian War, 209–205 B.C.', *Historia: Zeitschrift für alte Geschichte*, 51 (3), 268–97.

Eckstein, A. M. [2006]. *Mediterranean Anarchy, Interstate War, and the Rise of Rome*, Berkeley.

Edwell, P. [2011]. 'War Abroad: Spain, Sicily, Macedon, Africa', in D. Hoyos (ed.), *A Companion to the Punic Wars*, Oxford, 320–38.

Erskine, A. [2005]. 'Spanish Lessons: Polybius and the Maintenance of Imperial Power', in J. Santos Yanguas & E. Torregaray Pagola (eds), *Polibio y la Península Ibérica: Revisiones de Historia Antigua, IV*, Vitoria, 229–43.

Esteban Payno, M. [2021]. *Praxis diplomática y comunicación política en el mundo celtibérico (siglos III–I a.C.)*, PhD dissertation, Universitat de les Illes Balears, Palma de Mallorca.

François, P. [2006]. '*Externo more*: Scipion l'Africain et l'hellénisation', in *L'hellénisation en la Méditerranée occidentale au temps des guerres puniques (260–180 av. J.-C.)*, *Pallas*, 70, 313–28.

Fronda, M. P. [2010]. *Between Rome and Carthage: Southern Italy during the Second Punic War*, Cambridge.

Fronda, P. & Gauthier, F. [2018]. 'Italy and Sicily in the Second Punic War: Multipolarity, Minor Powers, and Local Military Entrepreneurialism', in

T. Ñaco & F. López Sánchez (eds), *Warlords: War and Interstate Relations in the Ancient Mediterranean 404 BC–AD 14*, Leiden, 308–24.

Garcés Estalló, I. [2007]. 'El empleo del ronzal caballar en el norte del Ebro durante la Edad del Hierro y la época ibérica', *Gladius*, 27, 67–84.

García Cardiel, J. [2019]. '*Animos barbarorum*: religión y comunidades locales en el frente hispano de la Segunda Guerra Púnica', in E. Sánchez Moreno & E. García Riaza (eds), *Unidos en armas: coaliciones militares en el Occidente antiguo*, Palma de Mallorca, 105–32.

García Cardiel, J. [2021]. 'Herakles as a Weapon of War: Religious Discourses and Local Responses in Ancient Iberia during the Second Punic War', *Aevum*, 95 (1), 87–109.

García Cardiel, J. & Sánchez Moreno, E. [2022]. 'Los Escipiones visitan a Afrodita: los santuarios hispanos de la diosa en el contexto de la Segunda Guerra Púnica', *DHA*, 48 (2), 303–26.

García Riaza, E. [1997]. 'La función de los rehenes en la diplomacia hispano-republicana', *Memorias de Historia Antigua*, 18, 81–108.

García Riaza, E. [1997–8]. 'La presencia cartaginesa en Hispania (237–206 a.C.): aspectos diplomático-militares', *Mayurqa*, 24, 17–31.

García Riaza, E. [2006]. 'Rehenes y diplomacia en la Hispania romano-republicana', in G. Bravo & R. González (eds), *Minorías y sectas en el mundo romano*, Madrid, 17–34.

García Riaza, E. [2007]. '*Tempus poenae*: represalias contra poblaciones sometidas durante la expansión romana en Hispania', in G. Bravo Castañeda (ed.), *Formas y usos de la violencia en el mundo romano*, Madrid, 19–30.

García Riaza, E. [2012]. 'Sobre los mecanismos de integración de los vencidos en el Occidente romano-republicano: algunas observaciones', in F. Marco, F. Pina & J. Remesal (eds), *Vae victis! Perdedores en el mundo antiguo*, Barcelona, 161–76.

García Riaza, E. [2015]. 'Foreign Cities: Institutional Aspects of the Roman Expansion in the Iberian Peninsula (218–133 B.C.)', in M. Jehne and F. Pina Polo (eds), *Foreign Clientelae in the Roman Empire: A Reconsideration*, Frankfurt am Main, 119–39.

Giral Royo, F. [2015]. 'Cartagineses y romanos en la Ilergecia: testimonios numismáticos', *Revista d'Arqueologia de Ponent*, 25, 83–101.

Gueye, M. [2013]. *Captifs et captivité dans le monde romain: discours littéraire et iconographique (IIIe siècle av. J.-C.–IIe siècle ap. J.-C.)*, Paris.

Helm, M. & Roselaar, S. T. (eds.) [2023]. *Spoils in the Roman Republic. Boon and Bane*, Stuttgart.

Hernández Prieto, E. [2014a]. *Roma y la Segunda Guerra Púnica en Hispania*, PhD dissertation, Universidad de Salamanca.

Hernández Prieto, E. [2014b]. 'Capturados vivos: hispanos, púnicos, mercenarios y rebeldes en las primeras décadas de la conquista romana de la Península Ibérica (218–201 a.C.)', in G. Bravo Castañeda & R. González Salinero (eds), *Conquistadores y conquistados: relaciones de dominio en el mundo romano*, Madrid, 377–98.

Hernández Prieto, E. [2019]. 'Las adhesiones hispanas a Escipión del 210–208 a.C. (Carthago Nova y Baecula)', in E. García Riaza & A.M. Sanz (eds), *'In fidem venerunt': expresiones de sometimiento a la República romana en Occidente*, Madrid, 27–57.

Herreros González, C. [2002]. 'Una nueva línea de investigación a propósito de la "Continencia de Escipión": el imperialismo escipiónico del s. II a.C. como modelo ideológico de las monarquías absolutistas de época moderna', *Iberia: Revista de la Antigüedad*, 5, 195–204.

Hoyos, B. D. [2001]. 'Generals and Annalists: Geographic and Chronological Obscurities in the Scipios' Campaigns in Spain 218–211 B.C.', *Klio*, 83, 68–92.

Ito, M. [2015]. *Informal Diplomacy and Rome from the First Macedonian War to the Assassination of Ti. Gracchus*, PhD dissertation, University of Edinburgh.

Jaeggi, O. [2004]. 'Vajillas de plata iberohelenísticas', in R. Olmos Romera & P. Rouillard (eds), *La vajilla ibérica en época helenística (siglos IV–III al cambio de era)*, Madrid, 49–61.

Keulen, W. [2019]. 'The "Controversial" Continence of Scipio in Literature and Art: Gellius' *Noctes Atticae* and Nicolò dell'Abate', in S. Finkmann, A. Behrendt & A. Walter (eds), *Antike Erzähl- und Deutungsmuster: wischen Exemplarität und Transformation*, Berlin, 595–615.

Lazenby, J. F. [1978]. *Hannibal's War*, Norman, OK.

Levene, D. S. [2010]. *Livy on the Hannibalic War*, Oxford.

Lillo Carpio, P. A., Page Pozo, V. del & García Cano, J. M. (eds) [2004]. *El caballo en la sociedad ibérica: una aproximación al santuario de El Cigarralejo*, Murcia.

Mayorgas Rodríguez, A. [2014]. 'Los bárbaros hispanos de Livio en la Segunda Guerra Púnica', in G. Bravo & R. González (eds), *Conquistadores y conquistados: relaciones de dominio en el mundo romano*, Madrid, 255–68.

Moret, P. [1997]. 'Les Ilergètes et leurs voisins dans la troisième décade Tite-Live', *Pallas*, 46, 147–65.

Ndiaye, S. [1995]. 'Le recours aux otages à Rome sous la République', *DHA*, 21 (1), 149–65.

Noguera Guillén, J., Ble Gimeno, E. & Valdés Matías, E. (eds) [2013]. *La Segona Guerra Púnica al nord-est de Ibèria: una revissió necessària*, Barcelona.

Olcina Doménech, M., Sala Sellés, F. & Abad Casal, L. [2016]. 'El camino de los Escipiones entre Saguntum y Cartagena', in M. Bendala Galán (ed.), *Los Escipiones: Roma conquista Hispania*, Alcalá de Henares, 149–61.

Olmos Romera, R. [1997]. 'Las incertidumbres de los lenguajes iconográficos: las páteras de plata ibérica', in R. Olmos Romera & J. Santos Velasco (eds), *Iconografía ibérica: iconografía itálica. Propuestas de interpretación y lectura*, Madrid, 91–102.

Olmos Romera, R. [2004]. 'Banquetes y vajilla en la Hispania republicana: algunos textos', in R. Olmos Romera & P. Rouillard (eds), *La vajilla ibérica en época helenística (siglos IV–III al cambio de era)*, Madrid, 1–4.

Olmos Romera, R. & Perea Cavea, A. [2004]. 'La "vajilla" de plata de Abengibre', in R. Olmos Romera & P. Rouillard (eds), *La vajilla ibérica en época helenística (siglos IV–III al cambio de era)*, Madrid, 63–76.

Padín Portela, B. [2017]. 'Héroes y traidores de la Antigüedad: dos arquetipos narrativos en la historiografía nacionalista española', *Hispania Antiqua*, 41, 389–428.

Pitcher, L. [2017]. 'Polybius', in K. De Temmerman & E. van Emde Boas (eds), *Characterization in Ancient Greek Literature*, Leiden, 191–206.

Quesada Sanz, F. [2005]. 'De guerreros a soldados: el ejército de Aníbal como un ejército cartaginés atípico', in B. Costa & J. H. Fernández (eds), *Guerra y ejército en el mundo fenicio-púnico: XIX Jornadas de Arqueología Fenicio-Púnica*, Ibiza: 129–62.

Quesada Sanz, F. [2012]. 'Sobre caballos, caballeros y sacrificios cruentos en la Roma republicana y en Hispania', in M. R. García Huerta & F. Ruiz (eds), *Animales simbólicos en la Historia: desde la Protohistoria hasta el final de la Edad Media*, Madrid, 111–32.

Quesada Sanz, F. & Zamora Merchán, M. (eds) [2003]. *El caballo en la antigua Iberia: estudios sobre los équidos en la Edad del Hierro*, Madrid.

Raddatz, K. [1969]. *Die Schatzfunde der Iberischen Halbinsen von Ende des dritten bis zur Mitte des ersten Jahrhunderts vor Chr. Geb.: Untersuchungen zur hispanischen Toreutik*, Berlin.

Rawlings, L. [2017]. 'Warlords, Carthage and the Limits of Hegemony', in T. Ñaco & F. López (eds), *War, Warlords, and Interstate Relations in the Ancient Mediterranean*, Leiden, 151–80.

Remedios Sánchez, S., Prados Martínez, F. & Bermejo Tirado, J. (eds) [2012]. *Aníbal de Cartago: historia y mito*, Madrid.

Richardson, J. S. [1986]. *Hispaniae: Spain and the Development of Roman Imperialism, 218–82 BC*, Cambridge.

Riera Vargas, R. & Principal Ponce, J. [2015]. 'Sitting on the Fence: Ilergetan Attitudes and Responses to Imperialist Strategies', in T. Ñaco, R. Riera &

D. Gómez (eds), *Ancient Disasters and Crisis Management in Classical Antiquity*, Gdańsk, 53–70.

Ritter, H. V. [1987]. *Röm und Numidien: Untersuchungen zur rechtlichen Stellung abhängige Könige*, Lüneburg.

Rivero Gracia, M. P. [2006]. *Imperator populi Romani: una aproximación al poder republicano*, Zaragoza.

Rodríguez Adrados, F. [1946]. 'La *fides* ibérica', *Emerita*, 14, 128–209.

Rodríguez Adrados, F. [1950]. 'Las rivalidades de las tribus del noreste español y la conquista romana', in *Estudios dedicados a Menéndez Pidal*, Vol. 1, Madrid, 563–87.

Romilly, J. de [1988]. 'Le conquérant et la belle captive', *Bulletin de l'Association Guillaume Budé*, 1 (mars 1988), 3–15.

Salinas de Frías, M. [2011]. 'Sobre la memoria histórica en Roma: los Escipiones y la traición de los celtíberos', *Studia Historica: Historia Antigua*, 29, 97–118.

Sánchez Moreno, E. [1997]. 'La mujer en las formas de relación entre núcleos y territorios de la Iberia protohistórica: I, Testimonios literarios', *Espacio, Tiempo y Forma. Serie II: Historia Antigua*, 10, 285–94.

Sánchez Moreno, E. [2005]. 'Caballo y sociedad en la Hispania céltica: del poder aristocrático a la comunidad política', *Gladius*, 25, 237–64.

Sánchez Moreno, E. [2011]. 'De la resistencia a la negociación: acerca de las actitudes y capacidades de las comunidades hispanas frente al imperialismo romano', in E. García Riaza (ed.), *De fronteras a provincias: interacción e integración en Occidente (ss. III–I a.C.)*, Palma de Mallorca, 97–103.

Sánchez Moreno, E. & Aguilera Durán, T. [2013]. 'Bárbaros y vencidos, los otros en la conquista romana de Hispania: notas para una deconstrucción historiográfica', in R. Cid López & E. García Fernández (eds), *Debita verba: estudios en homenaje al profesor Julio Mangas Manjarrés*, Vol. 1, Oviedo, 225–44.

Sánchez Moreno, E. & García Riaza, E. [2012]. 'La interacción púnica en Iberia como precedente de la expansión romana: el caso de Lusitania', in M. B. Cocco, A. Gavini & A. Ibba (eds), *Trasformazione dei paesaggi del potere nell'Africa settentrionale fino alla fine del mondo antico: l'Africa Romana*, 19, 1249–59.

Scullard, H. H. [1930]. *Scipio Africanus in the Second Punic War*, Cambridge.

Silber, I. F. [2007]. 'Registres et repertoires du don: avec mais aussi après Mauss?', in E. Magnani (ed.), *Don et sciences sociales: théories et pratiques croisées*, Dijon, 123–43.

Storm, E. [2001]. *Massinissa: Numidien im Aufbruch*, Stuttgart.

Taylor, M. J. [2022]. 'Conquest and Continence: Roman Sexual Politics at the Dawn of Empire', in H. Cornwell & G. Woolf (eds), *Gendering Roman Imperialism*, Leiden–Boston, 128–45.

Torregaray Pagola, E. [1998]. *La elaboración de la tradición sobre los Cornelii Scipiones: pasado histórico y conformación simbólica*, Zaragoza.

Torregaray Pagola, E. [2003]. 'La influencia del modelo de Alejandro Magno en la tradición escipiónica', *Gerion*, 21 (1), 137–66.

Torregaray Pagola, E. [2005]. 'Embajadas y embajadores entre Hispania y Roma en la obra de Tito Livio', in E. Torregaray & J. Santos (eds), *Diplomacia y autorrepresentación en la Roma antigua* (Anejos de Veleia, 6), Vitoria, 25–61.

Torregaray Pagola, E. [2017]. 'Les Scipions: la création d'une tradition politique fondée sur la victoire', in D. Álvarez Pérez-Sostoa & J. Lanz Betelu (eds), *The Aftermath in Rome: Preparing War, Managing Victory*, Zaragoza, 37–67.

Valenciano Prieto, M. C. & Polo López, J. [2017]. '*Phiale* de plata del *oppidum* de Titulcia', *Complutum*, 28 (1), 163–84.

Vallejo Ruiz, J. M. [2016]. *Onomástica paleohispánica: I, Antroponimia y teonimia. 1, Testimonios epigráficos latinos, celtibéricos y lusitanos, y referencias literarias*, Vitoria.

Walbank, F. W. [1957]. *A Historical Commentary on Polybius*, Oxford.

Walbank, F. W. [1967]. *A Historical Commentary on Polybius*, Volume 2: *Commentary on Books VII–XVIII*, Oxford.

Walker, C. [1980]. *Hostages in Republican Rome*, PhD dissertation, University of North Carolina, Chapel Hill.

Zecchini, G. [2002]. 'Scipione in Spagna: un approriccio critico alla tradizione polibiano-liviana', in G. Urso (ed.), *Hispania terris ómnibus felicior: premesse ed estii di un proceso di integrazione*, Pisa, 87–103.

Zimmermann, K. [2011]. 'Roman Strategy and Aims in the Second Punic War', in B. D. Hoyos (ed.), *A Companion to Roman Imperialism*, Leiden–Boston, 280–98.

11

Gold for the Romans
Booty, Gifts and Bribes during the Roman Conquest of the Western Iberian Peninsula*

Manuel Salinas de Frías

A bright but sinister thread runs through the history of the Roman conquest of the Iberian Peninsula like a Wagnerian leitmotif: it is the glitter of gold, by which the conquerors never felt quite satiated – gold in booty, gold in bribes or gold in diplomatic gifts to buy peace or to recognise the conqueror's supremacy. The purpose of this chapter is to study the forms assumed by this transfer of gold, and in general of precious metals, during the conquest of the western peninsula: its causes, its modalities and the consequences it had both for the indigenous societies and for the Romans.[1]

Booty

The Romans had many ways of obtaining the gold and precious metals in general that they so coveted; the spoils of war were the simplest and most direct way of doing so. Livy gives detailed references to the booty obtained

---

* This work has been developed within the research project PGC2018-096415-B-C21 'La expresión diplomática en el Mediterráneo occidental bajo la expansión romana: el regalo en su contexto ideológico y cultural', funded by the State Research Agency, Ministry of Science and Innovation, Government of Spain (MCIN/AEI/10.13039/501100011033) and ERDF 'A way of making Europe'.

[1] The Roman interest in gold and silver even reached the ears of Judas Maccabaeus: 1 Macc. 8:3; on Galba's and Lucullus' *avaritia* for precious metal: App. *Hisp.* 51–2, 54, 60; Decimus Brutus plundered the west to enrich his soldiers: App. *Hisp.* 71 and 75; the inhabitants of Cinginnia replied to the proconsul that they had no gold to give him but only iron to fight him: Val. Max. 6.4. On Caesar's rapacity in the province during his praetorship, going so far as to attack even his allies in order to obtain riches: App. *Hisp.* 102; Suet. *Iul.* 18 and 54; Plut. *Caes.* 11; Cass. Dio 37.52–3; Zonar. 10.6.

in the provinces of Hispania Citerior and Ulterior in the years 197–167 BC, and the figures for this booty have been the subject of study on various occasions.[2] Although the data relating to Hispania Ulterior are less abundant than those relating to Hispania Citerior, a rereading of Livy's text nevertheless allows us to draw conclusions that indicate the amount of wealth obtained from the province over a period of some thirty years.

The first report dates back to 198 BC, when L. Manlius Acidinus, who had been proconsul from 205 to 200 BC, paid into the *aerarium*, *ex Hispania*, 1,200 pounds of silver and almost 30 pounds of gold.[3] The following year, L. Stertinius, who had governed the provinces over the two years of 199–198 BC, brought in great riches which, according to Livy, cemented his hopes of holding a triumph (50,000 pounds of silver), as well as building, with the remaining fortune, two triumphal arches (*fornices*) in the Forum Boarium, in front of the Temples of Fortuna and Mater Matuta, and a third in the Circus Maximus, all three decorated with gold.[4] These figures show the great wealth extracted from the province despite the fact that there is no record of any major battles to justify significant booty. The Hispanians' unrest can therefore be understood, finding expression in the same year with an uprising in both provinces. In Hispania Ulterior this uprising involved various kings and *populi*, who were joined by the Phoenician cities.[5] Although the uprising could not be put down by the praetor of the province, M. Helvius, he paid into the *aerarium* 14,732 pounds of silver, as well as 121,441 in *argentum oscense* and 70,023 *bigati*.[6] There is a general consensus that *argentum oscense* refers to Iberian silver drachmae, while *bigati* were coins imitating Roman coins.[7] The situation could be brought under control only with the dispatch in 195 BC of a consular army under the command of the consul M. Porcius Cato, to whom both *Hispaniae* were assigned in an extraordinary command, with the praetor of Hispania Citerior as his assistant. The following year Cato deposited, from both provinces, booty of 25,000 pounds of unminted silver and 1,400 pounds of gold, as well as 123,000 *bigati* and 540 coins of *argentum oscense*.[8]

It is not until 194 BC, however, that we have the first reference to booty seized from the Lusitanians. The praetor of Hispania Ulterior in that year, Publius Scipio, attacked them on the pretext that they had plundered the

---

[2] Fatás Cabezas, 1973; Fernández Gómez, 1989; García Riaza, 1999a; 1999b.
[3] Livy 32.7.4.
[4] Livy 33.27.4–5.
[5] Livy 33.19.7, 33.21.6–9.
[6] Livy 34.10.4.
[7] Milne, 1944; Seltman, 1944; Neatby, 1951; Villaronga Garriga, 1979: 114.
[8] Livy 34.46.2.

province. He fought them not far from the city of Ilipa and, after defeating them, returned with an *opulentum exercitum*.⁹ In 191 BC, M. Fulvius Nobilior deposited, *ex Hispania Ulteriore*, 12,000 pounds of silver, 127 pounds of gold and 130 of *bigati*, which earned him an *ovatio*.¹⁰ Two years later, his successor in command, L. Aemilius Paullus – of whom we know explicitly that he fought the Lusitanians, since in the first year of his rule he was defeated by them – seized a booty of gold.¹¹

The next five years were spent in bitter battles against the Lusitanians and other peoples of the southern plateau, mainly the Vettones and Carpetani, until in 185 BC the praetors C. Calpurnius Piso and L. Quinctius Crispinus won a decisive victory at the Tagus River.¹² The two praetors each earned the triumph *de Lusitanis et Celtiberis*, and Calpurnius paid into the *aerarium* 12,000 pounds of silver and 83 gold crowns.¹³ We have no further data until six years later, when L. Postumius Albinus and T. Sempronius Gracchus received triumphs for their victories of 180–179 BC. Gracchus held his first, and Albinus did so the day after *de Lusitanis aliisque*, bringing in a booty of 20,000 pounds of silver. It is noteworthy that in the *fasti triumphales* Albinus' triumph appears as *[ex] Lu[sita]nia Hispaniaq(ue)*.¹⁴ Ten years later, in 169 BC, M. Claudius Marcellus, who had held the governorship of both provinces, deposited the sum of 100 pounds of silver and 10 pounds of gold.¹⁵

The loss of Livy's text from 167 BC makes it impossible to continue this series. Despite this, and the fact that the data are more fragmentary for the province of Ulterior than for the province of Citerior, we can nevertheless assess the amount of precious metal, gold and silver, extracted by the Romans from that province. The totals add up to 1,837 pounds of gold, 135,032 pounds of unminted silver, 121,981 pounds of *argentum oscense*, 193,153 of *bigati*, as well as 83 gold crowns, and the wealth necessary to finance the three triumphal arches erected by M. Helvius in 197 BC. These sums are obviously only a part of the wealth actually extracted, since many years' worth of data are missing. On the other hand, these figures probably reflect only what was paid into the *aerarium Saturni*, not counting

---

⁹ Livy 35.1.11–12.
¹⁰ Livy 36.39.1–2.
¹¹ Polyb. 31.22.3.
¹² On the military coalition: Sánchez Moreno, 2019a.
¹³ Livy 39.42.4. On the symbolic value of these *coronae aureae* as an element of ostentation whose frequency increased after the confrontation with the Hellenistic states, cf. García Riaza, 1999a: 129–30.
¹⁴ Livy 41.7.1–3; García Riaza, 2019a.
¹⁵ Livy 45.4.1.

the *manubiae* kept by the victorious general, the *stipendium* paid to the troops and various rewards.[16] In other words, the amounts requisitioned in the provinces must have been much higher. As García Riaza has rightly observed, moreover, the figures expressed can be understood only in the context of the performance of the ritual of victory.[17] The identification of the concepts mentioned by Livy raises problems that have yet to be satisfactorily resolved. On the one hand, there is the archaeologically attested silver and gold jewellery, some of which (single-hooked funicular torques and spiral bracelets) have been supposed to have functioned as pre-monetary currency, because their weights are standardised and their structure easily segmented – a function of pre-monetal currency – which relates them to the 'small cut-out silver sheets' mentioned by Strabo.[18] These objects could be hidden under the designations of *argentum infectum* or the *coronae* mentioned by Livy, who, in contrast, never mentions *viriae* or *torques*. On the other hand, there is the fact that no coins of the type known as Iberian denarii or imitation drachmae have appeared in Italy, which would be expected if these specimens are identified with the *argentum oscense* and the *bigati* mentioned by Livy. The explanation could be that these coins were immediately melted down and repurposed, probably into *argentum infectum*.[19]

These are not, however, the only mentions of the spoils of war. In other cases, we find references to it, although we do not know the exact amount. In 154 BC, for example, L. Mummius pursued the Lusitanians and Vettones, who, after sacking the province and attacking the cities of the Blastophoenicians, had crossed into North Africa. After defeating them, he distributed the booty that could be carried among the soldiers, and the rest he burnt in honour of the gods of war.[20] In another example, in 140 BC Fabius Maximus lost the booty (λεία) he was carrying when his army was attacked by two *lestarchoi*, Curius and Apuleius, who commanded an army of 10,000 men.[21]

The origin of this gold was mainly alluvial, although there is also evidence of mining activity for raw gold in those areas where other types of silver/lead or copper deposits were exploited, with which native and

---

[16] From very early on, however, the *stipendium* was collected among the indigenous Hispanians, as the reference to a *stipendium duplex* shows (Livy 29.3.5); cf. Salinas de Frías, 1995: 146–8.
[17] Strabo 3.3.7. Cf. García Riaza, 1999a: 121.
[18] García-Bellido, 1999: 369–70.
[19] García-Bellido, 1999: 371, 384.
[20] App. *Hisp.* 57.
[21] App. *Hisp.* 68.

visible gold was associated. As indicated, all literary references to peninsular gold that provide specific geographic data always mention a river.[22] Silver, on the other hand, was almost exclusively mined. The study of pre-Roman gold and silversmiths' work seems to show a preference for gold in the north-western Castreño world, while silver was preferred in the Meseta Central region. Comparing Livy's figures for booty for the decades 197–167 BC with the meagre booty that Scipio Aemilianus distributed to his soldiers after the fall of Numantia – 7 denarii per head – we can see the enormous deflation of wealth that the Roman levies meant for the peoples of central and western Hispania.[23]

Gifts

War with its booty was not the only way for the Romans to obtain wealth. The existence of an independent indigenous diplomacy, and diplomatic relations both between the Hispanian peoples and between them and the Mediterranean powers, have been studied by various historians and, recently, by Esteban Payno's doctoral thesis.[24] In the context of these relationships, gifts – and particularly gifts of precious metals, whether unrefined, minted or in the form of sumptuary objects – played a fundamental role. The diplomatic gift could be intended, in some cases, to guarantee or foster a climate of mutual goodwill between parties; secondly, to gain the benevolence of the other party, especially if that party was seen as superior or more powerful; and thirdly, it could also serve to ratify diplomatic agreements.

The Hellenistic world had developed sophisticated processes of diplomatic relations that not only protected the integrity of heralds, messengers and ambassadors (κήρυκες, πρέσβεις, *nuntii, legati*) and delegations (πρεσβεῖαι, *legationes*), but also, through highly elaborate formal codes of verbal communication, apparatus, dress and staging, established the status and roles of the various participants in diplomatic acts.[25] Operating in the Hellenistic East, Rome learnt these behaviours while introducing its own

---

[22] Sánchez Palencia, 1989: 21.
[23] Plin. *NH* 33.141: *Numantia quidem deleta idem Africanus in triumpho militibus denarios VII dedit*; Oros. 5.7.18: *aurum vel argentum, quod igni superesse potuisset, apud pauperes non fuit*. Salinas de Frías, 1986: 132–3.
[24] García Riaza, 2002; Torregaray Pagola, 2011; Sánchez Moreno, 2011b; Esteban Payno, 2022.
[25] Burton 2011: 114–22, on the performative character of the *deditio*; Torregaray Pagola, 2011; Rudolph, 2016: 4.

codes, especially regarding the categories of *socii* and *amici*.[26] For diplomatic relations to work, however, it was necessary for the various parties involved to share a lowest common denominator in terms of the codes used, to ensure that the intentions of the various parties and their objectives in establishing the diplomatic relationship were correctly understood. Despite all the elements in common, communication between Greeks and Romans was not always free of misunderstandings; for the same reason, the diplomatic relationship between Romans and Hispanians, who were culturally highly heterogeneous, was much more complicated and subject to greater confusion.[27] In accounts of the wars of conquest, the negotiations between the Romans and the Hispanians are often presented with an aspect of bad faith. For example, the consul Popillius Laenas, when entering into negotiations with Viriathus, first demanded certain conditions from him and only gradually revealed new requirements, until the demand to surrender arms was seen by the Lusitanians as unacceptable and they returned to a state of war.[28] It is possible, however, that this apparent bad faith was a consequence of a misunderstanding of the various stages of diplomatic negotiation. In these circumstances, the gift of quantities of gold and silver was an eloquent gesture of goodwill that smoothed over any difficulties.

For the west of the Iberian Peninsula, the information available is scarce and often ambiguous. It is possible, nevertheless, to discern clear behaviours of gift-giving in the course of conversations or negotiations that could be described as diplomatic, consisting in many cases of the giving (and acceptance) of gold and silver.

The exchange of gifts as a practice that served to open or maintain a state of good relations can be traced from an early phase of the conquest, in the relationships of Hannibal and Scipio with their allies,[29] and

---

[26] Sands, 1975 [1908]; Cimma, 1976; Salinas de Frías, 2010b; Burton, 2011.

[27] Diplomatic activity between Mediterranean states was a transcultural phenomenon that required training: on misunderstandings, cf. Lenfant, 2013, for Graeco-Persian relations; on transculturality and training, cf. Bonnefond-Coudry, 1989: 261–350; Torregaray Pagola, 2011: 21–2; García Riaza, 2011b, 2015a, 2015b; Sánchez Moreno, 2018; García Riaza & Sanz, 2019.

[28] Diod. Sic. 33.19; Cass. Dio, *fr.* 75; *De vir. ill.* 71. The same occurred in the case of the Lusitanians who sought peace with Galba. From Appian's account (*Hisp.* 59–60), a sequence can be deduced which includes a) diplomatic negotiations, b) surrender of arms, c) receipt of land. In Lucullus' negotiations with the Caucaei (App. *Hisp.* 52), a series of successive acts can also be observed: a) offer of gifts and 100 talents of silver, b) union of their cavalry with the Romans, c) admission of a Roman garrison.

[29] Story of Alucius: Livy 26.50.7; Polyb. 10.19.3–7; Val. Max. 4.3.1; Gell. *NA* 7.8.6; *de vir. ill.* 49.7–8; Walbank, 1967: 218–19; García Riaza, 2002: 166; Torregaray Pagola,

continued to be practised throughout the second century BC. In 151 BC, the Lusitanians agreed a peace treaty with the praetor M. Atilius.[30] The treaty included a distribution of land, as Appian states further on.[31] Land distributions were a constant feature of negotiations between the Romans and Hispanians during the second century BC. The demand for land was a response to the structural inequalities of the city-state as it was emerging in the central and western territories of the Iberian Peninsula during the second century BC. The causes of this situation did not disappear until well into the first century BC, in fact until after the time of Caesar, as this author has studied elsewhere.[32] The distribution of land to indigenous communities can be considered *sensu lato* as a gift intended to guarantee the status quo resulting from the new negotiations carried out between Hispanians and Romans and, therefore, as a diplomatic gift. One year later, in 150 BC, Galba repeated the same offer of land at the request of the Lusitanians, who wanted to renew the treaty made with Atilius.[33] Valerius Maximus, referring to Galba's offer, uses the expression *de commodis eius acturus*,[34] which means that he would act in their interest. Orosius also uses a similar expression: *simulans enim de commodis eorum se acturum fore*.[35] That such interests were contemplated in a diplomatic negotiation can be deduced from an earlier passage in Valerius Maximus which alludes to the accusation against Galba of having killed the Lusitanians *interposita fide*,[36] in spite of the *fides* agreed.

Again, in 147 BC, the Lusitanians sent emissaries to Vetilius with supplicant olive-branches requesting land, and he promised to give it to them and to sign an agreement (*synetítheto*), although the negotiations did not ultimately prosper after Viriathus alerted the Lusitanians to the Romans' *apistía* (bad faith).[37]

2005: 84–7; Salinas de Frías, 2011, with questions about the veracity of the passage; Sánchez Moreno & García Riaza, 2012: 1257; Hernández Prieto, 2019: 39. Reciprocity is made clear in Scipio's response: *amicus populi romani sis*. Additionally, see the chapter by E. Sánchez Moreno & J. García Cardiel in this volume.

[30] App. *Hisp*. 58; García Riaza, 2002, 101–3.
[31] App. *Hisp*. 59.
[32] Salinas de Frías, 2012a: 353–8; 2012b.
[33] App. *Hisp*. 59–60; Oros. 4.21.10. García Riaza, 2002: 103–13. On Galba's perfidy, his trial, and the promulgation of the *lex repentundarum*: Richardson, 1987; García Riaza, 2002: 292–6; 2008; Muñiz Coello, 2004; Salinas de Frías, 2010a.
[34] Val. Max. 9.6.2.
[35] Oros. 4.21.10.
[36] Val. Max. 8.1.2.
[37] App. *Hisp*. 61.

Another treaty about which we are exceptionally well informed is the *foedus* signed in 140 BC between Viriathus and Q. Fabius Maximus Servilianus. During the siege of Erisane by Servilianus, Viriathus managed to enter the city at night and, the next day, attacked the Roman army and encircled it in a position where he forced it to surrender. In exchange for Roman lives, Viriathus obtained a *foedus* ('treaty', Appian uses the Greek term συνθηκαι) with Rome, whereby Rome acknowledged that Viriathus was a friend of the Roman people and that all those under his command held the land they occupied (Οὐρίατθον εἶναι Ῥωμαίων φίλον, καὶ τοὺς ὑπ᾽ αὐτῷ πάντας ἧς ἔχουσι γῆς ἄρχειν).[38] Through this action, which for the Romans had a specific political significance, Rome placed the Lusitanian leader on the same level as other important allied kings such as, for example, Hieron II of Syracuse. From Viriathus' perspective, it meant that he was able to understand, at least in its essential aspects, the diplomatic codes that Rome had developed in its Mediterranean expansion.

The *foedus* between Viriathus and Servilianus conformed to many of the principles of the *foedera* of *amicitia* signed after a war.[39] On one hand, Viriathus' decision not to take advantage of his position of strength with Servilianus' army, which was trapped among cliffs, must be seen – as well as a sign of goodwill – also as one of the *officia* or services intended to support the request for *amicitia* from the Romans. Appian does not say that Viriathus became an ally (*symmachos*), but only a friend, *philos*, of the Romans, but this is not significant since *philos* is the term Appian uses most often, including to refer to kings whose status as allies is recorded. In any case, it is likely that the treaty obliged Viriathus to remain actively neutral towards the enemies of the Romans, if not to provide the Romans with troops and supplies, either because this was specified, or because it was what Rome expected its *amici* to do spontaneously. Another fact is that the treaty endowed the power of the Lusitanian leader with a stable and defined territorial basis. Appian expressly states that through this treaty, the Romans recognised Viriathus' sovereignty over the men who were with him. This must have meant the establishment of borders, and this type of delimitation was frequent when *amicitia* relations were established between Rome and the kings, above all when these relationships were the outcome of a peace treaty.[40] This was the case, for example, for the

---

[38] App. *Hisp.* 69. García Riaza, 2002: 149–59. On the figure of Viriathus: Gundel, 1968; Sánchez Moreno, 2006; Salinas de Frías, 2008a; Sánchez Moreno, 2019b.
[39] Cimma, 1976: 90–1. On *amicitia* as a consequence of a peace treaty, Cimma, 1976: 29–30; cf. Livy 8.2.1–2; 8.26.6; 32.39.10; 35.42.2; 42.12.5; 44.13.9; Cic. *Verr.* 2.3.123.
[40] Cimma, 1976: 91.

borders imposed on Antiochus III as a result of the peace of Apamea, or the territorial limits drawn between Carthage and the Numidian kingdom of Masinissa, which followed the line of the so-called *fossa Regia*.[41]

The negotiations between Viriathus and Servilianus involved several preliminary steps, among them the handing over of defectors by Viriathus to Fabius Maximus. Fabius earned a reputation for exceptional harshness by cutting off the hands of five hundred defectors.[42] This same condition seems to have been imposed in the subsequent negotiations between Viriathus and Popillius Laenas. The latter asked the Lusitanian to put the defectors and deserters to death, among them his own father-in-law, who commanded a troop of his own.[43] To the surrender of deserters or prisoners may be added the surrender of hostages: although Viriathus returned their wives and children, the Segovians preferred to remain loyal to the Romans.[44]

We can sequence the diplomatic negotiations, especially in the cases of *deditio* (surrender), in different ways, depending on the data that our sources make explicit and also on the data that they silence. In general, however, they all followed a common pattern: indigenous request for negotiations, exchange of mutual guarantees of the *fides* upon which the pacts were founded (handing over of arms, prisoners, etc.), fulfilment of the agreed conditions (handing over of arms, provision of troops, financial rewards, and, where applicable, land distribution) and, finally, religious sanction for the pacts.[45] The religious sanction can be deduced from Appian's reference to the Caucaei who, when they were killed by Lucullus in breach of the pact, invoked the pacts and the gods who witnessed them, execrating the perfidy of the Romans: οἱ μὲν δὴ πίστεις τε καὶ θεοὺς ὁρκίους ἐπικαλούμενοι, καὶ Ῥωμαίους ἐς ἀπιστίαν λοιδοροῦντες.[46] This religious sanction seems to have existed also in some international treaties agreed by Rome and by other states, such as the one concluded between Philip V and Carthage, however it is noteworthy that no mention at all is made of the gods in either of the two epigraphic documents that are direct evidence of a *deditio* to the Romans in Hispania: Aemilius Paullus' decree and

---

[41] Polyb. 21.43.14.
[42] Val. Max. 2.7.11: *omnium enim qui ex praesidiis Romanorum ad hostes transfugerant captique erant manus abscidit, ut trunca prae se brachia gestantes metum defectionis reliquis inicerent.* Frontin. *Str.* 4.1.42: *Q. Fabius Maximus transfugarum dextras praecidit*; Oros. 5.4.12 with an error, referring to the allies.
[43] Diod. Sic. 33.19; Cass. Dio 21, *fr.* 75; Astolpas' sacrifice: Livy *Per.* 54.
[44] Ps. Frontin. 4.5.22; cf. García Riaza, 2006.
[45] García Riaza, 2002: 175–226.
[46] App. *Hisp.* 52. García Riaza, 2002: 141–3.

the *deditio* of Alcántara. It is instead the senate and the Roman people, through the *de maiestate* clause, who appear as guarantors of the status quo upon which the diplomatic agreement is based. Except in the case of the treaty between Viriathus and Servilianus, in which the Lusitanian was the stronger party, in all other cases the surrender of arms, defectors, and hostages was always a demand imposed by the Romans.[47]

Given the opacity of our sources, however, care should be taken not to assume that everything that was handed over always fell within the category of diplomatic gifts. In this respect, there is a striking similarity between the demands of Decimus Brutus to the Talabrigenses and what, according to the epigraphic document known as the Bronze or *deditio* of Alcántara, a Lusitanian community, *the populus Seano...*, had to hand over to the praetor L. Caesius in 104 BC.[48] In it, the *populus Seano...* brings the *imperator L. Cesius captivos, equos, equas (...) agros, aedificia [et] leges*. Caesius, upon receiving them, and *de consilii sententia*, returned them so that they remained as they were *dum populus romanus senatusque vellet*. The detailed mention of *agros et adificia, equos et equas et leges*, in accordance with the casuistry of Roman juridical thought, implied the total surrender of all property, both movable and immovable, as well as of the community as a political-legal entity. Some of what was specified in the document, such as prisoners or livestock, may coincide with some items that were given as guarantees in earlier diplomatic negotiations, but arguably this case is not a diplomatic negotiation of any kind, but a pure and simple submission of a small *oppidum* of the Second Iron Age to Roman authority, far superior in strength.

Alongside the gifts that accompanied or sealed a diplomatic negotiation there are other individual gifts that seem to have served to establish interpersonal relationships that could fall within the realm of relationships of *amicitia* and *fides*, *hospitium* and *clientela*. Unfortunately, we have very little evidence about this, but within what we have, there is one story about Quintus Occius, legate of Caecilius Metellus in 143 BC, who defeated one Pirresus, undoubtedly a Celtiberian aristocrat, who surrendered his sword and his *sagulum* to him in the sight of both armies, while Occius for his part asked that the two be united by the law of *hospitium* when peace was

---

[47] App. *Hisp*. 71-2; 73; 75; Diod. Sic. 33.1.3. From Livy, *Per*. 55, it can be inferred that Caepio's successor, Decimus Brutus, also distributed land to *qui sub Viriatho militaverunt*. Perhaps however, this does not refer to those who fought under Viriathus' orders, who would therefore be Lusitanians, but to those who fought in Viriathus' times, using a temporal meaning of the preposition.

[48] López Melero *et alii*, 1984.

restored between the Celtiberians and the Romans.[49] This use of weapons as elements of prestige and exchange can be related to the almost exact coincidence between two panoplies of arms, pointed out by Sánchez Moreno, one from the necropolis of El Cabecico del Tesoro in Verdolay, Murcia, and the other in the necropolis of La Osera, in Chamartín de la Sierra, Ávila, as a presumable result of a hypothetical exchange of military equipment in the context of an interaction between elites.[50]

Bribes

The dividing line between gift and bribe is obviously very thin. We must be careful, moreover, not to attribute to antiquity political categories and criteria that belong to our current society, but which lack meaning in the ancient world and can lead to gross misrepresentations. An example of this is the relationships implicit in the institution of patronage. Clients owed *obsequium* to their patron and, within this concept, all kinds of gifts and presents were included, which were inherent to this institution and which, from our modern point of view, could appear to be cases of bribery. Client relationships were not always explicitly displayed, however, but often – above all in the field of international relations – masked by the concept of *amicitia*.

Originally, the term *amicitia* belonged more to the vocabulary of Rome's international relations with other states. The first known *amicitia* treaties date back to the third century BC, the first being the one concluded in 273 BC between Rome and Ptolemy III Euergetes, who sent an embassy requesting Roman *amicitia*.[51] During the Second Punic War, and later during the second century BC, we know of the existence of relations of *philia* or *amicitia* between Rome and Syphax in 210 BC[52] and between Rome and Masinissa, to whom Scipio gave Syphax's kingdom, which was later confirmed by the senate.[53] The friendship between Rome and Masinissa meant that the Romans imposed on Carthage their recognition of him as King

---

[49] Val. Max. 3.2.21: *Idem Pyrresum nobilitate ac virtute omnes Celtiberos praestantem, cum ab eo in certamen pugnae devocatus esset, succumbere sibi coegit. Nec erubuit flagrantissimi pectoris iuvenis gladium ei suum et sagulum utroque exercitu spectante trader, ille vero etiam petiit, ut hospitii iure se iuncti essent, quando inter Romanos et Celtiberos pax foret restituta.*

[50] Sánchez Moreno, 2011a: 176–7.

[51] Cimma, 1976: 37. Cf. Burton, 2011.

[52] Livy 24.48.2–13; 27.4.5–7, who tells us about the *amicitia* with Rome and a private *hospitium* with Scipio; in 213 the *amicitia* became a *societas*; Cimma, 1976: 41–52.

[53] Livy 30.17.10–12; Cimma, 1976: 46–52.

of the Numidians, and prohibited them from declaring war on him, as he was their *amicus*.[54] *Amicitia* relationships also existed between Rome and the kings of Illyria, in particular with Demetrius of Pharos; between Rome and the Aetolians; with Philip V[55] and with the Attalids of Pergamum.[56] During this time, the rise of Rome's power and the fact that many of these relationships were established as a result of some Roman victory, usually as part of a peace treaty that ended hostilities, meant that the relationship of *amicus populi Romani* gradually turned into one of dependence on the Romans themselves, akin to that of a client. On the other hand, the duty to assist the Romans militarily, whether voluntarily assumed by these *amici* or mandated in the peace clauses, meant that the relationship of *amicitia* became synonymous with that of *societas*, and that the expression *amici et socii populi Romani* was seen in the second century BC as the expression of the same type of relationship with the Romans.[57]

In the transition from Republic to Empire, the term also became generalised within interpersonal relationships, as a synonym for *clientela*, which was the word that tended to be used predominantly in its place. *Amicitia*, *clientela* and *patronatus* covered the range of interpersonal relationships of dependence in an imprecise and very often fluctuating manner, depending on the circumstances. Generally speaking, *amicus* indicated a more equal or less unequal relationship than *cliens*. Even if courtesy led to the treatment of an inferior as an *amicus*, however, as in the case of Augustus to Herod,[58] this did not prevent the clear establishment of the relative social position of each party. *Amici* were thus divided into different categories: *superiores*, *pares* and *inferiores*, and each category had an appropriate and characteristic mode of behaviour, so that inferior *amici* displayed a social behaviour that was practically the same as that of clients, characterised by the expression *colere et observare*.[59]

---

[54] Polyb. 15.18.4–5.
[55] Aetolians: Livy 26.24.8–9; Philip V: Livy 33.35.5. Sometime after the Battle of Cynoscephalae, Philip sought *amicitia* and *societas* from Rome, which was granted. This reference is important because in his case *amicitia* did not automatically derive from an agreed peace treaty and reveals the importance of having previously demonstrated goodwill towards the Romans: Cimma, 1976: 59–67.
[56] The alliance with Attalus I, signed in 212 BC, was an extension of the alliance signed between Rome and the Aetolians (Livy 29.11.2); that *societas* would later become an *amicitia*, as in Syphax's case.
[57] Cimma, 1976: 168 and 177; Sands, 1975: 12 and 15; 17, who indicates that in Polybius, the expression *philia kai synmachia* was gradually substituted by *philia*.
[58] Joseph. *AJ* 16.290; Cimma, 1976: 310–11.
[59] Saller, 1990: 57–8.

In the case of the western Iberian Peninsula, we know of only one obvious case of bribery (although of course there must have been many more), but it is sufficiently demonstrative. It is the bribe by which Servilius Caepio bought the loyalty of Viriathus' *philoi*, who put an end to his life.[60] According to Diodorus, three conspirators – Audas, Ditalkes and Nikorontes – seeing that Viriathus' supremacy was starting to be threatened by the Romans, resolved to enlist their benevolence by some service (*charis*), thus winning their own security.[61] In other words, the initiative came from them. Appian, on the other hand – who instead of Nikorontes mentions Minouros – does not specify from whom the initiative came, saying only that Caepio bribed the friends whom Viriathus had sent to negotiate peace with generous gifts and many promises.[62] Livy limits himself to stating that Viriathus was killed by traitors bought by Servilius Caepio;[63] and *De viris illustribus* is less precise and says that Caepio corrupted two servants with money, who then killed Viriathus.[64] Although the sources attribute the treachery of the Turdetanian aristocrats to bribery, it should be taken into account that Viriathus' father-in-law, Astolpas, had been killed a short time before as a result of the initial talks of the failed peace between Viriathus and Popillius Laenas. Both Astolpas and the assassins were Turdetanians, and most probably all from the city of Urso. A political motive, revenge or a consequence of the change of alliances after the rupture between Rome and Viriathus cannot therefore be ruled out as the cause of the Lusitanian leader's death. The sources, perhaps out of ignorance of the real motives, or to discredit the figure of Caepio, attributed it to a bribe.

The Exhibition of Gold: Viriathus' Wedding

This study will end by alluding to a paradigmatic occasion on which indigenous gold was exhibited before the Romans in exceptional circumstances: the wedding of Viriathus, to which we have no other reference than a passage in Diodorus.[65] He reports that Viriathus married the daughter of a rich Iberian named Astolpas, and at their wedding a great multitude of gold and silver vessels and all kinds of precious fabrics were exhibited. Viriathus, however, despised them all, for, rising and leaning on his spear, he said that all these riches of his father-in-law were subject to him who held the spear,

[60] On the onomastics of the characters: Salinas de Frías, 2013: 22–3.
[61] Diod. Sic. 33.21.
[62] App. *Hisp.* 74.
[63] Livy, *Per.* 54.
[64] *De vir. ill.* 71.
[65] Diod. Sic. 33.7.1.

and, therefore, that gratitude was due rather to him, since they gave him nothing, as he was the owner of everything. Then, without sitting down at table, he took the loaves and delicacies and divided them among his own party; and, after taking some of the food with his own hands, he asked for his wife to be presented to him. He sacrificed to his gods according to the rites of the Hispanians, Diodorus says, and mounting his bride on a horse, departed immediately for his dwelling, hidden in the mountains. At the sight of the riches on display, moreover, Viriathus asked Astolpas why the Romans invited to his table had not taken these riches even though they had the strength to do so. Astolpas replied that many had seen them but that no one had taken them or asked for them, and hearing this, the Lusitanian leader asked him why he had united himself to his own rusticity and obscurity, leaving to one side the powerful who would have allowed him freedom and the safe use of these goods.

It is difficult to imagine what the riches exhibited by Astolpas would have looked like. Schulten suggested that this goldware must have been the result of the Lusitanian raids in Baetica,[66] but undoubtedly the Lusitanians and Celtiberians had their own precious metal work, examples of which are, respectively, the torques of Berzocana (Cáceres) (Figure 11.1) and Sagrajas (Badajoz), and the hoards from Arrabalde (Zamora) and Fuentes de Valdepero (Palencia) (Figure 11.2), chronologically closer to the period we are studying (second to first century BC).[67] The Mogón hoard (Villacarrillo, Jaén) (Figure 11.3), datable to the early first century BC, presents an extraordinary collection of silver jewellery (torques, bracelets) together with 1,258 Roman Republican denarii, the most recent of which is dated to 101 BC. It has been assumed that this treasure belonged to an indigenous merchant who had become wealthy or, given the presence of several torques, to an individual from the military elite. The possession and display of these riches must be understood in the context of the κειμήλια that emphasised the aristocratic status of their owners. It is possible that the riches displayed by Astolpas on the occasion of Viriathus' wedding resembled the sumptuous silverware that makes up the Abengibre (Albacete) hoard (Figure 11.4).

Although Diodorus' account has an obvious fictional aspect, presenting an idealised image of Viriathus, there are arguably some basic facts that are not in doubt: firstly, the existence of the wedding itself. An important argument in this respect is the name of the father-in-law, Astolpas, or

---

[66] Schulten, 1937: 132.
[67] Fernández Gómez, 1989: 84; Delibes de Castro, 2001; on the typology of the jewellery: Pérez Outeiriño, 1989; Delibes de Castro & Esparza Arroyo, 1989.

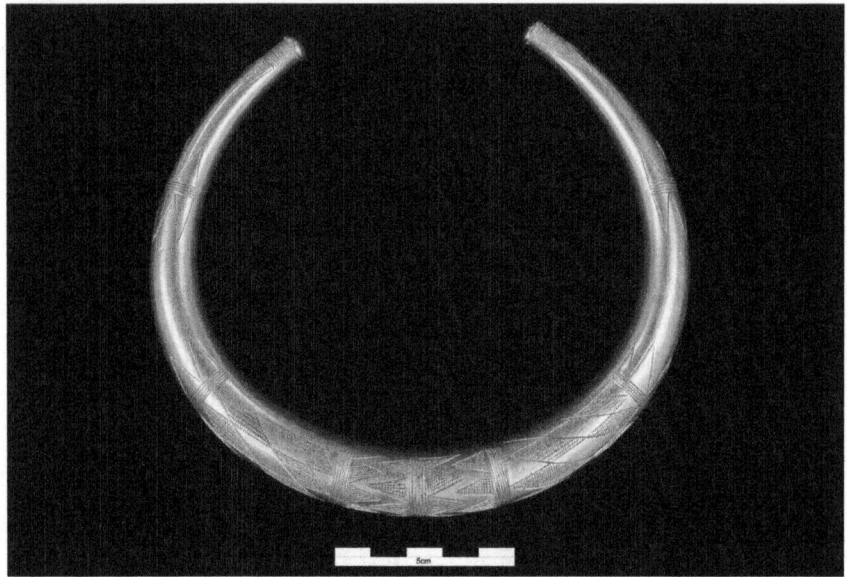

Figure 11.1 Torques from Berzocana, Cáceres (© Ministerio de Cultura y Deporte, Gobierno de España).

Figure 11.2 Torques from the Fuentes de Valdepero (Palencia) hoard (© Ministerio de Cultura y Deporte, Gobierno de España).

Figure 11.3 Pieces (funicular torques, filiform torques, belt plate) from the Mogón hoard, Villacarrillo, Jaén (© Ministerio de Cultura y Deporte, Gobierno de España).

Figure 11.4 Treasure and silverware from Abengibre, Albacete (© Ministerio de Cultura y Deporte, Gobierno de España).

Istolpas as García y Bellido preferred,[68] which has parallels in the pre-Latin toponymy and anthroponymy of the southern peninsula, with toponyms such as Astapa, Astigi and Asta, and anthroponyms such as Istolatios and Estopeles.[69] It is unlikely that a Greek author such as Diodorus would have invented a name so well adapted to Hispanian pre-Latin onomastics, and for this reason we believe that the gist of the story from the historical point of view – that is, that Viriathus married the daughter of a Turdetanian nobleman named Astolpas – is true.

Another important question is the motive or purpose of the wedding, for which its date is important. Gundel believed that it took place 'perhaps not long before 141', that is, when Viriathus was at war with the Romans.[70] According to Diodorus, however, the presence of the Romans at the wedding did not arouse any hostility, although the Lusitanian was understandably annoyed. Although hypothetically it could be imagined that there was some kind of sacred truce in connection with the ceremony, what we know is that Viriathus and the Romans met at the same table and that Viriathus celebrated his wedding and then left peacefully with his wife. This kernel of facts suggests that the wedding took place at a time when there had previously been peace between Viriathus and the Romans, and that time could only be the months between the signing of the treaty with Servilianus and the resumption of hostilities by Servilius Caepio, that is, approximately in the second half of the year 141 BC. In this period, Viriathus was at the height of his power, and the senate recognised his dominion over the lands he held at the time of the signing of the treaty. From what can be deduced from the sources, these territories consisted essentially of Celtic and Turdulian Baeturia, plus some cities in the Guadalquivir Valley such as Tucci or Urso.[71] As we have seen, the name Astolpas is related to the onomastics of this area, which allows us to think he was from there, like the *philoi* who later committed the assassination, who were from Urso. It is possible that the purpose of the wedding was to provide Viriathus, through kinship with some aristocratic family, with some sort of legitimacy, the nature of which we do not know. His marriage after a resounding victory somewhat recalls that of Hasdrubal, who after defeating the king of the Oretani married an Iberian princess and was proclaimed *stratēgos autocratōr* by

[68] García y Bellido, 1945: 575–7 and n. 14.
[69] Palomar Lapesa, 1957: 45; Albertos Firmat, 1966: 38, 94, 262, 274; Vallejo Ruiz, 2005: 188.
[70] Gundel, 1968: 187.
[71] Salinas de Frías, 2008a: 110. Tucci: App. *Hisp.* 66; Ituca: App. *Hisp.* 67; Escadia, Gemella and Obolcola: App. *Hisp.* 67–8.

all the Iberians, according to Diodorus.⁷² Hannibal also married a princess of Castulo, which seems to have strengthened his position among the Hispanians.⁷³ Diodorus' account, interested in presenting Viriathus as the model of the noble savage, uncorrupted by *luxus*, emphasises the contrast between wealth and frugality and, consequently, the economic features – but the main purpose of the marriage may have been quite different.

There is an obscure episode later on which could be of great interest in understanding the political complexity of Viriathus' marriage. Referring to the failed peace negotiations between Viriathus and Popillius Laenas, Dio Cassius says that Popillius demanded the death of some of the leading Roman deserters, among whom was his kinsman (ἐν οἷς καὶ ὁ κηδεστὴς αὐτοῦ), even though he had his own power (*dynamis*).⁷⁴ The word *kēdestēs* means inlaw. Schulten assumed that this was Popillius Laenas' brother-in-law,⁷⁵ but this interpretation makes no sense, since a Roman officer had no power of his own. The word *dynamis* means 'force', but also 'power', 'resources' or 'army', and the most likely scenario is that *kēdestēs* refers to the only inlaw we know of in this context, who was Astolpas, Viriathus' father-in-law. It is clear that Astolpas had a position of power within indigenous society, and that Viriathus could have taken advantage of this position to cement his own power through marriage.

Two well-studied aspects of the diplomatic gift coincide in the episode of Viriathus' marriage. On the one hand, the display of riches, which probably formed part of the bride's dowry and which Astolpas therefore offered Viriathus as a way of ratifying the political alliance; and, on the other hand, the meal at the wedding banquet, which constitutes another form of gift and lavish hospitality through the delicacies offered. Diodorus stresses that Viriathus distributed the delicacies among his party, in the same way as he distributed the spoils of war.⁷⁶

Viriathus' wedding, and the subsequent banquet, could have been the consequence of a diplomatic negotiation (perhaps the culmination of the peace treaty) between Rome, the Lusitanians and prominent members of the Turdetanian aristocracy, to which Astolpas belonged. Appian's summary of the circumstances that led to the signing of the *foedus* between Viriathus and Servilianus omits many events that must have occurred and focuses the attention on our hero, but it is possible that

---

[72] Diod. Sic. 25.12.
[73] Livy 24.41.7; Sil. *Pun.* 3.97–105 gives the princess' name, Himilce.
[74] Cass. Dio 22, fr. 75.
[75] Schulten, 1937: 324.
[76] Diod. Sic. 3.1, 33.5, 33.7; Cass. Dio 22, fr. 73; Cic. *Off.* 2.40.

prominent members of the Turdetanian aristocracy also played an important role since, when the events took place, Servilianus was besieging the Turdetanian city of Arsa. The fact that Viriathus subsequently sacrificed his father-in-law during the peace negotiations with Popillius Laenas can arguably only be interpreted as a symptom of the existence of internal problems in Viriathus' camp and the breakdown of the diplomatic alliance previously formed. These circumstances would explain his defensive attitude to Caepio's attack. It is a fact that his forces were intact and that he had not been defeated in any significant way, as attested by the fact that Caepio was denied a triumph because he had not won the victory in battle, and because the Romans did not approve of a leader dying at the hands of his own soldiers.[77]

Bibliography

Albertos Firmat, M. L. [1966]. *La onomástica personal primitiva de Hispania: Tarraconense y Bética*, Salamanca.

Bonnefond-Coudry, M. [1989]. *Le sénat de la république romaine. De la guerre d'Hannibal à Auguste: practiques délibératives et prise de decisión*, Rome.

Burton, P. J. [2011]. *Friendship and Empire: Roman Diplomacy and Imperialism in the Middle Republic (353–146 BC)*, Cambridge.

Cimma, M. R. [1976]. *Reges socii et amici populi Romani*, Milan.

Delibes de Castro, G. [2001]. 'La orfebrería', in M. Almagro Gorbea, M. Mariné Isidro & J. R. Álvarez Sanchís (eds), *Celtas y vettones*, Ávila, 149–57.

Delibes de Castro, G. & Esparza Arroyo, A. [1989]. 'Orfebrería celtibérica', in *El oro en la España prerromana*, Madrid, 108–29.

Esteban Payno, M. [2022]. *Praxis diplomática y comunicación política en el mundo celtibérico (siglos III al I Antes de Cristo)*, PhD dissertation, Universitat de les Illes Balears, Palma de Mallorca.

Fatás Cabezas, G. [1973]. 'Un aspecto de la explotación de los indígenas hispanos por Roma: los botines de guerra en la Citerior', *Estudios del Seminario de Prehistoria, Arqueología e Historia Antigua de la Facultad de Filosofía y Letras de Zaragoza*, 2, 101–10.

Fernández Gómez, F. [1989]. 'Orfebrería indígena en época prerromana', in *El oro en la España prerromana*, Madrid, 82–9.

García-Bellido, M. P. [1999]. 'Sistemas metrológicos, monedas y desarrollo económico', in F. Burillo (ed.), *IV Simposio sobre los Celtíberos: Economía. Homenaje a L. Argente Oliver*, Zaragoza, 363–85.

---

[77] Forces intact: *De vir. ill.* 71; expulsion of the assassins: *POxy.* 200; Eutr. 4.16; Oros. 5.4.14.

García Riaza, E. [1999a]. 'El cómputo del metal precioso en los botines de guerra hispanorrepublicanos', *Hispania Antiqua*, 23, 119–36.
García Riaza, E. [1999b]. 'Especie, metal, moneda: consideraciones en torno a la cuantificación de las exacciones romanas en Hispania republicana', in G. Mora Rodríguez, R. M. Sobral Centeno & Mª. P. García-Bellido (eds), *Rutas, ciudades y moneda en Hispania* (Anejos de *Archivo Español de Arqueología*, 20), Madrid, 39–46.
García Riaza, E. [2002]. *Celtíberos y lusitanos frente a Roma: diplomacia y derecho de guerra*, Vitoria.
García Riaza, E. [2006]. 'Rehenes y diplomacia en la Hispania romanorepublicana', in G. Bravo & R. González (eds), *Minorías y sectas en el mundo romano*, Madrid, 17–34.
García Riaza, E. [2008]. 'Las fronteras de la ley: Servio Sulpicio Galba y el gobierno provincial de Hispania', in G. Bravo & R. González (eds), *La corrupción en el mundo romano*, Madrid, 17–26.
García Riaza, E. [2011a]. 'Derecho de guerra en occidente durante la expansión romano-republicana: planteamientos metodológicos', in E. García Riaza (ed.), *De fronteras a provincias: interacción e integración en Occidente (ss. III–I a.C.)*, Palma de Mallorca, 31–66.
García Riaza, E. [2011b]. *De fronteras a provincias: interacción e integración en Occidente (ss. III–I a.C.)*, Palma de Mallorca.
García Riaza, E. [2015a]. 'Foreign Cities: Institutional Aspects of the Roman Expansion in the Iberian Peninsula (218–133 B.C.)', in M. Jehne and F. Pina (eds), *Foreign Clientelae in the Roman Empire: A Reconsideration*, Stuttgart, 119–39.
García Riaza, E. [2015b]. 'Le protocole diplomatique entre particularisme romain et universalisme: quelques réflexions sur l'occident républicain', in B. Grass & G. Stouder (eds), *La diplomatie romaine sous la république: réflexions sur une practique*, Besançon, 15–41.
García Riaza, E. [2019a]. '*[de Celti]beris Hispaneisqu(e), [ex] Lu[sita]nia Hispaniaq(ue)*: las campañas de Graco y Albino en las listas triunfales', in J. I. San Vicente González de Aspuru, C. Cortés Bárcena & E. González González (eds), *Hispania et Roma: estudios en homenaje al profesor Narciso Santos Yanguas*, Oviedo, 85–97.
García Riaza, E. & Sanz, A. M. [2019b]. '*In fidem venerunt*': expresiones de sometimiento a la republica romana en Occidente, Madrid.
García y Bellido, A. [1945]. 'Bandas y guerrillas en las luchas contra Roma', *Hispania*, 21, 547–605.
Gundel, H. G. [1968]. 'Viriato: Lusitano, caudillo en la lucha contra los romanos, 147–139 a.C.', *Caesaraugusta*, 31–2, 175–98.
Hernández Prieto, E. [2019]. 'Las adhesiones hispanas a Escipión del 210–208 a.C. (*Carthago Nova* y *Baecula*)', in E. García Riaza & A. M. Sanz (eds),

'In fidem venerunt': expresiones de sometimiento a la republica romana en Occidente, Madrid, 27–58.

Lenfant, D. [2013]. 'Les malentendus culturels entre Grecs et Perses', Revue des Sciences sociales, 50, 36–41.

López Melero, R., Sánchez Abal, J. L. & García Jiménez, S. [1984]. 'El bronce de Alcántara: una deditio del 104 a.C.', Gerión, 2, 265–323.

Milne, J. G. [1944]. 'Bigati', JRS, 34, 49–50.

Muñiz Coello, J. [2004]. 'El proceso de Galba, las quaestiones y la justicia ordinaria (Roma, siglos II/I a.C.)', L'Antiquité Classique, 73, 109–26.

Neatby, L. H. [1951]. 'The "bigatus"', American Journal of Archaeology, 55 (3), 241–4.

Palomar Lapesa, M. [1957]. La onomástica personal pre-latina de la antigua Lusitania, Salamanca.

Pérez Outeiriño, B. [1989]. 'Orfebrería castreña', in El oro en la España prerromana, Madrid, 90–107.

Richardson, J. S. [1987]. 'The Purpose and Date of the lex Calpurnia de repetundis', JRS, 77, 1–12.

Rudolph, H. [2016]. 'Entangled Objects and Hybrid Practices? Material Culture as a New Approach to the History of Diplomacy', in H. Rudolph (ed.), Material Culture in Modern Diplomacy from the 15th to the 20th Century, Berlin–Boston, 1–28.

Salinas de Frías, M. [1986]. Conquista y romanización de Celtiberia, Salamanca.

Salinas de Frías, M. [1995]. El gobierno de las provincias hispanas durante la República romana (218–27 a.C.), Salamanca.

Salinas de Frías, M. [2008a]. 'La jefatura de Viriato y las sociedades del occidente de la península Ibérica', Palaeohispanica, 8, 89–120.

Salinas de Frías, M. [2008b]. 'Urbem venalem! Provincias y corrupción política en la obra de Salustio', in G. Bravo Castañeda & R. González Salinero (eds), La corrupción en el mundo romano, Madrid, 43–52.

Salinas de Frías, M. [2010a]. 'El proceso contra Galba, la lucha de facciones en Roma y el gobierno de las provincias', in A. J. Domínguez Monedero & G. Mora Rodríguez (eds), Doctrina a magistro discipulis tradita: estudios en homenaje al profesor Dr. Luis García Iglesias, Madrid, 121–35.

Salinas de Frías, M. [2010b]. '[Fides ami]citiaque Bletisam(ensium)', in I. Sastre Prats & A. Beltrán (eds), El bronce de El Picón (Pino de Oro): procesos de cambio en el Occidente de Hispania, Valladolid, 137–44.

Salinas de Frías, M. [2010c]. 'In castreis Scipionis: ejército y política en Roma durante el siglo II a.C.', in J. J. Palao (ed.), Militares y civiles en la antigua Roma: dos mundos diferentes, dos mundos unidos, Salamanca, 15–30.

Salinas de Frías, M. [2011]. 'Sobre la memoria histórica en Roma: los Escipiones y la traición de los celtíberos', *SHHA*, 29, 97–118.
Salinas de Frías, M. [2012a]. 'Los lusitanos y los problemas de definición étnica en el Occidente peninsular', in J. Santos Yanguas & G. Cruz Andreotti (eds), *Romanización, fronteras y etnias en la Roma antigua: el caso hispano*, Vitoria, 335–58.
Salinas de Frías, M. [2012b]. 'La provincia Ulterior entre Décimo Bruto y Augusto', in J. M. Abascal Palazón, A. Cabellos Rufino, S. Castellanos García & J. Santos Yanguas (eds), *Estudios de Historia Antigua en homenaje al prof. Manuel Abilio Rabanal*, León, 105–22.
Salinas de Frías, M. [2013]. 'Personal Onomastics and Local Society in Ancient Lusitania', in J. L. García Alonso (ed.), *Continental Celtic Word Formation: The Onomastic Data*, Salamanca, 17–36.
Saller, R. [1990]. 'Patronage and Friendship in Early Imperial Rome: Drawing the Distinction', in A. Wallace-Hadrill (ed.), *Patronage in Ancient Society*, London, 49–62.
Sánchez Moreno, E. [2006]. 'Ex pastore latro, ex latrone dux ... Medioambiente, guerra y poder en el occidente de Iberia', in T. Ñaco & I. Arrayás (eds), *War and Territory in the Roman World (Guerra y territorio en el mundo romano)*, Oxford, 55–79.
Sánchez Moreno, E. [2011a]. 'Rebaños, armas, regalos: expresión e identidad de las élites vettonas', in G. Ruiz Zapatero & J. Álvarez Sanchis (eds), *Castros y verracos: las gentes de la Edad del Hierro en el occidente de Iberia*, Ávila, 159–90.
Sánchez Moreno, E. [2011b]. 'De la resistencia a la negociación: acerca de las actitudes y capacidades de las comunidades hispanas frente al imperialismo romano', in E. García Riaza (ed.), *De fronteras a provincias: interacción e integración en Occidente (ss. III–I a.C.)*, Palma de Mallorca, 97–103.
Sánchez Moreno, E. [2018]. 'Imperialism and Multipolarity in the Far West: Beyond the Lusitanians (237–146 B.C.)', in T. Ñaco del Hoyo and F. López Sánchez (eds), *War, Warlords and Interstate Relations in the Ancient Mediterranean*, Leiden–Boston, 326–50.
Sánchez Moreno, E. [2019a]. '*Carpetanorum, appendicibus Olcadum vaccaeorumque centum milia fuere*: estrategias de asociación de las poblaciones meseteñas entre Cartago y Roma (220–185 a.C.)', in E. Sánchez Moreno & E. García Riaza (eds), *Unidos en armas, coaliciones militares en el Occidente antiguo*, Palma de Mallorca, 71–104.
Sánchez Moreno, E. [2019b]. 'Imperialismo romano y resistencia hispana: Viriato como paradigma', in E. Sánchez Moreno (ed.), *Veinticinco estampas de la España antigua cincuenta años después (1967-2017): en torno*

a la obra de Antonio García y Bellido y su actualización científica, Seville, 197–222.

Sánchez Moreno, E. & García Riaza, E. [2012]. 'La interacción púnica en Iberia como precedente de la expansión romana: el caso de Lusitania', in M. Bastiana Cocco, A. Gavini & A. Ibba (eds), *L'Africa romana: trasformazione dei paesaggi del potere nell'Africa settentrionale fino alla fine del mondo antico*, Vol. 2, Rome, 1251–9.

Sánchez Moreno, E. & García Riaza, E. [2019]. *Unidos en armas: coaliciones militares en el occidente antiguo*, Palma de Mallorca.

Sánchez Palencia, F. J. [1989]. 'Los yacimientos auríferos de la península Ibérica', in *El oro en la España prerromana*, Madrid, 16–23.

Sands, P. C. [1908]. *The Client Princes of the Roman Empire under the Republic*, reprinted New York, 1975.

Schulten, A. [1937]. *Fontes Hispaniae Antiquae, fascículo IV: las guerras de 154–72 a. de J.C.*, Barcelona.

Seltman, C. [1944]. 'Argentum Oscense and bigati', *Numismatic Chronicle and Journal of the Royal Numismatic Society*, 4 (1/4), 77–82.

Torregaray Pagola, E. [2005]. 'Realidad histórica y elaboración retórica en los *exempla* hispanos de Valerio Máximo', in L. Troiani & G. Zecchini (eds), *La cultura storica nei primi due secoli dell' Impero romano*, Rome, 77–98.

Torregaray Pagola, E. [2006]. 'Embajadas y embajadores entre Hispania y Roma en la obra de Tito Livio', in E. Torregaray Pagola & J. Santos Yanguas (eds), *Diplomacia y autorrepresentación en la Roma antigua*, Vitoria, 25–62.

Torregaray Pagola, E. [2011]. 'En torno a la diplomacia como una forma de interacción en el occidente romano: un estado de la cuestión', in E. García Riaza (ed.), *De fronteras a provincias: interacción e integración en Occidente (ss. III–I a.C.)*, Palma de Mallorca, 15–30.

Vallejo Ruiz, J. M. [2005]. *Antroponimia indígena de la Lusitania romana*, Vitoria.

Villaronga Garriga, L. [1979]. *Numismática antigua de Hispania*, Barcelona.

Walbank, F. W. [1967]. *A Historical Commentary on Polybius*, Vol. 2: *Books 7–18*, Oxford.

12

Bonding Gifts
Material Exchange and Political Alliance during the Sertorian War*

David García Domínguez and
Diego Suárez Martínez

Introduction: The Diplomatic Gift in the Sertorian Context

Throughout the first century BC, Rome was scourged by a succession of internal conflicts that interrupted the usual exercise of *imperium* over the allies and subjects of the empire across the Mediterranean. The agreements and treaties signed with the Roman state still pertained, but it was unclear who was in a position to exercise the representation of that state, inasmuch as various mutually incompatible claims for legitimacy coexisted.[1] From the perspective of the various political entities that argued the right to rule over the empire, the challenge was to secure as many loyalties as possible, whether that was through diplomacy or force. The political actors situated on the periphery of Rome, meanwhile, faced a choice that would shape their future in the short and medium term.[2] At these crossroads, the offering and receiving of gifts came to satisfy various discursive and diplomatic needs. Broadly speaking, Roman leaders offered gifts to secure loyalties through the creation of obligation relationships,[3] while the political

---

* This work has been developed within the research project PGC2018-096415-B-C21 'La expresión diplomática en el Mediterráneo occidental bajo la expansión romana: el regalo en su contexto ideológico y cultural', funded by the State Research Agency, Ministry of Science and Innovation, Government of Spain (MCIN/AEI/10.13039/501100011033) and ERDF 'A way of making Europe'.
[1] Millar, 1984: 18–19; Crawford, 2008: 637; Börm, 2019: 150.
[2] Santangelo, 2016.
[3] e.g. Caes. *BCiv.* 3.4.5, 3.59.1–3; *BAfr.* 35.2; App. *BCiv.* 4.54; Suet. *Iul.* 28.1.

subjects they addressed used the receiving or giving of gifts to reveal their recognition of one of the parties.[4]

Each particular case nevertheless allows for specific readings where these 'framework functions' crystallised into more immediate political intentions. For this reason, we will focus our attention on Hispania affected by the Sertorian War (82–72 BC), the sources for which refer on various occasions to the exchange of gifts. This dossier is as attractive as it is problematic: the *Life* that Plutarch dedicates to the exiled Cinnan provides most of the relevant material; it does so, however, in a strongly apologetic context that tends to overrepresent the 'peaceful' methods by which Sertorius obtained local collaboration.[5] Appian, in turn, takes the opposite stance: from a hostile perspective towards the exile, he silences the constructive episodes in which Plutarch revels. In fact, the only reference of his that is useful for our dossier refers to a point after the death of Sertorius himself.[6] Faced with this 'screen of prejudice and propaganda',[7] we cannot limit ourselves to analysing the sources' accounts literally. On the contrary, focus should be on cutting across every class of distortion and a priori reasoning to glimpse the diplomacy latent in the exchanges.

There is, in any case, no reason to deny the obvious: provision of gifts played an important role when it came to establishing the tenor of relationships between Sertorius and his local allies. The objective of this chapter is to clarify the reasons for this circumstance, while analysing the material and symbolic functions that the diplomatic gift satisfied throughout the conflict.

Establishing the Alliance

Quintus Sertorius arrived on the Iberian Peninsula in late 83 or early 82 BC.[8] Both the date of his praetorship and the identification of the province(s)

---

[4] e.g. Cic. 2 *Verr.* 4.64; Plut. *Sull.* 26.3, *Luc.* 2.6–3.1; Cass. Dio 51.6.6.
[5] Plut. *Sert.* 11.3–7 (= Gell. *NA* 15.22; Polyaenus, *Strat.* 8.22), 14.2, 14.4–5. The tradition favourable to Sertorius possibly started in Sallust (La Penna, 1963); but Plutarch takes it to a new level through anecdote and reorganisation of the information (Konrad, 1994: xxx–xli; recently, Santangelo, 2019: 332–3).
[6] App. *BCiv.* 1.114. Appian seems to work from sources different from Plutarch's, with a strong Livian influence (Gabba, 1956: 89–101), although that does not prevent his complementary use of other references (Gabba, 1956: 89–101; Westall, 2015: 156 and n. 106).
[7] Badian, 1962: 51.
[8] During his crossing of the Pyrenees, Sertorius agreed to pay a toll to the communities that controlled the passes (Plut. *Sert.* 6.5–6). According to Plutarch, both he and his immediate circle saw this exchange in terms of a commercial transaction, in

over which he held command are subject to debate.⁹ It is clear, nonetheless, that the civil dispute that was unfolding in Italy at the same time put the legality of his magistracy in doubt. The praetors whom he met in the peninsula seem to have shown reticence in ceding power to him, a recalcitrance that Sertorius managed to defeat with the assistance of Roman and Celtiberian troops.¹⁰ If this report by Appian is credible, we should assume that the locals showed themselves willing to collaborate with the Cinnan representative of Rome from the very moment he set foot in the province. The reasons for this behaviour are opaque, although it is true that Plutarch mentions the discontent that spread through the province as a result of the greed of its previous governors.¹¹ Exuperantius, an epitomist of Sallust who preserves the most accurate narrative of any that refer to this period, claims that local feeling vacillated over the arrival of the new praetor, and that he knew how to incline them towards collaboration with his faction through protection and flattery (*tuendo atque blandiendo*).¹² In this context, we would expect an active effort from Sertorius to attract the civic elites by creating personal networks, a process in which gifts would have formed a key part. In fact, Plutarch's account mentions certain meetings with those in power (ἀνελάμβανεν ὁμιλίᾳ τε τοὺς δυνατούς) which would have attracted them to his cause, but does not clarify the level of formality of those meetings nor the role that materiality or commensality could have played in them.¹³ Along with this diplomatic work, we know that Sertorius adopted administrative measures designed to nourish collective benevolence towards his version of the Roman Republic: once again according to Plutarch's account, he offered fiscal exemptions to 'the majority' and suspended the burdensome custom of *hospitium sub tectis*.¹⁴ It is unfortunate that our sources adopt an abbreviated approach and that we have no

---

this case rejecting the idea of a 'gift' – possibly because they were not creating a personal and lasting relationship between the proconsul and the 'miserable barbarians' of the Pyrenees. This certainly explains their apparent passivity in the armed clashes between Sertorians and Sullans which scourged the region the following year (Plut. *Sert.* 7.1–3).

⁹ Konrad, 1994: 74–6; Brennan, 2000: 502–3. The proconsular nature of his powers, however, is not debatable in the light of the compelling epigraphic evidence: Beltrán Lloris, 1990; García González, 2019: 195–7.
¹⁰ App. *BCiv.* 1.86, 1.108.
¹¹ Plut. *Sert.* 6.7.
¹² Exup. 8.51.
¹³ Plut. *Sert.* 6.7.
¹⁴ On this institution, see Ñaco del Hoyo, 2001. It is important to bear in mind that Sulla had drawn upon *hospitium militare sub tectis* during his Greek wintering in 85 (Plut. *Sull.* 25.2; App. *Mith.* 61). In the context of an interconnected Mediterranean,

explicit information on the possible actions that could have been taken by the pro-Sullan praetors to counter these moves, nor on the possible expressions of loyalty that both Sertorius and his enemies could have demanded from the local *civitates*.

Sertorius' tenure did not remain undisputed for long. Overwhelmed by Sullan forces, he left Hispania from Carthago Nova and roamed around the Mediterranean until some Lusitanians summoned him back to the westernmost part of the Iberian Peninsula. The dispatch of successive Sullan governors to confront him transplanted the diplomatic customs characteristic of a civil conflict to Hispania,[15] obliging the *civitates* of the south and south-east of Hispania to choose between the two versions of Rome that were available to them.

This choice was carried out on a city-by-city basis and under the pressure of potentially severe retaliations. It is important to remember that local actors were primarily characterised by their pronounced political atomisation.[16] Despite that, it is ethnic labels that dominate the narrative focus in our sources, a phenomenon of radical homogenisation that reflects the attitudes and interests of Roman imperialism.[17] This way of presenting reality operates as a filter capable of obscuring the subtleties of local diplomatic praxis, blurred by the fallacious 'ethnic positioning' that modern historiography has tended to endorse.[18] It becomes necessary to suspect the way in which Plutarch evaluates the action of those Lusitanian spokespeople (πρέσβεις) who sought Sertorius' leadership (ἡγεμονίᾳ) in that phase of the conflict:[19] although we cannot specify the scope of their representative capacity, we can sense that it did not extend throughout the entirety of the evanescent and fragmented Lusitanian region. In fact, the dispersion of positions in the far west of the peninsula can be read between the lines in Plutarch's own account, which mentions the way in which Sertorius 'brought the neighbouring parts of Iberia into subjection.

Sertorius could have been sending an important political message of global reach with this decision.

[15] Brennan, 2000: 505–7; Díaz Fernández, 2015: 362–3, 390–3; Manchón Zorrilla, 2016.

[16] Sánchez Moreno, 2011a: 98; Salinas de Frías, 2012: 344.

[17] 'That of Lusitanians is a supra-ethnic category handled by the Greco-Roman narrative from the position of cultural antagonism and military conflict' (Sánchez Moreno, 2018: 328).

[18] Spann, 1987: 58–62; Konrad, 1994: 116–17. García Morá, 1991, in turn, changes the 'ethnic positioning' for a reading in terms of social banditry.

[19] Plut. *Sert.* 10.1.

Most of the people' – therefore not all – 'joined him of their own accord.'[20] Further on, the progressive increase in Sertorian influence is mentioned, which was fed by the conquest of numerous urban centres (πόλεις εἷλε πολλάς).[21] Again, it is inferred that these cities did not belong to the initial nucleus of his followers – and that he used violence to force the reluctant cities into obedience.

In these circumstances, it is unsurprising that some communities may have hurried into making a public profession of their position, thereby anticipating events and providing themselves with the protection of one of the parties in the civil conflict.[22] Local communities tapped into their knowledge of the pan-Mediterranean diplomatic codes to overcome their vulnerability.[23] Among those codes, the gift would have functioned as an expression of formal recognition, freeing the communities that offered it from any hint of suspicion and, therefore, from the risk of *oppugnatio*.

The conspicuous episode of the white fawn might be read along these lines: according to Plutarch, this was a gift (δῶρον) that Sertorius received from the hands of an 'ordinary Lusitanian' (<Λυ>σιτανὸς ἀνὴρ δημότης).[24] Plutarch implies that this would be just an example of a much broader

---

[20] Plut. *Sert.* 11.2. The militancy of locals on the Sullan side is made clear by the remains of arms and personal decorations exhumed in Cáceres el Viejo (Ulbert, 1984: 50–71, 109, 114–16, plates 7–11, 25; Fernández Ibáñez, 2021: 157–8). Caution is nevertheless advised, as local and Roman panoplies converge very strongly at this time (Quesada Sanz & Uroz Rodríguez, 2020: 52) and lost or broken materials could have been refurbished with replacements acquired on local circuits (Heras Mora, 2018: 579).

[21] Plut. *Sert.* 12.3. See Mataloto & Elliott, 2021: 230, 247 for a risky attempt at cross-reading archaeological and literary sources that might link some archaeologically attested episodes of urban destruction to this chronological context.

[22] We know for certain that both Sertorius and Metellus used coercion to recruit the *civitates* reluctant to collaborate: Sertorius' aggression has been mentioned above, while Metellus involved himself in various siege operations. Among them, it is worth recalling the assault on the city of Langobriga, justified by the help that that city had lent to Sertorius (Plut. *Sert.* 13.7). Sallust is very clear about the punitive actions taken by Metellus at this time: Sall. *Hist.* 1.112–13M (1.111LP, 1.135MG).

[23] See García Riaza, 2002: 99–101; 2009: 211–13; Sánchez Moreno & García Riaza, 2012: 1253, 1257; Sánchez Moreno, 2020.

[24] García Morá, 1993: 170–1. We follow Ziegler's emendation to read <Λυ>σιτανὸς, rather than Σπανός, which is favoured in Perrin's edition. Aulus Gellius' text, derived from Sallust's independently of Plutarch, supports this hypothesis (*NA* 15.22, *cerva alba ... a Lusitano ei quodam dono data est*; see Konrad, 1994: 123–4). Polyaenus alone describes the parties that sent the gift as hunters (κυνηγων), which may perhaps be a rationalisation of the peculiar nature of the gift. Álvarez Pérez-Sostoa offers a lucid reflection on the terminology used by the sources when they describe episodes of 'informal diplomacy' (2015: 107).

mode of action, and so we learn that Sertorius 'gladly received everything in the way of game or produce that was brought him as a gift', and that he reacted with generosity to these demonstrations of attention (φιλοφρόνως ἀμειβομένου).²⁵

The meaning of this report is ambiguous, even more so as we have no other sources that can refine our understanding: Spann believes that the gifts were a simple demonstration of the admiration his Lusitanian allies held for Sertorius, while Roth has suggested that receiving supplies could have formed part of a deliberate campaign to source provisions.²⁶ The hypothesis about accumulating stores has some merit, but it is arguably also important to consider the possibility that these exchanges served to express the local *civitates*' allegiance to the Sertorian cause.²⁷ In this respect, it seems highly probable that our source, Plutarch, was responsible for a reinterpretation of the material that was available to him, stripping it of its diplomatic content and converting it into a barbarising tale in which the rusticity of the indigenous environment and Sertorius' capacity to adapt to these circumstances is emphasised first and foremost.²⁸

There is every reason to question, firstly, the actual identity of the givers – presumably accomplished political actors – but also the innocence that Plutarch attributes to all the participants in this episode. Far from being a succession of happy coincidences, Sertorius' readiness to receive gifts and the willingness of the locals to bring them seem to be better explained as a consequence of Sertorius' efforts to establish his power in the south-west of Hispania. We therefore propose that the gifts – including the fawn – were the recognition of the sovereignty that the Republican leader never ceased to proclaim through all the channels at his disposal.²⁹ It is possible that the Sullan generals found themselves approached with similar gestures; the evidence for this, however, is sparse and problematic.³⁰

---

²⁵ Plut. *Sert.* 11.4.
²⁶ Spann, 1987: 63; Roth, 1999: 233.
²⁷ With nuances, Pailler, 2000: 52–3.
²⁸ Konrad, 1994: xxvi–xxxvii, 124. On the stereotypical nexus that associated barbarism with superstition in the ancient world, see Gordon, 2008: 83–4, 91–3. Transcending stereotypes, the divinatory processes used by pre-Roman Hispanian peoples have been studied by García Cardiel, 2019b.
²⁹ Beltrán Lloris, 1990; Santos Yanguas, 2009: 187–9. In the future, the demand for hostages (Plut. *Sert.* 14.3) and the celebration of a *conventus omnium sociorum* (Livy, fr. 22.6 Jal) would fulfil a similar function to that of the expedient analysed here, in the sense that they all served to keep track of the political position of the local communities (García Riaza, 2002: 180; 2016: 243).
³⁰ A unique passage exists in which Q. Caecilius Metellus is the object of a triumphal reception given by an unidentified people from Hispania Ulterior (Sall. *Hist.* 2.70M

The question then arises of whether the exact type of the gifts exchanged was meant to deliver a specific message beyond the already discussed gesture of political compliance. This kind of analysis is only possible for the white fawn, whose nature is described to us in detail by the sources. As it happens, deer possessed a strong symbolic value for the inhabitants of the western peninsula, which makes it plausible to think that this was a carefully chosen gift. Justin has preserved a valuable piece of local myth that relates the fawn to the semantics of sovereignty.[31] Independent iconographic evidence confirms this approach.[32] Even acknowledging the fact that Justin's version is a heavily Hellenised version of indigenous tales, we can unproblematically retain the core idea that the fawn had some transcendent, sovereignty-related meaning for the populations of the Guadalquivir Valley.[33] The very nature of the gift, therefore, might have contained an assertion of Sertorius' authority to exercise power, which in turn reinforces the general hypothesis that the locals bestowed gifts upon the exiled Cinnan as an expression of allegiance and commitment.

We may lastly raise some points about the counter-gifts given by Sertorius. The act of reciprocating should not be understood as an obligation, but as a choice that adds nuance to the exchange: on the one hand, it confirms the success of the initial gesture; on the other, it inverts the relationship of inequality created by that initial gesture by transforming the recipient into the giver, and vice versa.[34] It is significant that Plutarch emphasises Sertorius' largesse when it came to reciprocating the gifts received: he deliberately offered a contribution of considerable value, sanctioning a hierarchy of power at the cusp of which was situated the Roman leader.[35] It is ambiguous who exactly was obliged by this hierarchy: it may be expected that the aristocracies that undertook the representation of the local communities saw themselves as personally connected with the sender of the (counter-)gift, including if they received it during the course

---

(2.59MG); Val. Max. 9.1.5; Plut. *Sert.* 22.2–3). All the versions descend from Sallust's defamatory libel, which makes it difficult to draw thorough conclusions about the possible diplomatic content of this episode.

[31] Just. *Epit.* 44.4; see Moret & Pailler, 2002: 117–24. More careful, García Moreno (1979) reduces to a minimum the indigenous traces that may survive in the heavily Hellenised version preserved for us by Justin.

[32] García Cardiel, 2020: 327.

[33] Justin's reworking of the tale: García Moreno, 1979.

[34] Burton, 2011: 63–75.

[35] Sánchez Moreno, 2002: 151–2, 169; 2011b: 174–5; Baray, 2007: 53–4.

of their work in the service of the community.³⁶ It is possible that the client ties that the sources mention under the name *devotio*/*κατάσπεισις*³⁷ had their origin specifically in the exchange of this type of gift and/or in the distribution of other similar *beneficia*. The hope of receiving distinctions, benefits or future honours would have created a similar effect. This hypothesis harmonises the apparent tension between two phenomena observed equally in the sources of the time: the prominence of the *civitates* and the importance of the aristocracies in the Sertorian movement.³⁸ At all times – including during the civil wars – these aristocracies were the meso level that mediated between the local political entities and the representatives of Rome.³⁹ The strong internal competitiveness that characterised these collectives must have translated, during the civil wars, into different orientations towards the sides in conflict, a dynamic documented by Sallust for the Sertorian War and clearly observed in other similar scenarios around the same time.⁴⁰ The inescapable conclusion of this latter observation is that the success of the public relationship that the parties were attempting to build depended, in a way, upon strengthening the political power of the aristocrats who were disposed to collaborate with Sertorius. Certain (counter-)gifts could have served this end.⁴¹

From the late second and early first centuries BC, it is possible to discern an increasing value attributed by the locals to Romano-Italic material culture.⁴² The essential requirement for this process was contact between locals and Italians in commercial and military contexts,⁴³ and its fundamental impetus was the unquestionable consolidation of Roman power. This generated new value systems in which status was expressed through the route of the 'Italianisation' of traditions of cuisine, ornamentation and

---

³⁶ Two contemporary parallels illustrate this confusion: both Lucullus in Plut. *Luc.* 2.6–3.1 and Appius Claudius Pulcher in Plut. *Luc.* 21 are conscious of the overlap of public and private in their representational activities, which conditioned their attitude when it came to reacting to the provision of gifts by their interlocutors.

³⁷ Sall. *Hist.* 1.112M, 1.125M (1.102MG, 2.70MG); Plut. *Sert.* 14.5–6. See Dopico Caínzos, 1998; Greenland, 2006; Aguilera Durán, 2019.

³⁸ Ñaco del Hoyo & Principal Ponce, 2018: 388.

³⁹ Sánchez Moreno, 2011a: 97.

⁴⁰ Sall. *Hist.* 2.92M, 2.93M (2.75MG, 2.76MG). The same situation repeatedly recurred during the conflict between Caesar and Pompey in Hispania: *BHisp.* 2.1 (Corduba, 46/5), 3.2 (Ulia, 46/5), 13.3–6 (Ategua, 45), 20.2 (Ucubis, 45), 22 (Bursavo, 45).

⁴¹ Plut. *Sert.* 14.1–2. A similar phenomenon has been observed in contemporary civil conflicts (Kalyvas, 2006: 96–7; see also n. 24).

⁴² Berrocal Rangel, 1997: 130–3; Barrandon, 2011: 83–5; García Cardiel, 2019a.

⁴³ Barrandon, 2011: 87–91; García Riaza & Sánchez Moreno, 2014.

armaments.⁴⁴ In this context, the fact that Plutarch mentions the distribution of 'Roman arms' (Ῥωμαϊκοῖς ὁπλισμοῖς) to Sertorius' followers cannot fail to draw our attention. Through the use of an adverb with the sense of emphatic addition (ἔτι), Plutarch adds to this equation a whole series of particularly sumptuous rewards that were included in a scale of recognition, raising themselves above the rest through their exceptionality and ostentatiousness: decorated shields and helmets (κράνη τε κατεκόσμει καὶ θυρεούς), brightly coloured cloaks and tunics (χλαμύσιν ἀνθιναῖς καὶ χιτῶσι).⁴⁵ The element that united all these material goods was their conspicuousness, a quality that meant they would be displayed in public as a sign of distinction.⁴⁶ Once again, Plutarch distorts the probable diplomatic content of this material exchange with an interpretation plagued by prejudices about the barbarism of local customs.⁴⁷ Putting to one side the limitations of his approach, this passage reveals to us the way in which the civil war brought unprecedented opportunities to those locals who were prepared to commit to a cause, acting as agents for that cause within their own communities of origin – and promoting themselves socially in the process.⁴⁸

The Connection Thereafter

The blurring between public and private does not cast doubt upon the official nature of the connections built by Sertorius and the Hispanian political entities.⁴⁹ In fact, there is abundant evidence that Sertorius retained at all times a legitimist attitude in which the official nature of his magistracy – and therefore his right to demand obedience from the *Hispani* – occupied

---

⁴⁴ The importance of a good relationship with Rome – and its usefulness on a domestic level – has been well studied for Greek cities: Börm, 2019: 63 and n. 76 with additional bibliography.
⁴⁵ Plut. *Sert.* 14.1–2.
⁴⁶ 'In a visual world quite different from ours, ... weapons – particularly swords, often with highly decorated scabbards, hilts and pommels – were visually striking ... and spoke of their owner's deeds and status' (Pérez Rubio, 2017: 90).
⁴⁷ According to Plutarch, Roman weapons would modernise the local forms of combat (modern research has shown otherwise: Quesada Sanz, 2003; 2006; Cadiou, 2003). Sumptuous goods, in turn, attempted to educate the barbarians 'in the taste for beauty' (συμφιλοκαλῶν ἐδημαγώγει).
⁴⁸ Selective grants of citizenship could have completed this symbiotic dynamic, although this hypothesis is not without difficulties: see Espinosa Espinosa, 2014: 109.
⁴⁹ On the inadequacy of 'charismatic' interpretations of the evidence, see García Riaza, 2015.

centre stage in his discourse.⁵⁰ As we have argued, however, these official connections might have been underpinned by interpersonal alliances capable of bringing Sertorian control into an unfathomable myriad of *civitates*. This would have been particularly important in a volatile context such as a civil war: Sertorius' legitimist discourse would have been mirrored by his enemies, which put local communities at serious risk of denunciation as traitors if they did not pledge allegiance to whichever actor was putting pressure on their territory.⁵¹ The aforementioned blurring between public and private, i.e. the existence of individual agents materially motivated to reinforce their community's commitment to official obligations – including at times of danger, and under siege or enemy offensive – would be a key condition for the functional performance of (civil) war.

It is instructive at this point to jump forward in time to observe what happened in the final stages of the conflict, when Sertorius himself disappeared from the equation: according to Plutarch, 'most of the Iberians immediately went away, sent ambassadors to Pompey and Metellus, and delivered themselves up to them'.⁵² As Konrad indicates, this is a radical compression of events – although essentially accurate, given that resistance lasted barely a year longer and Perperna himself committed to a decisive battle under inferior conditions, an unmistakable sign of his precarious position.⁵³ Appian gives a more detailed picture of the transfer of power, confirming the difficulties of the new Cinnan leader in getting to grips with the situation. He also allows us to glimpse that succession to Sertorius occurred as part of a highly formalised picture, passing into the hands of Perperna because 'he held the next rank to Sertorius' (μετὰ Σερτώριον εἶχεν ἀξίωμα).⁵⁴ Had there been institutional continuity, it is hard to imagine that the official ties acquired by the local *civitates* would have been considered extinct: in spite of everything, Perperna considered himself obliged to undertake a new campaign to build interpersonal connections of his own.⁵⁵

⁵⁰ García González, 2019: 200–2.
⁵¹ On the transversality of legitimist discourse, see the bibliography cited in n. 1. Around the exercise of violence against provincials in the age of civil wars, see García Domínguez, 2022.
⁵² Plut. *Sert.* 27.1. Appian mentions the wrath that spread among the 'Lusitanians' (*BCiv.* 1.114).
⁵³ Spann, 1987: 133–6; Konrad, 1994: 216–17.
⁵⁴ Other sources seem to describe an ordered transition of power (Livy, *Per.* 96.5; Plut. *Pomp.* 20.2; Oros. 5.23.13). On the existence of a bona fide Cinnan government in Hispania, with its own administrative apparatus and formal procedures, see among others Gabba, 1973: 427–32 and, recently, Crawford, 2008: 635; *contra*, Konrad, 1994: 183–7.
⁵⁵ Illustrative of this point: Hernández Prieto, 2019: 30–1, 33, 48–9.

As we shall see, gifts do reappear on this occasion. Why so? How is this situation to be explained, and what does it tell us about the connection between the Hispanians and Sertorius with his 'alternative state'?[56]

The situation is better understood based on two previous considerations. On the one hand, there was the enormous shift in the balance of forces that had occurred since 76 BC, which put in doubt the viability of Sertorian control and which invited the cities to seek a unilateral exit from the conflict.[57] On the other hand, there was the agency of the locals when it came to representing their own interests in the ambiguous situation created by the dual content – public and private – of the relationship they had with Sertorius. Aligning both ideas, it can easily be conceived that Sertorius' death was an opportunity to justify, internally and externally, a pragmatic diplomatic attitude: hence, we suggest, the embassies of Plutarch's account sent to Pompey and Metellus; hence Perperna's difficulties in consolidating his own leadership in spite of the persisting institutional connections. The interpersonal infrastructure cultivated by Sertorius had created an ideological curb that bound numerous individuals to a cause in bad times: with the disappearance of the individual, a tie disappeared that, among other things, had been built with gifts.

The actions adopted by Perperna to reverse this process of dissolution are completely coherent with what has been observed until now. Appian, the only source who reports these events, claims that he

> bestirred himself, making gifts [δώροις] to some and promises [ὑποσχέσεσι] to others. Some he terrified with threats and some he killed in order to strike terror into the rest ... [He] released from confinement some whom Sertorius had imprisoned, and dismissed some of the Iberian hostages.[58]

The deliberate brevity of this passage means we miss Plutarch's anecdotalism: indeed, we have no indication about the nature of the gifts mentioned, nor who received them. This narrative approach possibly tries to censure Perperna's actions, implying they come close to bribery, by passing over any detail that could justify the distribution of goods or root that distribution in an affective context.[59] Looking beyond the frequent criticisms, both ancient and modern, that are made of Perperna, we can see that his behaviour did

---

[56] 'Alternative states': Crawford, 2008: 636.
[57] Spann, 1987: 123–31.
[58] App. *BCiv.* 1.114.
[59] Carlà & Gori, 2014: 7–9.

not differ substantially from that adopted by Sertorius some years earlier. In fact, it seems like the conscious reproduction of the strategy pursued by the latter: the giving of gifts served precisely to restore the private infrastructure that supported the institutional ties, while the threat of violence weighed on those who were reluctant to collaborate. In this case, another element comes to light: the return of those infants whom Sertorius had gathered in the city of Osca as hostages. The position of those subjects had always been ambiguous, as they were the object of extraordinary distinctions[60] at the same time as becoming guarantors of their progenitors' allegiance. As the alliance destabilised, Sertorius executed or enslaved some of these individuals.[61] In returning the rest, Perperna was putting distance between himself and the repressive excesses of his predecessor in the final stages of his activity, and trying to re-establish the mutual trust that should act as a base for further interpersonal relationships.[62]

It is difficult to weigh the effectiveness of these measures, because our sources for the military campaign of the following year are extremely scanty. The evidence is, moreover, highly contradictory: the fact that Metellus did not consider it necessary to participate in the operations against Perperna seems an invitation to downplay its scale, but Appian claims that a great battle was fought (ἀγὼν μέγιστος).[63] However it was, the observations made are sufficient to document that Perperna harboured the intention of restoring the model for diplomatic interaction espoused by Sertorius years previously: no better case could be made for its success.

---

[60] According to Plutarch, they were gifted, for the pleasure of their parents, *bullae* and togas fringed with purple (*Sert.* 14.3). These *insigniae pueritiae* raised the *obsides* – and through them, their parents – above their peers, in the promise that they would soon be able to lay down the trappings of infancy to take possession of full legal competence in the eyes of Rome (Rawson, 2003: 111, 144). These gifts can logically be considered beyond their material dimension as a promise of legal elevation. Once again, the materialisation of the discourse in conspicuous goods redoubles their value in the eyes of the locals, who aspire *to be perceived as* favourites of Rome within their communities of origin.

[61] Plut. *Sert.* 25.4. As it appears in the sources, this killing is part of the polemical subject of the *crudelitas Sertorii* (Diod. Sic. 37.22a; Livy, *Per.* 96.4; Oros. 5.23.2, 7). On the place of hostages in Roman diplomatic praxis, García Riaza, 2002: 188–9; 2006: 30.

[62] It remains possible that other motives also influenced this decision: see Álvarez Pérez-Sostoa, 2015: 109–10.

[63] App. *BCiv.* 1.115. Always in accordance with his narrative purposes, Plutarch summarises the events of this phase of the war (*Sert.* 27.2–3; *Pomp.* 20.2–3).

Conclusions

A considerable proportion of the phenomena observed in the Sertorian Iberian Peninsula should be understood within the peculiar strategic circumstances created by the civil war. The frequent recourse to diplomatic gifts is not an exception: in a context marked by uncertainty, the offering and acceptance of gifts seems to have served to map the scattered loyalties of allies and subjects. The sources indicate that Sertorius, at least, satisfied this need by receiving gifts.

An official tie was thereby recognised which, nevertheless, could be subject to fierce tensions according to the progress of armed operations. The external demands for loyalty to the allies of the opposing side involved constant danger, which in turn generated internal disputes and processes of στάσις capable of questioning the original position. In this context, personal connections were instrumental in upholding public relationships. Once again, the sources let us see that Sertorius – and, after his death, Perperna – used gifts to create private networks of obligation within the communities loyal to them. These connections did not work independently of the official relationship, but in synergy with it. From the point of view of the locals, such gifts were the materialisation of Roman favour and therefore an important asset in achieving power over their respective communities.

These conclusions demonstrate the importance of the diplomatic gift in this chronological context, at the same time as revealing the coexistence of various functions overlapping within the same gift: one single object becomes the expression of public connections, the support of an underground interpersonal infrastructure that united local aristocracies with Roman power, and a key piece in local power discourses. It would be desirable to develop this approach transversally throughout the period of the civil wars, following the theme of gifts and expanding the focus to other forms of recognition and retribution. Such research would inevitably meet the parallel question of the coercive use of violence, which is simply the flip side of diplomatic languages orientated towards fostering integration and collaboration. This kind of work, lastly, should understand civil war as a peculiar political ecosystem which, in this case, affected the entire Mediterranean basin that looked towards Rome.

Bibliography

Aguilera Durán, T. [2019]. 'El hombre fiera: la etnografía hispana en las estampas de Antonio García y Bellido', in E. Sánchez Moreno (ed.), *Veinticinco estampas de la España antigua cincuenta años después (1967–2017): en torno a la obra de Antonio García y Bellido y su actualización científica*, Seville, 163–78.

Álvarez Pérez-Sostoa, D. [2015]. '*Clementia* o "visión diplomática": devolución voluntaria de los cautivos en la república romana', in B. Grass & G. Stouder (eds), *La diplomatie romaine sous la République: réflexions sur une pratique*, Besançon, 107–25.

Badian, E. [1962]. 'Waiting for Sulla', *JRS*, 52 (1–2), 47–61.

Baray, L. [2007]. 'La question du don dans les sociétés celtiques', in E. Magnani (ed.), *Don et sciences sociales: théories et pratiques croisées*, Dijon, 29–70.

Barrandon, N. [2011]. *De la pacification à l'intégration des Hispaniques (133–27 a.C.)*, Bordeaux.

Beltrán Lloris, F. [1990]. 'La *pietas* de Sertorio', *Gerión*, 8, 211–26.

Berrocal Rangel, L. [1997]. 'À propos des peuples, des armes et des sites pendant les Guerres Lusitaniennes: une vision d'ensemble', in M. Feugère (ed.), *L'équipement militaire et l'armament de la République (IVe–Ier s. avant J.-C.)* (*JRMES*, 8), 123–36.

Börm, H. [2019]. *Mordende Mitbürger: Stasis und Bürgerkrieg in griechischen Poleis des Hellenismus*, Stuttgart.

Brennan, T. [2000]. *The Praetorship in the Roman Republic*, Vol. 2, New York.

Burton, P. J. [2011]. *Friendship and Empire: Roman Diplomacy and Imperialism in the Middle Republic (353–146 BC)*, Cambridge.

Cadiou, F. [2003]. 'Sertorius et la guérrilla', in C. Auliard & L. Bodiou (eds), *Au jardin des Hésperides: histoire, société et épigraphie des mondes anciens. Mélanges offerts à Alain Tranoy*, Rennes, 297–314.

Carlà, F. & Gori, M. [2014]. 'Introduction', in F. Carlà & M. Gori (eds), *Gift Giving and the 'Embedded' Economy in the Ancient World*, Heidelberg, 7–47.

Crawford, M. [2008]. 'States Waiting in the Wings: Population Distribution and the End of the Roman Republic', in L. de Ligt & S. Northwood (eds), *People, Land and Politics: Demographic Developments and the Transformation of Roman Italy 300 BC–AD 14*, Leiden–Boston, 631–43.

Díaz Fernández, A. [2015]. *'Provincia et imperium': el mando provincial en la República romana (227–44 a.C.)*, Seville.

Dopico Caínzos, M. D. [1998]. 'La *devotio* ibérica: una revisión crítica', in J. Mangas Manjarrés & J. Alvar (eds), *Homenaje a José Mª Blázquez*, Vol. 2, Madrid, 181–93.

Espinosa Espinosa, D. [2014]. *Plinio y los 'oppida de antiguo Lacio': el proceso de difusión del Latium en Hispania Citerior*, Oxford.

Fernández Ibáñez, C. [2021]. 'Reflexiones preliminares sobre la revisión del conjunto armamentístico del final de la República en el campamento de

Cáceres el viejo (Cáceres, España)', in C. Pereira, P. Albuquerque, Á. Morillo, C. Fabião & F. Chaves (eds), *De Ilipa a Munda: guerra e conflito no sul da Hispânia*, Lisbon, 151–66.

Gabba, E. [1956]. *Appiano e la storia delle guerre civili*, Florence.

Gabba, E. [1973]. *Essercito e società nella tarda Repubblica romana*, Florence.

García Cardiel, J. [2019a]. 'Revestir el poder en tiempos de cambio: el uso de la toga entre las élites ibéricas (ss. II–I a.C.)', *AEA*, 92, 155–71.

García Cardiel, J. [2019b]. 'Agentes locales y prácticas oraculares durante la conquista romana de Hispania: el caso de las comunidades ibéricas', in S. Montero Herrero & J. García Cardiel (eds), *Santuarios oraculares, ritos y prácticas adivinatorias en la Hispania antigua*, Madrid, 183–218.

García Cardiel, J. [2020]. 'La cierva de Sertorio en su contexto (ibérico): poder, adivinación e integración en la Hispania tardorrepublicana', *Latomus*, 79 (2), 317–39.

García Domínguez, D. [2022]. 'Del control a la colaboración: los locales hispanos ante el conflicto cesaropompeyano (49–45 a.C.)', *Antesteria*, 11, 137–55.

García González, J. [2019]. '*Quintus Sertorius pro consule*: connotaciones de la magistratura proconsular afirmada en las *glandes inscriptae Sertorianae*', *Anas*, 25–6, 189–206.

García Morá, F. [1991]. *Un episodio de la Hispania republicana: la guerra de Sertorio*, Granada.

García Morá, F. [1993]. 'Entre la leyenda y la realidad: la cierva de Sertorio', in *'In memoriam' J. Cabrera Moreno*, Granada, 163–92.

García Moreno, L. A. [1979]. 'Justino 44,4 y la historia interna de Tartessos', *AEA*, 52, 111–30.

García Riaza, E. [2002]. *Celtíberos y lusitanos frente a Roma: diplomacia y derecho de guerra*, Gasteiz.

García Riaza, E. [2006]. 'Rehenes y diplomacia en la Hispania romano-republicana', in G. Bravo & R. González (eds), *Minorías y sectas en el mundo romano*, Madrid, 17–34.

García Riaza, E. [2009]. 'La política romana de atracción de las élites indígenas: el caso de la Galia cesariana y sus antecedentes hispánicos', in G. Bravo Castañeda & R. González Salinero (eds), *Formas de integración en el mundo romano*, Madrid, 209–24.

García Riaza, E. [2015]. 'Foreign Cities: Institutional Aspects of the Roman Expansion in the Iberian Peninsula (218–133 BC)', in M. Jehne & F. Pina Polo (eds), *Foreign Clientelae in the Roman Empire: A Reconsideration*, Frankfurt am Main, 119–39.

García Riaza, E. [2016]. 'Une institution politique dans le contexte de l'impérialisme romain: les *conuentus omnium sociorum* dans les références hispaniques de Tite-Live ', *Ktéma*, 41, 243–61.

García Riaza, E. & Sánchez Moreno, E. [2014]. '¿Del mercado al tratado? El papel del comercio itálico en las relaciones celtíbero-romanas anteriores a la provincialización', in F. Burillo Mozota & M. Chordá Pérez (eds), *VII Simposio sobre los celtíberos: nuevos hallazgos, nuevas interpretaciones*, Teruel, 435–44.

Gordon, R. [2008]. '*Superstitio*, Superstition and Religious Repression in the Late Roman Republic and Principate (100 BCE–300 CE)', in S. A. Smith & A. Knight (eds), *The Religion of Fools? Superstition Past and Present (Past & Present*, Suppl. 3), Oxford, 72–94.

Greenland, F. [2006]. '*Devotio Iberica* and the Manipulation of Ancient History to Suit Spain's Mythic Nationalist Past', *G&R*, 53 (2), 235–51.

Heras Mora, F. J. [2018]. *La implantación militar romana en el suroeste hispano (siglos II–I a.n.E.)*, Madrid.

Hernández Prieto, E. [2019]. 'Las adhesiones hispanas a Escipión del 210–208 a.C. (Carthago Nova y Baecula)', in E. García Riaza & A. M. Sanz (eds), *'In fidem venerunt': expresiones de sometimiento a la República Romana en Occidente*, Madrid, 27–58.

Kalyvas, S. N. [2006]. *The Logic of Violence in Civil War*, Cambridge.

Konrad, C. F. [1994]. *Plutarch's Sertorius: A Historical Commentary*, Chapel Hill–London.

La Penna, A. [1963]. 'Le *Historiae* di Sallustio e l'interpretazione della crisi repubblicana', *Athenaeum*, 41 (3–4), 201–74.

Manchón Zorrilla, A. [2016]. '*Generales enviados contra él*: actores secundarios en el sur peninsular a comienzos de la guerra sertoriana. Una aproximación a las operaciones militares de 81 a.C.–78 a.C.', *Saldvie*, 63–71.

Mataloto, R. & Elliott, A. M. [2021]. 'From the *Baetis* to the *Tagus*: Traces of Warfare in the Alentejo in the Late 2nd/Early 1st Century BC', in C. Pereira, P. Albuquerque, Á. Morillo, C. Fabião & F. Chaves (eds), *De Ilipa a Munda: guerra e conflito no sul da Hispânia*, Lisbon, 225–50.

Millar, F. [1984]. 'The Mediterranean and the Roman Revolution: Politics, War and the Economy', *P&P*, 102, 3–24.

Moret, P. & Pailler, J.-M. [2002]. 'Mythes ibériques et mythes romains dans la figure de Sertorius', *Pallas*, 60, 117–31.

Ñaco del Hoyo, T. [2001]. '*Milites in oppidis hibernabant*: el *hospitium militare* invernal en ciudades peregrinas y los abusos de la hospitalidad *sub tectis* durante la República', *DHA*, 27 (2), 63–90.

Ñaco del Hoyo, T. & Principal Ponce, J. [2018]. 'Q. Sertorius: A Warlord in Hispania?', in T. Ñaco del Hoyo & F. López Sánchez (eds), *War, Warlords and Interstate Relations in the Ancient Mediterranean*, Leiden–Boston, 380–414.

Pailler, J.-M. [2000]. 'Fabuleux Sertorius', *DHA*, 26 (2), 45–61.

Pérez Rubio, A. [2017]. 'Singing the Deeds of the Ancestors: The Memory of Battle in Late Iron Age Gaul and Iberia', in N. Roymans & M. Fernández Götz (eds), *Conflict Archaeology: Materialities of Collective Violence from Prehistory to Late Antiquity*, London–New York, 89–101.

Quesada Sanz, F. [2003]. 'Innovaciones de raíz helenística en el armamento y tácticas de los pueblos Ibéricos desde el siglo II a.C.', *CuPAUAM*, 28, 69–94.

Quesada Sanz, F. [2006]. 'Armamento indígena y romano republicano en Iberia (siglos III–I a.C.): compatibilidad y abastecimiento de las legiones republicanas en campaña', in Á. Morillo Cerdán (ed.), *Arqueología militar romana en Hispania II: producción y abastecimiento en el ámbito militar*, León, 75–96.

Quesada Sanz, F. & Uroz Rodríguez, H. [2020]. 'El armamento de época iberorromana de Libisosa (Lezuza, Albacete): un conjunto excepcional', *Gladius*, 40: 19–72.

Rawson, B. [2003]. *Children and Childhood in Roman Italy*, Oxford.

Roth, J. P. [1999]. *The Logistics of the Roman Army at War (264 B.C.–A.D. 235)*, Leiden–Boston–Cologne.

Salinas de Frías, M. [2012]. 'Los lusitanos y los problemas de definición étnica en el Occidente peninsular', in J. Santos Yanguas & G. Cruz Andreotti (eds), *Romanización, fronteras y etnias en la Roma antigua: el caso hispano*, Vitoria, 337–58.

Sánchez Moreno, E. [2002]. 'Algunas notas sobre la guerra como estrategia de interacción social en la *Hispania* prerromana: Viriato, jefe redistributivo (I)', *Habis*, 32, 149–69.

Sánchez Moreno, E. [2011a]. 'De la resistencia a la negociación: acerca de las actitudes y capacidades de las comunidades hispanas frente al imperialismo romano', in E. García Riaza (ed.), *De fronteras a provincias: interacción e integración en Occidente (ss. III–I a.C.)*, Palma de Mallorca, 97–103.

Sánchez Moreno, E. [2011b]. 'Rebaños, armas, regalos: expresión e identidad de las elites vetonas', in G. Ruiz Zapatero & J. Álvarez-Sanchís (eds), *Castros y verracos: las gentes de la Edad del Hierro en el occidente de Iberia*, Ávila, 159–89.

Sánchez Moreno, E. [2018]. 'Imperialism and Multipolarity in the Far West: Beyond the Lusitanians (237–146 BC)', in T. Ñaco del Hoyo & F. López Sánchez (ed.), *War, Warlords and Interstate Relations in the Ancient Mediterranean*, Leiden–Boston, 326–50.

Sánchez Moreno, E. [2020]. '¿Truco o trato? El reparto de tierras a los lusitanos, un opaco en la expansion romana en el Occidente hispano', in E. Torregaray Pagola & J. Lanz Betelu (eds), *Algunas sombras en la diplomacia romana*, Gasteiz, 107–48.

Sánchez Moreno, E. & García Riaza, E. [2012]. 'La interacción púnica en Iberia como precedente de la expansión romana: el caso de Lusitania', in M. Bastiana Cocco, A. Gavini, & A. Ibba (eds), *L'Africa romana: trasformazione dei paesaggi del potere nell'Africa settentrionale fino alla fine del mondo antico*, Rome, 1251–9.

Santangelo, F. [2016]. 'Performing Passions, Negotiating Survival: Italian Cities in the Late Republic', in H. Börm, M. Matheis & J. Wienand (eds), *Civil War in Ancient Greece and Rome: Contexts of Disintegration and Reintegration*, Stuttgart, 127–48.

Santangelo, F. [2019]. 'Plutarch and the Late Republican Civil Wars', in C. Lange & F. J. Vervaet (eds), *The Historiography of Late Republican Civil War*, Leiden–Boston, 320–50.

Santos Yanguas, J. [2009]. 'Sertorio: ¿un romano contra Roma en la crisis de la República?', in G. Urso (ed.), *Ordine e sovversione nel mondo greco e romano*, Pisa, 177–92.

Spann, P. O. [1987]. *Quintus Sertorius and the Legacy of Sulla*, Fayetteville.

Ulbert, G. [1984]. *Cáceres el Viejo: ein Spätrepublikanisches Legionslager in Spanisch-Extremadura*, Mainz.

Westall, R. [2015]. 'The Sources for the *Civil Wars* of Appian of Alexandria', in K. Welch (ed.), *Appian's Roman History: Empire and Civil War*, Swansea, 125–67.

Epilogue
Gifts at the Edges of the World
Diplomatic Exchanges in the Roman West and Early Colonial Chile*

Tomás Aguilera Durán

Introduction

It is generally agreed that the anthropological basis of research into gifts in Antiquity is constructed upon comparisons with modern and contemporary ethnology. This chapter will not focus on the possibilities and problems posed by handling sources that are so disparate or the generalisation of models in this subject, since they have already been discussed by anthropology itself and by ancient history.[1] It will instead offer a comparative study along those lines, but without attempting to establish closed parallels, find universal laws or apply restrictive concepts, but rather, will provide certain reflections on transversal problems. The focus will specifically be on diplomatic gifts – the exchange of goods in contexts of political negotiation – in two historical settings which have until now never been considered together: the western expansion of the Roman Republic, where the question has been raised recently with some vigour,[2] and the beginning of Spanish colonialism in Chile in the sixteenth century.

Spanish presence in Chile is marked by the Arauco War (1550–1641). After the relatively rapid colonisation of the north and centre of Chile (1540–5), the Mapuche resistance in the south-central region ended with

---

* This work has been developed within the research project PGC2018-096415-B-C21 'La expresión diplomática en el Mediterráneo occidental bajo la expansión romana: el regalo en su contexto ideológico y cultural', funded by the State Research Agency, Ministry of Science and Innovation, Government of Spain (MCIN/AEI/10.13039/501100011033) and ERDF 'A way of making Europe'.
[1] Sykes, 2005; Verboven, 2014, respectively.
[2] Auliard, 2009; Grass, 2015.

the establishment of a border along the River Biobío, and the retention of their autonomy throughout the whole colonial period. The continuation of the conflict nonetheless definitively shaped both the political and legal ordering of Chile within the Viceroyalty of Peru and also the indigenous peoples' ways of life, generating a frontier reality that was unique in the Hispanic world.[3]

This study focuses on the first stage, from Pedro de Valdivia's expedition, which began in 1540, until the end of the century, when the Araucanian border was consolidated. This period was the most intense in terms of war, and, moreover, the early contacts entailed interesting phenomena of diplomatic improvisation and adaptation. Contemporary accounts will provide the main sources, written by soldiers, administrators and evangelists, direct participants who knew other witnesses and documents.[4] The general problems of these sources will not be examined, only interpretative questions that concern our specific theme. It is likewise obvious that the fragments discussed contain a certain literary licence, so a simple criterion for plausibility will be applied: almost all the situations described are repeated in multiple passages and authors, so that – independently of the precise details in each specific episode – it seems reasonable to assume that this type of exchange, in general, did really take place in that context. On the other hand, only occasional use will be made of later accounts, literary sources and contemporary ethnology, in which problems of bias and anachronism multiply and would require greater discussion.

Wherever possible, these accounts will be compared with archaeology, always bearing in mind the fragmentary nature of research into this period. Two big questions dominate the ethnohistorical and material study of these societies, particularly for the problematic south-central region. The first emphasises the degree of social complexity: communities were decentralised and scattered; structures were predominantly familial; material culture, austere; prior to the Spanish invasion, there was a process of demographic growth, hierarchisation and proto-state institutional consolidation which was reflected in public buildings and the diversification of burial patterns (the El Vergel Complex, 1000–1550).[5] The second question explores the impact of the Spanish presence on this process: theories of pericentrism and hybridism emphasise the importance of the agency of local communities, phenomena of mutual transformation and regional variability, furthermore considering their integration into a broad Andean

[3] Boccara, 2009; Bengoa, 2018.
[4] Orellana Rodríguez, 2017.
[5] Dillehay, 2007; 2017; Campbell, 2011.

and Trans-Andean universe. More traditional perspectives are thus being questioned, which either exaggerate Mapuche isolation and particularism, or conceptualise Spanish acculturation as a unidirectional and definitive influence.[6]

Gifts sit at the heart of these big questions. Among the factors in the unprecedented Mapuche resistance, their effective capacity to coordinate seems fundamental. In a heterogeneous landscape, fragmented communities established networks of collaboration and leadership structures solid enough to be able to execute large joint offensives successfully, but flexible enough to regenerate rapidly after serious defeat. There has therefore been focus on the importance that must be attributable to mechanisms designed to maintain and renew ties between the kinship groups, whose daily functioning would have been essentially autonomous. We know the regular practice of intercommunity meetings (*ngillatun, kawiñ, koyang* etc.) in established spots, for various reasons, often intermingled (marriages, prayers, trade, assemblies etc.) and heavily ritualised, to the point of indicating a real obsession for symbolic gesture related to sociability.[7] Gifts of course formed an essential part of these protocols. The anthropology of contemporary communities has emphasised the importance of ritualised exchange in maintaining connections over a large distance, redistributing surpluses and complementing the resources of different natural niches.[8] Even at the local and quotidian level, it is thought that the traditional formulae for the exchange of basic goods between families in fact constitute the basis of the Mapuche social fabric and its most characteristic and persistent mark of identity.[9]

These networks of reciprocity were without doubt the basis for activating forms of political and military collaboration. In the face of the Spanish irruption, traditional institutions expanded in importance and functions to give a joint response to the threat, which included an intensification of the connectivity between families and regions, and a transposition of the patriarchal headships into large coalition leaderships (*toqui*).[10] This process interwove with the potentiation and homogenisation of common ethno-cultural elements (language, material culture etc.), in what some consider a real phenomenon of ethnogenesis.[11] These inter-community gatherings thus became larger and more common, to establish alliances, decide moves

[6] Dillehay, 2017, 69–71.
[7] Bengoa, 2018: 109–29.
[8] Bohme, 2014.
[9] Kradolfer, 2011; Tereucán-Angulo *et alii*, 2016.
[10] Goicovich, 2006; Boccara, 2009: 31–118; Dillehay, 2017: 33–48.
[11] Boccara, 2009.

and choose leaders. The accounts speak of constant 'juntas de indios' before and after each important event, although the references tend to be vague and mediated by an ethnocentrist filter which converted them into simple 'borracheras (boozing)'.[12] Negotiations with the Spanish were undoubtedly also accompanied by rites of exchange and commensality, but the chroniclers tend to record few details, probably considering them irrelevant. We know quite a lot about the large diplomatic parliaments already institutionalised in the seventeenth century,[13] but very little about the preceding formulae of negotiation upon which they were based and which were probably adaptations of the indigenous models for meeting.[14]

Against this backdrop, the comparisons proposed between the Roman West and the Chilean case pivot around certain relatively similar circumstances which, in any case, pose common methodological problems: to consider the place of diplomatic gifts in contexts characterised by deadlock in conflicts of long duration and the formation of complex border realities. What functions did the diplomatic gifts fulfil in the relationship between fragmentary entities and in scenarios of precarious colonial control? What do they tell us about the processes of ethnogenesis and the formation of war leaderships derived from this climate of unrest? What can they contribute to the reassessment of the concepts of assimilation and resistance, centre and periphery, in reconsidering colonial interactions and cultural hybridism?

Chaquira: Hybridism and Mutual Appropriation

> Oída esta razón, el Teopolicán se levantó y se quitó de su cuello la chaquira que tengo dicho que hacen de hueso, que es lo más preciado que ellos tienen, y se lo puso al anacona, y le mandó dar un vestido, y le dijo: 'Hermano, eso que dices cumplirlo heis vosotros. Yo te prometo que si tú lo haces, que yo te haré señor'.[15]

It was 1558, next to the Spanish fort of Cañete, in the province of Arauco. A yanacona (or 'ancona', an indigenous person in the service of the Spanish)

---

[12] Bengoa, 2018: 109–29.
[13] Zavala *et alii*, 2020.
[14] Contreras Painemal, 2007: 60–72.
[15] 'Hearing this reason, Teopolicán got up and took off of his neck the chaquira, which, I have said, is made of bone, which is the most precious thing they have, and he put it on the *anacona*, and ordered that he be given a garment, and told him: "Brother, you must fulfil what you say. I promise you that if you do it, I will make you lord."' Vivar, 135.

concocted a plan to lift the siege that the Mapuche were staging against the enclave. He pretended to have escaped and, when caught by the besiegers, claimed to have a proposal for the powerful toqui, Teopolicán (or Caupolicán). He convinced him that he would betray the Spanish and open the gates to the fort while they slept. The gift of a necklace, with the promise of future awards, compensated him for his services and symbolised the trust placed in the agreement, which would eventually kill him. In other versions of the same episode, the yanacona received, instead, 'un lucido llauto de oro puro / y un grueso mazo de chaquira prima' ('a splendid *llauto* of pure gold / and a thick bunch of raw chaquira') or 'un cesto de chaquira, que cabría un celemín' ('a basket of chaquira that holds a celemín').[16]

One way or another, the chaquira appears as the Mapuche's gift *par excellence*. A little later, in 1563, various communities in the province organised to attack the fort of Arauco and named the toqui, Colocolo, as leader, offering him a joint reward: 'para el efeto hicieron derrama, a su usanza, de mucha chaquira y ropa' ('for this purpose they collected, according to their custom, a lot of chaquira and clothes').[17]

What exactly is the chaquira? Its importance led the chroniclers to include ethnographic notes about it.[18] It refers to small beads, pierced pieces of different materials (stone, bone, shell, metal and, after the Spanish arrival, glass), used in necklaces, textiles and other ornaments. The chroniclers indicated regional preferences in material, although the most valued pieces were of green stone. In any case, the evidence is confused and contradictory. For a start, 'chaquira' is an exogenous term, perhaps of Central American provenance, adopted by the Spaniards to refer generally to the multiple types of beads that existed in America.[19] Some authors, however, when referring to this region, use 'llanca', derived from *llangka*, local Mapudungun vocabulary. In fact, the terms overlap and are interchangeable, generating confusion about the possible differences, although the distinction itself suggests a certain local particularism.[20]

It is also difficult to elucidate its use and meaning. The chroniclers are apparently projecting their gender stereotypes when they claim that it was an ornament for women, but in specific accounts almost always attribute

---

[16] Ercilla, 31.29; Góngora Marmolejo, 28. A 'llauto', derived from the Quechua *llawt'u*, is a decorative headband. 'Celemín' is a traditional Spanish unit of volume, approx. 4.6 litres.
[17] Góngora Marmolejo, 38.
[18] Vivar, 105 and 109; Góngora Marmolejo, 49; González de Nájera, 1.3.4; Rosales, 1.28.
[19] Puerta Sánchez, 2021: 239.
[20] González-Caniulef, 2019: 7–9.

it to men.²¹ One idea, however, is very clear – its high value: 'tenida en más que entre los cristianos el oro' ('it is more appreciated by them than gold is by Christians').²² This translated into social prestige conferred upon the owner by certain pieces. We have seen this with Caupolicán's necklace. In order to unite troops for his attack at Villarrica, another toqui, Vilinango, sent messengers throughout the region, 'y con ellos un collar suyo de piezas de oro y perlas y turquesas, que por ser muy conocido en la provincia lo envió por señal' ('and with them his necklace made of pieces of gold, pearls and turquoises, which he sent as a guarantee because it was well known in the region').²³ It constituted a distinctive emblem of his person and guaranteed the trustworthiness of the embassy. Like Caupolicán's, moreover, there are indications it could be transferred on special occasions, leaving a trace of the memory of its owners; on Catiray: 'Él tiene el rico llauto de chaquira / Que fue del venerable Pailataro' ('He has the *llauto* of chaquira / which belonged to the venerable Pailataro').²⁴ In any case, its use appears to be polyfunctional: apart from diplomatic exchange and honouring leaders, the chroniclers mention it in association with religious, funerary and matrimonial rituals, including as indemnity for victims of war or crime.²⁵

The Spanish, however, also offered beads, in their case of glass. There are various allusions to the gift of the chaquira or, explicitly, 'cuentas de vidrio', on the part of the Spanish, from the early encounters in the north and centre,²⁶ and also in business dealings on the south coasts, where they were also used by the Dutch.²⁷

In fact, European colonisers used glass beads as exchange in all corners of the earth; specifically, the Spanish trade in these objects in the sixteenth century is well known,²⁸ as well as their particular deployment in territories like New Spain, Peru and Argentina.²⁹ They constituted a real catch-all because of their balance of exoticism with familiarity; glass was a novel and striking material outside Europe, while the form of beads, similar to other local pieces, made them easy to recognise and assimilate. Their use in Chile was therefore not an improvised or innovative strategy, but the result

---

[21] González-Caniulef, 2019: 10–11.
[22] Góngora Marmolejo, 28, also Vivar, 105 and 109; Góngora Marmolejo, 38; Mariño de Lobera, 1.38.
[23] Mariño de Lobera, 3.4.
[24] Oña, 13.
[25] González-Caniulef, 2019: 13.
[26] Vivar, 14; Mariño de Lobera, 1.19 and 1.38.
[27] Rosales, 1.10, 1.12, 2.18.
[28] Smith & Good, 1982.
[29] Martins, 2019; Menaker, 2016; Tapia & Pineau, 2011, respectively.

of a lesson learnt through previous experiences, applied in America from Christopher Columbus' very first contacts, Hernán Cortés' relationship with Moctezuma, and that of Francisco Pizarro with Atahualpa.[30]

We do not know the distinction that the peoples of Chile made between autochthonous and imported pieces, although a late source points to a possible discriminatory use:

> Se adornan la cabeza ... con ciertas piedras, que por lo menos son unas falsas esmeraldas, que hasta ahora no se sabe de donde las saquen. Estimanlas infinito y las conocen tan perfectamente, que habiéndolas procurado falsear con vidrio teñido del mismo color, ellas entre mil separan una de estas y desechan las otras.[31]

It is necessary to turn to archaeology to compare with the written sources. Discoveries of pre-Hispanic beads are limited; it is not known whether that is because of the incipient nature of the research or a genuine rarity of the object.[32] Examples can, however, be found in most of the Chilean territory, including in the south-centre, from very early periods, the majority in funerary offerings, which reinforces the idea of their function as social differentiators. In the period immediately prior to the Spanish arrival, moreover, a new phenomenon seems to have arisen. A compositional analysis on Mocha Island demonstrates the simultaneous use of beads in autochthonous materials (bone and shell), and others in turquoise and bronze, which implies exchanges over distances greater than 2,500 km. This appears to be associated with the above-mentioned process of growing social complexity, so that certain groups or individuals were competing for control of these networks and the possession of sumptuous ornaments whose value was increased by the distance the material had travelled.[33]

On the other hand, the finds from the early colonial period confirm the simultaneous use of glass and autochthonous pieces. Although also sporadic, there are examples from across the Chilean region.[34] The case of a burial in Chalupén 5, in the province of Cautín, stands out, as it contained

---

[30] Martins, 2019: 163–89; Menaker, 2016: 90, respectively.
[31] Gómez de Vidaurre, 6.10. 'They embellish their heads ... with certain gemstones, which are false emeralds at least, and to this day it is unknown where they get them from. They esteem them infinitely and know them so perfectly that, having tried to falsify them with glass tinted in the same colour, they can distinguish one of those among a thousand and reject the others.'
[32] Campbell *et alii*, 2018: 223; González-Caniulef, 2019: 9.
[33] Campbell *et alii*, 2018: 219–28.
[34] Soto Rodríguez *et alii*, 2019: 16.

beads of both glass and green stone.³⁵ This combination of Spanish and traditional beads has also been attested in Peruvian finds.³⁶

Ultimately, the entrance of the Spanish into the circulation of chaquira in Chile cannot be interpreted as a unidirectional phenomenon.³⁷ It has long been argued that the use of exotic objects in colonial interactions always involves a dynamic of reciprocal appropriation and resignification.³⁸ In this case, it is very clear that the Spanish harnessed an extensive substrate of pre-existing social practices around *llangka*, while the local communities used and adapted the new material in their own symbolic universe, without, moreover, abandoning the traditional variants. From this perspective, bead ornaments reveal themselves to be an ideal artefact for the generation of hybrid practices due to their intercultural adaptability.

The examination of phenomena of mutual appropriation in this type of exchange is applicable to multiple colonial contexts. In fact, analysis of glass beads in the Peruvian context has already indicated a theoretical parallelism with the study of cultural hybridism in ancient Sardinia.³⁹ The case studied in this chapter includes the circumstance that, in both the Araucanian and Sardinian worlds, the stereotype of indigenous isolation and resistance to external influences has been a fundamental assumption, fed by barbarising discourses in the Spanish and Graeco-Latin sources respectively. This preconception has, for example, conditioned the interpretation of the ethnic character of the Sardo-Punic uprisings in the face of Roman provincialisation, while careful study of the material culture suggests a much more complex reality around the true cultural impact of the Italian presence.⁴⁰ Local integration of foreign objects of value – whether they were glass beads in Mapuche burials or Campanian vessels in Sardo-Punic rituals – demonstrates the complex effects of colonial interaction, above all if we take into account the agency of local actors beyond the simple dichotomy of resistance or assimilation.

Curiously, glass beads have also prompted reassessment of the Roman Empire's Caledonian border. The simultaneous presence of local and Roman beads has entered, through typological and compositional study, into the substantial problem of cross-border relations in a region notable for prolonged periods of conflict and coexistence.⁴¹ From the earliest campaigns,

---

35 Berdichewsky & Calvo 1972–3: 542.
36 Menaker, 2016.
37 González-Caniulef, 2019: 13–18.
38 Thomas, 1991; Cipolla, 2017.
39 Menaker, 2016: 89.
40 Van Dommelen, 2007.
41 Macinnes, 1989; Bertini *et alii*, 2011.

and later with the establishment of the Antonine *limes*, the relatively sporadic presence of Roman luxury objects and silver coin hoards has been interpreted as evidence of a combined strategy of a certain form of taxation and personal diplomatic gifts that strengthened the loyalty of the border elites.[42] Against the idea of a simple, passive collection of exotic artefacts, it is possible to perceive a dynamic of selective acceptance of objects and techniques, according to the region, whether that was because the material was considered valuable in itself, or because its form was easily adaptable to local dress, symbols and rites; the glass beads constitute a good example of the latter.[43] In the far north of the Roman Empire and the far south of the Spanish Empire, they provided a good hard currency for negotiating.

Hats, Trinkets and Feathers: Exoticism and Mastery of Symbolic Language

> Demandóle el capitán indio qué seguridad tendrían los señores y él de aquello que allí les decía y prometía. El general Valdivia le dio en señal un sombrero que en la cabeza tenía con una medalla de oro con una pluma. Y esto le envió en señal de paz, que era mucho para un indio, el cual lo recibió, y tomándolo en las manos, lo besó y lo puso en su cabeza, y lo dio a un indio que traía sus armas para que se lo guardase.[44]

It worked. It was 1540, and Valdivia had just entered Copiapó, in the north of Chile. Four days later, the representatives of the various communities returned and named Valdivia 'apo', as they had with the Incan rulers. His manoeuvres did not end there; he also invited them to a banquet to continue feting them: 'dioles chaquira y tijeras y espejos y cosas de nuestra España, especialmente cosas de vidrio que ellos tienen en mucho' ('They gave them chaquira, scissors, mirrors and things from our Spain, especially glass things, which they value very much').[45] The chronicler uses an interesting simile, comparing the conquistador with Thrasybulus, the tyrant of Miletus, who entertained the Lydian king Alyattes ostentatiously, showing

---

[42] Breeze, 2006: 120–5.
[43] Campbell, 2018.
[44] Vivar, 13. 'The Indian captain asked him what assurance he and the lords had of what he told and promised. General Valdivia gave him the hat with a gold medal and a feather that he had on his head as a guarantee. And he sent it as a sign of peace, which was a lot for an Indian, who received it, and taking it in his hands, kissed it and put it on his head, and gave it to an Indian who carried his weapons to keep it.'
[45] Vivar, 14.

an exaggerated prosperity to make him believe he was stronger than he really was.[46]

Clothing, trinkets and beads were often combined. Already in the Araucanian territory, and in order to attract the communities in the Los Ríos region peacefully, Valdivia also 'los regaló con algunas cosillas y en particular con tijeras y cuchillos y alguna chaquira' ('he gifted them some little things and in particular scissors and knives, and some chaquira').[47] The judges of the Real Audiencia likewise used this strategy to pacify the situation in Concepción in 1557: 'dieron a los caciques y a los presos bonetes de grana, camisetas de fina lana y otros vestidos y cosas que ellos estiman' ('they gave the chiefs and the prisoners scarlet caps, fine wool shirts and other clothes, and things that they appreciate').[48] The peoples of Mocha Island and Paicaví apparently supplied the Spanish with cattle and crops, and 'se contentan con un pequeño retorno de cascabeles, peines, cuchillos, añil, cuentas de vidrio y cosas deste porte' ('they are pleased with a small reward of bells, combs, knives, indigo, glass beads and that sort of thing'), as well as wedges and iron axes.[49]

In another famous negotiation, a striking hat came into play again, this time on Mapuche initiative. In 1556, during his drive towards Santiago, the powerful toqui Lautaro parleyed with the captain Marco Veas. Defiant, he demanded various highly valuable items in exchange for a truce, one of them very specifically: 'me habéis de dar esa medalla que traéis en el sombrero; la cual vos soléis llamar la medalla de Quinto Curcio' ('you need to give me the medallion that you wear on your hat, which you usually call the medallion of Quintus Curtius').[50] Did Veas wear a coin of Quintus Curtius on his hat?[51] Such an ornament would not have been rare on a Renaissance gentleman. The specificity of the detail confers a certain credibility and, moreover, Lautaro was raised among the Spanish, and it seems that he and Veas were old acquaintances.[52] In any case, Lautaro was not unfamiliar with Spanish social codes, and it is possible that he was aware in some way of the stamp of antiquity and prestige with which that medallion was imbued, which would allow it to protect and sanction their pact.[53]

[46] Diog. Laert. 1.83, from Hdt. 1.21–2.
[47] Mariño de Lobera, 1.38.
[48] Rosales, 4.36.
[49] Rosales, 2.18.
[50] Mariño de Lobera, 1.3.54.
[51] RRC 285/2–7.
[52] Rosales, 4.7.
[53] On the diplomatic use of medallions, already analysed, in the North American sphere, see Depkat, 2016.

Lautaro also demanded of Veas thirty 'capas de grana fina' ('fine scarlet capes').[54] It seems that European attire, derived from gifts or booty, was desirable to local leaders, and they used them as a demonstration of authority. When Juan Gómez de Almagro fled after surviving a skirmish near the Fort of Purén, he ran into the son of a local leader, whom he tricked by giving him his 'sayete de terciopelo morado con botones de oro' ('purple velvet tunic with gold buttons').[55] At one point, Caupolicán was described 'con una capa de grana, como si fuera un español muy autorizado así en su traje como en el mandar' ('with a scarlet cape, as if he were a very authoritative Spaniard, both in his suit and his command').[56] Alonso de Ercilla represented him with the rich apparel seized from Valdivia, adding that 'Todos los capitanes señalados / a la española usanza se vestían ... / por inútil y bajo se estimaba / el que español despojo no llevaba' ('All prominent captains / dressed in the Spanish manner ... / who did no wear Spanish spoils / was considered useless and poor'). In another passage, he catalogued the collection of ornaments and clothes with which the Spaniards had gifted the chiefs of an embassy led by Millalauco: 'ropas de mil colores diferentes, / jotas, llautos, chaquiras y listones / insignias y vestidos competentes / a nobles capitanes y varones' ('clothes of a thousand different colors, / sandals, *llautos*, chaquira and ribbons, / badges and dresses characteristic / of noble captains and gentlemen').[57] Although less detailed, there are other generic mentions of the gift of clothes, from Spaniards and also amongst the Mapuche themselves.[58]

Often in these cases, the chroniclers' discourse revolves around deceit and disproportion, the shrewdness of the Spaniards who achieved valuable objectives in exchange for more or less quotidian possessions and clothes ('cosillas', 'cosas deste porte'), bamboozling some indigenous people who had a very primitive understanding of the value of objects. The same occurred when they marvelled at the unusual value that was accorded to chaquiras, equivalent for the Spaniards to gold, which indigenous people disregarded.[59] The games of omission and emphasis, the underestimation of those objects and the exaggeration of indigenous innocence and passivity in the face of Spanish Machiavellianism turned trinkets into an archetypal

---

[54] Mariño de Lobera, 1.3.54; a hundred, according to Rosales, 4.7; thirty green ones and thirty purple ones, according to Ercilla, 12.14.
[55] Góngora Marmolejo, 15.
[56] Mariño de Lobera, 2.1.4.
[57] Ercilla 8.13–14, 17.15.
[58] Vivar, 135; Góngora Marmolejo, 38; Mariño de Lobera, 2.13.
[59] Góngora Marmolejo, 28 and 38.

element in the discourse of othering the original peoples.[60] This ambivalent condescension owed much to Classical ethnography; in fact, chroniclers sometimes sought explicit parallels to explain the phenomenon.[61] In reality, the attitude of the Mapuche described in the chronicles does not differ much, for example, from that attributed by Diodorus to the Balearic mercenaries, who rejected precious metals and settled for women and wine.[62]

Beyond ethnographic topics, the reality behind this type of gift is more complex if we observe the local motivations and Spanish adaptations necessary for such mechanisms to be operative. The degree of improvisation was probably not as great nor the value of the objects as insignificant as it seems. Leaving the glass and fabrics to one side for the moment, almost all are metal possessions and ornaments, whose functional and symbolic usefulness should not be underestimated.[63] Working metal in central and south-central Chile was relatively recent (tenth century) and highly selective, a prestige technology, above all of copper, and particularly dedicated to personal adornment. The Spanish presence profoundly altered this panorama, modifying the rationales for extraction, circulation and valuation.[64] In the new context, metal objects, especially of iron, soon started to be sought in sieges and booty for reuse to the extent that, at least from the early seventeenth century, Mapuche warriors already carried steel arms and had Spanish blacksmiths in their service.[65]

Bearing this in mind, the gift of knives, scissors and metal ornaments takes on a new meaning. It is therefore not unusual that the yanacona who tricked Caupolicán, when he went to meet the most important people in the area, offered them the only thing he was carrying, an axe for chopping wood, and they received it with pleasure. On the other hand, when the toqui was captured, he tried to buy his freedom by offering to return Valdivia's personal objects that were in his possession: his sword, his helmet and a gold chain with a crucifix.[66] In the same account, those innocent Mapuche who supposedly accepted any rubbish were later capable of identifying the priorities and codes of the Spanish and using them in their favour.

Negotiation with fundamentally symbolic objects is, furthermore, multidirectional. After the toqui Michimalonco razed the burgeoning

[60] Martins, 2019: 160–3.
[61] Valenzuela Matus, 2016: 210–11.
[62] Diod. Sic. 5.17.4.
[63] See, for example, the study of the processes of dissemination and resignification of sleigh bells in North America (Ivas, 2014).
[64] Campbell, 2004.
[65] González de Nájera, 2.3.3 and 2.4.
[66] Góngora Marmolejo, 28.

city of Santiago in 1541, he engaged in negotiation with Valdivia and Inés Suárez. In order to ingratiate herself with Michimalonco, Suárez: 'le dio algunas preseas, como peines, tijeras, chaquira y un espejo. En recompensa de lo cual sacó él una pluma, y se la dio, diciendo que la tuviese en mucho' ("She gave him some precious things, such as combs, scissors, chaquira and a mirror. In return he took out a feather, and gave it to her, saying that she should hold it in high regard').[67] He then explained that it came from a bird raised among the volcanoes, and that the feather had fireproof qualities. After that, we hear an interesting detail in the story: Michimalonco had saved it to give to the Inca as thanks for having him at his table in a meeting in Cuzco some time previously. We have already seen how the inhabitants of Copiapó attributed authority formulae to Valdivia that dated back to Incan rule, which suggests a phenomenon of transposition of the political and diplomatic mechanisms in the north and centre of Chile, which increasingly appears to have been integrated into the Incan Empire.[68] In any case, the nature of the exchange (metal and glass for a magical feather) reaffirms the relativisation of the rationalist rhetoric of simple trickery.

Rather than deceiving with exotic objects, the Spanish harnessed the dynamics of exchange that had already functioned previously, although they strengthened certain elements and introduced other new ones in their interest. Their reception, however, was not merely passive; instead, it is possible to identify selective criteria defined by both material value and symbolic prestige, reinforced by the biography of the object, its antiquity, the distance it had travelled, its rarity and its previous owners, whether it was a Roman coin, a feather intended for an Inca, or Valdivia's arms.

On the recurrence of garments in exchanges, there is an interesting supplementary attestation from the early seventeenth century. The work by González de Nájera, Maestro de Campo in the Arauco War, is a series of proposals for putting an end to the conflict. It bestows critical importance upon 'indios amigos', border communities who collaborated with the Spanish in military matters, retaining a certain degree of autonomy and privilege, such as exemption from taxation and provision of work, which normativised over time.[69] In order to retain their indispensable support, Nájera recommended establishing a system of agreed gifts: 'a cada un cacique de los indios amigos, para tenerlos gratos, se le dé cada dos años una capa de paño azul y un sombrero de fieltro; ... ellos lo tienen por adorno grande y autoridad cacical' ('that each chief of the indios amigos, to please them, be

---

[67] Mariño de Lobera, 1.19.
[68] Cornejo & Saavedra, 2018; Urbina *et alii*, 2019.
[69] Ruiz-Esquide Figueroa, 1993.

given a cape of blue cloth and a felt hat every two years; ... they consider them a great ornament and a sign of chief authority').[70] They would offer their warriors 'un sombrero azul cada año' ('a blue hat every year'), when it was their turn to take up arms. He completes the proposal by offering a helmet as a reward for any exceptional exploits. With this formula, they would be compensated for their services without great expense, at the same time as strengthening their commitment to the Spanish, motivating them to compete for achievements and fostering a certain group identity.

The details are important. He proposed adorning the hats with 'toquillas de vidrios de colores' ('bands of pieces of coloured glass'), that is, chaquira, as some local communities already did with their headdresses.[71] The hats and cloaks had to be blue, moreover; in fact, he recommended that this colour should be removed from Spanish equipment so that the 'indios amigos' perceived them as exclusive. He stated that the idea had arisen from a personal anecdote: a Mapuche offered the Spaniard a horse in exchange for a blue cloth he possessed that had no value; after making a cloak with it, they all followed him and many went to ask him for more 'paño de señores' ('cloth of lords').[72] Apart from his supposed discovery, we have already seen mentioned the fact that the Spanish gifted indigo. We know that blue has always held great importance in the Mapuche cosmovision and is very present in the chromatic codes of the fabrics and body paints used in rituals.[73] Nájera's proposal therefore tried to harness the attraction of European attire, adapting it to local symbolic codes with significant ornaments and colours. In this way, it reinforced their authority within their community at the same time as incentivising loyalty to the Spanish as guarantors of that ongoing favourable status quo.

In this respect, it is apposite to reflect on the importance of mastering symbolic language in the colonisation of America: a large proportion of the successes and failures in the Spanish expansion can be explained by the conquistadors' capacity to observe and understand the communicative mechanisms of the original peoples and to apply them to the process of domination. This applies to language per se – through interpreters and bilingualism – and also to the attention given to gestures, attire and rites, in order to understand better the opponent's signals and, at the same time, retain greater control over the non-verbal messages sent.[74]

---

[70] González de Nájera, 5.4.5.
[71] Vivar, 137.
[72] González de Nájera, 5.4.5.
[73] Bengoa, 2018: 11–15.
[74] Todorov, 2010: 120–53. On the colonial politics of clothes in Peru, Decoster, 2005.

More generally, the idea of the colonial instrumentalisation of ethnographic observation can be applied to multiple contexts. The Second Punic War, for example, provides numerous demonstrations of the complex game of obligation networks used by Carthaginians and Romans to win the indispensable support of the local peoples in the various conflict arenas. Polybius reports that Hannibal organised a duel between the Alpine prisoners in order to cheer his troops, using Gaulish princely arms and offering horses and luxury tunics as a prize for the winner; such strategies have been interpreted as a skilful use of indigenous diplomatic languages directed at his mercenaries.[75] The use of discourses, gestures and religious iconography of Ibero-Phoenician origin by the Barcas and Scipios to promote alliances and legitimise their authority with respect to the Hispanian elites has been understood in the same way.[76]

Parallels can also be found in the local elites' use of the colonial power's garbs of authority. Rome's relationship with the Numidians is highly striking in this respect, in that the entire diplomatic game with them was sanctioned with multiple gifts, amongst which were various types of togas and tunics as worn by the Roman aristocracy: they are present in the alliance with King Syphax, Massiva's liberation by Scipio, the alliance with Masinissa and the embassy sent to the latter by the senate in 200 BC.[77] Sertorius' strategy of Romanising the Hispanian elites disposed towards his cause, teaching them to use the toga and tunic while detaining their children to give them a Roman education, is likewise well known.[78] These accounts, combined with the iconographic evidence of indigenous use of Roman garments, have been interpreted, through the theory of colonial hybridity, as revealing a bidirectional phenomenon which helped Rome to strengthen the bonds of *amicitia* with its allies, while the local elites used them to imbue themselves with additional prestige and legitimise their privileges.[79]

In such complex contexts, a sharp distinction between the foreign and the indigenous is contrived, since their elements quickly interlaced (in hybrid garments and ornaments), used by various agents (colonisers, rebels and collaborators, mestizo or not) and whose layers of bestowed value (material, exoticism and symbolism) are difficult to calibrate.

---

[75] Polyb. 3.62; see Sánchez Moreno, 2005: 239.
[76] García Cardiel, 2019a; 2021.
[77] Livy 27.4.8 (and just after, the same with other African kings, Livy 27.4.9–10), 27.19.12, 30.15.11–12, 31.11.11. For further details, see the chapter by E. Sánchez Medina & G. Roselló Calafell in this volume.
[78] Plut. *Sert.* 14.
[79] García Cardiel, 2019b. See also the chapter by D. García Domínguez & D. Suárez Martínez in this volume.

Their meaning, furthermore, is always mediated by previous colonial experiences: Spanish diplomacy in Chile cannot be understood without considering Incan intervention, in the same way as Roman diplomacy in Hispania is unintelligible without the Phoenicio-Punic component.

Horses and Dogs: Between the Pragmatics of War and Social Symbolism

When Lautaro asked Veas for his medal and some capes, that was not all; he also wanted 'treinta caballos blancos con los mejores jaeces que se hallaren entre vosotros ... y una docena de perros grandes de esos conque vosotros soléis aperrear a los indios' ('thirty white horses with the best harnesses you have and a dozen large dogs of those you usually employ to *aperrear* the Indians').[80]

The offer of horses and dogs to strengthen agreements also appears on certain occasions, and they were not only given by the Spanish. When Pedro de Villagra led his campaign through Reinohuelén, the local communities coordinated to confront him:

> Los indios habían enviado a llamar a todos los comarcanos les viniesen a ayudar, pues los habían pagado a su usanza, y para esta paga habían juntado ochocientos perros y gran cantidad de chaquira ... Los perros quiérenlos para cazar, y desto se aprovechan dellos, y cuando no son de provecho se los comen.[81]

The allusion to dogs is important. Góngora did not specify, but Mariño de Lobera seems to refer to European dogs. There are many uncertainties around the characteristics of the extinct autochthonous dogs, but it is well attested that large European dogs were significant in the course of the war, as a shock force in battles, to track enemies, guard camps and terrorise communities through their punitive use ('aperrear indios'); particularly useful were the 'cebados en indios', those fed with human flesh to increase their ferocity. These practices were common throughout America in the early years of the conquest,[82] but endured an especially long time in Chile

---

[80] Mariño de Lobera, 1.3.54; ten of each, according to Rosales, 4.7; twelve and six, according to Ercilla, 12.15.
[81] Góngora Marmolejo, 49. 'The Indians had called on all the locals to come and help them, since they had paid them according to their custom, and for this pay they had collected 800 dogs and a large amount of chaquira ... They want dogs to hunt, and use them for this, and eat them when they are not useful.'
[82] Bueno Jiménez, 2011.

due to the deadlock in the conflict and the precarious hold on the area.[83] We should understand their presence in negotiations in this context, wherein the harsh conditions of violence and supply problems converted these animals into a valuable asset for survival and balancing power between opponents.

Horses were more pivotal. They had been vital to the Spanish for a long time for both combat and logistics, above all given the uneven terrain and long distances. Indeed, sources constantly reflect the problem of their supply, the gravity of equine casualties in battle and the significance of the theft of these animals in incursions into enemy camps. On the other side, the Mapuches' rapid learning and adaptation of techniques for mounting and rearing radically marked their military tactics; in the 1550s they already used cavalry, and by the early seventeenth century, theirs was bigger than the Spanish one.[84] It also constituted a fundamental element in their economic transformation. In the pre-Hispanic period, their societies were essentially agrarian and communication networks were structured around the extensive river network in the region; however, instability and the dismantling of their supply chains fostered a new setting which privileged farming and trade, and brought a demographic displacement towards more rugged territories, where mobility on horseback became indispensable.[85] In this context, it is unsurprising that the Mapuche requested horses from the Spanish in negotiations, and that they also offered them as a sign of goodwill.[86]

With their military and economic implications, the adoption of horses interwove decisively into Mapuche sociopolitical structure. Superimposed over the process of hierarchisation that these societies were already experiencing, a new non-productive masculine social group emerged, dedicated exclusively to combat, whose role in the community was sustained through the reinforcement of the pre-existing martial ideology. In this context of unrest and semi-nomadic economy, *malones* – horseback raids for looting and robbing livestock – were deployed from very early on as a combined military tactic, method of survival and way of validating these groups and their leaders.[87]

The possession of and control over horses, especially in the early days when their availability was more restricted, therefore became an

---

[83] Góngora Marmolejo, 20 and 47; Mariño de Lobera, 2.21. See Varner & Varner, 1983: 175–91.
[84] González de Nájera, 2.3.1; see Leiva, 1981–2.
[85] Bengoa, 2018: 147–53.
[86] González de Nájera, 3.1.2.
[87] Boccara, 2009: 118–97, 309–15.

indisputable symbol of prestige. Significantly, Lautaro – who before breaking cover was a groom for the Spanish – did not simply request horses, but 'caballos blancos con los mejores jaeces' ('white horses with the best harnesses'); Caupolicán was also described as mounted on 'un caballo blanco' ('a white horse').[88] Did the Mapuche assume so early the social significance and differentiating signs that the Spanish attributed to their horses, or is this a case of literary licence? What is certain is that, a few decades later, González de Nájera recounted that the principal warriors reserved the best horses for themselves, and that they covered them with luxurious tack, trophies and distinctive insignia, 'en lo cual imitan a nuestros españoles'.[89] It makes sense that that elite, defined by military capacity and merit, should seek formulae for distinguishing their mounts through the exclusive use of the rarest breeds and most sumptuous equipment, and that in doing so they quickly imitated Spanish codes, bearing in mind the radically new character of the phenomenon.

The circulation of horses as prestige goods is an excellent indication of the social structure and its transformations. In the study of the pre-Roman West, the analysis of equestrian ideology constitutes one of the main topics for understanding the functioning of military leaderships and the structure of their warrior *ēthos*. Along these lines, the existence of an entire equestrian iconographic tradition on objects of social distinction in Hispania and Gaul has been widely studied, as well as the habitual presence of equine remains with all their equipment in aristocratic graves.[90] The possibility has even been raised that in some cases, these animals could have been imported, which would have augmented their exclusive character, the fruit of exchanges between elites from different territories.[91] Discussion has likewise encompassed the complex interweaving of mechanisms of inter-regional hospitality with dynamics of livestock movement and the incidence of raids by semi-nomadic groups, especially in periods of instability.[92]

Obviously, there the equestrian ideology was established before the arrival of Rome, but it was strengthened in the context of war, which also left its imprint on diplomatic negotiations. As an example, in the Second Punic War, Scipio gave 300 horses to the Ilergetan leader Indibilis for his help in the Battle of Baecula; Scipio also included a harnessed horse among

---

[88] Mariño de Lobera, 2.1.4.
[89] González de Nájera, 2.3.3.
[90] Méniel, 2001; Quesada Sanz & Zamora Merchán, 2003; Sánchez Moreno, 2005.
[91] Sánchez Moreno, 2005: 238–43.
[92] Sánchez Moreno, 2011.

the presents for Massiva, the Numidian.[93] In the context of the Macedonian Wars, when Gaulish auxiliary troops were decisive, three Gaulish leaders likewise received richly caparisoned horses and collections of equestrian armour, among other gifts, in two embassies to Rome.[94] These are highly disparate scenarios, but the gift of horses, in addition to their evident usefulness, constituted – especially in cases of individuals – an excellent symbolic recognition of those elites whose position was strengthened precisely within a climate of escalating war.

There is one final general reflection to be made. It is striking that Góngora framed the gift of dogs and horses among the Mapuche as a 'paga' ('pay'),[95] as he did when he spoke of the 'paga y salario' ('pay and salary') of chaquira and clothes which they gave to Colocolo when he assumed leadership.[96] It is reasonable to think that the Spanish, with their military and mercantile mentality, interpreted as an employment relationship – a hiring of mercenaries – what perhaps could be better understood as a system of gifts within these reciprocity networks that operated to foster collaboration between fragmented communities.[97] Such gifts helped to mobilise reluctant groups or individuals; in the case of animals, furthermore, they used goods that had acquired a new importance and were fundamental for effective involvement in conflict. In such complex diplomatic contexts, nevertheless, the boundary between symbolic and economic compensation is certainly fuzzy and generates inevitable problems of conceptualisation.

For the ancient world as well, the difficult contrast of hypothetical archaeological interpretation, source bias and the preconceptions of modern research has led to similar dilemmas which are difficult to resolve. The interpretation of the circulation of crowns and other gold and silver pieces in Gaul has been framed along these critical lines. Certainly, their exchange and amassing can be related to distinct reciprocity mechanisms, family connections and political alliances. The standardisation of weights and shapes, however, invites reconsideration of the phenomenon from an economic perspective, as a form of pre-monetal transaction, which takes on even more meaning in contexts of generalised unrest, such as the Roman expansion, when the need to develop fluid systems of compensation for the payment of mercenaries or logistical services intensified. In cases like this,

---

[93] Livy 27.19.7, 27.19.12.
[94] Livy 43.5.8, 44.14.2, 53.5.8.
[95] Góngora Marmolejo, 49.
[96] Góngora Marmolejo, 38.
[97] González-Caniulef, 2019: 12–13.

interpretation could have been tainted by a schematic and primitivist application of the anthropological model of gift and counter-gift – in fact very dependent on emic explanations (both Posidonius' Gaulish informants as well as the indigenous sources of contemporary anthropologists) – which makes it difficult to create sufficient analytical distance.[98] There is no easy answer for either of the two cases, which are otherwise very different. The call for caution in extrapolating from pre-established models to address problems of this type, however, seems to remain pertinent.

As signposted at the start of this chapter, all these common examples do not try to establish universal rules about the meaning of the diplomatic gift. An enormous geographical, cultural and chronological distance separates the two contexts; for a start, to a greater or lesser degree, Rome shared with the European and North African peoples common codes that had to be built between the Spanish and original American peoples. Arguably, however, comparative study can be useful, at least, as a pretext for reflection on general methodological and interpretative problems relating to interaction in scenarios of prolonged unrest and precarious colonial rule. The diplomatic gift in such contexts reveals itself to be a valuable indication of the phenomena of mutual adaptation and appropriation of prestige elements (such as chaquira), the importance of mastering the symbolic language of the other in interethnic relationships (such as the use of clothes and insignia), and the construction of profound social transformations (such as the horse). It likewise makes us conscious of the multiple determinants, ancient, modern and contemporary, that we should avoid when analysing complex human interactions.

Bibliography

Auliard, C. [2009]. 'Cadeaux et marchandages diplomatiques à Rome jusqu'au début de la conquête méditerranéenne', *Veleia*, 26, 63–73.

Bengoa, J. [2018]. *Historia de los antiguos mapuches del sur: desde antes de la llegada de los españoles hasta las Paces de Quilín, siglos XVI y XVII*, Santiago de Chile.

Berdichewsky, B. & Calvo, M. [1972–3]. 'Excavaciones en cementerios indígenas de la región del Calafquén', in *Actas del VI Congreso de Arqueología Chilena*, Santiago de Chile, 529–58.

Bertini, M., Shortland, A., Milek, K. & Krupp, E. M. [2011]. 'Investigation of Iron Age North-Eastern Scottish Glass Beads Using Element

---

[98] Lewuillon, 1992; 1999. On the circulation of prestige goods in Gaul, see the chapter by A. Pérez Rubio in this volume.

Analysis with LA-ICP-MS', *Journal of Archaeological Science*, 38 (10), 2750–66.
Boccara, G. [2009]. *Los vencedores: historia del pueblo mapuche en la época colonial*, Antofagasta.
Bohme, E. [2014]. 'El *Nguillatún* de los mapuches: antropología económica de un hecho social total', *Revista de Historia y Geografía*, 30, 37–56.
Breeze, D. [2006]. *Roman Scotland: Frontier Country*, London.
Bueno Jiménez, A. [2011]. 'Los perros en la conquista de América: historia e iconografía', *Chronica Nova*, 37, 177–204.
Campbell, L. [2018]. 'Culture Contact and the Maintenance of Cultural Identity in Roman Scotland: A Theoretical Approach', in L. Campbell, D. Wright and N. A. Hall (eds), *Roots of Nationhood: The Archaeology and History of Scotland*, Oxford, 75–92.
Campbell, R. [2004]. *El trabajo de los metales en la Araucanía (siglos X–XVII d.C.)*, Santiago de Chile.
Campbell, R. [2011]. *Socioeconomic Differentiation, Leadership, and Residential Patterning at an Araucanian Chiefly Center (Isla Mocha, AD 1000–1700)*, Pittsburgh.
Campbell, R., Carrión, H., Figueroa, V., Peñaloza, Á., Plaza, M. T. and Stern, C. [2018]. 'Obsidianas, turquesas y metales en el sur de Chile: perspectivas sociales a partir de su presencia y proveniencia (1.000–1.700 d.C.)', *Chungará (Arica)*, 50 (2), 217–34.
Cipolla, C. [2017]. *Foreign Objects: Rethinking Indigenous Consumption in American Archaeology*, Tucson.
Contreras Painemal, C. [2007]. *Koyang: parlamento y protocolo en la diplomacia mapuche-castellana. Siglo XVI–XIX*, Berlin.
Cornejo, L. & Saavedra, M. [2018]. 'El centro político inka en el extremo austral del *tawantinsuyu* (Chile central)', *Boletín del Museo Chileno de Arte Precolombino*, 23 (1), 133–57.
Decoster, J. J. [2005]. 'Identidad étnica y manipulación cultural: la indumentaria inca en la época colonial', *Estudios Atacameños*, 29, 163–70.
Depkat, V. [2016]. 'Peace Medal Diplomacy in Indian–White Relations in Nineteenth-Century North America', in H. Rudolph & G. Metzig (eds), *Material Culture in Modern Diplomacy from the 15th to the 20th Century*, Berlin–Boston, 80–99.
Dillehay, T. [2007]. *Monuments, Empires, and Resistance: The Araucanian Polity and Ritual Narratives*, Cambridge.
Dillehay, T. [2017]. *La organización política temprana de los Mapuche: materialidad y patriarcado andino*, Santiago de Chile.
Dommelen, P. van [2007]. 'Beyond Resistance: Roman Power and Local Traditions in Punic Sardinia', in P. van Dommelen & N. Torrenato (eds),

Articulating Local Cultures: Power and Identity under the Expanding Roman Republic, Portsmouth, RI, 55–69.

Ercilla, A. [2018] (1569–89). *La Araucana*, ed. I. Lerner, Madrid.

García Cardiel, J. [2019a]. '*Animos barbarorum*: religión y comunidades locales en el frente hispano de la Segunda Guerra Púnica', in E. Sánchez Moreno & E. García Riaza (eds), *Unidos en armas: coaliciones militares en el Occidente antiguo*, Palma de Mallorca, 105–32.

García Cardiel, J. [2019b]. 'Revestir el poder en tiempos de cambio: el uso de la toga entre las elites ibéricas (ss. II–I a.C.)', *AEA*, 92, 155–71.

García Cardiel, J. [2021]. 'Herakles as a Weapon of War: Religious Discourses and Local Responses in Ancient Iberia during the Second Punic War', *Aevum*, 95 (1), 87–109.

Goicovich, F. [2006]. 'Alianzas geoétnicas en la segunda rebelión general: génesis y dinámica de los *vutanmapus* en el alzamiento de 1598', *Historia (Santiago)*, 39 (1), 93–154.

Gómez de Vidaurre, F. [1889] (1789). *Historia geográfica, natural y civil del reino de Chile*, ed. J. Toribio Medina, Santiago de Chile.

Góngora Marmolejo, A. [2019] (1575). *Historia de todas las cosas que han acaecido en el reino de Chile y de los que lo han gobernado*, ed. M. Donoso Rodríguez, Santiago de Chile.

González-Caniulef, E. [2019]. 'Cuentas vítreas y llangka: nuevas miradas desde la antropología histórica', *Bajo la Lupa*, s.n., 1–29.

González de Nájera, A. [2017] (1614). *Desengaño y reparo de la guerra del reino de Chile*, ed. M. Donoso Rodríguez, Santiago de Chile.

Grass, B. [2015]. 'Les présents diplomatiques à Rome (IIIe–Ier siècle av. J.-C.)', in B. Grass & G. Stouder (eds), *La diplomatie romaine sous la République: réflexions sur une pratique*, Besançon, 147–73.

Ivas, A. [2014]. 'Hawk Bells Revisited: The Intriguing Lives of Historic Trade Bells in the American South, 1521–1776', *Southern Quarterly*, 51 (4), 103–21.

Kradolfer, S. [2011]. *Quand la parenté impose, le don dispose: organisation sociale, don et identité dans les communautés mapuche de la province de Neuquén (Argentine)*, Bern.

Leiva, A. [1981–2]. 'La araucanización del caballo en los siglos XVI y XVII', *Anales de la Universidad de la Frontera*, 3 (140), 181–203.

Lewuillon, S. [1992]. '"Contre le don": remarques sur le sens de la réciprocité et de la compensation sociale en Gaule', *DHA*, 18 (1), 105–56.

Lewuillon, S. [1999]. 'Le pesant d'or: dépôts fastueux et trafics barbares', in A. Villes & A. Bataille-Melkon (eds), *Fastes des Celtes entre Champagne et Bourgognes aux VIIe–IIIe siècles avant notre ère*, Reims, 427–46.

Macinnes, L. [1989]. 'Baubles, Bangles and Beads: Trade and Exchange in Roman Scotland', in J. Barrett, A. P. Fitzpatrick and L. Macinnes (eds),

Barbarians and Romans in North-West Europe from the Later Republic to Late Antiquity, Oxford, 108–66.

Mariño de Lobera, P. [1960] (1598). 'Crónica del Reino de Chile', in F. Esteve Barba (ed.), *Crónicas del Reino de Chile*, Madrid, 225–562.

Martins, C. [2019]. *Lo que cuenta un abalorio: reflejos de unas cuentas de vidrio en la Nueva España*, Madrid.

Menaker, A. [2016]. 'Las cuentas durante el colonialismo español en los Andes peruanos', *Boletín de Arqueología PUCP*, 21, 85–97.

Méniel, P. [2001]. *Les Gaulois et les animaux: élevage, repas et sacrifices*, Paris.

Oña, P. [1917] (1596). *Arauco domado*, ed. J. Toribio Medina, Santiago de Chile.

Orellana Rodríguez, M. [2017]. *Pensamiento historiográfico chileno (siglos XVI y XVII)*, San Pedro de Atacama.

Puerta Sánchez, A. [2021]. *Estudio lingüístico de la Crónica y relación copiosa y verdadera de los Reinos de Chile, de Jerónimo de Vivar (1558)*, Murcia.

Quesada Sanz, F. & Zamora Merchán, M. (eds) [2003]. *El caballo en la antigua Iberia: estudios sobre los équidos en la Edad del Hierro*, Madrid.

Rosales, D. [1877–8] (1674). *Historia general de el reyno de Chile, Flandes Indiano*, ed. B. Vicuña Mackenna, Valparaíso.

Ruiz-Esquide Figueroa, A. [1993]. *Los indios amigos en la frontera araucana*, Santiago de Chile.

Sánchez Moreno, E. [2005]. 'Caballo y sociedad en la Hispania céltica: del poder aristocrático a la comunidad política', *Gladius*, 25, 237–64.

Sánchez Moreno, E. [2011]. 'Rebaños, armas, regalos: expresión e identidad de las elites vetonas', in G. Ruiz Zapatero & J. Álvarez-Sanchís (eds), *Castros y verracos: las gentes de la Edad del Hierro en el Occidente de Iberia*, Ávila, 159–89.

Smith, M. & Good, M. E. [1982]. *Early Sixteenth Century Glass Beads in the Spanish Colonial Trade*, Greenwood, MS.

Soto Rodríguez, C., Latorre Blanco, E. & Olguín, B. [2019]. '"Chiches" olvidados: caracterización y puesta en valor de la colección de adornos del Museo Regional de Rancagua', *Bajo la Lupa*, s.n., 1–28.

Sykes, K. [2005]. *Arguing with Anthropology: An Introduction to Critical Theories of the Gift*, London.

Tapia, A. & Pineau, V. [2011]. 'Diversidad de las cuentas vítreas: los hallazgos de la misión de Santiago del Baradero (siglo XVII)', *Arqueología*, 17, 119–36.

Tereucán-Angulo, J., Briceño-Olivera, C. & Gálvez-Nieto, J. [2016]. 'Equivalencia y valor en procesos de reciprocidad e intercambio entre los mapuches', *Convergencia*, 23 (72), 199–220.

Thomas, N. [1991]. *Entangled Objects: Exchange, Material Culture and Colonialism in the Pacific*, London.

Todorov, T. [2010]. *La conquista de América: el problema del otro*, Madrid.
Urbina, S., Uribe, M., Agüero, C. & Zori, C. [2019]. 'De provincia inca a repartimiento: Tarapaca en los siglos XV y XVI (Andes Centro Sur)', *Estudios Atacameños*, 61, 219–52.
Valenzuela Matus, C. [2016]. *Grecia y Roma en el Nuevo Mundo: la recepción de la antigüedad clásica en cronistas y evangelizadores del siglo XVI americano*, Barcelona.
Varner, J. G. & Varner, J. J. [1983]. *Dogs of the Conquest*, Norman, OK.
Verboven, K. [2014]. 'Like Bait on a Hook: Ethics, Etics and Emics of Gift Exchange in the Roman World', in F. Carlà & M. Gori (eds), *Gift Giving and the 'Embedded' Economy in the Ancient World*, Heidelberg, 135–53.
Vivar, J. [1988] (1558). *Crónica de los reinos de Chile*, ed. A. Barral Gómez, Madrid.
Zavala, J. M., Dillehay, T. D. & Payàs, G. (eds) [2020]. *The Hispanic–Mapuche Parlamentos: Interethnic Geo-Politics and Concessionary Spaces in Colonial America*, Cham.

Index

Note: Page numbers in *italics* indicate illustrations.

Abelux *see* Abilyx, 215
Abigail, biblical figure, 21
Abilyx, 215–19
Abimelek, biblical figure, 20, 21
Achaean League, 133–9, 144
Achaemenid Empire, 29, 43–4
Achilles, 64, 65
Adherbal, 178–9, 182
Aedui, 191
Aeginetans, 138
Aelian, 44
Aelius, Gaius, tribune of the plebs, 84
Aelius Tubero, Quintus, 123
Aemilius Paullus Macedonicus, Lucius, 122, 123, 126, 149–50, 244, 250–1
Aemilius Scaurus, Marcus, 179–80
Aeschines, 39, 51
Aetolian League, 88, 89, 108–9, 123, 124, 156, 253
Agamemnon, 60, 65
agriculture, 195, 299
Ahab of Israel, 27
Ahaz of Judah, 28, 29
akinakes, 199
Alabanda, 81–2, 94, 101
Alcibiades, 37
Alexander the Great, 65, 92, 97
Alexandria, 93, 97, 114–16, 232
Allobroges, 191
Alucius, 120, 161, 224–5, 226
Amasis, pharaoh, 66–7, 70
Ambiorix, 195

Ambracia, 95, 156
Amel-Marduk, 17
amici, 247, 249, 253
amicitia, 3, 219, 222, 225, 228, 249, 251, 252–3, 297
  Numidia, 172, 176, 177, 179, 185
Amphictyonic Council, 89
Amyclae, 65–6
Amynander of the Athamanes, 156
Androtion, 86, 90, 91
Anonimum Vaticanum, 113
Antigonus Monophthalmus, 87, 89, 92
Antiochus of Arcadia, 47, 50
Antiochus III, 78, 80, 82, 95, 98, 121, 176, 233, 250
anxiety, 132–3, 138, 140–1, 143, 144
Apollonidas of Sicyon, 133, 137, 139
Appian, 79, 151, 172, 177, 248, 249, 250, 254, 259–60, 266, 267, 274, 275, 276
Aquitania, 191, 201–2
Arauco War (1550–1641), 283–6, 302
  gifts of animals, 298–300, 301
  gifts of chaquira, 286–91
Arch of Trajan, 96–7
argentum infectum, 245
Argos, 64–5
Ariarathes V of Cappadocia, 83, 91, 100–1
Ariovistus, 192, 195, 197
Aristophanes, 44
Ark of the Covenant, 20

arms
  Celtic, 195
  as diplomatic gifts, 57–62, 66–70, 135–6, 199, 221, 251–2
  as relics, 60, 61–6, 68, 70
  in sanctuaries, 62–70
Arrian, 65
Arverni, 191
Asa, biblical king of Judah, 26–7
Asia Minor, 81–2
Assyria, 28–9
Astolpas, 254, 255–8, 259
Atahualpa, 289
Athenaeus, 51
Athens
  ambassadors, 36, 37, 44, 45, 49, 50–3, 54
  crowns, 83, 86, 87–8, 89–91
athletic contests, 85
Attalids, 78–9, 99, 138, 144, 253
Attalus I of Pergamum, 78, 79, 94, 138
Audoleon of Paeonia, 87–8, 89
Augustus, 84–5, 125, 198, 253
austerity, 119–20, 126, 143; *see also* frugality

Baasha, biblical king of Israel, 26–7
Babylon, 17, 21–2, 29, 32
Baecula, Battle of, 155, 158, 194, 228–33
Balanos, 192, 193
Bantius, Lucius, 159–60
Bastarnae, 130, 139–44
beads
  chaquira, 287–8, 289–90, 292, 293, 295, 296, 298, 301, 302
  glass, 288–91
Ben-hadad I of Syria, 26–7
Benjamites, biblical tribe, 20, 22
Bible
  Joshua, 18–20, 30–1, 32
  Judges, 20
  Kings, 23–4, 32
  1 Maccabees, 98
  Samuel, 20–1, 22–3
Biblia Hebraica Stuttgartensia (BHS), 18
Boii, 190–1
booty, 158, 162, 189, 197, 202, 224, 242–6, 293, 294

Deuteronomistic history, 20, 30, 31
diplomatic gifts, 155, 158, 173, 220, 221, 226–7
Homeric epic, 61
refusal of, 122
Bostar, 214, 215, 216, 217, 218
bows, 59, 61–2
Brasidas, 85
bribery, 21, 32
  Gaul, 190, 191
  Iberian Peninsula, 242, 252–4, 275
  Jugurthine War, 178, 179, 180, 181, 185
  Macedonia, 39, 48, 53–4, 108–9
  Roman view of, 109, 116, 118, 122, 125
  suspicions of, 49–53, 108–9
bullion, 96, 98, 226

Caecilius Metellus Numidicus, Quintus, 181, 182–3
Caecilius Metellus Pius, Quintus, 274, 275, 276
Caesar's civil war, 196
Caesius, Lucius, 251
Callimachus, 64–5
Callixenus of Rhodes, 93, 97
Calpurnius Bestia, Lucius, 180
Calpurnius Piso, Gaius, 244
Campanians, 148–9, 161, 290
Canaan, 19–20, 21
Capitol (Rome), 78, 80, 81, 90, 93–4, 99, 100, 101–2
Capua, 148–9, 161
Carpetani, 244
Carthage, 83, 119, 177, 189, 212, 214, 216, 218
  fall of, 175, 184
  treaties, 250
Carthago Nova, 120–1, 153, 154, 155, 158, 214, 215, 219–27, 228, 234, 268
Cassander of Aegina, 133, 137–9
Cassius Longinus, Gaius, 192–3
Cato the Elder, 117–18, 119, 120, 122, 123–4, 125, 126, 151, 154–5, 243
Cato the Younger, 123
cattle, 50, 52
Caucaei, 250
Caupolicán, 286, 287, 288, 293, 294, 300

cavalry
  Celts, 194, 195–6
  Macedonia, 141
  Thessaly, 141
Celtiberians, 214, 227, 251–2, 255, 267
  captives, 120, 222, 224, 225, 226
Celtiberian Wars, 176
Celts, 188–94, 203–4
  cavalry, 194, 195–6
  horses, 141–2, 194–6
  as mercenaries, 190–1, 194, 195, 202
  torques as diplomatic gifts, 196–203
censors, 110, 120, 125
chairs, 83, 162, 169, 170, 171, 173, 183, 192, 232
chaquira, 287–8, 289–90, 292, 293, 295, 296, 298, 301, 302
Chile, 283–6
  beads, 287–90, 292, 293, 295, 296, 298, 301, 302
  gifts and symbolic language, 291–6, 297–8
  horses and dogs, 298–300, 301
  inter-community gatherings, 285–6
Chios, 88, 89
Chronicle of Lindos, 64
Cicero, 113, 117, 124, 132
Cincibilus, 192–3
Cineas, 111–13, 119, 124, 125
Cinna(n), 266, 267, 271, 274
Cirta, 172, 178, 179–80
Claudius Caecus, Appius, 111, 113
Claudius Marcellus, Marcus, 159–60, 244
Cleopatra, 171
clientela, 251, 253
cloaks, 123, 192, 193, 194, 203, 232, 273, 296
Clondicus, 142–3, 194
Columbus, Christopher, 289
comitatus, 195, 196
Commius, 195
concilia, 148, 162
conloquia, 148
Constantine Porphyrogenitus, 78
constructivism, 2
continentia, 118, 120–1, 123, 126, 222–4
contiones, 162
Convictolitavis, 191

Cornelius Scipio, Gnaeus, 168–9, 170, 213, 214, 215, 216, 217, 219
Cornelius Scipio, Publius, father of Scipio Africanus, 168–9, 170, 214, 215, 216–17, 219
Cornelius Scipio Aemilianus, Publius, 122, 124, 126, 175, 177–8, 246
Cornelius Scipio Africanus, Publius, 150, 151, 157, 158–9, 173–4, 192, 194, 217, 229–31, 243–4, 300
  criticism by Cato, 124
  refusal of gifts, 120–2
  return of hostages, 120–1, 153, 154, 155, 203, 220–6, 228–9, 232–3, 297, 300–1
corruption, 48, 54, 108–9, 116, 118, 122–5; *see also* bribery
Cortés, Hernán, 289
Cos, 90
counter-gifts, 35, 43, 60, 188, 271–2, 302; *see also* reciprocity
Croesus of Lydia, 67–8, 70
crowns
  Gaul, 301
  gifts to Numidia, 169, 183, 194
  in Greek honorific culture, 85–91
  Iberian Peninsula, 244
  Numidian iconography, 171, 172, 175
  presentation to Rome, 77, 78–85, 93–4, 96–102
  recognition of sovereignty, 192, 194, 198–9, 271
  refusal of, 115, 134–5
  Roman camps, 156–7
  value and weight, 78, 80, 81, 91–8, 102
cups, 39, 44, 60, 193, 199
Curius Dentatus, Manius, 117–18, 122, 123, 124, 125, 126
Cynoscephalae, Battle of, 108
Cyrus II of Persia, 29, 40–1

Dabar, 181, 182
David, biblical king of Judah and Israel, 21, 22–3
deditiones, 155, 213, 214, 229, 250–1
deer, 24, 269–70, 271
Delilah, biblical figure, 20, 21

Delphi, 67, 68, 70, 89, 195
Demetrius I, Seleucid king, 79, 80, 82–3, 101
Demetrius I of Macedon, 99
Demetrius of Pharos, 253
Demos, son of Pyrilampes, 44, 54
Demosthenes, 39, 48, 51, 53, 86, 90, 91
Deuteronomistic history, 17–18, 31–2
    diplomatic exchange in Judaean/Israelite Territory, 19–22
    historiography, 21–2, 32
    Kings and diplomatic gifts, 22–9
    theological aspect of the diplomatic gift, 30–1
diadems, 171, 172, 175
Didyma, 67
Dio Cassius, 80, 114, 198, 259
Diocles of Sidon, 92
Diodorus Siculus, 136, 203, 254–9, 294
Dionysius of Halicarnassus, 112, 114, 115, 119–20, 170
Dionysius of Syracuse, 83
diplomatic materiality, 3–4
disciplina, 113, 118, 126
dogs, 298–9, 301
dōra, 46–7, 48, 49, 61, 66, 70
dōrodokia, 49, 53
Dumnorix, 195

Edeco, 154, 222
Edesco *see* Edeco
Egypt, 26, 28, 29
    relations with Rome, 114–16, 170–1
elephants, 176, 180, 182
eleutheria, 135, 137, 144
Elisha, biblical figure, 27
Emporion, Battle of, 154–5
Endios, 37
Ennius, 113, 117, 120, 126
Ercilla, Alonso de, 293
escorts, 82, 101, 152, 163, 170, 173, 182, 184, 221, 232
Etruscans, 69, 170
euergetism, 3
Eumenes II of Pergamum, 79, 133, 135, 137–8, 144
exchange phenomenon, 131

exempla, 51, 113, 117, 119, 120, 122–3, 125, 126, 222–4
Exuperantius, 267

Fabius Maximus Servilianus, Quintus, 159, 245, 249, 250, 251, 258, 259–60
Fabricius Luscinus, Gaius, 119, 120, 123, 125, 126
fibulae, 189, 192, 202–3, 204, *205*, 232
fides, 111, 215, 225, 248, 250, 251
Flaminius, Gaius, 98, 197
forum, 162, 164
frugality, 110, 117, 118, 120, 123, 124, 125, 126, 259; *see also* austerity
Fulvius Centumalus, Gnaeus, 148, 149
Fulvius Nobilior, Marcus, 95, 156–7, 244

Gaesatae, 190–1
Gala, 173, 232
Galatians, 95, 130, 151
Gauda, 181, 182–4, 185
Gaul, 188–94, 202–4
    cavalry, 194, 195–6
    fibulae as diplomatic gifts, 202–3, 204, *205*
    horses as diplomatic gifts, 193–4, 196
    torques as diplomatic gifts, 193–4, 196–202, 203, *204*, *205*
Gelon of Sicily, 68–9, 70
Gentius of Illyria, 155–6, 194
Germani, 191
Germanicus, 123
Gibeonites, 19, 21, 22
Gideon, biblical figure, 20
gifts
    cultural context, 4–5
    cycle of gift exchange, 131–3
    refusal of, 39, 109, 111–20, 121–4, 125–6, 131, 134–5, 136–8, 142–4
    symbolic communication, 233–4, 291–6, 297–8
gold, alluvial, 245–6
Gómez de Almagro, Juan, 293
Góngora Marmolejo, Alonso de, 298, 301
González de Nájera, Alonso, 295–6, 300
graffiti, 200–1, 202
grain, 21, 23, 87, 98, 176

Great Plains, Battle of, 173
Greece
    appointment of envoys, 36–7
    crowns in honorific culture, 85–91
    honours and titles, 36–7, 38
    hospitality gifts, 34–6, 39, 48, 58–9
    hospitality meals, 37–8
    presentation of crowns to Rome, 77, 78–85, 93–4, 96–102
    relations with Macedonia, 38–9, 48, 49, 53–4
    relations with Persia, 38, 39–40, 44–8, 49, 54
    role of diplomatic gifts, 34–5, 38, 53–4, 131–2
    role of gifts in Homeric epic, 34, 35, 36, 46, 48, 58–62, 66, 70
guard posts, 148, 149, 161, 164
guides, 154, 163
Gulussa, 178, 180

Hadadezer, biblical king of Zobah, 22–3
Hannibal, 84, 159, 172, 190, 213, 228, 229–30, 234, 247, 297
    marriage, 259
    taking of hostages, 214–15
Hasdrubal Gisco, 173, 258–9
Hazael of Syria, 27, 28
Hellenisation, 110, 113
Hellenistic symbolism, 170, 171–2, 174–5
helmets, 59, 64, 66, 69, 273, 294, 296
Helvius, Gaius, 156–7
Helvius, Marcus, 243, 244
Heraclea, Battle of, 111–13, 119
Hernici, 83
Herodotus, 66, 67–8
heroes, Greek, 36, 37, 58–60
    relics, 60–2, 63–6
Hezekiah of Judah, 28–9
Hiempsal, 178–9, 182
Hieron I of Syracuse, 69, 98
Hieron II of Syracuse, 66, 249
Hieronymus of Cardia, 112
Hiram I of Tyre, 22, 24–5
Hispania Citerior, 231, 243
Hispania Ulterior, 243–4

hoards, 191, 197, 227, 255, 291
Homer, 35, 36, 46, 48, 58, 70
    Iliad, 58–60
    Odyssey, 34, 59, 60, 61–2
honours, 3
    cult, 82, 85, 87
    Greek cities, 36–7, 38, 49
    hope of receiving, 272
    solicitation of, 182–4
    see also crowns
horses
    Chile, 299–300, 301
    as gifts, 25, 41, 58, 141–2, 169–70, 193–4, 196, 203, 229–30, 298, 299–301, 302
    iconography, 175, 231
    importance to the Celts, 141–2, 194–6
    importance to the Iberians, 231
    Macedonia, 141
Hoshea of Israel, 28, 29
hospitality gifts, 34–6, 39, 48, 58–9
hospitality meals, 37–8
hospitium, 251–2, 267
hostages
    release with gifts, 152, 155, 163, 203, 232–4, 297
    return by Scipio, 120–1, 153, 154, 155, 203, 220–6, 228–9, 232–3, 297, 300–1
    Roman camps, 151, 152–6
    status, 218, 222, 224
    taken by Hannibal, 214–19, 229–30
    see also prisoners

Ilergetes, 194, 222, 228, 229–31, 300
Ilion, 65
Illyrians, 130, 194, 253
Illyrian War, 155–6
Inca, 291, 295, 298
Indibilis, 152, 153–4, 158, 194, 222, 228, 229–31, 300
Induciomarus, 191
Insubres, 190–1
Iunius Brutus, Decimus, 251

Jeconiah, biblical king of Judah, 17
Jehoahaz, biblical king of Judah, 29
Jehoash of Judah, 27–8, 29

Jehoiakim of Judah, 29
Jericho, 18–19, 22, 30
Jesse, biblical figure, 21
jeu de l'honneur, 132, 143
Josephus, 98
Judaeans, 21–2
Jugurtha, 158, 178–9, 180, 181–2, 183, 184–5
Jugurthine War, 177, 179–3
Julius Caesar, 192, 195–6
Justin, 115, 271

keimēlia, 61–2, 63, 65, 66, 70
kraters, 60, 66

La Tène, 195, 202
Labienus, Titus, 196
Laelius, Gaius, cos. 190 BC, 150, 151, 157, 158–9
Lampsacus, 81–2, 94
Latins, 83
Lautaro, 292–3, 298, 300
League of Islanders, 92, 93, 94, 97
Leon, Athenian ambassador, 52
Licinius Crassus, Publius, 196
Licinius Lucullus, Lucius, 250
lions, 176
livestock, 20, 23, 50, 52, 251, 299, 300
Livy, 78, 124–5, 148, 149–50, 151, 160, 254
    on booty, 242–3, 244, 245, 246
    on crowns, 78, 79, 80, 81, 83–4, 93–4, 95, 96, 98, 99, 100
    on Gaul, 190, 192–3
    on Numidia, 168–9, 170–1, 173, 176, 232
    on the Second Punic War, 214, 218, 219, 221, 222–6, 229, 230
llanca *see* chaquira
Lusitanians, 243–4, 245, 247, 248–9, 250, 251, 254–8, 259–60, 268, 269–70
luxuria, 110, 116, 124, 125
Lysimachus, 92, 94

Macedonia, 39, 48, 49, 51, 53–4
Macedonian Wars, 301
    First, 79
    Second, 78, 79–80, 108, 176

Third, 80–1, 82, 93, 139–44, 148, 176
Machiavellianism, 218, 293–4
Mandonius, 152, 153–4, 222, 228
Manlius Acidinus, Lucius, 243
Manlius Vulso, Gnaeus, 151
Mapuche, 283–4, 287, 292–4, 296, 299–300, 301
    networks of reciprocity, 285–6
    use of chaquira, 287–8, 289–90
Mariño de Lobera, Pedro, 298
Marius, Gaius, 183, 184, 185
Masinissa, 172, 176, 181, 182, 185, 250, 252–3
    capture and release of nephew, 152, 155, 163, 203, 232–3, 297
    gifts and honours, 158, 160–1, 169–70, 173–5, 183, 192, 193, 194, 297
    iconography, 169, 174–5
    will, 175, 177–8
Massiva, grandson of Masinissa, 180–2, 185
Massiva, nephew of Masinissa
    gifts, 155, 163, 173, 194, 203, 232–3, 297, 299–1
    as hostage, 152, 155, 163, 203, 232, 233
Mastanabal, 178, 181, 182
Mauretania, 175–6
medallions, 292
Menahem of Israel, 28, 29
Menander Rhetor, 100
mercenaries, 20, 21, 67, 95, 294, 297, 301–2
    Bastarnae, 139–44
    Celts, 190–1, 194, 195, 202
Meriones, 59, 64
Mesha of Moab, 27
Michimalonco, 294–5
Micipsa, 177, 178, 184
Millalauco, 293
mining, 245–6
Moagetes, tyrant of Cibyra, 156–7
Moctezuma, 289
monkeys, 24
Mummius, Lucius, 245
Mytilene, 84–5

Nebuchadnezzar II, 29
Necho II, pharaoh, 29, 67

Nicomedia, 64
Nitiobroges, 200–2
Numantia, 158, 176, 178, 246
Numidia
  iconography, 169, 171–2, 174–5, 177
  relations with Rome, 151, 152, 155, 163, 168–71, 172–4, 175–85, 192, 194, 203, 232–3, 252–3, 297, 300–1

Occius, Quintus, 251–2
Odrysian Kingdom, 43–4, 46–7, 53
Odysseus, 59, 61, 62
Olloviconus, 202
Olympia, 64, 68, 69–70
Opimius, Lucius, 179
oracles, 67
Orophernes of Cappadocia, 83
ostriches, 176

Pamphylia, 81–2, 94, 95, 101
panthers, 176
parrhēsia, 135, 137, 144
Parthenon, 89, 92
paterae, 170, 173, 192, 193, 202, 226–7, 232
patronage, 3, 138, 252
Pausanias, 64, 68–9, 195
peacocks, 24, 45, 54
Peloponnesian War, 85
Perperna, 274, 275–6, 277
Perseus of Macedon, 80, 82, 139–44, 148, 193, 194
Persian Empire
  conquest of Babylon, 29
  diplomacy beyond Greece, 43–4
  relations with Greece, 38, 39–40, 44–8, 49, 54
  role of gift-giving, 40–3, 44
Peru, 288, 290
phalerae, 141, 169–70, 194
Phaselis, 64
phiales, 44, 46, 54, 66, 227
Philip II of Macedon, 39, 48, 51, 53–4, 81, 95, 141
Philip II of Spain, 57, 62
Philip V of Macedon, 66, 78, 79–80, 93, 94, 108–9, 139, 142, 143, 250, 253

Philistines, 20–1, 22
Philocrates, 39, 53
Philopoemen, 109, 133, 134–5, 137, 139, 144
Pindar, 69–70
Piraeus, 87, 88
Pizarro, Francisco, 289
Plato, 122, 124
Pliny the Elder, 66, 84, 112, 117
Plutarch, 50–3, 95, 111–12, 113, 117, 119, 124, 139, 159
  on the Sertorian War, 266, 267, 268–70, 271, 273, 274, 275
Polybius of Megalopolis, 78, 134–5, 136–7, 162, 197
  on crowns, 79, 82, 84, 93, 94, 95–6, 97, 100–1
  on Roman values, 108–9, 121, 122–4, 126
  on the Second Punic War, 190, 214–15, 216, 219, 221, 222, 229, 232, 297
Pompey, 274, 275
Popillius Laenas, Marcus, 247, 250, 254, 259, 260
Posidonius, 188, 302
Postumius Albinus, Lucius, 244
'potlatch' communities, 188–9
poultry, 24; *see also* peacocks
praetorium, 149, 150, 152, 153, 160–1, 162–4
Priene, 92, 94, 97
principia, 149, 161, 162, 164
prisoners
  double standards, 228
  duels, 297
  negotiations, 112–13, 119, 151, 152–6, 162, 220, 229, 250
  release with gifts, 233–4
  status, 218, 222, 224, 233
  see also hostages
processions, 40, *41*, 65, 93, 96–7, 101
proxenos (title), 36–7, 38
Ptolemy I Soter, 97, 135–6, 144
Ptolemy II Philadelphus, 92, 94, 114–16
Ptolemy III Euergetes, 252
Ptolemy IV Philopator, 171, 232
Ptolemy V Epiphanes, 98

Punic Wars, 77
　Second, 150, 191, 212–13, 300–1
　　Baecula, 155, 158, 194, 228–33
　　Carthago Nova, 219–227
　　coinage, 202
　　obligation networks, 297
　　Roman relations with Numidia, 168–9, 172–3, 176, 177, 184, 252–3
　　Saguntum, 84, 213–19
　Third, 176
purple, 170, 171, 192, 232, 293
Pydna, Battle of, 148
Pyrilampes, 45, 54
Pyrrhic War, 110–14, 117, 119–20
Pyrrhus of Epirus, 66, 95, 111, 112, 113–14, 117, 119–20

quaestorium, 153, 162
Queen of Sheba, 25, 31
Quinctius Crispinus, Lucius, 244
Quinctius Famininus, Titus, 108–9

Rahab, biblical figure, 19, 21, 22
rats, 21, 22
reciprocity, 188–9, 224–5, 234, 271–2, 285
　anthropological models, 131–3, 290, 301–2
　Greece, 35–6, 60, 70, 131–2, 133–4, 138, 139, 143, 144
　Third Macedonian War, 140–1, 142–4
reconaissance dance, 131–2, 142
Rehoboam, biblical king of Judah, 26, 29
relics, 60, 61–6, 68, 70
reward goods, 85–6, 219, 225, 226, 245, 273
　Bible, 20, 23
　Chile, 287, 292
　Persian Empire, 40, 54
　Roman camps, 148, 152, 157–9, 164
Rezin of Syria, 28
Rhodes, 64, 66–7, 70, 82, 84, 88–9, 93, 94, 99, 102, 149
rings, 20, 169, 173, 203, 232
robes, 25, 27, 30, 40; *see also* togas; tunics
Roman camps
　diplomatic and political role, 147–50, 161–4

　hostage/prisoner exchange, 152–6
　importance of gifts, 151–2
　new alliances, 152, 156–7
　reaffirmation of friendship or alliance, 157, 159–61
　reward goods, 148, 152, 157–9, 164
Romanisation, 272–3, 297
Rome
　appointment of envoys, 114–15
　changing approach to diplomacy, 4, 170–1
　expansionism, 2, 4, 119, 301
　as new dominant power, 77–8
　presentation of crowns, 77, 78–85, 93–4, 96–102
　refusal of diplomatic gifts, 109, 111–20, 121–4, 125–6
　relations with Egypt, 113–16, 170–1
　relations with Numidia, 151, 152, 155, 163, 168–71, 172–4, 175–85, 192, 194, 203, 232–3, 252–3, 297, 300–1
　value system, 108–9, 111, 113, 116–17, 118–21, 122–5, 126
Romulus, 230

Sabines, 117, 118, 125
sacrifices, 65, 80, 100, 101, 102, 231, 255
Saguntum, 84, 100, 214–19, 228–9, 234
Sallust, 178, 180–1, 182, 267, 272
Samnites, 83, 117, 118
Samson, biblical figure, 20
sanctuaries, 62–70, 89, 96, 197, 201, 202
　negotiations, 217
Saul, biblical king of Judah and Israel, 21
scabbards, 195
Scepsis, 81, 87, 89, 92
sceptres, 60, 65, 83, 169, 173, 174, 183, 192
Scipiones, 170, 174, 214, 216, 217, 219; *see also* Cornelii Scipiones
scythes, 195
Scythians, 43
Second Athenian Confederacy, 88, 89
Seleucid War, 233

Seleucus, 135, 136–7, 144
sella, 182, 183
Sempronius Gracchus, Tiberius, cos. 177, 163 BC, 100–1, 244
Seneca, 131
Sennacherib, 28–9
Sertorian War, 266–9, 273–4
   diplomatic gifts, 266, 269–73, 275–7
Sertorius, Quintus, 266–70, 271–2, 273–4, 275–6, 277, 297
Servilius Caepio, Quintus, 254, 258, 260
Shalmaneser V, 28
Sheshak, pharaoh, 26, 29
shields, 26, 64, 66, 68, 70, 98, 135–6, 273
ships, 136
Siceliot rulers, 68–70
Sicyon, 64
Sitalkes, 44
Smyrna, 88
So, biblical pharaoh, 28
socii, 169, 192–3, 247, 253
Socrates, 124
Solomon, biblical king of Judah and Israel, 23–6, 31
Sophonisba, wife of Syphax, 160
sovereignty, symbolism of, 192, 194, 198–9, 271
Sparta, 36, 47, 66, 67, 109, 133–5
Spartans, 109, 134–5, 139
Spartocids, 89–91
spices, 25
Statorius, Quintus, centurion, 169
status anxiety, 132
Stertinius, Lucius, 243
Strabo, 203, 245
Suessiones, 203, *204*
sumptuary laws, 125
sumptus, 124
swords, 294
   Celtic, 195
   gifts, 59, 61, 66, 199, 221
   relics, 64
   surrender of, 251–2
Syphax, 150, 151, 157, 160, 168–73, 174, 176, 185, 232, 252, 297
   iconography, 169, 171–2
Syracuse, 88–9
Syria, 28, 29

Tabula Peutingeriana, 201, 202
Tacitus, 195
Talabrigenses, 251
Tarentum, 110
Tarpeia, 125
Tarquin the Elder, 170
Tarraco, 151, 153, 154, 155, 157, 214, 219, 221–2, 228
taxation, 28, 29, 95, 190, 291, 295
Temple of Athena Lindia, Rhodes, 64, 66–7, 70
Temple of Jupiter Capitolinus, Rome, 78, 80, 81, 83, 84, 96, 98, 100, 101–2
Teopolicán, 286, 287, 288, 293, 294, 300
Teutomatus, 195, 202
Thebes, 47, 52, 68, 70
Thessaly, 90, 141
Thisbe, 80–1
Thrace, 43–4, 46–7, 53
Thracians, 35, 44, 46, 130
Thrasybulus of Calydon, 85–6
Thrasybulus of Miletus, 291–2
Thucydides, 44, 46–7
Thurii, 84
Tiglath-Pileser III, 28
Timaeus of Tauromenium, 113
Timagoras, Athenian ambassador, 50, 51–3
togas, 169, 170, 173, 192, 232, 297
torques, 189, 193–4, 198–202, 203, *204*, 245, 255, *256*, *257*
   importance to the Celtic world, 196–7
   Persia, 40, 41, *43*, 44, 198–9
   as symbol of sovereignty, 194, 198–9
Trasimene, 98
treaties, 102, 112, 248, 249–51, 252–3, 265
   Bible, 24, 27, 32
   Gaul, 197
   Roman camps, 153, 156
   with Viriathus, 249, 250, 251, 259–60
Treveri, 191
tribunals, 149–50, 160–1, 162, 173
triumphal arches, 243, 244
triumphs, 96, 118, 197, 244
Trojan War, 63–4, 65
tryphē, 122

tumours, 20–1, 22
tunics, 169, 170, 173, 175, 192, 203, 232, 273, 293, 297
Turdetanians, 254, 258, 259–60

Utica, Battle of, 158

Valdivia, Pedro de, 284, 291, 292, 293, 294, 295
Valerius Maximus, 51, 114, 115, 117, 123, 232, 248
vases, *42*, *227*
Veas, Marco, 292–3, 298
Vercingetorix, 191, 195
Vergina, 91, 92, 95
Vermina, 172
Vettones, 244, 245
Villagra, Pedro de, 298
Viriathus, 176, 247, 248, 254

treaty with Rome, 249, 250, 251, 259–60
wedding, 254–9

women, 20, 21, 22, 294
jewellery, 197, 287–8
Roman morality, 124–5
wreaths, 85, 95
golden, 68, 151, 152, 156, 157, 158, 159, 162, 173, 174, 192

xenía (friendship pacts), 3, 34–5, 37, 39, 46, 47–8, 53–4, 67, 70
xénia (hospitality gifts), 34–6, 37–8, 39, 48
Xenophon, 45, 47, 52

Zonaras, 80

EU Authorised Representative:
Easy Access System Europe Mustamäe tee 50, 10621 Tallinn, Estonia
gpsr.requests@easproject.com

Printed and bound by CPI Group (UK) Ltd, Croydon, CR0 4YY
29/03/2026
02080666-0007